SCYRI(?)

GELONI

GEPIDAE

NEURI

URGUNDIANS

BASTARNAE

ALANS

OSTROGOTHS

SCYRI (?)

H U N S

A C A T Z I R I

Margus

R. Danube

E A S T E R N   E M P I R E

Constantinople

Alexandria

THE BARBARIAN INVASIONS
OF THE ROMAN EMPIRE

THE BARBARIAN INVASIONS
OF THE ROMAN EMPIRE

VOLUME II

The Huns and the Vandals

THOMAS HODGKIN

Introduced by Peter Heather

LONDON

The Folio Society

2000

Thomas Hodgkin's *The Barbarian Invasions of the Roman Empire,
Volume II: The Huns and the Vandals* was first published, under the
title *Italy and her Invaders, Volume II: The Hunnish Invasion, The Vandal Invasion,
and the Herulian Mutiny*, by the Clarendon Press in 1880. A second edition,
containing substantial revisions by the author, was published in 1892.
This edition follows the 1892 version of the text.

Introduction © Peter Heather 2000

Maps drawn by Reginald Piggott

Binding illustration: Attila the Hun invades Northern Italy, in 452. From
Stefanoni's *Storia d'Italia*, 1885. (*Mary Evans Picture Library, London*)
Slipcase: Rome is sacked by the Visigoths, by an unidentified
artist, 19th century. (*Mary Evans Picture Library, London*)
Frontispiece: the large eagle-shaped *fibula* from a Gothic hoard found at
Pietroasa, Rumania, dating from the period of the Hunnic empire

Typeset at The Folio Society in Monotype Poliphilus
Printed on Grosvenor Book Wove paper at The Bath Press, Bath,
and bound by them in quarter buckram with printed boards

CONTENTS

ILLUSTRATIONS

Maps

INTRODUCTION TO VOLUME II

The Huns and the Vandals

VOLUME II OF *THE BARBARIAN INVASIONS OF THE Roman Empire* is divided into two parts, each one centred on a separate incursion. The first deals with the Huns and the invasion of Gaul and Italy launched by Attila in 451. The second discusses the background to and main events of the Vandals' sack of Rome in 455, before taking the story of the Western Roman Empire down to the Herulian mutiny – by which Hodgkin meant the *coup d'état* of the Roman army of Italy commanded by the barbarian soldier Odovacar* – which deposed the last emperor Romu‑ lus Augustulus on or about 4 September 476.

In keeping with his usual method, Hodgkin's treatment of these two invasions and a mutiny is highly discursive. Since, in charting the trans‑ formation of western Europe – and of Italy in particular – the invaders were just as important as the invaded, he needed to spread his net wide to bring the subject effectively before his readership.† Consequently, more than half of the first part of *The Huns and the Vandals* is spent addressing the controversy over Hunnic origins, and in telling the story of Attila's cam‑ paigns in the Balkans, before the narrative is able to turn to the Huns' invasion of Gaul and Italy (chapters iii and iv). Likewise, in the second part, the fall of the Hunnic empire (chapter v), early Vandal history (the first section of a long chapter vi), and the history of the Roman West (chapters vii–xi and xiii) are all fully explored in order to provide the con‑ text Hodgkin desired for his portrayals of the Vandal attack on Rome (the final portion of Chapter vi) and Odovacar's *putsch* (chapter xii).

All of Hodgkin's excellent qualities as a historical writer are on display

---

* As Hodgkin carefully analyses in chapter xii (pp. 298–302), all the indications suggest that since the 450s the army of Italy had come to be dominated by Germanic and espe‑ cially Herulian mercenaries.

† See my general introduction to this Folio edition of *The Barbarian Invasions of the Roman Empire* in vol. i, p. xii.

in *The Huns and the Vandals*. His incisive and lively prose consistently enter-
tains the reader – I greatly enjoyed his vignette of nineteenth-century
history done in the rather sparse style of a late Roman chronicler
(pp. 174–5). Furthermore, as a good ancient historian in the tradition of
Herodotus and Thucydides, his visits to the scene of various parts of the
action furnish another dimension to his narrative.* He was clearly especially keen to work out exactly where, west of Paris, the Roman general
Aetius and his allies had managed to defeat Attila's hordes in the summer
of 450 (see pp. 366–8), and he also spent large amounts of time hunting for
the genuine site of the villa of one of his primary authorities, the Gallo-
Roman nobleman Sidonius Apollinaris (pp. 180–1). '

At every turn, Hodgkin reveals himself a masterful judge of how much
extra information and explanation to blend into his sources so that a general reader can grasp the significance of what they say. Priscus' account of
the embassy that he accompanied to Attila is quite expertly glossed, it seems
to me; and Hodgkin is equally successful in his provision of background
material on Roman North Africa to contextualise his picture of Vandal
Carthage.† His extensive section of translations from the correspondence
of Sidonius Apollinaris (chapter vii) is also very acute. Full of colourful
vignettes, these letters allow *The Huns and the Vandals* to escape the dryness of
the chroniclers and to illuminate a great many aspects – expected and
unexpected – of life in fifth-century Gaul. To have made a smooth, read-
able narrative, complete with delightful changes of pace and subject,
despite the huge variations in the nature of his sources is a major literary
achievement.

Not that history was at any point sacrificed to literature. *The Huns and the
Vandals* exhibits every sign of the concern for accuracy which its author sustained over more than twenty years of work on *The Barbarian Invasions of the
Roman Empire*. Hodgkin went out of his way to exploit all obtainable primary sources, some of which – such as fragments of the history of John of
Antioch (Joannes Antiochenus) – were only being published for the first
time as he was writing. He also interrogated his sources closely in order
both to fit together fragmentary and contradictory evidence – as his excellent digression on the chronology of the Vandal kings of Africa demon-
strates (pp. 375–82) – and to test hyperbolical rhetoric against the available

* Autopsy – being an eyewitness – was a prime virtue in the classical historiography that
Hodgkin had studied when a student at University College London.
† See pp. 37–59 for the former; for the latter, especially pp. 138–44.

facts. His reconstruction of the Vandal ruler Gaiseric's religious policy from the vitriol of Victor of Vita (Victor Vitensis) is especially well done (pp. 159–68).

In addition, Hodgkin immersed himself completely in the secondary literature of his day and the issues with which it was concerned, whether of greater or lesser significance. The opening chapter of *The Huns and the Vandals* attests to up-to-date knowledge of the debate surrounding the origins of the Huns and whether they could be equated with the Hsiung-Nu (or Hiong-nu) whose attacks plagued China in the centuries either side of the birth of Christ. At the other end of the scale, between the first and second editions he corrected the date of one of the truces between the Roman state and the Vandals – from January to February 435. And throughout, this meticulousness is reinforced with the excellence of Hodgkin's historical judgement. The despatch with which he dismisses medieval and early modern traditions linking the origins of both Hungary and Venice to Attila's escapades is, for instance, exemplary.* His discussion of the significance of the regime of the emperor Avitus could hardly be bettered either (pp. 222–32).

The most striking expression in *The Huns and the Vandals* of Hodgkin's qualities as a historian, however, is provided by its final chapter, which is composed of his reflections upon the fall of the Western Roman Empire. The directness and simplicity of its opening gambit will startle, I think, many modern readers. The Roman Empire fell, in Hodgkin's opinion, because it was God's will that this should be so. The Empire had given western European humanity civilisation and prepared it for accepting Christianity, but had done so at the price of human freedom, and had therefore to fall so that this great fault might be rectified. As a lifelong Quaker of great personal faith, Hodgkin believed in the straightforward operation of divine providence in human history. This, of course, is a level of analysis that readers will either accept or deny according to their own beliefs. Hodgkin then moved on to consider what he termed 'secondary causes'. These have a very modern ring, ranging from economic dislocation caused by oppressive tax systems, to internal disaffection arising from slavery and the political oppression of the curial classes, the divisive rivalry prompted by separating the Empire into eastern and western halves, and the varied and sometimes subtle effects of the adoption of Christianity. On this last subject Hodgkin is much less hostile than his forebear Gibbon, as

* On Hungary see pp. 110–11; on Venice, pp. 99–104 and 368–73.

one would indeed expect of a lifelong Christian. He does give some emphasis, as did Gibbon, to monastic withdrawal, but also highlights the adverse consequences of a – to him – unholy combination of Christianity and state-enforced religion.

No one would dispute, I think, that all these topics have some bearing on Imperial collapse, but what strikes me is that they are all internal. This would suggest that, for Hodgkin, the invaders were effect and not cause of change, and sometimes his narrative implies as much. The admission of the Goths into the Empire in 376 he portrays as a mistake on the part of the emperor Valens which could have been avoided.* On the other hand, his defence of Stilicho, as having done everything that circumstances allowed to preserve the Empire, presents a somewhat different view.† The debate between 'internalists' and 'externalists' continues down to the present.‡

As one might expect (or at least hope!), an interval of more than a century has altered scholarly opinions from some of those held by Hodgkin. No one now believes the contemporary slander passed on by the Byzantine historian Procopius that Count Bonifacius invited the Vandals to North Africa as part of his struggle for power (p. 133). The very careful work of Otto Maenchen-Helfen has produced a different and much more convincing chronology for Attila's Balkan campaigns out of some very intractable Byzantine materials,§ and the dispute over Hunnic origins continues to rumble on.¶ On the archaeological front, the developments have in some ways been less dramatic than in the case of the Goths, the invaders in Hodgkin's first volume. The Vandals can reasonably be associated with the Przeworsk culture of southern Poland in the Roman period, but this was a material cultural system shared by many groups, and, once on the move (from the early fifth century), the Vandal conquerors of North Africa left no detectable archaeological traces of their passage across Europe.** The nomadic Huns are similarly invisible apart from a very few rich burials.

* See vol. i, pp. 134–7.   † See vol. i, pp. 432–4.
‡ An outline of my own views on the subject can be found in P. Heather, 'The Huns and the End of the Roman Empire in Western Europe', *English Historical Review*, vol. cx (1995), pp. 4–41.
§ For Hodgkin's version see pp. 30–4. Cf. O. J. Maenchen-Helfen, *The World of the Huns* (1973), pp. 86–103.
¶ Compare F. Altheim (ed.), *Geschichte der Hunnen*, 5 vols (1959–62) with again Maenchen-Helfen, *The World of the Huns*.
** See K. Godlowski, *The Chronology of the Late Roman and Early Migration Periods in Central Europe* (1970).

On the other hand, more indirect materials aplenty have been unearthed. The UNICEF-sponsored excavation of abandoned Carthage has advanced immensely our knowledge of the city in both the late Roman and Vandal periods. Likewise, while the Huns themselves are difficult to find, the world of the Germanic subject peoples of the Huns has emerged with great clarity in the gold-strewn burials of the middle Danube region.* All of this would have thoroughly delighted Hodgkin, and given him the means with which to make his history even more compelling.

PETER HEATHER

* On Carthage see e.g. the illustrations in A. Ennabli, *Carthage retrouvée* (1995). On the archaeology of the Hunnic Empire see I. Bona, *Das Hunnenreich* (1991).

EDITORIAL NOTE

B OTH THE 1880 AND THE 1892 EDITIONS OF *THE Huns and the Vandals* included much annotation that was intended, in the author's words, 'almost exclusively' for a contemporary academic audience. In the interests of providing a more uncluttered, reading edition, only that material which is likely to be most informative or entertaining to present-day non-specialists has been retained. However, so that readers can observe the ways in which Hodgkin deployed his authorities, all source references have been kept, and have been expanded or standardised where helpful. The often detailed discussions concerning his sources with which Hodgkin originally preceded each chapter – and the lengthy notes on more technical subjects that he appended to the ends of many – have been collected together and placed at the back of the volume, in order to avoid disrupting the narrative flow. Translations have been added (in square brackets) only where it was felt they would be useful. No attempt has been made to amend the substance of Hodgkin's scholarship: in particular, his sterling equivalents for sums of money have not been updated.

The Hunnish Invasion

CHAPTER I

Early History of the Huns

There is a race on Scythia's verge extreme
Eastward, beyond the Tanais' chilly stream.
The Northern Bear looks on no uglier crew:
Base is their garb, their bodies foul to view;
Their souls are ne'er subdued to sturdy toil
Or Ceres' arts: their sustenance is spoil.
With horrid wounds they gash their brutal brows,
And o'er their murdered parents bind their vows.
Not e'en the Centaur-offspring of the Cloud
Were horsed more firmly than this savage crowd.
Brisk, lithe, in loose array they first come on,
Fly, turn, attack the foe who deems them gone.

Claudian, *In Rufinum*, i.323–31

SUCH IS THE ACCOUNT WHICH THE COURTIER-poet of Rome gave of the Huns half a century before the name of Attila became a terror to the nations. In the fifth chapter of the first book* we witnessed the effect which the appearance of these wild Tartar hordes produced upon the Gothic warriors. The swarthy faces, without either beard or whisker, the twinkling black eyes, the squat figures, the perfect understanding which seemed to exist between the riders and their little steeds, were there described in the words of the Gothic bishop, Jordanes, and we heard what he had to say concerning their *execranda origo* [cursed origin], descended, as he believed them to be, from Gothic sorceresses and from evil spirits.

The German professor of today emerges from his library to gaze at the descendants and representatives of the Huns, and liking them as little as his primeval kinsmen did, brands them with a term of deeper condemnation than Jordanes' epithets of 'witch-born' or 'fiend-begotten' — the terrible name, Turanian.†

* Vol. i, p. 130.
† It is true that this term, Turanian, seems to be going somewhat out of fashion in

For by thus defining their ethnological position he cuts them off from all connection with the great Aryan stem whose branches have overspread Europe, America, and Australia, Persia, and India; he equally destroys their claim to share in any of the glory of the Semitic races through whose instrumentality Judaism, Christianity, and Mohammedanism were given to the world; and he shuts them up with a multitude of dull barbarians, mighty in destruction, powerless in construction, who have done nothing for the cause of civilisation or human progress, and who, even where they have adopted some of the varnish of modern customs, have remained essen-tially and incurably barbarous to the present day.*

Now this Turanian (or, to speak popularly and with less accuracy, Tar-tar) race which burst upon the affrighted Goths in the reign of the emperor Valens (376), being a people of unlettered nomads, neither cared to give, nor probably could give to the European nations whom they terrified, any information as to their history in the remote past. Some traditions of a myth-ical kind as to the origin of their race they probably possessed, and had they established themselves in Europe permanently, these might, like the Scandi-navian sagas, have floated down into a literary age and been so preserved. But the Huns vanished out of Europe almost as suddenly as they came, leav-ing no trace behind of their history, their language, or their religion. But for one somewhat disputed source of information, all is dark concerning them. That source is the history of China. If the Huns be the Hiong-nu, whose ravages are recorded in that history, then we have a minute account of their doings for centuries before the Christian era, and we know, in fact, far more about them than about the inhabitants of Gaul or Britain before the time of Julius Caesar: if they are not, our ignorance is complete.

A learned and laborious Frenchman, M. Deguignes, in the middle of last century, conceived the idea that the Huns might be thus identified, and with infinite pains he wrote out their history from Chinese sources, and exhibited it in its connection with that of the various Tartar conquerors

ethnological circles, and that it is confessedly a merely conventional designation. But either it or some other similar name will apparently be always required to denote those races in Europe and Asia which are neither Aryan nor Semitic, and which speak what are called 'agglutinative languages'.

* This statement will be admitted to be generally true of all the Turanian tribes. There are however two honourable exceptions, the Finn and the Magyar. The Tartar sovereigns of India and China conformed to the civilised tastes of their subjects, but cannot claim the merit of having originated them. [For more information on the chief 'Turanian' races in history see table i, p. 397.]

who, since their day, have poured down upon the civilised kingdoms of Europe and Asia, and wasted them.

This identification has been questioned, and it must be admitted that mere similarity of name is dangerous ground to build upon in the history of barbarous races.* But as the hypothesis though looked upon with much less favour than it received a century ago, does not seem to be yet absolutely disproved, we may be permitted to spend some pages on the history of the Hiong-nu, in the possibility that we are thus contemplating the formation of that volcano which hurled forth Attila.

From the description which physical geographers give of central Asia, it would surely be one of the most striking features of our globe, in the sight of any visitor who might be approaching us from another sphere. East-wards from longitude 73° it rises, we are told, to the almost incredible average height of eight thousand feet, bearing the character of a vast insu-lated upland, and, its extent and average elevation being taken into account, it may be said to form on the whole the most considerable projec-tion on the surface of our planet.

From this mighty upraised altar great rivers flow down in all directions, the Obi, Yenisei, and Lena through Siberia into the Arctic sea, the Amour and the two great rivers of China, the Hoang-ho and Yangtse-kiang, into the Pacific; the Irawaddy, Brahmahputra, Ganges, Indus, into the Indian ocean; the Oxus and Jaxartes into the sea of Aral. Rivers of its own it has none (or only one, the Yar-kiang), having apparently no deep valleys: the small streams which it does possess find their way to some insignificant inland lake, and are lost there.

Four great mountain chains, limiting or traversing it, run from west to east. The mountains of Altai mark it off from Siberia on the north. The Thian Shan, or mountains of heaven, pass across the middle of it at about the forty-second parallel of latitude. The Kuen-Lun fence off what is now Chinese Tartary from Tibet. The Himalayas bound the great plateau to the south.

No mountain chain of any importance appears to intersect the country from north to south till we reach the Bolor mountains (longitude 73°), which are its western boundary, and which form a kind of step down into the lower, but still lofty plateau (four thousand feet high) of eastern Turkestan.

* [For more information on the identification of the Hiong-nu with the Huns see appen-dix i, pp. 365–6.]

The dominions of the Hiong-nu at the time of their greatest supremacy reached over the whole of the northern and central sections of this plateau – from Mount Altai, that is, to the Kuen-Lun. And westwards, their rule extended beyond the Bolor mountains down into Turkestan, down lower still to the old seabed between Lake Aral and the Caspian, nay, even across the Ural mountains to the Volga. In its more contracted state, their empire still touched the Irtish (long. 80°) on the west; but it seems to have receded to the Thian Shan mountains on the south; and the proper home of the race – if nomads can be said to have a home – was that district between China and Siberia bounded on the east by the Inshan mountains (long. 115°), which is marked in modern maps Mongolia. Very roughly estimated, it is probably about as large as Germany and Austria put together. Across the centre of it stretches the great sandy desert of Gobi or Shamo.

Here, then, if we may trust our French guide, the nation of the Huns was roaming before the date usually assigned to the call of Abraham. In winter they crowded down upon the northern frontier of China, which lies in the latitude of Madrid; in summer they drove their cattle northwards, across the great desert of Gobi, and took refuge from the heat in the cool valleys under the mountains which lie to the south of Lake Baikal, and which are in the same latitude as London.

Under the first two historic dynasties of China (the Hia, 2207–1767 BC, and the Shang, 1767–1122 BC), the Huns – if it be indeed the same race – are spoken of under the name of Chan-yong (barbarians of the mountains) and Tchong-yo. Their country was called Kuei-fang, 'the country of spirits', so denominated by the same unchanging nation which at this day calls us Europeans 'foreign devils'.

About one hundred years before the building of Solomon's Temple, the Chow dynasty ascended the Chinese throne, and slumbered there for nearly nine centuries, till the year 258 BC. These were the Carolingians of China, monarchs nominally supreme, but really overshadowed and over-awed by their great feudatories; in their personal character debauched and cruel – in short, conspicuous offenders against the golden-mean maxims of morality so dear to the Chinese heart. This cycle of anarchy (it would probably have lasted but a century in Europe) was the harvest-time of the Northern barbarians, who are now spoken of as Hien-yun. The three northern provinces of the Chinese empire, Shen-se, Shan-se, and Petche-li (which comprise an area about equivalent to the whole of Great Britain) seem to have been in a state of perpetual border warfare with these savage enemies, who after each inroad retired laden with booty to the northern portion of their own territory. Their fleet ponies and trackless wildernesses rendered hopeless any attempt on the part of regular troops to pursue or to avenge.

At length, about the middle of the third century BC, the long-smouldering light of the Chow dynasty went out, and the Tsin dynasty succeeded. Ching-wang, otherwise Che-Hwang-te, the greatest monarch of this new house, the Napoleon of China, united her warring provinces into one compact empire, took the title of *hwang-te* (universal emperor) instead of *wang* (king), which had been borne by all previous monarchs, drove back the Hiong-nu (for such is now the name of the barbarians) to their deserts, and finally, about the time of the second Punic war, completed the Great Wall of China (portions of which had been already built by two provincial sovereigns) in order to protect the northern frontier from their incursions. Thus then (if only the theory of Deguignes be true) this great work, 1,500 miles long, the name of which has been familiar to all of us from our childhood, was really built to guard the civilisation of eastern Asia from the inroads of the ancestors of Attila, and might as fairly be called the Huns' wall as Hadrian's barrier across the Northumbrian isthmus is called by many the Picts' wall.

Che-Hwang-te in the course of his great career found himself frequently thwarted by the traditions, the etiquette, the state maxims of the literati, who seem to have been even then a powerful class in China. To recur to a former simile, the Napoleonic idea could not be made to accord with the Bourbon tradition. Violently breaking with the past of his country, he ordered, it is said, that all the books of history which could be found should be destroyed, sparing however those on medicine, agriculture, astrology, and other branches of science.*

This strange story may be the invention of national vanity, unable to trace up the written history of China beyond the third century BC. In this case, all that has been hitherto said as to the early history of China and the Hiong-nu must be relegated to dreamland, for an oral transmission of the events of sixteen centuries may be set aside as an impossibility.

On the other hand, if the story be true, and if Che-Hwang-te was in the main successful in his onslaught on the works of the earlier historians, it does not follow that Chinese history must necessarily begin with him. For

* The very name of Che-Hwang-te (the beginning emperor) was meant to set forth this claim of his to be the beginning of Chinese greatness.

if the Chinese were by this time a literary nation, which the story seems to imply, no mere destruction of books would avail to wipe out from the fully formed historical consciousness the general outlines of their past national life. Had every roll of manuscript perished out of the world at the time of the Peloponnesian war, the Greeks of that period would still have been able to reconstruct, with sufficient distinctness, by an act of memory, both the mythical and the historical record of previous ages which they had read from their childhood. Considering the apparently early development of the literary character in this enigmatic nation with which we are dealing, one is inclined to conjecture that this is the true view of the subject, and that there is at least some historic value in the Chinese annals previous to the third century BC.

From this time onwards, at any rate, the chronicle seems to be complete, and full, to the reader's exhaustion, of the doings of the robber-nation, the Hiong-nu. These latter had now 'taken to themselves a king after the man-ner of the nations'. He was called the *tan-jou*, which we are told is a contraction of the formidable title *tcem-li-ko-to-tan-jou* (mighty son of heaven*). The *tan-jou*'s queen was always called Yen-chi. All the great commands of the state were filled up in duplicate, one officer for the right and one for the left. Characteristically enough, as showing how their faces were ever set towards the fertile and opulent south, the left with them meant the east and the right the west. The left was, as we are informed that it is still with their Tartar nephews at Constantinople, the post of honour; and thus *hien-wang* (which signifies 'wise-king') being the highest grade of office under royalty, the '*hien-wang* of the left', or viceroy of the east, was the next greatest person to the *tan-jou*, and the office was generally held by the heir-apparent of that monarch.

In their prosperous days the sovereigns of the Hiong-nu trampled upon the civilised and literary pride of the Chinese emperors with the greater pride of the uncouth barbarian. On tablets, the exact size of which had been prescribed by generations of masters of the ceremonies, the Chinese monarch thus wrote with the vermilion pencil, 'The emperor respectfully begs the great *tan-jou* of the Hiong-nu, etc.' To which, on much larger tablets, the *tan-jou* replied, 'The great *tan-jou* of the Hiong-nu, born of the heavens and the earth, established by the sun and moon, respectfully begs the emperor of China, etc.'

Frequently an invading *tan-jou* would ask for the hand of a Chinese

* *Tan-jou* = mighty; *ko-to* = son; *tcem-li* = heaven.

princess as the price of his return to his own land, and the court, not unwilling to plant by the side of the robber-king a representative of its own interests, would comply with the request. National vanity however will not allow the Chinese historians to confess that one of the princesses of the blood-royal was really given in marriage to a barbarian, and they accordingly relate that a custom prevailed of adopting for the occasion a female slave into the family of the emperor, giving her the title of *kum-tcheou*, or princess of the blood, and then sending her off to be the bride of the *tan-jou*. An improbable story doubtless; but what is certain is that the transition from the highly civilised luxurious life of a Chinese palace to the squalor of the *tan-jou*'s home would be keenly felt by the sufferer, whatever her station in life might be, and perhaps even more by the domestic than by the mistress. Here is the melancholy outpouring in verse of one of these victims of policy, sent indeed not to a king of the Hiong-nu but to a prince of the neighbouring nation, the Ou-sioun, whose mode of life was indistinguishable from theirs:

> Me to a husband have my kindred tied,
> And in a far-off land have bid me bide;
> A wretched tent is now my palace-hall,
> And a rough paling is its only wall.
> Raw flesh must now my hunger satisfy,
> And curdled milk, my thirst: nought else have I.
> O native land! I still must think of thee,
> And my heart's wound bleeds ever inwardly.
> Why am I not a happy bird of air
> To thee, dear home, that I might straight repair?

The Hiong-nu were ignorant of the art of writing, but the Chinese historians, with a candour which we should scarcely have expected, admit that when they had verbally pledged themselves to a treaty they generally showed strict good faith in the observance of it. The children were early trained in the use of missile weapons. It is said that they were first taught to ride on the wild scampering moorland sheep, and to shoot with their little bows at birds and mice. As boys they hunted hares and foxes, as young men they assumed the weapons of war. They were not deemed full-grown men till they had slain a foe. When they reached old age they fell into poverty and contempt, all the good things being reserved for the active warriors of the nation. Flight was, as hinted in the verses of Claudian, a great part of their strategy. Like the Parthians they would discharge a cloud of arrows at the pursuing foe, and even if their rapid return failed to throw his ranks into confusion, they easily vanished into the terrible solitudes of those trackless deserts whither for many generations their harassed neighbours feared to pursue them.

Of the two chief residences of the *tan-jou*, one appears to have been situated in the north of their dominions, under the continuation of the Altai mountain range, and near the place which, as the capital of later Tartar chieftains, was known as Karakorum; the other near the Inshan mountains on the eastern frontier, where a large manufactory of bows and arrows was established.

At the first moon of each year there was a general assembly of all the officers of the kingdom and army at the *tan-jou*'s court, and a solemn sacrifice was then offered up. They met again in the fifth month, and sacrificed to the heavens, the earth, and the spirits of their ancestors. At another assembly held in the autumn they numbered the people and their flocks, thus taking stock, and striking a balance of the profit or loss of the summer's operations in the way of plunder.

Every morning the *tan-jou* issued from his tent on the left hand of the camp to pay his devotions to the sun, and in the evening he offered similar adoration to the moon, presumably during that part of the month only when she was visible. Such was the simple and primitive nature-worship of this tribe. We are informed that one of the other tribes of central Asia stuck a naked sabre hilt downwards into the earth, and then gathered round to adore it.

The great aim of the Hiong-nu in war was to take as many prisoners as possible. They reduced them, of course, to a state of slavery, and employed them to tend their flocks and herds, that they themselves might be left more free to practise the one art of the barbarian — war. If one of their number fell in battle, the comrade who succeeded in carrying off his dead body (as in the Homeric combats) to a place of safety, might claim his inheritance. In the later days of the Hiong-nu empire (40 BC), when we might have expected that their contact with the Chinese would have exerted some civilising influence upon them, we find the *tan-jou* Hou-han-sie confirming an oath by drinking blood from the skull of a hostile chief who had been slain by one of his ancestors 130 years before.

Such was the general character of the relations between the Hiong-nu and their southern neighbours. A few striking features of the history of the two nations, selected from a mass of monotonous details, will sufficiently explain the movement which eventually launched the Hunnish nation, not upon Peking, but upon Rome.

In China the Tsin dynasty, founded by the book-destroying Che-Hwang-te, was of short duration, like that of the Bonapartes, to which it has been already compared.

In the year 207 BC another period of anarchy was ended by Kaou-te, who, gathering up again all China under his rule, founded the celebrated Han dynasty, which flourished till AD 220, or, roughly speaking, from the days of Hannibal to those of Caracalla.

Contemporaneously with Kaou-te in China, the terrible Mé-té-tan-jou reigned over the Hiong-nu. His father, his stepmother, his half-brother, all atoned to him with their lives for an abortive attempt to exclude him from the succession. Yet, fierce as he had shown himself against his own flesh and blood, he appeared to submit with patience to the accumulated insults of the Sien-pi, a nation perhaps of Tungusic origin on the east of his dominions. Mé-té had in his stable a horse of fabulous speed and endurance, which could travel, it was said, 150 miles in one day. The Sien-pi sent to ask for this horse; he gave it up to them. Emboldened by this act of submission, they demanded one of his wives; she was sent to their king's tent. Then came a requisition for some wastelands, on a disputed frontier between the two nations, and at last the pent-up rage of Mé-té burst forth, 'Whatever touched my own honour or profit I have given up for the sake of peace, but of the land of my people I will not surrender to you a foot's-breadth.' And he smote the people of the Sien-pi with a great destruction, and pursued them till they took refuge in the mountains of Manchuria, where they remained a crippled and enfeebled remnant, but ever brooding over their wrongs, till, after the lapse of nearly three centuries, they sallied forth to enjoy their long-delayed vengeance.

Towards China, Mé-té assumed an attitude of permanent hostility. He fixed his court at Ta-tum-fou, or Tai-tong, just south of the Great Wall, and pushed forward his *hien-wang* of the left as far as Changkow, and him of the right to Yen-gan, both apparently from one to two hundred miles within the Chinese frontier.

The emperor Kaou-te levied an army of 320,000 men and marched against him, but was outmanoeuvred, and shut up in a fortress near Ta-tum-fou, where for seven days his army was left without provisions. By the favour of the *tan-jou*'s wife he escaped from this perilous position; but those seven days of semi-starvation were long remembered by the sleek Chinese troops. Peace of some sort was patched up between the two powers, but after the death of Kaou-te an audacious *hien-wang* of the right pushed his inroads so far that his barbarian hordes came almost within sight of Sin-gan-fou (in the province of Shen-si), which was then the capital of the empire. The Chinese court complained, and the *tan-jou* sent his too zealous viceroy of the west on a tour of conquest through central Asia. Tibet, all that we now call eastern and western Turkestan, and part of Siberia, were made subject to Mé-té's domination, and it is even said that the conquering Hiong-nu reached on this occasion as far as the Volga itself. With a great show of cour-tesy, the *tan-jou* sent an embassy to inform the Chinese emperor of these con-quests, by which he had become the greatest potentate in Asia; and hereupon, after a copious exchange of compliments, the emperor, we are informed, concluded to accord to him a renewal of the treaty of peace. As it is clear that at this time China was almost helpless in the hands of her bar-barian foe, the *tan-jou*'s humble supplications for peace, and the gracious concession of it by the emperor, were probably recorded by the literati of that day, the contemporaries of Hannibal, with about as much accuracy as may be evinced by some Chinese historian, upon whom in our own day may have devolved the duty of chronicling the destruction of the Summer palace, and the treaty graciously conceded to El-gin and Mon-to-ban.

From the death of Mé-té-tan-jou, which occurred in 174 BC, we have, for the space of 260 years, a history of the wars of China and the Huns, almost as detailed and circumstantial as the records of Roman conquest during the same period. Happily for the reader there is no necessity to repro-duce these details here. The same kind of events repeat themselves with monotonous regularity. 'The *tan-jou* sought for peace from the Chinese emperor. A wife was sent to him, and presents were exchanged. The Hiong-nu at once recommenced their inroads and ravaged a great belt of country in the three provinces of Shen-se, Shan-se, and Petche-li. The emperor sent three armies, amounting to two hundred thousand men, into the country of the Hiong-nu. Two of the generals obtained great successes, the third lost all his men in a march through the desert. He ought to have returned to China, and there submitted to degradation from all his posts of honour, and afterwards committed suicide. But he preferred to take refuge at the court of the *tan-jou*, where the information which he gave as to the move-ments of the troops and the strength of the frontier cities proved extremely injurious to the interests of China. The *tan-jou* now supplicated for peace; rich presents were exchanged, and various complimentary speeches were made, but both parties understood that there was no reality in the peace thus arranged. A Chinese princess was sent as a wife for the heir-apparent, the *hien-wang* of the left. The Hiong-nu recommenced their invasions of the three provinces of Shen-se, Shan-se, and Petche-li,' and so on as before.

There was however during all this period a pretty steady decline of the power of the barbarians, and an equally steady increase in that of their civilised neighbours. Especially noteworthy in this respect was the long reign of the great emperor Woo-te, which lasted from 140 to 86 BC, or, shall we say, from the time of Cato the Censor to that of Cicero. This monarch Woo-te, whose victorious arms extended to Pegu, Siam, and Bengal, and who was a zealous patron of the morality of Confucius, was contemporary with seven successive *tan-jou*, and, but that his prosperity did not desert him at the end of his reign, he might, not inaptly, be called the Louis XIV of China.

The lives of three of his servants may be briefly noticed here for the sake of the light which they throw on the history of the Hiong-nu.

Chang-kiao was instructed (in 138 BC) by his master to establish communications with the Yue-ché, a Tartar people whom the Hiong-nu had driven from the east to the west of central Asia, and who had now established themselves in great force between the Oxus and Jaxartes, and even within the confines of the present Persian kingdom. Chang-kiao was made prisoner by the Hiong-nu while seeking to pass through their country in disguise. After ten years of captivity he escaped, reached the country of the Yue-ché (the modern Khorasan), remained there some time, storing up a large amount of valuable political information, and returned by way of Tibet, but even so was unable to escape from the Hiong-nu. His second captivity however was of short duration. Under cover of the troubles of a disputed succession, he again made his escape, and after an absence of twelve years, returned to his master's court.

Li-kwang-li, one of the bravest of the Chinese officers, was for sixty years (144–85 BC) perpetually giving and receiving hard blows in the wars with the Northern barbarians. They themselves so highly esteemed the skill and rapidity of his movements that they called him 'the winged general'. Once, it is said, at the head of one hundred horsemen, he put a large body of their cavalry to flight. Yet even he, after a defeat, had to endure the systematic ingratitude of his countrymen, and after counterfeiting death on the field of battle, was on the point of receiving it at the hands of the execu-tioner. He was permitted, however, to redeem his life by the payment of a large sum of money, but was degraded from all his dignities. But in the very next year the emperor found himself compelled to restore him to the chief military command, so pressing was the danger from the Northern invaders.

In the decline of life, this veteran soldier had the misfortune to see the honour of his family tarnished by the treason of his grandson Li-ling, one of the many Chinese generals who after defeat fled to the court of the *tan-jou*, and sold their knowledge of the strategic combinations of their countrymen for honours and offices in the barbarian court.

About nine years later (90 BC), the brave old general, who must now have been fully eighty years of age, again headed a grand attack upon the Hiong-nu. He met at first with complete success, and pushed the foe before him to the mountain barrier at the extreme north of their dominions. The forced marches, however, across the terrible desert of Gobi had too much weakened his troops. The *tan-jou* brought fifty thousand fresh men into the field, dug in the night a deep ditch in the rear of the Chinese forces, and thus added to the disorder and panic of their flight after the defeat of the morrow.*

Li-kwang-li was compelled to surrender at discretion, and taken pris-oner to the court of the *tan-jou*, who treated him with such marked favour (partly, perhaps, on account of his relationship to the already exiled Li-ling) that all the barbarian officers became jealous of his predominating influence.† Superstition was enlisted on the side of envy; in a dangerous ill-

* The historians, consulted by Mr Wylie [in his translation of the Han annals], put a somewhat different colour on this campaign of Li-kwang-li. According to them, Li-kwang-li, in the midst of a victorious expedition against the Hiong-nu, received a message, brought him by his servant Hoo-A-foo, to the effect that his wife and family had all been sentenced to death on account of Li-ling's defection. (This defection had hap-pened nine years before, but was perhaps only now bearing fruit manifestly in Li-ling's command of the Hiong-nu troops.) Hereupon Li-kwang-li, determined to do a desper-ate deed and either conquer fate or die, planned his march across the great desert. The chief historian of the Chinese army warned his comrades that the general was fighting wildly and staking his all on a single throw. He therefore advised them to seize Li-kwang-li, who however was beforehand with his critic, and cut off the chief historian's head. According to these writers the trench was cut by the Hiong-nu in front of the Chinese troops and the attack was made in their rear.
† One of the chief calumniators of Li-kwang-li, and he who eventually succeeded in getting him offered up as a sacrifice, was Wei-leuh, who had himself many years before deserted from the Chinese service, and who was bitterly jealous of the favour shown to the newcomer.

ness of the queen mother, the soothsayers declared that the gods of the Hiong-nu were offended because they received no more human sacrifices as of yore, but prisoners of war were now preserved alive, and even received into favour. Li-kwang-li was seized and sacrificed; a terrible succession of snowstorms followed, which destroyed a vast number of cattle, and pre-vented the seeds from germinating in the earth. Then they changed their minds and said that they had mistaken the will of the gods; but the fine old warrior, after his sixty years of battle, was beyond the reach of their repen-tance.

Woo-soo was sent (in 100 BC) by the emperor Woo-te upon one of those endless embassies for the arrangement of 'a lasting and honourable peace', which vary with their monotony of fraud the monotony of blood-shed. In the course of the discussions on this subject, he addressed himself to one of the Chinese fugitives, who had been promoted to a subordinate kingship in western Siberia, and reproached him so bitterly for his treason and want of patriotism, that the tan-jou, disregarding the sanctity of an ambassador's person, seized him and cast him into a ditch. There he lived for several days, exposed to all the rigour of the climate, and feeding only upon snow and the offal of the camp. The barbarians conceived that there must be something divine in the nature of a man who could endure such hardships, but they chose a singular means of testifying their admiration. They carried him off to the inhospitable shores of Lake Baikal, in the east of Siberia, where he dragged out life for nineteen years, his food being mice and the bitter fruits of the desert. Some of his countrymen, deserters, tried to reconcile him to his lot, and to persuade him to accept, as they had done, the bounty of the barbarian. 'No,' said he, 'I will remain true to my coun-try, whatever tortures her enemies may inflict upon me. A minister owes to his king the same affectionate duty which a child does to his parent.' And when he heard of the death of his master, the great Woo-te, he turned his face to the beloved south, looked towards China, and burst into tears. The remorse which the tan-jou felt for the death of Li-kwang-li turned out bene-ficially for Woo-soo, who, after his weary captivity, was at length restored to his country.

In the early days of the conquering tan-jou, Tibet appears to have felt their influence, and the whole of eastern Turkestan (or what Deguignes calls 'Little Bukharia') seems to have been in complete dependence upon them. Even then, however, for some reason which is not explained, but which is probably connected with the physical geography of the country, their invasions of China were always made on the north, never on the west frontier. If they thus missed an opportunity of taking their enemy in flank, he, when his turn of superiority came, showed more skilful strategy; and the great triumph of the reign of Woo-te was the series of conquests and alliances by which he turned the south-west flank of the Hiong-nu position.

Anyone who now looks at the map of Asia will see a long thin slice of territory stretching forth at the north-western angle of China (from the Hoang-ho to Su-chow, long. 98°). This is ground won from the barbar-ians, and made strong by the Chinese monarchs for the defence of the empire. It is, in fact, an arm stretched forth into the desert, by which China seems to say, 'Not this way, barbarians of the North! fight, if you will fight, fairly, face to face; but you shall not come round to my left side, and there deal me stealthily an assassin's blow.'

After the conquest of this territory came the secret mission of Chang-kiao through Tibet, to the country between the Oxus and Jaxartes, and this produced immense results. Where the stealthy emissary had gone, victori-ous armies followed. Khotan, Yarkand, Kashgar accepted the alliance, or became the subjects of the Chinese emperor. The Ou-sioun, a powerful people, kindred with but hostile to the Hiong-nu, and dwelling to the south of Lake Balkhash, were encouraged to lean on China for protection against the common intervening foe: and a Chinese governor was perma-nently established at Aksou, under the steeps of the Thian Shan (about 78° long. and 42° lat.).

In the year 71 BC a great army amounting, it is said, to two hundred thousand men, was sent against the Hiong-nu under the command of seven generals. Notwithstanding the mismanagement and cowardice of some of the generals, this expedition seems, more than anything else, to have broken the power of the Hiong-nu.

It was not without some protest from the timid conservatism of the Chinese ministers that this energetic policy was pursued. When Siven-ti, the great-grandson of Woo-te, was meditating an expedition, half-hostile, half-friendly, to the country of the Ouigours (near Turfan, long. 89°) he was met by the outspoken remonstrances of a wise old counsellor named Goei-siang. This sage appears not to have been perplexed by any of those difficulties as to the triumph of injustice and the downfall of the good which have troubled the sages and seers of other nations.

'There are five sorts of wars,' said he. 'The first, for the suppression of civil tumult. This is a war of justice, and it is sure to be successful. The second, in which you oppose a foreign invader, is a war of necessity, and is generally crowned with victory. In the third kind of war, one of rage and fury, in which men take up arms about mere trifles, one is often beaten. To invade the lands of others for the sake of spoil is the fourth species of war, that of avarice, and in this success is not to be expected. But when a monarch fights only in order to acquire glory, to render his family illustrious and become a terror to his neighbours, that is a war of ambition and pride, the results of which are uniformly disastrous. These five points are so many maxims founded on the dealings of heaven. At present the Hiong-nu desire peace, while our own internal condition is far from satisfactory. It is no rare occurrence to see a son murder his father, a younger brother the elder, a wife her husband. Twenty-two crimes of this kind have occurred in the course of the past year. We ought to apply a remedy to these social disorders instead of carrying war into the country of our neighbours.'

Notwithstanding these excellent remarks, the policy of war and annexation prevailed. The Ouigours became tributary, and the Hiong-nu felt the predominant influence of China all round their southern and western frontiers. The barbarians saw that their empire was departing from them, and fell into confusion and anarchy. In the year 58 BC five tan-jou were warring against one another. Hou-han-sie, apparently the rightful heir, at length emerged from the contest, sole tan-jou; but, almost immediately after, had to enter upon a new and fiercer contest with two fresh competitors, one of them his own brother. The upshot of the whole business was, that he humbly presented himself at the court of the Chinese emperor, promised subjection and tribute, and received from this hereditary enemy assistance which at length enabled him to reign without a rival.*

In a feeble and crippled state, the Hiong-nu empire lasted on for a century and a half from this time (58 BC to AD 93), but never again as the equal foe, generally as the vassal, occasionally as the revolted subject of the court of China.

About the middle of the first century after Christ, the nation became finally divided into two hostile sections – a northern and a southern.

---

* On the death of Hou-han-sie, 31 BC, a generous rivalry took place between his children, which should not succeed him. Besides other wives he had married two sisters, daughters of his prime minister. The elder sister, chief in rank, had the younger children, and this led to a discussion whether the dignity of the mother or the age of the children ought to be most regarded. Eventually all the four sons in question succeeded, first the two

Doubtless the dwellers in the immediate neighbourhood of China became more dependent on the good things which accompany civilisation than the wild nomads of the north-west; and then the physical barrier of the great desert of Gobi would probably intensify and perpetuate the moral division. From this time forwards the *tan-jou* of the south becomes one of the most eager enemies of the northern kingdom, ever besieging the ear of the Chinese emperor with cries for its demolition.

At the same time a new enemy pressed upon them from the east. The neighbouring tribe of the Sien-pi whom the great *tan-jou* Mé-té had cooped up in the mountains of what is now called Manchuria, after brooding for three centuries over their wrongs, now found the longed-for opportunity of vengeance. After forty years of more or less constant warfare with this triple league of foes, symptoms of dissolution began to show themselves in the northern kingdom. Vast hordes of the Hiong-nu, in one case amounting to a quarter of a million of fighting men, went over bodily to the Chinese. A terrible famine, the work of some locust-like insect, then wasted the country. A combined invasion of the Chinese and the southern Hiong-nu on a large scale took place in the year AD 89. The Chinese general, Teou-hien, put the *tan-jou* to flight, and having advanced one thousand miles into his kingdom, left upon one of the mountain ranges an inscription composed by the historiographer who accompanied the expedition, recording the success of his arms. In two years however even this effort was surpassed: the Chinese troops reached the Irtish, the western frontier of the dominions of the Hiong-nu, the *tan-jou* had again to take shelter in some Siberian desert, and his mother was taken prisoner.

Teou-hien, though victorious, recommended his imperial master to spare his fallen foes. But on his death sterner counsels prevailed. A new *tan-*

---

elder by the inferior wife, and then the two younger by the chief consort. Their regal names were as follows, and as they are a fair type of their class, the reader will perceive the reason for so often speaking of the *tan-jou* by his title and not quoting his name:

(1) Feou-tchou-loui-jo-ti (*jo-ti* = the Greek *philopator* [father-lover])
(2) Seou-hiai-jo-ti
(3) Tche-ya-jo-ti
(4) Ou-tchou-lieou-jo-ti

In course of time two more sons of Hou-han-sie succeeded to the throne:

(5) Ou-loui-jo-ti and
(6) Hou-tou-ulh-chi-tao-jo-ti

It is perhaps an unworthy Aryan prejudice which finds a certain amount of uncouthness in these Turanian names.

jou who had been raised to the throne was driven into revolt, a revolt hope-less from the first (AD 93). He himself fell into the hands of the Chinese forces, and was beheaded. The Sien-pi poured into the defenceless country like a torrent. Great multitudes of the Hiong-nu consented to pass under their yoke and bear their name, the rest fled westwards across the Irtish, set-tling by the Ural river and near the modern Russian government of Orenburg. Thus did the great barbarian empire, which for two thousand years had been measuring its forces against the civilisation of China, fall, with apparently irretrievable ruin.

All this occurred in the reign of Domitian. It was not till nearly three centuries later (AD 376) that the Huns, during the reign of Valens, crossed the sea of Azov or the stream of the Volga, and fell upon the affrighted and disgusted Gothic subjects of King Hermanric. This long interval of qui-escence and of obscurity is the weak place in the identification of the Hiong-nu and the Huns. It is impossible not to feel that many changes might have occurred during that time, and that mere similarity of name is a slight clue by which to traverse so vast a distance.

The Chinese historians necessarily give during this interval far scantier information than previously as to the affairs of central Asia. The expulsion of the northern Hiong-nu appears to have been a 'victory of Pyrrhus' for the Chinese empire. The southern Hiong-nu and the Sien-pi, under vari-ous barbarous names, formed settlements within its limits and erected dynasties which disputed the throne of China itself with its native princes. In such a state of things the historians of that country had but little induce-ment or opportunity to record the revolutions of western Asia. We are enabled however, dimly and at long intervals, to trace the continued exis-tence of a Hiong-nu people along the line of the Volga and the northern shores of the Caspian.

To the west of them, but separated by one fierce Tartar people, the Chi-nese historians placed the great kingdom of Ta-Tsin. Their description of this kingdom is so curious that a few of its leading features may be here inserted. 'It is a country of large extent with many dependent kingdoms. The walls are built of stone; inns are placed along the lines of road. All sorts of trees and plants are found there. The inhabitants are given to agri-culture, and even understand how to keep silkworms. They cut their hair and wear very fine clothes. They have all sorts of chariots with white cover-ings: in war they have drums, flags, and tents. The capital is thirty-four miles in circumference; it contains five palaces by the waterside, supported

on pillars. Every day the king goes to one or other of these palaces to administer justice. Before his chariot walks an officer holding an open bag in
which are placed the petitions of all who present themselves, which are
examined by the king when he enters the palace. Thirty-six generals of the
army form a council of state to deliberate on the affairs of the empire. The
king does not always hold his office for life; they generally endeavour to
choose a wise man, but should any extraordinary calamity occur, for
instance any great whirlwind or inundation, they change their ruler, and he
who is thus deposed appears to descend into private life without a sigh.

'Gold, silver, precious stones, rich and beautifully embroidered vest-
ments abound in this country. They have both gold and silver money: ten
pieces of the latter are equivalent to one of the former. They trade both with
the Parthians and Indians. They have often endeavoured to enter into direct
commercial relations with China, but have always been prevented by the
Parthians. Recently' (in the year corresponding to AD 166) 'the king of the
Ta-Tsin named Gan-tun succeeded in sending ambassadors, who were
followed by merchants, to China by way of India. The inhabitants of Ta-
Tsin are tall and well made like the Chinese, whence their name' (Ta =
great: Tsin = China or the Chinese). This last sentence will probably
have disclosed to the reader the real name of the country in question. Only
the Romans of that day could be considered worthy of being called by a
Chinese historian 'great as the Chinese'. He has been reading a description
of *imperium Romanum** by a Chinese pen, and the king, Gan-tun, is the
emperor Marcus (Aurelius) Antoninus.

The question will naturally be asked, 'Why, if these Hiong-nu,
marauders as they were by nature, had wandered so near to the confines of
this alluring kingdom of Ta-Tsin, did they allow three centuries to elapse
before they commenced their invasions of that empire?' Dimly and vaguely,
through the faint twilight of their history, we may conjecture the following
reasons for their quiescence: there may have been a hundred others which
are to us undiscoverable.

First, their eyes were still turned eastwards; their expeditions still sometimes reached as far as Khamil (long. 95° E), and for generations they seem
to have cherished the hope of once more ravaging the valley of the Hoang-
ho. At length their old enemies, the Sien-pi, under the dynasty of the Topa,
built up, in the old country of the Hiong-nu, a sufficiently solid empire to
check all eastward incursions on their part.

* [The Roman Empire.]

But, secondly, between their new home and western civilisation a strong barrier was presented by the fierce nation of the Alani, Turanian nomads like themselves, who, under the name of Alanna, are spoken of by the Chinese historians as occupying the country of Yen-Tcai, the extensive district which is bounded by the Volga on the north, the Caucasus on the south, the sea of Azov and the Don on the west, and the Caspian and Volga on the east. These are the people who for so many generations adored a naked sabre stuck into the earth as their only divinity. They were at length, after contests the duration and severity of which are hidden from us, overcome by those neighbours of theirs whom we may now without fear of contradiction venture to call the Huns. Some, the Alani of the Don, became amalgamated with the armies of the conqueror, others fled west-wards and bore a part, recognised in history, in the subversion of the Roman Empire, though it did not fall to their lot to found any enduring kingdom within its borders.

Hopes of Chinese spoil on the east, the reality of Alan resistance on the west, were doubtless two reasons for the long sojourn of the Hiong-nu east-wards of the Volga. A third, which it is sufficient merely to indicate, is the prestige, slowly and with difficulty impaired, of the Roman Empire, of that 'Ta-Tsin' which 'Gan-tun' and his immediate predecessors had ruled so wisely and made so strong.

A fourth is the utterly broken and dispirited state of the Hiong-nu themselves. After their flight from their old home in central Asia, they seem to have ceased to elect tan-jou; the unity of the nation was gone, the degree of organisation, the semblance of a polity which they had before possessed, probably vanished. Removed from the civilising influences of contact with China they doubtless sank lower and lower into mere squalid savagery, becoming a loosely united bundle of roving hordes, until at length increase of numbers brought with it confidence, the remembrance of past su-premacy stirred up shame at their present abject condition, the success of their conflict with the Alans assured them of victory, and turning their backs definitively on the east, they crossed the Cimmerian Bosporus – whether guided by a demon stag or not we need not enquire – to work, both directly and indirectly, more ruin and greater changes in the fair king-doms of Ta-Tsin than their mightiest tan-jou had ever done in the often-wasted provinces of the real China.

This chapter was commenced by Claudian's poetical description of the Huns; at its close let us listen to the historian Ammianus Marcellinus, a soldier, and more strictly a contemporary, describing in what guise they showed themselves when first 1,500 years ago, they burst upon Europe.

'The nation of the Huns, little known to ancient records, but spreading from the marshes of Azov to the icy sea, surpasses all other barbarians in wildness of life. In the first days of infancy, deep incisions are made in the cheeks of their boys, in order that, when the time comes for whiskers to grow there, the sprouting hairs may be kept back by the furrowed scars: and hence they grow to maturity and to old age beardless as eunuchs. They all, however, have strong and well-knit limbs and fine necks. Yet they are of portentous ugliness and so crook-backed that you would take them for some sort of two-footed beasts, or for the roughly chipped stakes which one sees used for the railings of a bridge. And though they do just bear the likeness of men (of a very ugly pattern), they are so little advanced in civilisation that they make no use of fire, nor of any kind of relish, in the preparation of their food, but feed upon the roots which they find in the fields, and the half-raw flesh of any sort of animal. I say half-raw, because they give it a kind of cooking by placing it between their own thighs and the backs of their horses. They never seek the shelter of houses, which they look upon as little better than tombs, and will only enter upon the direst necessity: nor would one be able to find among them even a cottage of wattled rushes: but wandering at large over mountain and through forest, they are trained to bear from their infancy all the extremes of cold, of hunger, and of thirst.

'They are clad in linen raiment, or in the skins of field mice sewn together, and the same suit serves them for use indoors and out. However dingy the colour of it may become, the tunic which has once been hung round their necks is never laid aside nor changed till through long decay the rags of it will no longer hold together. Their heads are covered with bent caps, their hairy legs with the skins of goats; their shoes, never having been fashioned on a last, are so clumsy that they cannot walk comfortably.

'On this account they are not well adapted to pedestrian encounters; but then on the other hand they are almost welded to their horses, which are hardy, though of ugly shape, and on which they sometimes ride women's fashion. On horseback every man of that nation lives night and day; on horseback he buys and sells; on horseback he takes his meat and drink, and when night comes he leans forward upon the narrow neck of his horse and there falls into a deep sleep, or wanders into the varied fantasies of dreams.

'When a discussion arises upon any matter of importance they come on horseback to the place of meeting. No kingly sternness overawes their deliberations, but being upon the whole well contented with the disorderly guidance of their chiefs, they do not scruple to interrupt the debates with anything that comes into their heads.

'When attacked, they will sometimes engage in regular battle. Then, going into the fight in order of columns, they fill the air with varied and discordant cries. More often, however, they fight in no regular order of battle, but being extremely swift and sudden in their movements, they disperse, and then rapidly come together again in loose array, spread havoc over vast plains, and flying over the rampart, they pillage the camp of their enemy almost before he has become aware of their approach. It must be owned that they are the nimblest of warriors; the missile weapons which they use at a distance being pointed with sharpened bones admirably fastened to the shaft: when in close combat, they fight without regard to their own safety, and while their enemy is intent upon parrying the thrusts of their swords, they throw a net over him and so entangle his limbs that he loses all power of walking or riding.

'Not one among them cultivates the ground, or ever touches a plough handle. All wander abroad without fixed abodes, without home, or law, or settled customs, like perpetual fugitives, with their wagons for their only habitations, in which their wives weave their foul garments, and bring forth children, and rear them up to the age of puberty.* If you ask them, not one can tell you what is his place of origin; he was conceived in one place, born in another, educated perhaps in some yet more distant one. They are great truce-breakers, fickle, always ready to be swayed by the first breath of a new desire, abandoning themselves without restraint to the most ungovernable rage.

'Finally, like animals devoid of reason, they are utterly ignorant of what is seemly and what is not; they are tricksters with words, and full of dark sayings; they are never moved by either religious or superstitious awe; they burn with unquenchable thirst for gold, and they are so changeable and so easily moved to wrath, that many times in the day they will quarrel with their comrades on no provocation, and be reconciled having received no satisfaction.'

* The squalid prototype of the gorgeous harem of the Ottomans.

CHAPTER II

Attila and the Court of Constantinople

FOR HALF A CENTURY AFTER THE IRRUPTION of the Huns into Dacia, they exercise but little direct influence on the course of Roman history. Occasionally they made a predatory inroad into the Empire, as, for instance, in the year 395, when, at the instigation, it was said, of the prefect Rufinus, they moved southwards from Caucasus upon Armenia, and pressed on through Cappadocia and Cilicia,* until

> The pleasant fields of Syria waste were laid,
> And hostile chargers trampled down the glade
> Of soft Orontes, to her children's dance
> And song more used than war's dread dissonance.†

And thirteen years later, under the guidance of a chief named Uldis,‡ they crossed the Danube and penetrated far into Bulgaria. When the prefect of Thrace sought humbly for peace, Uldis proudly pointed to the sun and said, 'All that he shines upon I can conquer if I will.' But in the midst of his boastings his power was undermined: the Imperial emissaries were at work among his troops, contrasting the hard life of a Hunnish marauder with the ease and the dignity of a stipendiary of Rome. So large a part of his army yielded to these suggestions that Uldis was obliged to fly, and escaped but with life to the Dacian shore.

Upon the whole, during this period, while their enemies the Visigoths and other Teutonic tribes were still hovering about the Danube and the eastern ranges of the Alps, the attitude of the Huns seems to have been more often friendly than hostile to the Romans, in whose armies we saw them serving when Honorius decreed the overthrow of Stilicho, and when

---

* See vol. i, p. 375.   † Claudian, *In Rufinum*, ii.32–5.

‡ Perhaps the same person as Uldin, Stilicho's Hunnish auxiliary in the campaign against Radagaisus (405).

Aetius came too late to the succour of Joannes against Placidia.

And, mere barbarians as they remained to the end of their history, it is easy to see that this half-century of intercourse with Rome had taught them some few of the needs and enjoyments of civilised life. The whole character of Attila's court and camp was sensual, but the sensuality was by many degrees less squalid and less disgusting than that of the men who first crossed the sea of Azov, and whose habits were described by Ammianus.

Doubtless it was the interposition of the Teutonic nations which, during this half-century, prevented the Huns from coming to close quarters with the Roman power. After the Visigoths, the Vandals, and the Suevi had settled in Spain, the Alans in Gaul, the Burgundians in that province which yet bears their name, the Huns, having only the Danube and the Alps between them and the Empire, began to make the two Augusti, but especially him of Constantinople, feel their heavy hand.

In 432 we find a certain Roua or Rugula reigning over the Huns, and receiving from Theodosius II an annual payment, which might be called either subsidy or tribute, of 350 pounds weight of gold (£14,000 sterling). Finding that the Romans had dared to make alliances with some barbarous tribes, dwellers by the Danube, whom he claimed as his subjects, Roua in great wrath declared that all his treaties with Rome should be at once made null and void unless the emperor renounced his alliance with these nations. Another question of a more personal nature also arose now, if it had not arisen before, and was the subject of ceaseless negotiation for the next seventeen years. Many deserters had fled from the harsh yoke of Roua, and taken shelter on Roman territory. The demand was made, and was pressed home with every circumstance of insult upon the trembling Theodosius, 'Restore to me my fugitives.' Imagine such a request having been hinted, ever so courteously, to any Roman magistrate who in the old days sat upon the curule chair, with his lictors and fasces round him. Had it not been better for the omnipotent mistress of the nations to have died rather than live on to endure such degradation?

But Theodosius II, who was a meek man and an excellent illuminator of manuscripts, if not a born king of men, was preparing to send an embassy to mitigate the wrath of Roua, when tidings arrived that he was dead, and that the kingdom of the Huns had devolved upon his two nephews, sons of his brother Mundzuk, men in the vigour of early manhood, named Attila and Bleda.

It was in the year 433 that the two brothers ascended the throne. Bleda is to us the mere shadow of a name, but it is far otherwise with Attila.

It is almost needless to say that no coin, or picture, or bust remains to bring before us the lineaments of the terrible savage. Yet he seems almost to live again in the pages of Jordanes and Priscus. We see him short of stature, with the small, bead-like eyes, and snub nose and swarthy skin of his Tartar ancestors, yet with a haughty step, and a fierce way of darting his glances hither and thither, as though he felt himself lord of all, and were perpetually asking of the bystanders, 'Who is he that shall deliver you out of my hand?' He had a broad and well-formed chest and a large head, a scanty beard, like most of the Tartar race, and his hair was early sprinkled with white.

Few men that ever lived have had such a power of inspiring fear in the minds both of their subjects and their enemies as this Turanian chieftain. Enthusiasm, loyalty, gratitude, these were not the motives by which he swayed mankind, but the amount of abject, slavish fear which this little swarthy Kalmuck succeeded in instilling into millions of human hearts is not to be easily matched in the history of our race.

Whether he had much military talent may be doubted, since the only great battle in which he figured was a complete defeat. The impression left upon us by what history records of him is that of a gigantic bully, holding in his hands powers unequalled in the world for ravage and spoliation, by the mere threat of loosing which he extorts from trembling Caesars every concession which his insatiable avarice, or his almost superhuman pride, requires, and by the same terror compelling Ostrogoths and Gepidae, and other Germanic races far nobler than his own, to assist in drawing his triumphal chariot. But of true constructive genius, of any notion of the right way to found an enduring empire, of the statesmanship of Ataulfus, or even of Alaric, he shows not a trace. To drink out of vessels of gold and silver, to put his foot upon the neck of his enemies, to be the terror of the world, these seem to be his only delights as a ruler of men.

Some doubt has recently been thrown on the received accounts of the wide extent of Attila's power. So much of our information, it is said, is derived from Gothic sources, and a proud nation like the Goths had so obvious an interest in magnifying the might of the monarch by whom they themselves had been humbled, that we are bound to make considerable deductions from their statements, and may perhaps reduce the dominions of the worldwide conqueror to an extent not quite equal to that of the modern Austrian empire. But it may fairly be urged on the other hand that the

Greek historian Priscus confirms, or even amplifies the statements of the Goth. According to him, when the ambassadors from the Eastern and Western Empires were met in trembling conference, consulting how they might possibly obtain a reasonable answer from the haughty barbarian, the Romans said, 'His head is turned by his successes. No ruler of Scythia or of any other country has ever achieved so much in so short a time as he has. He rules over the islands in the Ocean' (by which we must probably under-stand the Scandinavian islands and peninsulas*); 'he has made the whole of Scythia his own; he has put the Roman Empire to tribute, and he thinks of renewing his attacks upon Persia. The road to that eastern kingdom is not untrodden by the Huns; already they have marched fifteen days' journey from a certain lake' (the sea of Azov the Romans thought, but more prob-ably the Caspian), 'and have ravaged Media.'†

Add to this apparently trustworthy statement of Priscus the firm belief of Deguignes that he has found traces in the historians of China of a con-federacy between Attila and the rulers of that country, and we have reasons for not lightly abandoning the old belief in the wide extent of the empire of Attila. The prince who felt China on his left, who threatened Persepolis, Byzantium, Ravenna in front, who ruled Denmark and its islands in his rear, and who ultimately appeared in arms on the soil of Champagne on his right, was no minor monarch, and had his empire been as deep as it was widespread, he might worthily have taken rank with Cyrus and Alex-ander.

At the same time it is well to remember that over far the larger part of this territory, Attila's can have been only an overlordship, Teutonic, Slavonic, and Tartar chieftains of every name bearing rule under him. His own personal government, if government it can be called, may very likely have been confined nearly within the limits of the modern Hungary and Transylvania.

For nineteen years, from 434 to 453, the sullen might of Attila lay like a

* It is perhaps deserving of consideration whether, if this northward impetus of Attila's subjects and allies really carried them to the Baltic and far into Denmark, it may not have something to do with the migrations of the English into Britain between the years 430 and 450. What they had before done against the *litus Saxonicum* ['the Saxon shore', i.e. the coasts of the Channel and lower North sea] had been apparently mere piracy and rob-bery. Now the whole nation migrates, a proceeding to which we can easily imagine them to have been stirred by the Teuton's loathing dread of the Mongol. And thus Attila may have been the unconscious founder of the English as well as of the Venetian dominion.
† Priscus, excerpt 11.

thundercloud over Europe. During that time the Eastern and Western courts were so closely united, as well by the bonds of relationship as by the overwhelming sense of their common danger, that it is not possible to dis-entangle their histories. Let us give a glance at the chief personages in the two courts.

The younger Theodosius, son of Arcadius, and emperor of the East, was in the twenty-fifth year of his age when we met with him (in 425), lead-ing his people from the Hippodrome to the basilica, to return thanks for the victory of his generals at Ravenna, which replaced his kinsfolk of the West on the Imperial throne. The fatuous dullness of his father and uncle no longer repels us in this member of the Theodosian family; he has some other employment than hunting; he illuminates sacred manuscripts with such skill as to earn the title of 'the calligrapher'; and he does not rush from blind confidence in his ministers to equally blind suspicion, with the in-stability which was so conspicuous in Arcadius and Honorius. Still, he is not a true king; he possesses no real momentum in the affairs of the state: as a rule, every important measure is decided upon by his sister Pulcheria, who is two years older than himself, who governs the East – as her aunt Placidia governs the West – respectably, but without genius, powerless to stem the quick-rushing torrent of barbarian ravage and change, but not conspicuously adding to the calamities of Rome by vices of her own.*

Theodosius himself, all through these years of political trouble and anx-iety, is much engrossed in the controversy concerning the union of the divine and human natures in Christ; but he does not win from it the same ecclesiastical renown which the council of Constantinople brought to his more celebrated namesake and grandfather. At the council of Ephesus he appears (through his ministers) to favour the heresy of Nestorius; at the close of his reign he leans towards the opposite heresy of Dioscorus and Eutyches, which is, immediately after his death, condemned by the great council of Chalcedon. At no time does he conspicuously defend the nar-row *via media* of orthodoxy.

It is strange that the marriages of the emperors of this family, which were daring and unconventional, did not remove from the race that effete

---

* It should be said that the historian Eunapius (excerpt 72) gives a terrible picture of the evils which afflicted the state 'under the empress Pulcheria'. But he does not appear to attribute them to her personal agency, and the root evil of all, the sale of public offices and the frightful corruption of the ministers of state, is spoken of in precisely similar terms a generation earlier, in the days of Arcadius and the eunuch Eutropius.

and worn-out character which attaches to its later scions. The mother of Theodosius II was a Frankish princess, beautiful and impetuous, who bore the name of Eudoxia. His wife, the equally beautiful but portion-less daughter of an Athenian rhetorician, brought up in the worship of the Olympian gods, was known in childhood by the name of Athenais, which, on her conversion to Christianity, she exchanged for that of Eu-docia. She was twenty-seven when her marriage with Theodosius, who was seven years her junior, raised her to the Imperial throne (421); but her influence seems never to have outweighed that of her sister-in-law Pul-cheria, and after twenty-three years of married life, at the mature age of fifty, she incurred a suspicion of unfaithfulness to her husband, and was ban-ished to Jerusalem, where she died in 460, after an exile of sixteen years.

The only child of this marriage, with whom history has to concern itself, is a daughter, a third Eudoxia (for that name and Eudocia seem to be interchangeable), who, as we have seen, was betrothed in her babyhood, and in the sixteenth year of her age (437) married, to Valentinian III, son of her father's aunt, but her own contemporary, with whom we have already made acquaintance as emperor of the West, reigning, but not gov-erning, under the tutelage of his mother Placidia.

After one more granddaughter of the great Theodosius has been named, the sketch of the two Imperial groups in the East and West will be complete. Besides her son Valentinian III, Placidia had a daughter Hon-oria (born 418), whose name was, for nearly twenty years, a byword and a horror in the two courts of Ravenna and Constantinople. Inheriting the coarse and sensual temperament of her father Constantius, and, like him, probably chafing at the restraints imposed on all the family of the 'sacred' emperors, she was detected in a low intrigue with one of the chamberlains of the palace (434). Her mother sent her to Constantinople, where for the next sixteen years of her life, she was kept more or less closely guarded, at the court of her cousin Theodosius. The foolish girl, who was but in the seventeenth year of her age, filled with wild resentment against her family and her native land, hating the calm and sorrowful face of her mother, hat-ing the severe dignity of Pulcheria, the psalmodies, the weaving, the visitations of the poor, in which she and her sisters passed their lives,*

* Sozomen, who was a contemporary historian, writes thus concerning Pulcheria and her sisters Arcadia and Marina: 'They all pursue the same mode of life, are sedulous in their attendance in the house of prayer, and evince great charity towards strangers and the poor. These sisters generally take their meals and walks together, and pass their days and

looked away to the gloomy North for vengeance, and called upon the squalid Hun to be her deliverer. She contrived to send a ring to Attila, who had become king of the Huns in the year preceding her disgrace, and begged to be considered as his wife, or rather, probably, as one of his wives, for the Huns, unlike the Goths, were polygamists. It was the wild act of a girl of sixteen, perhaps half-crazy with passion. We hear nothing of Attila's reply, nothing of any renewed applications on Honoria's part for his assistance. Probably her apartments in the palace at Constantinople were thenceforward too strictly guarded to allow of her repeating the message. But Attila treasured the ring, and in after-days pulled through that tiny circlet long threads of diplomacy and a bloody skein of war.

Immediately upon Attila's accession, an embassy from Theodosius waited upon him and Bleda, in order to settle the various questions which had been raised between the emperor and their deceased uncle Roua. The ambassadors met the kings at Margus, a town which stood at the point where the Morava, now the chief river of Serbia, empties itself into the Danube. Not only the Hunnish kings, but all their retinue, remained seated on horseback, and, that the dignity of Rome might not suffer in their persons, the ambassadors did the same. Yet, though etiquette might be maintained, Plinthas and Epigenes, the Roman envoys, did not win any very brilliant diplomatic triumph for their master. The *honorarium*, or stipend, or by whatever name the Romans chose to style that yearly payment which Attila, with ever-increasing frankness, called by its true designation, tribute, was raised from £14,000 to £28,000; the fugitive Huns and Romans were to be surrendered, or a fine of £8 per head paid for each who was not forthcoming; there were to be free markets at which the Romans and Huns should meet on equal terms, and any barbarian tribe upon which Attila might choose to levy war, was to be excluded from the alliance of Rome. In compliance with this treaty, two children of the royal blood of the Huns were surrendered by the Roman officers, and crucified on Roman territory by the orders of Attila. Their only crime was flight.

The next eight years are a blank in the Roman annals, as far as the Huns are concerned. It was at this time probably that Attila made those extensive conquests northwards and eastwards to which reference has already been made, that he pushed his dominion to the shores of the German ocean, and

their nights together in singing the praises of God. Like other exemplary women, they employ themselves in weaving and in similar occupations, avoiding idleness as unworthy of the life of virginity to which they have devoted themselves' (ix.4).

sent his armies fifteen days' march from the Caspian into Media.* According to some accounts, he also, during the same interval, marched into the country watered by the Rhône, and fought the Burgundians. However this may be, in 441 the curtain again lifts, and the first scene of conflict is that same Serbian town of Margus on the Morava, where we last saw Attila doubling the Roman tribute and discussing terms of peace with Plinthas and Epigenes. The bishop of this place had crossed the Danube on a marauding expedition, and robbed one of the royal treasure-houses of the Huns of the wealth deposited therein. Naturally this imitation of their own predatory tactics excited the fierce wrath of the barbarians. At the time of one of the great markets by the banks of the Danube, which were arranged for by the last treaty, the Huns made a savage attack on the unsuspecting Romans. To the expostulations of the Imperial court but one reply was returned: 'Give us up our refugees, and with our refugees the marauding bishop of Margus.' It began to be discussed among prefects and chamberlains whether it might not be better to give up this one rash bishop, that the whole nation should not perish. The rumour reached the ears of the reverend prelate, who determined to be beforehand with fate. Stealing across to the camp of the barbarians, he undertook to put them in possession of the city of Margus if the kings of the Huns would hold him harmless. Clasping his right hand, they swore to confer upon him all sorts of benefits if he would fulfil this promise. Then, having planted the barbarian host in a well-selected ambuscade on the northern shore of the Danube, he returned into the city, unsuspected by his fellow citizens, and at a given signal opened the gates to his new allies. They rushed in and sacked the place, and one of the chief border cities of Moesia was thus lost to the Empire.

An incident like this seems worth recording, since it marks the rapidly changing manners and positions of men during this century of barbarian invasion. Of course the occupant of the see of Margus was no fair specimen of his order, either in his first marauding expedition, or in his subsequent treachery: but when we look back over two centuries, from the time we have now reached to the days of Cyprian, or over one century to the courtly theologian disputants who hurried to the numberless councils of Constantius, and compare them with this mitred combatant, we feel that

---

* This may have been an earlier invasion. Priscus uses very vague language concerning it, and attributes it to 'Basik and Cursik, men belonging to the royal family of Scythia [the Huns] who commanded a great multitude of followers, and afterwards entered into alliance with Rome' (excerpt 11).

we have already passed from ancient history into the Middle Ages: we might imagine ourselves standing before the warrior-bishop of Beauvais, or one of the robber-bishops of the Rhine.

Out of the invasion, for which the fall of Margus gave the signal, another ecclesiastical complication, this time not with the Eastern but the Western Empire, took its rise. The town of Sirmium on the Save, situated in what is now the Austrian province of Slavonia, though it has left no modern representative of its former glories, was once one of the most important cities of Pannonia. The bishop of Sirmium, seeing his city invested by the Hunnish army (442), gathered together the chalices and patens and other sacred vessels of his church, all of gold, and apparently of considerable value, and contrived to send them secretly to one Constantius, a Gaul, who was at that time officiating as Attila's secretary. The object of the trust hereby created was to liberate the bishop if he should survive the capture of the city, or if he should die, then to ransom as many as possible of the citizens. The city was taken, and what became of the bishop we know not; but Constantius, ignoring the trust reposed in him, went off to Rome on private business, and there pawned the golden chalices for a large sum of money to a silversmith, named Silvanus.* Meanwhile his masters, Attila and Bleda, who probably did not like this journey to Rome on urgent private affairs, came to the conclusion that their secretary was playing the traitor, and soon after Constantius' return, he was crucified. Some time afterwards, the story of the embezzlement of the golden chalices came to the ears of Attila, and filled him with wrath. 'Had my secretary', said he, 'not deposited these chalices at Rome, they would have come into *my* possession on the death of the swindler. Silvanus therefore has really stolen my property, and unless the emperor of the West can restore the chalices, I insist that he shall surrender Silvanus to my vengeance.' How the affair, which dragged on for many years, at length terminated we know not, but we shall meet hereafter with an embassy from Valentinian III commissioned to treat on this important subject.

Three years after these events Bleda died (445), and Attila became sole ruler of the Huns. Historians have accepted, perhaps too readily, a version of the story which attributes to the great Hun the guilt of fratricide, not in passion, but with premeditation and cunning. With all his vices, treachery and

---

* This Silvanus held some official position, but what, it is difficult to say. He was 'president of the board of silver at Rome'. This may mean either that he was a *praepositus argentariorum*, or *primicerius scrinii ab argento*, probably the latter (see *Notitia Occidentis*, 10).

secret assassination scarcely seem consonant with the rest of his character.*

In the year 447, Attila led his barbarian warriors on the most formidable of all his expeditions against the Eastern Empire. No detailed account of it has been preserved, but it is evident that no inroad of so destructive a kind had pierced the provinces between the Adriatic and the Aegean since Alaric met Stilicho in the Peloponnesus. The Huns pushed southwards as far as Thermopylae, and eastwards to the shore of the Dardanelles, where, at Gallipoli, they inflicted a disastrous defeat on the Roman troops.† The walls of Constantinople, on this occasion as on so many subsequent ones, saved the very existence of the Empire. But though the tide of barbarian invasion rolled back into its old bed when there was nothing more left to ravage in the open country, a panic fear seized the rulers of the state, who submitted with abject eagerness to every demand which their master, for such they now considered him, might please to make upon them. Anatolius, a man of high rank who had held the office, still regarded with some of its old veneration, of Roman consul, was sent to Attila's camp to negotiate terms of peace. The yearly tribute, which had been doubled at Attila's succession, was now tripled, and stood at £84,000, and at the same time £240,000 in gold were handed over as a settlement of past arrears. In order to raise this sum, all the usual fiscal expedients of a weak, yet tyrannical government were resorted to. To have the reputation of wealth was the surest passport to misery. Each senator was assessed upon a certain sum, often greatly in excess of his real fortune; but the amount which stood opposite to his name had to be provided, whether he possessed it or not. Blows and insults enforced the demands of the officers of the Imperial exchequer, and the upshot of the whole was that in some cases the family jewels of ladies of high rank, or the articles of household furniture of men who had passed all their lives in affluence, were exposed for sale in the market-place; while in other yet more desperate cases, the unhappy Roman noble escaped by the aid of a cord, or by the slower process of self-starvation, into a land whither even the ministers of Theodosius could not follow him. And all this time the misery of the

* Marcellinus and Jordanes, the chief authorities for the story of the fratricide, were separated by an interval of nearly a century from the event. On the other hand Priscus, the contemporary and guest of the king, speaks of Bleda's death casually and calmly, and does not hint at any tragedy connected with it. But it is true that only fragments of his history remain.

† It need hardly be observed that, in the language of the historians of the time, the inhabitants of Thrace, of Syria, and of Egypt are still as uniformly spoken of under the name of Romans as those who were born and died by the banks of the Tiber.

situation was aggravated by the thought that while the defence of the country was neglected, and, in consequence, these frightfully heavy subsidies had
to be paid to her invaders, 'the country's wealth and the royal treasures were
being applied, not to their proper uses, but to ridiculous shows, tawdry
pageants, and all the pleasures and all the extravagances of sensuality, such
as no sensible man would have wasted money upon, even had the state
been in the height of prosperity. Far less ought these men to have thus acted,
who had so far neglected the military art that not only the Huns, but all the
other barbarous tribes round had bound the Roman state to the payment of
tribute.'*

The ruler of the Huns marked well the abject terror of the Byzantine
court, and traded upon it with the low cunning of a savage. Scarcely had
the treaty of Anatolius been concluded, when Attila sent ambassadors to
Theodosius, demanding, in the usual formula, 'the surrender of the fugitives'. The Roman emperor could only reply, 'We have surrendered all who
were in our power'; but in order to secure powerful friends in the Hunnish
encampment, he not only treated the ambassadors with splendid hospitality, but loaded them with rich presents on their departure. Again, and
again, and again, four times in the space of a twelvemonth, did Attila
repeat this process, selecting always for his ambassador some needy favourite
whom he had a desire to enrich, and inventing such ridiculous pretexts for
his embassies that all could see his real motive in sending them. This plan of
pacific invasion began to tire out the patience of the meek emperor and his
ministers. His sister Pulcheria no longer now exercised a predominant
influence in the affairs of state. Theological discussions seem to have
divided the Imperial pair. She adhered to that side which was eventually, at
the council of Chalcedon, decreed to be the side of orthodoxy; while the
rival, and now reigning influence at court was that of the eunuch
Chrysaphius, godson and partisan of Eutyches, the fanatic asserter of the
absolute oneness of the nature of Christ even during the time of his incar-
nation. Judging by the acts of Chrysaphius, we may safely conclude that
any opinion of his on such a question was as valuable as the opinion of an
Australian savage concerning the philosophy of Plato.

In the year 448, yet another embassy arrived at Constantinople, more
famous and more fateful than any which had preceded it. Let us observe
well the names of the two chief ambassadors, for these are men who either
by themselves or by their offspring will make a deep and ineffaceable mark

* Priscus, excerpt 9.

on the history of their time. Edecon is introduced to us as a 'Scythian', that is, a Hun,* 'who had accomplished mighty deeds in war'. He was evidently also one of the most intimate counsellors of Attila. No small degree of jealousy existed between him and his colleague Orestes. This man, as we might have inferred from his name, was not of barbarian extraction. He was of 'Roman' descent (a term which is of course consistent with any provincial nationality within the limits of the Roman Empire), and 'he dwelt in that part of Pannonia which borders on the Save', that is to say, within the limits of the modern Austrian province of Slavonia. He was at this time a regular subject of Attila, his country, which was included in the Western emperor's share of Illyricum, having recently been ceded by Aetius to the Huns. He married the daughter of a certain count Romulus, who dwelt at Poetovio in Noricum, the place which is now called Pettau. From this marriage was born to Orestes, probably about ten years after the date at which we have now arrived, a son who was named after his maternal grandfather Romulus, and upon whom history has fastened the unkind nickname of Augustulus. The other ambassador, Edecon, was probably already the father of a son whom he had named Odovacar (Odoacer). These two ambassadors, on arriving at the Imperial court, presented the letters of their lord, in which, as usual, he expressed his high displeasure at the conduct of the Romans with reference to the refugees. War, immediate war, was threatened unless these were surrendered. Further, there must be no attempt on the part of the Romans to cultivate the district which would in later times have been called the march of the Danube. This was a belt of territory about one hundred miles wide on the southern side of the great stream,† which Attila claimed to have annexed by right of conquest after his recent campaign. If this condition were not observed, war. The position of the great market for the interchange of Roman and Hunnish

---

* As before remarked, the term Scythian, as used by the Greek historians, is of no ethnological value whatever. In classical times it meant probably sometimes Slavonic tribes, sometimes a race with Thracian affinities. Zosimus uses it regularly of the Goths, and now, in Priscus, it is the accepted equivalent for the Huns. Probably it was not intended to mean more than 'the barbarians (of whatever race) living north of the Danube and the Euxine'.

† Its width was 'five days' journey for a well-trained pedestrian'. This certainly would not mean less than twenty miles a day. It was to reach from Pannonia (now Attila's by treaty with Aetius) on the west to Novae, now Sistova, in Bulgaria on the east. Eastward of Novae probably commenced the territory of the imperfectly subdued Acatziri. The dimension of the march from west to east would be about three hundred miles.

commodities must be shifted. It had been fixed at Margus, on the Danube; now it was to be at Naissus, the modern Nish, 150 miles up the Morava, in Serbia. And, lastly, ambassadors were to be sent to Attila, to talk over the points in dispute; and these were to be no men of second-rate position in the state, but men who had sat in the curule chair of the consuls, and the most eminent even among them. If these high dignitaries were afraid to under-take so long and wild a journey, he, the great king, would condescend to come as far as Sardica to meet them. Such was the imperious mandate of Attila, uttered by the lips of Edecon, and translated by the interpreter Vig-ilas to him, who was saluted by the names, once so mighty, *imperator* and *Augustus*. Edecon then went to the house of Chrysaphius to confer with that minister as to the subject of his embassy. On his way he said to the interpreter, Vigilas, 'How beautiful is the emperor's palace, how richly adorned with all precious things, and how happy must be the lives of the lords of such magnificence.' Vigilas repeated the remark to Chrysaphius, and with the words a wicked thought entered the mind of the Monophysite eunuch. He said to Edecon, 'You, too, might sit under gilded ceilings of your own, and be lord of vast wealth, if you would leave the party of the Huns and take up ours.'

Edecon. 'I could not do that, being another man's servant, without my lord's consent.'

Chrysaphius. 'Have you free access to your lord's person?'

Edecon. 'Yes. I am one of the nobles selected for the purpose of keeping watch in arms over his person. We serve for so many days and then are relieved.'

Chrysaphius. 'If you will promise secrecy, I can tell you something very greatly to your advantage. Come to dine with me, without Orestes and your other colleagues, and we can talk the matter over at our leisure.'

So a secret meeting was arranged at the house of the eunuch, and there in the presence and by the assistance of Vigilas, evidently a Byzantine dragoman of the worst type, a vile plot was hatched. Chrysaphius first swore that what he had to say should in no case injure Edecon. Edecon swore a counter-oath that he would not reveal, even if he could not accom-plish, the designs of the minister; and then Chrysaphius at length uttered the fatal secret. 'If when you return to Scythia you will slay Attila and then come to us, you shall have a happy life here and vast wealth.'

Edecon. 'I promise to do so. But I shall want some small sum of money to be paid me in advance, say about fifty pounds of gold [£2,000], in order to ensure the co-operation of the common soldiers under my command.'

Chrysaphius. 'There will be no difficulty about that. You shall have the money at once.'

Edecon. 'No, I will not take it at once, for Attila will ask me on my return, as he asks all his ambassadors, how much the mission has been worth to me; and I could not deceive him because all my colleagues will know what weight of gold I am carrying back. You must let me return to report the answer of your master as to the refugees, and Vigilas must come with me to receive the rejoinder of mine. Then, through Vigilas, I will send you word how the rest of the gold (beyond the ordinary gratuity to an ambassador) had better be sent to me.'

This plan met with the full approval of the eunuch, who, as soon as he had dismissed his guest, hurried away to the palace to inform Theodosius of the new prospect of an early termination of Attila's embassies. The Imperial calligrapher, the illuminator of sacred manuscripts, at once accepted the proposal, and calling in Martialius, the *magister officiorum*, and chief of what we should call the secret service department, consulted with him what shape the return embassy to Attila should now assume. Of a truth many things were changed, and not altogether for the better, since the consul Fabricius handed over to Pyrrhus the traitor who proposed to purchase the favour of Rome by administering poison to his master.

In order to cloak the atrocious scheme thus concocted, the emperor and his minister decided to send to the court of Attila a sham embassy, in whose train the intending murderers might travel unsuspected, regardless, of course, of the danger to which they exposed the innocent envoy, who in the event of the plot being discovered was likely to plead in vain the sanctity of an ambassador's person. The man selected for this post was Maximin, an officer of high, but not the highest, rank, and of illustrious lineage, but whose name had not figured in the consular *fasti* [official register]. He invited Priscus 'the sophist', or, as we should say, professor of rhetoric and man of letters, to accompany him, and it is to the diary of the embassy kept by Priscus, and afterwards interwoven by him into his history, that we are indebted for almost all trustworthy details of the court and camp of Attila.* He assures us emphatically, and the whole course of the history tends to confirm his statement, that the murder secret was not confided

* Many of the details which Priscus gives as to the movements of the ambassadors are so unnecessarily minute as to suggest the conclusion that they were jotted down from day to day and almost from hour to hour while the embassy was still proceeding.

either to him or to his patron, but that the ostensible object of their mission was to them the real one. As both Maximin and Priscus seem still to have adhered to the worship of the Olympian divinities, we are driven, however reluctantly, to the conclusion that by this time the traitors, the time-servers, and the hypocrites had ranged themselves on the side of successful Chris- tianity, and that when the emperor wanted a man of indisputably high character and sterling honesty to mask by his innocence a dark and nefari- ous design, his thoughts naturally turned to the few remaining pagan statesmen, who probably held at his court a position not unlike that of the Roman Catholics under Queen Elizabeth or the Huguenots under Louis XIII.

The message which was entrusted to Maximin was couched in a less servile tone than the recent replies of Theodosius. As if they already saw the knife of the assassin piercing the heart of the great Hun, the emperor and the eunuch began to express their weariness of Attila's perpetual rec- lamations. 'You ought not to overleap the obligations of treaties and invade the Roman territory. As for fugitives, besides those already surrendered, I now return you seventeen, and I really have no more.' So ran the letter. Verbally Maximin was instructed to say that Attila must not expect ambas- sadors of any higher rank than him who now spoke to be sent to him, since this had not been the usage with his own ancestors or any of the other Northern rulers, but the custom had hitherto been to send any chance person, soldier or letter-carrier, whose services were available. And as for the king's proposition to come and meet an ambassador of consular rank at Sardica, he himself had made that impossible by his sack of that very town. Such was the contemptuous reply of the Byzantine to the Hunnish court as it was intended to have been delivered; but not such was the actual message which reached the ears of Attila; for, as we shall see, like good wine it mellowed considerably on the journey.

The first fortnight of travel seems to have been pleasant and uneventful enough. During all this time the Roman and barbarian ambassadors were passing through the comparatively tranquil and prosperous province of Thrace. At the end of it they reached Sardica, about 350 miles from Con- stantinople, and the first city of Dacia Mediterranea. This was the place at which almost exactly a century before (343) the celebrated council had been held which enunciated again the Nicene creed, and gave to the see of Rome the right of deciding whether a bishop had been lawfully deposed. Other matters, however, than theological wrangles had of late forced themselves on the attention of the unhappy inhabitants of Sardica. As we have just heard from the lips of Theodosius, the town had been terribly pillaged and laid waste by Attila. The destruction, however, was not complete. There were still houses and some inhabitants from whom it was possible for the ambassadors to buy sheep and oxen. These they killed and roasted; and having prepared a goodly repast, they thought it would be but courteous to ask Edecon and the barbarians attending him to partake with them. As they sat long over the meal, conversation turned upon the greatness and majesty of their respective masters. The Huns, of course, magnified the might of Attila; the Romans tried to extol their great Augustus. At this point of the conversation, Vigilas, with an indiscretion which can only be accounted for by supposing that he had plied the winecup too freely, said, 'I cannot think it right to compare gods and men together. Attila, after all, is but a man, while Theodosius I look upon as a god.' At these words the Huns started up with flushed cheeks and angry eyes; and the pleasant diplomatic banquet was on the point of ending in bloodshed. Priscus and Maximin however succeeded in silencing their noisy colleague, guided the conversation into safer channels, and by their civility mollified the wrath of the Huns. That there might be no chance of any rancorous feeling remaining in their minds, Maximin, when the banquet was over, made handsome presents, both to Edecon and Orestes, of silken raiment and 'Indian jewels'.*

The bestowal of these presents led to another curious outburst of angry feeling. Orestes sat out all his companions, and when they were gone came up to Maximin and thanked him heartily for his presents. 'You', said he, 'are a wise man, of a most excellent disposition. You are not like those insolent courtiers at Byzantium, who gave presents and invitations to Edecon but none to me.' 'When? where? how?' gasped out the puzzled ambassador; but Orestes, vouchsafing no more particular statement of his grievances, stalked moodily out of the room.

Next day, on the journey, Maximin and Priscus reported this strange conversation to Vigilas. He, of course, knew well enough to what it referred, but did not choose to explain. He only said, 'Orestes has no business to be offended. He is but a secretary, a mere squire of Attila: Edecon is of course differently treated. He is a great warrior and a Hun by birth, and far superior in position to the other.' Already then, in the estimation of a Byzantine dragoman, to be 'a Hun by birth' was a higher position than that

* Were these diamonds, or pearls?

of a well-born Roman provincial. Vigilas afterwards repeated this conversation to Edecon and had much difficulty, so he told his companions, in
soothing the barbarian's resentment against the pretensions of Orestes to be
put on an equality with him.

A further hundred miles of travel brought the ambassadors to Naissus
(now Nish, on the confines of Serbia), and here they found such traces of
the ravage of the Hun as his Turkish kinsman has often in later days left
behind him in the same regions. A city utterly empty of inhabitants, in the
churches a few sick folk too weak to fly, every place down to the river's
bank full of human bones and skulls: that is how the Turanian leaves his
mark. 'But we found', says Priscus, with simplicity, 'a clean spot a little
above the river, and there we rested for the night.'

Near to this city, which had become a tomb, lay the Imperial 'army of
Illyricum', under the command of the general-in-chief, Agintheus. Five
out of the seventeen fugitives, whom Theodosius had promised to surrender to Attila, were there, imagining themselves safe under the shelter of the
eagles. But the emperor's orders were clear. The Roman general had to give
up the five suppliants to the Roman ambassador for him to hand over to the
Hunnish king. Agintheus spoke kindly to them; but as they knew, in all
probability, that they were going to a death of torture, kind words from the
ghost of the old Roman war-wolf were not much to the purpose.

At length the ambassadors reached the shores of the Danube. The roads
leading down to the river were crowded with Huns; and ferrymen were
plying across the stream in their uncouth boats, each made of a single tree
roughly hollowed out. They were thus without delay transported to the
northern bank of the river; but if they had supposed that all this stir was
made in expectation of their own arrival they were soon undeceived. The
barbarian king had announced that he meant to cross over into the
Romans' land to hunt, and the expectation of his coming had caused this
stir among his subjects. Like the Percy's 'Hunting of the Cheviot', Attila's
hunting meant war, war over the endless grievance of the unsurrendered
refugees. It was in fact the barbarian's device to accomplish what the modern strategist calls mobilisation.

On the second day after crossing the Danube, the Roman party came in
sight of the numerous tents of Attila, and were about to pitch their own on
a hilltop near. But this the Huns around them would by no means permit:
'they must come down and pitch their tents in the plain: it would be quite
improper for the Roman ambassador to occupy the hill while Attila was

below in the valley.' When this difficulty was settled, the Romans, as it was still early afternoon, expected doubtless an audience that day with Attila. Instead of this, however, several of the Hunnish nobility came, together with Edecon and Orestes, to their tent, and demanded to know the tenor of their message to the king. Naturally the ambassadors replied that their commission was for Attila alone, and they would disclose it to no other person. At that reply, Scotta, one of the Hunnish magnates, burst out with a passionate question, 'Do you take us for busybodies, who came here out of our own prying curiosity? Attila sent us, and we must have your answer.' The ambassadors firmly declined, pleading the invariable usage of their profession. Whereupon the Huns galloped away, and soon returned, ominous exception, without Edecon. 'Your commission', said they, 'to our king is so and so; such concessions about refugees, such messages about future ambassadors. Deny that this is the purport of your instructions if you can. If you have nothing to add to this, return at once to your own country.' In vain did the Romans try to maintain the proper official reserve and refuse to say whether this was indeed a true summary of their instructions or not. Their faces doubtless showed that the arrow had hit the mark: the barbarians' version of their commission was correct in the smallest particulars, and to all further protestations of the Romans the Huns had but one reply continually repeated, 'Begone directly.'

Maximin and Priscus were bewildered, as well they might be, by this strange innovation on the customs of diplomacy. Vigilas, who knew that for his part, the darker part of the enterprise, access to the court of Attila and some days' sojourn there were essential, bitterly complained of his colleagues' truthfulness. 'They might have vamped up some other matter, and declared that the Huns had not revealed the whole of the commission. It would have been better to be detected eventually in a falsehood, than to return without even seeing Attila.'

Little did the false interpreter guess upon what a volcano he himself was standing. The true cause of Attila's strange demeanour was that Edecon had revealed the plot. Either he had only feigned compliance from the first – the more probable supposition – or else that wild conversation at Sardica and the tidings which Vigilas himself had brought him, of the rage and jealousy of Orestes, had satisfied him that the risk was too great to run, with such an unwise person as the interpreter for confederate, and with such an angry rival as the secretary for spy on his movements. And therefore, at the very first opportunity when he found himself alone with Attila, he rehearsed to him the whole plan for his intended assassination, and at the same time furnished him with the particulars of the intended Roman reply, which Edecon had, no doubt, received from Chrysaphius.

It was night when the party of the ambassadors received their peremptory orders to depart. With heavy hearts they were watching their attendants loading the beasts of burden, when they received another message, giving them an ungracious permission to remain where they were till daybreak. A present of an ox for roasting, and some fish, salted, no doubt, as it came from the Euxine, attested the surly hospitality of Attila. Next morning, they thought, 'Surely some act of kindness and gentleness will now be shown to us by the barbarian.' But no: there came only the same harsh command, 'Begone, if you have no other commission to unfold.' Hereupon Priscus, seeing the deep dejection of his patron, resolved to try what prayers and promises could accomplish with one of Attila's ministers. His chief minister, Onégesh, who was well known by the Romans, and on the whole favourably inclined towards them, was absent; but Scotta, the brother of Onégesh, was in the Hunnish camp, and to him Priscus betook himself, using another interpreter than Vigilas. He enlarged on the advantages to the two nations, but still more to the house of Onégesh, which would result from the peaceful outcome of the negotiations, on the presents which were in store for Onégesh at Constantinople, and on those which Maximin would immediately bestow on Scotta. And finally, he wound up with a diplomatic appeal to the vanity of the Hun. 'I have heard', said he, 'that Attila pays great deference to the advice of Scotta, but I shall never believe it if you cannot accomplish so small a matter as to obtain for us this interview.' 'Doubt not that I can do it,' he answered: 'my influence with the king is just as great as my brother's.' And with that he mounted his horse and galloped off to the king's tent. The faithful Priscus returned to his master, who was lying on the grass with Vigilas, while again the packing of the horses was going forward. As soon as they heard of the slight hope which had arisen, and of the influence which Priscus had brought to bear on the mind of Attila, they sprang to their feet, and while warmly commending the sophist for his happy inspiration, began to discuss what they should say to the king, and how the presents of Theodosius and of Maximin himself should be offered for his acceptance.

Soon Scotta returned and escorted them to the royal tent. 'When we obtained admittance,' says Priscus, 'we found the monarch seated on a wooden stool.* We stood a little way off from the throne, but Maximin went forward, and after making obeisance to the barbarian, and handing him the emperor's letter, said, "Our sovereign prays for the safety of thyself and all around thee." Attila answered, "May the Romans receive exactly what they desire for me." Then, turning sharp round to Vigilas, "Shameless beast!" he said. "How have you dared to come to me, knowing, as you do right well, the terms of peace which I settled with you and Anatolius; and how I then said that no more ambassadors were to come to me till all the fugitives were given up." When Vigilas replied that the Romans no longer had with them any refugees of Scythian origin, since we had surrendered all that were with us, Attila grew still more furious, and shouted out with a loud voice every opprobrious epithet that he could think of; "I would impale you," he roared out, "and leave you as food for vultures, if it were not for your sacred charac- ter of envoy, which I would not seem to outrage, fitting as the punishment would be for your impudence and your reckless falsehoods. As for Scythian refugees, there are still many among the Romans." And here he bade his sec- retaries read out their names, inscribed on a roll of paper. When they had rehearsed them all, he bid Vigilas depart without delay. With him was to go Eslas the Hun, commissioned to order the Romans to restore all the fugitives who had gone over to them from the days of Carpilio, son of Aetius, who was sent as a hostage to his court, and had escaped. "For", continued Attila, "I will never endure that my own servants should come forth and meet me in battle, all useless though they may be to help those with whom they have taken refuge, and who entrust to them the guardianship of their own land. For what city, or what fortress has any of these men been able to defend when I have determined on its capture?" '

After this outburst the king condescended to accept the presents which Maximin had brought, and then he repeated his commands as to the future conduct of the negotiations. Having satisfied himself, probably, in the course of this interview that Maximin was an honest man, and guiltless of any complicity in the design against his life, he felt that he could safely indulge in the pleasures which such an embassy brought to him – gifts for himself, gifts for his dependants, and the gratification of trampling on the pride of Rome by exhibiting the Imperial ambassadors as frightened sup- pliants for his favour. All, therefore, except Vigilas, received orders to repair to his palace in the interior, and there to wait for the written reply which he would send to Theodosius.

* δίφρος. Perhaps something like the *sella curulis* [official chair] of the Romans.

Vigilas, on the other hand, whose presence doubtless suggested, even to the brave Hun, uncomfortable thoughts of midnight alarms and the assassin's dagger, was ordered to return at once to Constantinople with the routine message and menace concerning the refugees. Eslas went with him as a spy on his movements: Edecon visited him immediately after the interview in the royal tent, to assure him that he was still true to the plot, and to press him to bring back the promised gold. At the same time, with considerable ingenuity, Attila issued a proclamation 'forbidding Vigilas to purchase any Roman captive or barbarian slave, or horses, or anything else but necessary food until the differences between the Romans and Huns should be arranged'. The effect of this proclamation was to deprive Vigilas of any plausible pretext for bringing back any large amount of gold from Constantinople. If, notwithstanding this prohibition, he still brought gold with him, that gold could only be the blood money of Attila.

There is no need to trace the return of the base and blundering Vigilas to Constantinople, whither he went still entirely unwitting that Attila had sapped below his mine. We follow honest Maximin and his friend as they journey northwards into the recesses of Hungary. For a certain distance they travelled in the train of the barbarian; then they received orders to turn off into another road. Attila was about to visit a certain village, and there add to his numerous harem another wife, the daughter of one Escam;* and apparently he did not choose that the courtly Byzantines should look on the rude wedding festivities of a Hunnish polygamist. The ambassadors had to cross three large rivers in the course of their journey. The names of these rivers are not easy to recognise, but they may possibly be represented by the Drave, the Temes and the Theiss. They crossed them, as before, in tree-trunk boats; while, for the smaller streams and the marshes, they availed themselves of the convenient rafts which the Huns always carried about with them on their wagons in all their journeys through that often inundated country. They were kindly entertained in the Hunnish villages, and received such provisions as the inhabitants had to offer; no wheat, indeed, but millet, for food, and for drink *medus* and *camus*, two beverages which seem to correspond to our mead and beer.

One night, after a long day's march, they pitched their tent beside a lake

* Some authors understand that the new bride's name was Escam, and that she was herself Attila's daughter. But the Greek does not absolutely require this interpretation, and if it had been correct, such an incestuous union would probably have called forth stronger comment on the part of Priscus.

which offered them the advantage of good and sweet water. 'Suddenly', said Priscus, 'there arose a great storm of wind, accompanied by thunderings and frequent flashes of lightning and torrents of rain. Our tent was blown down, and all our travelling furniture was rolled over and over into the waters of the lake. Terrified by this accident and by the din of the storm which filled all the air, we left the spot and soon wandered away from each other, everyone taking what he supposed to be the right road. At length, by different paths, we all reached the neighbouring village, and turned into the huts for shelter. Then, with loud outcry, we began enquiring into our losses. Roused by our clamour, the Scythians started up, kindled the long reeds which serve them for candles, and which threw a good light upon the scene, and then asked us what on earth we wanted that we were making such an uproar. The barbarians who were with us explained how we had been thrown into confusion by the storm, whereupon they kindly called us into their houses, and by lighting a very great number of torches did something to warm us.

'The chieftainess of the village, who was one of the wives of Bleda [Attila's brother], sent us a supply of food, of which we gladly partook. Next morning, at daybreak, we set about searching for our camp furniture, and were fortunate enough to find it all, some in the place where we pitched our tents, some on the shore, and some in the lake itself, from which we succeeded in fishing it up. The whole of that day we spent in the village, drying our things, for the storm had now ceased and the sun was shining brightly. After attending to our beasts, we visited the queen, saluted her respectfully, and repaid her for her hospitality with presents. These were three silver bowls, some red skins, Indian pepper,* dates, and other articles of food, which the barbarians prize as foreign to their climate. Then we wished her health and happiness in return for her hospitality to us, and so we departed.'

At length, after seven days' journey, they reached a village, where they were ordered to stop. Their road here joined that by which the royal bridegroom would be approaching, and they were not to presume to proceed till Attila should have gone before them. In the little village where they were thus detained they met some unexpected companions. Primutus,† the Roman governor of Noricum, Count Romulus of Pettau, the father-in-law

---

* It will be remembered that both these two kinds of goods, red skins and pepper, figured forty years before this in the ransom which Alaric exacted from Rome.
† Possibly a mistake for Promotus.

of Orestes, and Romanus, a general of legionaries, with probably a long train of attendants, were already testing, perhaps somewhat severely, the resources and accommodation of the Hunnish village. They, too, had come on an embassy: they represented the emperor of the West, and it is needless to say that the subject which they had come to discuss was that interminable one, the sacred vases of Sirmium. The father of Orestes, and Constantius the Roman secretary of Attila, journeyed, in an unofficial capacity, with the ambassadors. It was certainly a striking scene: the ambassadors from Ravenna and Constantinople, the representatives of the dignity of the two Imperial courts, the functionaries who between them could set forth the whole majesty that might still survive in the title *senatus populusque Romanus*,* meeting in a dingy little village in Hungary, and waiting with abject submission till a snub-nosed Kalmuck should ride past and contemptuously toss them a permission to follow in his train. It is difficult to resist the conclusion that Attila, who had a genius for scenic effect in the enhancement of his glory, not unlike that which our century has witnessed in the Napoleons, had purposely arranged this confluence of the two embassies, and partly for this cause had invited Maximin to follow him into Hungary.

After crossing a few more rivers, the united embassies came in sight of the village in which was situated the palace of Attila. Students have discussed whether this Hunnish capital is represented by the modern city of Pest, by Tokay, or by some other less-known name; but we may dismiss with absolute indifference the enquiry in what particular part of a dreary and treeless plain a barbarian king reared his log-huts, of which probably, twenty years after his death, not a vestige remained.

As Attila entered the village he was met by a procession of maidens in single file wearing linen veils, thin and white, and so long that under each veil, held up as it was by the hands of the women on either side of the path, seven maidens or more were able to walk. There were many of these sets of girls, each set wearing one veil; and as they walked they sang national songs in honour of the king. The last house which he reached before his own was that of his favourite and chief minister Onégesh,† and as he passed it the

---

* [SPQR: the senate and people of Rome.]

† Priscus calls him Onegesius, and Thierry remarks, *Onégèse dont le nom grec indiquait l'origine* [Onegesius, whose Greek name betrayed his origin] (*Histoire d'Attila*, i.98). But everything seems to show that Onegesius was a pure Hun. His brother's name was Scotta. The dialogue at Sardica, in which Vigilas compared the positions of Edecon the

wife of the owner came forth with a multitude of attendants bearing food
and wine – 'the highest honour', says Priscus, 'which one Scythian can pay
to another' – saluted him, and begged him to partake of the repast which
she had provided as a token of her loyalty. The king, wishing to gratify the
wife of his most trusted counsellor, partook accordingly, without dis-
mounting from his horse, his attendants holding high before him the silver
table on which the banquet was spread. Having eaten and drunk he rode
on to his palace.

This edifice, the finest in all the country round, stood on a little hill, and
seemed to dominate the whole settlement. Yet it was in truth, as has been
already said, only a log-hut of large dimensions. Externally it seems that it
was built of half-trunks of trees, round side outwards, and within, it was
lined with smoothly planed planks. Round the enclosure in which the
dwellings of the king and his wives were placed ran a wooden palisading,
for ornament, not defence; and the top of the palace was fashioned into the
appearance of battlements. Next to the king's house in position, and only
second to it in size, rose the dwelling of Onégesh. The only stone building
in the place was a bath, which Onégesh had built at a little distance from
his palisading. The stone for this building had been brought from quarries
in the Roman province of Pannonia; and in fact all the timber used in the
settlement had been imported likewise, for in the vast and dreary plain
where the nomad nation had pitched its camp, not a tree was growing, not a
stone underlay it. With the building of the bath of Onégesh a grim jest was
connected. The architect, a Roman provincial, who had been carried captive from Sirmium, hoped that his ingenuity would at least be rewarded
by the boon of freedom, if no other architect's commission was paid him.
But no such thoughts suggested themselves to the mind of Onégesh. When
he had completed his task, the architect was rewarded by being turned
into bath-man, and had to wait upon his master and his master's guests
whensoever they had a mind for the pleasures of the *sudatorium* and the *tepi-
darium*.* Thus, as Priscus remarks, with a hint, no doubt, at the personal

---

Hun and Orestes the Roman provincial, shows how impossible it would have been for
any but a full-blooded barbarian to attain to the rank which Onegesius held. And the
name of Oebar*sius*, Attila's paternal uncle, recorded by Priscus (excerpt 14), shows his
habit of Graecising the names of undoubted Huns. We may therefore conclude that
Onegesius is the similarly Graecised form of some such name as Onégesh, by which it
seems better to call him in order to mark his barbarian origin.

* [The sweating-bath and the tepid bath.]

uncleanliness of the Huns, the unhappy man of science 'had prepared for himself unconsciously a worse lot than that of ordinary servitude among the Scythians'.

Onégesh himself, who was absent when Priscus sought an interview with his brother Scotta, had now returned to his master's court. He had been engaged in quelling the last remains of independence among the Acatziri, a people possibly of Slavonic origin, who dwelt on the lower Danube. The Byzantine ministers had endeavoured to parry Attila's attack by stirring up some of the petty chieftains of this nation against him. But, with their usual tendency to blunder, they had sent their most costly and honourable presents to the wrong man, and consequently Curidach, the real head of the confederacy, having received only the second gift, called in the aid of Attila to avenge the insult and beat down the power of his associ-ated kings. The Hun was nothing loath, and soon succeeded in quelling all opposition. He then invited Curidach to come and celebrate their joint tri-umph at his court; but that chieftain, suspecting that his benefactor's kindness was of the same nature as the promised boon of Polyphemus to Ulysses, 'I will eat Outis last',* courteously declined. 'It is hard', he said, 'for a man to come into the presence of a god; and if it be not possible to look fixedly even at the orb of the sun, how shall Curidach gaze undis-tressed upon the greatest of gods?' The compliment served for the time, but Attila understood what it was worth, and at a convenient season sent his grand vizier, Onégesh, to dethrone Curidach and to proclaim the eldest son of Attila king of the Acatziri in his stead. From this expedition the prime minister had now just returned successful and in high favour with his master.

The ambassadors were hospitably entertained by the wife and family of Onégesh. He himself had to wait upon the king to report the success of his mission, and the only drawback which had befallen his party, an accident namely to the young prince, who had slipped off his horse and fractured some of the bones of his right hand. At nightfall Maximin pitched his tents a little way off the enclosure of the royal dwellings, and next morning he sent Priscus early to the house of Onégesh with servants bearing presents both from himself and from Theodosius. The zealous rhetorician was actually up before the barbarian. The house was still close-barred and there was no sign of anyone stirring.

While Priscus was waiting, and walking up and down before the pal-

* *Odyssey*, ix.369.

isading which surrounded the house of Onégesh, a man, with the dress
and general appearance of a Hun, came up and saluted him with a well-
pronounced Greek χαîρε (How d'ye do?). A Hun speaking Greek was
an anomaly which aroused all the attention of the sophist, for, as he
says, 'though it is true that this people, who are a kind of conglomerate of
nations, do sometimes affect the speech of the Goths, or even that of the
Italians, in addition to their own barbarous language, they never learn
Greek, except indeed they be inhabitants of Thrace or Dalmatia, who have
been carried captive into the Hunnish territory. And these captives or their
offspring may be easily known by their ragged garments and scabby
heads, and all the other tokens of their having changed their condition for
the worse. But this man seemed like a flourishing Scythian, handsomely
dressed, and having his hair neatly clipped all round his head. So, returning his salutation, I asked him who he was, and from what part of the
world he had come into that barbarian land to adopt the Scythian life.
"What has put it into your head to ask me such a question as that?" said he.
"Your Greek accent," answered I. Then he laughed and said, "'Tis true I
am of Greek parentage, and I came for purposes of trade to Viminacium, a
city of Moesia, on the Danube" [about sixty miles below Belgrade].
"There I abode for a long time, and married a very wealthy wife. But on the
capture of the city by the Huns I was stripped of all my fortune, and
assigned as a slave to this very Onégesh before whose door you are standing.
That is the custom of the Huns: after Attila has had his share, the chiefs of
the nation are allowed to take their pick of the wealthiest captives, and so
Onégesh chose me. Afterwards, having distinguished myself in some
actions with the Romans and the Acatziri, I surrendered to my master all
the spoils which I had taken in war, and thus, according to the law of the
Scythians, I obtained my freedom. I married a barbarian wife, by whom I
have children: I am admitted as a guest to the table of Onégesh, and I consider my present mode of life decidedly preferable to my past. For when war
is over, the people of this country live like gentlemen, enjoying themselves to
the full, and free from worry of any kind. But the people in Roman-land
are easily worsted in war, because they place their hopes of safety on others
rather than themselves. Their tyrants will not allow them the use of arms,
and the condition of those who are armed is even more dangerous, from the
utter worthlessness of their generals, who have no notion of the art of war.
Then, too, peace has its injuries not less severe than war. Think of all the
cruelties practised by the collectors of the revenue, the infamy of informers,

and the gross inequalities in the administration of the laws. If a rich man offends, he can always manage to escape punishment; but a poor man, who does not know how to arrange matters, has to undergo the full penalty, unless indeed he be dead before judgement is pronounced, which is not unlikely, considering the intolerable length to which law-suits are pro-tracted. But what I call the most shameful thing of all is that you have to pay money in order to obtain your legal rights. For a man who has been injured cannot even get a hearing from the court without first paying large fees to the judge and the officials who serve him." '

In reply to this angry outburst, Priscus entered into a long and sophis-tical disquisition on the advantages of division of labour, the necessity that judges and bailiffs, like men of other occupations, should live by their call-ing, and so on. It is easy to see that Priscus felt himself to be talking as sagely as Socrates, upon whose style his reply is evidently modelled; but that reply has the fault so common with rhetoricians and diplomatists, of being quite up in the air, and having no relation to the real facts of the case. His conclu-sion is the most interesting part of the speech: ' "As for the freedom which you now enjoy, you may thank fortune for that and not your master, who sent you to war, where you were likely to have been killed by the enemy on account of your inexperience. But the Romans treat even their slaves better than this. True, they correct them, but only for their good as parents or schoolmasters correct children, in order that they may cease to do evil and behave as is suitable for persons in their station. The Roman master is not allowed, as the Hun is, to punish his slave so as to cause his death. Besides, we have abundant legal provisions in favour of freedom, and this gift may be bestowed not only by men who are in the midst of life, but also by those who are on the point of death. Such persons are allowed to dispose of their property as they please, and any directions of a dying man concerning the enfranchisement of his slaves are binding on his heirs." Thus I reasoned with him. He burst into tears, and said, "The laws are beautiful, and the polity of the Romans is excellent; but the rulers are not like-minded with the men of old, and are pulling down the state into ruin." '

By the time that this conversation was ended, the household of Onégesh had awoken, and the door was unbarred. Priscus obtained an interview with the minister and delivered the presents, which were graciously received. It is needless to transcribe the memoranda, almost tediously minute, which Priscus has kept of his various conversations. The general drift of them was, on the Roman side, to press for an interview with the king of the Huns, and to urge Onégesh to undertake in person the return embassy, and win for himself eternal glory and much wealth by bringing his candid and impartial mind to bear upon the points in dispute, and set-tling them in favour of the Romans. Onégesh indignantly repudiated the idea that any arguments of the Romans could ever induce him to betray his master, to forget his Scythian life, his wives, and his children, or to cease to consider servitude with Attila preferable to wealth among the Romans. He could be far more useful to them, he said, by remaining at Attila's court and mollifying his resentment against their nation, than by coming to Byzan-tium and negotiating a treaty which his master might very probably disavow. On the other hand, he pressed them repeatedly with the question, 'What man of consular dignity will the emperor send as ambassador?' The fact that Maximin, a man who had never filled the office of consul, should have been selected as envoy, evidently rankled in the mind of the barbarian king, sensitive, as all upstarts are, about his dignity. And at length, Attila having named three, Nomus, Anatolius and Senator, any one of whom would be, in the language of modern diplomacy, a *persona grata* at his court, declared that he would receive no one else. The envoys replied that to insist so strongly on the selection of these three men would bring them into suspi-cion at the Imperial court; a charming piece of inconsistency in the men who were constantly petitioning that Onégesh and no one else might undertake the return embassy. Attila answered moodily, 'If the Romans will not do as I choose, I shall settle the points in dispute by war.'

While diplomacy was thus spinning her tedious web, the ambassadors saw some sights in the barbarian camp which deserved to be recorded by the careful pen of the professor of rhetoric. One day he had an audience of the queen Kreka, the chief in dignity of the wives of Attila, and mother of three of his sons. Her palace was built of well-sawn and smoothly planed planks, 'resting on the ends of logs'.* Arches at certain intervals, springing from the ground and rising to a pretty considerable height, broke the flat surface of the wall.† Here Kreka was to be found, lying on a soft couch, and with the floor around her covered with smooth felts to walk upon. Carpets were evidently still an unwonted luxury in Hun-land. There was no trace of the oriental seclusion of women in the palace of Kreka. A large number of menservants stood in a circle round her, while her maids sat on

* The meaning of this clause is not very clear.
† This seems to be the purport of the sentence. But what part arches can have played in an architecture dealing only with planks and logs it is not easy to see.

the floor in front, and were busied in dyeing linen of various colours, intending afterwards to work it up into ornamental costumes of the barbarian fashion.

When Priscus had offered his gifts and emerged from the queen's dwelling, he heard a stir and a clamour, and saw a crowd of men hurrying to the door of Attila's palace. These were the signs that the king was coming forth, and the rhetorician obtained a good place to watch his exit. With a stately strut Attila came forth, looking this way and that. Then he stood with his favourite Onégesh in front of the palace, while all the multitude of his people who had disputes one with another came forward and submitted them to him for his decision. Having thus in true oriental fashion administered justice 'in the gate', he returned into the interior of his palace in order to give audience to some barbarian ambassadors who had just arrived at his court.

Scarcely was this scene ended when Priscus fell in with the ambassadors of the Western Empire, with whom he naturally began to compare notes. 'Are you dismissed', said they, 'or pressed to remain?' 'The very thing', he answered, 'that I myself want to know, and that keeps me all day hanging about near the palisading of Onégesh. Pray has Attila vouchsafed a gentle answer to your petition?' 'No; nothing will turn him from his purpose. He declares he will either have Silvanus or the sacred vessels, or else will make war.' Priscus then expressed his wonder at the folly of the barbarian; and Romulus, who was an old and experienced diplomatist, answered, 'His extraordinary good fortune and unbounded power have quite turned his head: so that he will listen to no argument which does not fall in with his own caprices. For no former ruler of Scythia or of any other land has ever achieved so much in so short a time as this man, who has made himself master of the islands in the Ocean, and besides ruling all Scythia has forced even the Romans to pay him tribute.' Then Romulus proceeded to tell the story of Attila's intended Persian campaign, to which reference has already been made. The Byzantine ambassadors expressed their earnest desire that he would turn his arms against Persia and leave Theodosius alone; but Constantiolus, a Pannonian in the retinue of Romulus, replied that he feared if Attila did attack and overcome, as he assuredly would, the monarch of that country, 'he would become our lord and master instead of our friend. At present,' said he, 'Attila condescends to take gold from the Romans and call it pay for his titular office of general in the Roman armies. But should he subdue the Parthians, and Medes, and Persians, he would not endure to have the Roman Empire cutting in like a wedge between one part and another of his dominions, but would openly treat the two emperors as mere lackeys, and would lay upon them such commands as they would find absolutely intolerable. Already he has been heard to remark, testily, "The generals of Theodosius are but his servants, while my generals are as good as emperors of Rome." He believes also that there will be before long some notable increase of his power; and that the gods have signified this by revealing to him the sword of Mars, a sacred relic much venerated by the Huns, for many years hidden from their eyes, but quite lately rediscovered by the trail of the blood of an ox which had wounded its hoof against it, as it was sticking upright in the long grass.'*

Such was the conversation between the representatives of Ravenna and Constantinople, amid the log-huts of the Hungarian plain. Later on in the same day they all received an invitation to be present at a banquet of the great conqueror.

'Punctually at three o'clock we, together with the ambassadors of the Western Romans, went to the dinner and stood on the threshold of Attila's palace. According to the custom of the country, the cup-bearers brought us a bowl of wine, that we might drink and pray for the good luck of our host before sitting down. Having tasted the bowl, we were escorted to our seats. Chairs were ranged for the guests all round the walls. In the centre Attila reclined on a couch, and behind him a flight of steps led up to his bed, which, hidden by curtains of white linen and variegated stuffs tastefully arranged, looked like the nuptial bed, as the Greeks and Romans prepare it for a newly wedded couple.

'The seat of honour on the right hand of Attila's couch, was occupied by Onégesh. We did not receive even the second place, that on his left, but saw Berich, a Hun of noble birth, placed above us there. Opposite to Onégesh, on a double chair, sat two of the sons of Attila. His eldest son sat on the king's couch, not near to him, however, but on the very edge of it, and all through the banquet he kept his eyes fixed on the ground in silent awe of his father.

'When we were all seated the cup-bearer came in and handed to Attila his ivy-wood drinking-cup, filled with wine. Remaining seated, the king saluted the one nearest to him in rank. The slave standing behind that person's chair advanced into the centre of the hall, received the cup from the

* Compare the worship of a naked sabre fixed hilt downwards in the earth, as practised by the Alans (see p. 21).

hand of Attila's cup-bearer, and brought it to the guest, whom etiquette required to rise from his seat and continue standing till he had drained the cup and the slave had returned it into the hands of Attila's cup-bearer.' This process of salutation and drinking was gone through with each guest and in the intervals of every course. The length of the solemnity, and perhaps the tediousness of it, seem greatly to have impressed the mind of Priscus, who describes it in much detail. After the banqueters had all been 'saluted' by Attila, the servants began to bring in the provisions, which were set upon little tables, one for every three or four guests, so that each could help himself without going outside the row of seats. 'For all the rest of the barbarians', says Priscus, 'and for us, a costly banquet had been prepared, which was served on silver dishes; but Attila, on his wooden plate, had nothing else save meat. In all his other equipments he showed the same simple tastes. The other banqueters had drinking-cups of gold and silver handed to them, but his was of wood. His clothes were quite plain, distinguished by their cleanness only from those of any common man: and neither the sword which was hung up beside him, nor the clasps of his shoes (shaped in the barbarian fashion), nor the bridle of his horse, was adorned, as is the case with other Scythians, with gold or jewels, or anything else that is costly.

'When evening came on, torches were lighted, and two barbarians coming in, stood opposite to Attila and chanted verses in praise of his victories and his prowess in war. The banqueters, looking off from the festal board, gazed earnestly on the minstrels. Some gave themselves to the mere delight of the song; others, remembering past conflicts, were stirred as with the fury of battle; while the old men were melted into tears by the thought that their bodies were grown weak through time, and their hot hearts were compelled into repose.' After tears laughter, and after the tragedy a farce. A mad Hun next came in, who by his senseless babble made all the guests laugh heartily. Then entered a Moorish dwarf named Zercon, humpbacked, club-footed, with a nose like a monkey's. Almost the only anecdote that is preserved to us about Bleda, Attila's brother, records the inextinguishable mirth which this strange creature used to awaken in him, how he had him always by his side at the battle and in the banquet, and how when at last the unlucky dwarf tried to make his escape together with some other fugitives, Bleda disregarded all the others, and devoted his whole energies to the recapture of the pygmy. Then when he was caught and brought into the royal presence, Bleda burst into another storm of merriment at seeing the queer little creature in the dignity of chains. He questioned him about the cause of his flight: the dwarf replied that he knew he had done wrong, but there was some excuse for him because he could get no wife in Hun-land. More delicious laughter followed, and Bleda straightway provided him with a wife in the person of a Hunnish damsel of noble birth who had been maid of honour to his queen, but had fallen into disgrace and been banished from her presence.* After Bleda's death, Attila, who could not abide the dwarf, sent him as a present to Aetius. He had now come back again, apparently to beg to have his wife restored to him, a prayer which Attila was not inclined to grant.

This strange being came into the banquet hall, and by his grotesque appearance, his odd garb, his stuttering voice, and his wild promiscuous jumble of words, Latin, Hunnish, Gothic, hurled forth pell-mell in unut-terable confusion, set every table in a roar. Only Attila laughed not; not a line in his rigid countenance changed till his youngest son Ernak came, laughing like everybody else, and sat down beside him. He did not shrink away like his elder brother and sit on the edge of the couch. His bright, happy eyes looked up into the face of his father, who gently pinched his cheek and looked back upon him with a mild and softened gaze. Priscus expressed aloud his wonder that the youngest son should be so obviously preferred to his elder brethren: whereupon one of the barbarians who sat near him, and who understood Latin, whispered to him confidentially that it had been foretold to Attila by the prophets that the falling fortunes of his house should by this son be restored.

The drinking bout was protracted far on into the night, and the ambas-sadors left long before it was over. At daybreak next morning they again sought an interview with Onégesh, and petitioned that without further loss of time they might receive Attila's answer and return to their master. Onégesh set his secretaries, Roman captives, to work at the composition of the letter of reply. Then they preferred another request, for the liberation of the widow and children of a certain Sulla, a citizen of Ratiaria,† who had apparently been killed at the same time when they were taken captive and their home destroyed. Onégesh entirely refused to hear of their gratuitous liberation, but at length, when the ambassadors begged him to reflect on

* This anecdote is preserved by Suidas. The commentator Valesius thinks he took it from a portion of the history of Priscus now lost to us: but there are some slight divergences in the story which seem to point to a different conclusion.
† Now Arzar Palanka on the Danube.

their former prosperity, and to pity their present misfortunes, he laid the matter before Attila, and obtained a reluctant consent to send the children back as a present to Theodosius. As to the widow the Hun remained inex-orable: the price of her freedom was fixed at £500. Such abject entreaties to a squalid barbarian for the liberation of the family of a Roman bearing the name of him

> whose chariot rolled on fortune's wheel,
> Triumphant Sulla,

seem to intensify the force of Byron's magnificent apostrophe –

> Couldst thou divine
> To what would one day dwindle that which made
> Thee more than mortal? and that so supine
> By aught than Romans Rome should thus be laid?
> She who was named Eternal, and array'd
> Her warriors but to conquer – she who veil'd
> Earth with her haughty shadow, and display'd,
> Until the o'er-canopied horizon fail'd,
> Her rushing wings – Oh! she who was Almighty hail'd!*

Another visit to Attila's chief wife† beguiled the tedium of the ambas-sadors' sojourn in the royal village. 'She received us', says Priscus, 'both with honeyed words and with an elaborate repast. And each of the com-pany wishing to do us honour in Scythian fashion, arose and presented us with a full cup of wine; and when we had drunk it they put their arms round us and kissed us, and then received it back from our hands.'

A final supper with Attila himself followed. The monarch seems to have had an increasing appreciation of the worth and honesty of Maximin: and now that the 'shameless beast', Vigilas, was gone, and Attila no longer had the unpleasant sensation as of the near presence of a venomous reptile, which was always suggested by his false smile and cringing salutation, the companionship of the Roman ambassadors agreeably diversified the monotony of the barbarian carousals. This time the relative who shared his

---

* *Childe Harold*, iv.84.
† Here called Recan: apparently the same name as the Kreka of whom we have already heard (p. 51).

royal divan was not one of his sons but Oébarsh, his uncle. Attila treated
the ambassadors during this meal with great politeness, but at the same time
frequently reminded them of a grievance which for the moment absorbed
all his thoughts, to the exclusion of the Hunnish refugees and the vases of
Sirmium. Aetius, who was continually sending presents to the Hunnish
monarch or receiving them from him, had consigned to him, perhaps in
exchange for the Moorish dwarf, a Latin secretary, named Constantius.
This secretary, the second of that name who had entered Attila's service,
was eager, like all the adventurers who hovered on the confines between
barbarism and civilisation, to consolidate his position by marrying one of
the 'enormously wealthy' heiresses who were to be found among the
Romans. Such a one seemed to be within his grasp when he was sent a few
years before as an embassy to Constantinople, and when he succeeded in
smoothing some of the negotiations between Theodosius and the Hun.
The emperor, a facile promiser, undertook to bestow upon the secretary the
hand of the daughter of Saturninus, a man of high lineage and fortune,
who held the office of *comes domesticorum*. Shortly after, however, Eudocia
the empress revenged herself on Saturninus for having, in obedience to
her husband's commands, put two favourite ecclesiastics of hers to death,
by sending him to join them. The fortunes of the house of Saturninus
declined, and a powerful general, Zeno, bestowed the daughter of the
fallen minister in marriage on one of his creatures named Rufus.* The disappointed secretary, Constantius, who had doubtless boasted not a little of
the 'enormously wealthy' bride that was to be assigned to him, besieged the
ear of Attila with his clamours, and even promised him money if he would
still obtain for him one of the longed-for heiresses. All through this banquet therefore Attila urged the fortune-hunter's claims upon Maximin,
saying repeatedly, 'Constantius must not be disappointed. It is not right for
kings to tell lies.'†

Three days after this banquet the ambassadors from the Eastern court,
after receiving presents which Priscus acknowledges to have been 'suitable',
were at length dismissed under the escort of Berich, the Hunnish noble-

* This intrigue is well illustrated by a curious 'title' in the Theodosian Code (iii.6): *Si
provinciae rector, vel ad eum pertinentes sponsalia dederint* [If the governor of a province or his
people present a betrothal gift]. It is directed against the abuse of their power by provincial governors, who terrified the parents or guardians of wealthy heiresses into betrothing
them to the governor's sons or dependants.

† Compare the words of Aspar to the emperor Leo I, some twenty years after this time:
'Emperor, he who is clothed with this purple robe should not be a deceiver.'

man who had sat above them at their first repast in Attila's presence. It is singular that we hear nothing as to the success or failure of the embassy of the West.

The return journey of Maximin and Priscus was not marked by any striking adventures. They saw a Scythian refugee, who had crossed the Danube and returned into his own country as a spy, subjected to the cruel punishment of impalement, common among these Turanian nations. And two Scythian slaves who had murdered their masters were put to death by crucifixion, a mode of execution which the Christian empire, from religious rather than humane sentiment, had by this time abandoned. But the only other incidents of their journey were caused by the testy and capricious humour of their companion Berich, who seemed bent on picking a quarrel with them. His ill-temper was chiefly shown by his violent resumption of the horse which, at Attila's command, he had presented to Maximin. Indeed all the Hunnish nobility had been ordered to make tender of their horses to the ambassador; but he had shown the wise moderation of his character by accepting only a few. Among these few however was Berich's; and considering the centaur-like union which had for generations existed between the Huns and their steeds, we may conjecture that it was the pain of daily beholding his favourite horse bestridden by an unwarlike stranger which caused the irritability of the Hunnish nobleman.

Vigilas had started from Constantinople before the return of the ambassadors, and met them on their road. They communicated to him the final answer of the barbarian, and he continued his route. As soon as he reached the camp of Attila, a detachment of Huns, who had been watching for his arrival, made him their prisoner, and took from him the £2,000 which he was bringing, as he supposed, to Edecon as the price of blood. They carried him at once before the king, who enquired why he travelled with so much money about him. 'To provide for my own wants and those of my attendants,' said Vigilas, 'lest by any mischance my embassy should lack its proper splendour. Also for the redemption of captives, since many persons in the Roman territory have begged me to purchase the liberation of their kinsfolk.' 'Evil beast!' said Attila, 'thou in truth shalt not blind justice by all thy quibbles, and no pretext shall be strong enough to enable thee to escape punishment. Thou hast provided far more money than could possibly be wanted for the purchase of beasts of burden and for the redemption of captives, which last I expressly forbade thee to undertake when thou camest hither with Maximin.'

With these words he signalled to his attendants to seize the son of Vigilas, who had for the first time accompanied his father on this journey. 'Next
moment,' said Attila, 'hew him down with the sword, unless his father
will say to whom and for what purpose he has brought this money into my
territory.' Vigilas burst into passionate lamentations, begged the executioner to slay him instead of his son, and when he saw that all was of no
avail, confessed the whole plot, told how Chrysaphius had originated it,
how Edecon had accepted it, how Theodosius had sanctioned it, and then
once more earnestly entreated Attila to put him to death and to spare his
son. The king, who from his previous information knew that Vigilas had
now disclosed the whole truth, coldly replied that for the present he should
be loaded with chains and await, in close confinement, the return of his son
who must start at once for Constantinople to obtain another sum of
£2,000, which, with that already taken from him, should constitute their
joint ransom.

Leaving Vigilas in this dangerous predicament, let us now see what
kind of messages Theodosius had to listen to from the king of the Huns.
Maximin seems to have been instructed to dwell principally on the
emperor's breach of promise to Constantius. 'No one', Attila argued,
'could have dared to betroth the daughter of Saturninus to another than
Constantius without the emperor's consent. For either he who had presumed to do such a deed would have suffered condign punishment, or else
the affairs of the emperor were in such a state that he could not manage his
own servants, against whom therefore, if he desired it, Attila would be
ready to grant him the advantage of his alliance.' The taunt, which must
surely have proceeded from the lips of Berich, not of Maximin, struck
home; and Theodosius showed his anger by confiscating the fortune of the
'enormously wealthy' young lady whose matrimonial affairs had caused
him so much annoyance. This act was of course followed by a loud outcry
from her husband Rufus and his patron Zeno, whose position towards his
Imperial master was in fact pretty accurately described by the sneers of
Attila. Zeno chose however to attribute the whole incident to the machinations of Chrysaphius, and began to clamour for the eunuch's life.

Such was the position of affairs at Constantinople when the two special
ambassadors of Attila, Orestes and Eslas, arrived (449). Their message
was yet harder to digest than that which had preceded it. When they
appeared in the Imperial presence, Orestes wore, suspended round his
neck, the purse (or rather the large bag) in which the blood-money had

been packed. Turning first to Theodosius and then to the eunuch, he asked each of them: 'Dost thou recognise this bag?' Then Eslas, the Hun, took up his parable, and said roundly, 'Theodosius is the son of a well-born father. Attila too from his father Mundzuk has inherited the condition of noble birth, which he has preserved. Not so Theodosius, who fell from the estate of an *ingenuus* [free man] and became Attila's slave, when he submit-ted to pay him tribute. He has now conspired against the life of a better man than himself, and one whom fortune has made his master. This is a foul deed, worthy only of a caitiff slave, and his only way of clearing himself from the guilt which he has thus contracted is to surrender the eunuch to punishment.'

How this harangue, every word of which had been composed by Attila himself, was received by Theodosius, as he sat surrounded by his courtiers, we know not. The general expectation of the court was that it would go hard with Chrysaphius, whose punishment was thus simultaneously demanded by the two men whom the emperor most feared, Zeno his gen-eral, and Attila his torment. But 'threatened men live long', and the eunuch seems to have been not unpopular with the other courtiers, who exerted themselves zealously for his deliverance.

Anatolius and Nomus were selected as the new ambassadors to the Hunnish court. Both had been named by Attila as persons of sufficiently exalted rank to visit him, such as he would be willing to welcome.* Ana-tolius, who had been the chief figure of the embassy of 447, was a man of high military rank, in fact, general of the household troops. Nomus, a patrician as well as his colleague, was in the civil service as master of the offices, renowned not only for his wealth, but for his willingness to spend it lavishly, and moreover kindly disposed towards Chrysaphius. They were commissioned to employ money freely, to deprecate Attila's resentment against the eunuch, and to assure Constantius that he should yet have a wealthy Roman bride, though the law would not permit the emperor to give him the daughter of Saturninus, as she was married to another man from whom she did not desire to be divorced. The trifling circumstance of the confiscation of her property appears not to have been mentioned in the instructions of the ambassadors.

This embassy was completely successful. Attila came as far as the river Drave,† in order to testify his respect for the persons of the envoys, and to spare them the fatigue of too long a journey. At first his speech was full of

* See p. 51.   † A conjectural translation of Δρέγκων.

arrogance and wrath, but when he saw the beautiful things which the ambassadors had brought for him, the presents of Theodosius, the presents of Chrysaphius, the presents of the lavish Nomus, the child nature in the heart of the barbarian asserted itself, his eyes gleamed with pleasure, and he suffered himself to be mollified by their gentle words. Peace was concluded pretty nearly on the old terms: in fact, he seems even to have surrendered his claim to the belt of territory, five days' journey wide, south of the Danube. He promised to worry the emperor no more about any refugees whom he might have received in past times; 'only', he said, 'Theodosius must receive no more of these men in future.' Vigilas was liberated, his son having brought the £2,000 of ransom; and the demand for the head of Chrysaphius seems to have been quietly withdrawn. Of his own accord, in order to mark his special esteem for Anatolius and Nomus, he liberated many captives without ransom; and he made them presents of several horses (whether belonging to himself or to his courtiers we are not informed), and of the skins of wild beasts, 'such as the royal family among the Scythians wear by way of ornament'. For once, diplomacy really prevented war.

The important question of satisfying the noble longings of Constantius for a wealthy bride was soon solved. He returned with the ambassadors to Constantinople, and was there mated to a lady of very high birth and large fortune, the widow of a certain Armatius, who had died when on service against some of the fierce tribes of Libya, and the daughter-in-law of Plinthas (consul 419), who had headed the first embassy to Attila in the year 433. Thus the last point in dispute between the son of Mundzuk and the son of Arcadius was disposed of.

In the following year (450) Theodosius II died in the fiftieth year of his age and the forty-third of his reign. His death was the result of an accident in hunting, his horse having run away, swerved aside into a stream and thrown him off. He was carried home to his palace in a litter, but he had received a fatal injury to the spine, and died on the following night (28th July, 450). He left no male offspring, and his sister Pulcheria ascended the throne, which she shared with a brave and honest soldier, Marcian, whom, for the good of the state, she consented to call her husband.

The immediate results of this change were, the calling together of the council of Chalcedon (451), at which the orthodox Roman view of the union of the two natures in Christ was finally adopted; the execution of Chrysaphius, whether as maladministrator, as Eutychian heretic, or as private foe to the new Augusta, we are not informed; and, lastly, the assumption of an altered and more manly tone in reply to the intolerable pretensions of Attila. When that monarch claimed his arrears of tribute (450), the new emperor sent as ambassador to his court, Apollonius, the brother of that Rufus who had married the 'enormously wealthy' bride, for whose fortune Constantius had languished. Apollonius crossed the Danube, but when Attila learned that he had not brought the tribute, which – to use the words of the Hun – 'had been promised to him by better and more king-like men* than the present ambassador', he refused to grant him an audience. Attila said expressly that he acted thus in order to show his contempt for the envoy, whom, nevertheless, he ordered, on pain of death if he refused, to hand over the presents which the emperor had sent. 'Not so,' said Apollonius, who spoke with a boldness worthy of old Rome, and in a tone which was now strange to Scythian ears. 'The Huns may kill me if they like, and then my presents will be spoils of war (if they choose to call murder warfare). Or they may receive me as ambassador, and then I willingly offer my gifts. But if not admitted to an audience, I do not part with these presents while I live.' The boldness of the ambassador prevailed. He returned with his gifts and his message alike undelivered, but Attila saw that he had now at length men to deal with at Constantinople, and that the policy of braggadocio would avail no longer. He did not care for a campaign in the often harried plains of Moesia, but looked out for some richer if not easier prey. And thus, with a dignity which we had ceased to hope for in any emperor of Byzantium, the long negotiations terminate, and we close the chapter of the doings of Attila in the East.

* Anatolius and Nomus.

CHAPTER III

Attila in Gaul

A STORY OF VERY DOUBTFUL AUTHORITY*
represents the monarch of the Huns as sending, shortly before the
death of Theodosius II, a Gothic messenger to each of the two Roman
emperors, with this insulting mandate, 'Attila, thy master and mine, bids
thee to prepare a palace for his reception.' Whether any such message was
actually sent or not, the story indicates not inaptly the attitude which the
great Hun maintained for the ten years between 440 and 450, hovering like
a hawk over the fluttered dovecotes of Byzantium and Ravenna, and enjoying the terrors of the Eastern and the Western Augustus alternately.

Now that the palace by the Bosporus was occupied by an inmate whose
beak and claw looked more like those of the old Roman eagle than any that
had been seen there for the last half-century, the barbarian began to turn his
thoughts more definitely to the hapless pigeon of the West. He needed to be
at no loss for pretexts in making war on Rome. Whether the great grievance
of the communion plate of Sirmium was still unredressed we cannot say,
for history, after wearying us with the details of this paltry affair, forgets to
tell us how it ended, whether the vases were surrendered to the service of the
king or the silversmith to his rage, or whether the latter was deemed to be 'a
bona fide holder of the goods for valuable consideration', and his title
respected accordingly.

But the grievances of the princess Honoria undoubtedly still remained,
possibly even were increased by the death of the easy-tempered Theodosius
and the accession to the Byzantine throne of that severe model of feminine
virtues, the Augusta Pulcheria, who was now fifty-one years of age, while
her cousin was but thirty-two, a juniority which was in itself almost treason
against a female sovereign. It is possible that the unhappy princess was

* The story rests only on the authority of the *Alexandrian Chronicle* and John Malalas. The
former was composed during the reign of Heraclius, about 630; the date of the latter historian is uncertain, not earlier, however, than 600, and not later than 900.

removed at this time (450) from the Eastern to the Western court, for we find Attila sending one of his usual insulting embassies to Valentinian III, 'to say that Honoria, whom he had betrothed to himself, must suffer no harm, and that he would avenge her cause if she were not also allowed to wield the Imperial sceptre'. The Western emperor replied, 'that Honoria could not enter into the married state with him, having been already given to a husband' (to whom, when, or under what circumstances, we are not informed); and they met the audacious claim set up on behalf of the princess by an equally audacious misstatement of their own customs, daring to assert in the face of the still existing royalty of Placidia and Pulcheria, 'that Honoria ought not to receive the sceptre, since the succession to the throne among the Romans was vested not in females, but in males'. Both parties probably felt that the claim was an unreal one: the Hun was determined on war, and would have it, whether he redeemed the ring of Honoria or no. One more embassy takes place, in which Attila prefers the modest claim to one half of the Western Empire, 'as the betrothed husband of Honoria, who had received this portion from her father, and was wrongfully kept out of it by her brother's covetousness'. This request is of course refused. Then Honoria too, like the vases of Sirmium, fades out of history; whether she ever saw the fierce face of her affianced when he wasted Italy in her name, nay even whether she was present at the deathbed of her mother Placidia, who expired at Rome in the same year as Theodosius (450), and there received and conferred a mutual forgiveness, we know not.

Two more pretexts for war must Attila accumulate, or at least two more alliances must he conclude, and then all would be ready for his great westward movement.

One was with a Frankish prince. A certain king of the Franks, whose name is not recorded, had just died, and there was strife between his sons as to the succession to his rude royalty. The younger son was the candidate whom the Romans favoured. He had been to Rome (probably some years before) on an embassy from his father. He had gazed there, doubtless, on the still undiminished glories of the Palatine and the forum and the great Flavian amphitheatre, and while he gazed, the observant eye of the rhetorician Priscus, who happened to be at Rome, had likewise gazed on him. A young warrior, with not even the first down of manhood on cheek or lip, but with a cloud of yellow hair descending thickly upon his shoulders, such is the appearance of the first Frankish king whom we meet with in history. Whether he was Meroveus himself, the half-mythical ancestor of the

Merovingian dynasty, may be doubted, and cannot now be ascertained,* but that long tawny *chevelure* identifies him with the race who reigned in France for 250 years, till the hair of the last fainéant king fell beneath the scissors of Pepin.

The all-powerful Aetius regarded this young Frankish chief with favour. He loaded him with presents, conferred upon him the title of his adopted son, and sent him back to his father as the bearer of a treaty of friendship and alliance. It may have been this title of adopted son of the great Aetius which suggested ambitious thoughts to the mind of the young prince. At any rate, on the death of his father, he, though the younger son, with Roman help, made good his claim to the succession to the kingdom. His elder brother fled to the court of Attila, who undertook to recover for him his lost inheritance.

The other alliance of Attila was with Gaiseric, king of the Vandals. This monarch was now undisputed master of the whole Roman province of Africa, had ravaged Sicily, and was making the name of Carthage, his capital city, as terrible to Italian hearts as ever it had been in the days of Hannibal. There can be little doubt that if the Hunnish hordes by land, and the Vandal pirates by sea, had simultaneously attacked the Western Empire, they must have achieved a complete and crushing success. But for some reason or other, perhaps because neither nation wished to share so rich a booty with a rival, this united action was not taken; and though the Hunnish king received large sums of money by way of subsidy from the Vandal, it may be doubted whether he did not lose far more than he gained by an alliance which made him accessory after the fact to a cruel and impolitic outrage. For Theodoric, king of the Visigoths, who was at this time far the most powerful ruler in the Gaulish provinces, had bestowed his daughter in marriage on Huneric, the son of Gaiseric. Gaiseric chose to suspect, apparently on very trifling grounds, that the new bride had attempted to poison him; and with a cruelty which seems to have been characteristic of the Vandal nature, he cut off the nose and ears of the Visi-gothic princess, and in this condition sent her back to the palace of Theodoric, a living and daily remembrancer of the vengeance due to the

* Meroveus is the so-called grandson of Pharamond and grandfather of Clovis; but no names of the Frankish kings before Childeric, father of Clovis, are now accepted as thor-oughly historical. The silence of Gregory of Tours as to some of these earlier kings and the hesitating way in which he speaks of others seem almost conclusive against the preten-sion of the medieval genealogists to trace their names and pedigree.

Vandal, and therefore an argument against any co-operation with Attila, who was that Vandal's friend.

One more, not ally, but summons to war must be mentioned, which may perhaps have assisted powerfully in turning the hosts of Attila towards Gaul rather than towards Italy. The iniquities of judges and the exactions of tax-gatherers, which were so loudly complained of by the barbarianised Roman in the camp of Attila, had in Gaul stirred up the peasants to a tumultuary war not unlike that which the medieval knights termed a jacquerie. The name given to the peasant warriors with whom we are now concerned was Bagaudae;* and their insurrection, a striking proof of the hollowness of the fabric of Roman prosperity, had smouldered for more than a century and a half, ever since the days of Diocletian. A man, of whom we would gladly know more than the few lines which the chron-iclers bestow on him, was the link between these marauders within the Empire and the great barbarian without. In the year 448, as we learn from the pseudo-Prosper, 'Eudoxius, a doctor by profession, a man of evil,

* The authorities quoted by Ducange (*Glossarium Mediae et Infinae Latinatis*, under the heading 'Bagaudae') imply that the name was of Celtic origin and meant 'robbers' or 'native oppressors'. He suggests a derivation from *bagat*, which, he says, is the Welsh for a mob of men, and the Breton for a flock or herd. The monastery of Fossat, four miles from Paris, was called in the time of Charles le Chauve [the Bald], *castrum Bagaudarum* [the fort of the Bagaudae]. Salvian (*De Gubernatione Dei*, v.6) draws a striking picture of the judi-cial and fiscal iniquities which had driven men into the ranks of the Bacaudae (as he spells the word), *De Bacaudis nunc mihi sermo est: qui per malos judices et cruentos spoliati, afflicti, necati, postquam jus Romanae libertatis amiserant, etiam honorem Romani nominis perdiderunt. Et imputatur his infelicitas sua? Imputamus his nomen calamitatis suae? Imputamus nomen, quod ipsi fecimus? Et vocamus rebelles? Vocamus perditos, quos esse compulimus criminosos? Quibus enim aliis rebus Bacau-dae facti sunt, nisi iniquitatibus nostris, nisi improbitatibus judicum, nisi eorum proscriptionibus, et rapinis, qui exactionis publicae nomen in questus proprii emolumenta verterunt et indictiones tributarias praedas suas esse fecerunt* [Now I come to the Bagaudae. Robbed, oppressed and murdered by evil and bloody judges, with the rights of Roman freedom they lost also the honour of being called Romans. Can we attribute to them the cause of their wretched condition, blame them for what was done by us? Can we call them rebels? Is 'criminal' the term for those we have driven to crime? They became Bagaudae through the iniquities of judges, the proscriptions and thefts of those who turned the collection of taxes into money-making for themselves, and put tribute payments into their own pockets]. Compare also the following interesting notice in Tiro's chronicle, 435: *Gallia ulterior Tibatonem principem rebellionis secuta, a Romana societate discessit, a quo tracto initio omnia paene Galliarum servitia in Bagaudam conspiravere* [Further Gaul followed the lead of the rebel Tibato and abandoned the alliance with Rome. After this beginning almost all the slaves in both Gauls joined the Bagaudae].

though cultivated intellect, being mixed up with the movements of the Bagaudae at that time, fled to the Huns.'* It is probable enough that we have here to do with a mere selfish adventurer such as float ever upon the surface of revolutionary change: yet before condemning the man of 'evil though highly cultured intellect', who flashes thus for a moment upon the page of history, we would gladly have known whether he too may not have been in his day an apostle of 'the enthusiasm of humanity', whether the miseries which Eudoxius saw among the pillaged peasants of Gaul were not the original cause of his being condemned as a Bagauda by delicately living senators and prefects, and forced to appeal against the injustices of civilisation at the bar of its terrible antagonist.

At length, in the spring of 451, the preparations of Attila were completed, and the huge host began to roll on its way towards the Rhine. This army, like those which modern science has created, and under which modern industry groans, was truly described as a nation rather than an army; and though the estimates of the chroniclers, which vary from half a million to seven hundred thousand men, cannot be accepted as literally accurate, we shall not err in believing that the vast multitude who looked to the tent of Attila for orders were practically innumerable. Sidonius describes how the quiet life of the Roman provincial senator was suddenly disturbed by the roar of a mighty multitude, when barbarism seemed to be pouring over the plains of Gaul all the inhabitants of the North. If his enumeration of the invading tribes, which no doubt partakes of some of the vagueness of his style of poetry, be at all correct, the Geloni from the shores of the Volga, the Neuri and Bastarnae from the Ukraine, the Scyri, whom we are in doubt whether to place near Riga on the Baltic or Odessa on the Euxine, were serving in that army.† The ethnological affinities of these obscure tribes are very doubtful. Some of them may have been of Slavonic origin. The Teutonic family was represented by the Rugii from Pomerania, the Bructeri from the Weser; one half of the Frankish people from 'the turbid Neckar'; the Thuringians (Toringi) from Bavaria, and the Burgundians — these too only a portion of the tribe who had lingered in their old homes by the Vistula. The bone and marrow of the army were of course the Huns themselves, and the two powerful Teutonic tribes, enemies to the Hun in

* Tiro, for the year 448.
† Apollinaris Sidonius, *Panegyric of Avitus*, 319–25. The Geloni are probably only inserted because their name fits in nicely into a hexameter and has a classical ring about it, as having been used by Horace.

the past and to be his enemies in the future, but for the present his faithful allies and counsellors, the Gepidae and the Ostrogoths. Thus if we go back to the old story of the Gothic migration from 'the island of Sweden', we have the crews of two of the ships being led on to attack their fellows in the other vessel, the Ostrogoths and the 'Torpid' Gepidae marching right across Europe at the bidding of a leader whose forefathers came from Siberia, to overwhelm their Visigothic brethren, who are dwelling by the Garonne. The Ostrogoths, who possibly occupied a territory in the north of Hungary, were commanded by three brothers, sprung from the great Amal lineage, Walamir and Theudemir and Widemir; 'nobler', as the patriotic Jordanes observes, 'than the king whose orders they obeyed'. The Gepidae, whose land probably bordered on the northern confines of the Ostrogothic settlement, were led to battle by Arderic, bravest and most famous of all the subject princes, and him on whose wise and loyal counsels Attila chiefly relied.

While this vast medley of nations are hewing down the trees of the Thüringer Wald, in order to fashion their rude boats and rafts for the pas-sage of the Rhine,* let us glance for a moment at the tribes, scarcely less various and not so coherent, which, on the Gaulish side of the river, are awaiting their dreaded impact.

Near the mouths of the Rhine, the Scheldt, and the Somme, that is to say, in the modern countries of Belgium and Picardy, clustered the great confederacy of the Salian Franks. Their Ripuarian brethren held the upper reaches of the great river, and it is to these probably that Sidonius refers when he places them by the turbid Neckar, and describes them as furnishing a contingent to the army of Attila. All the Franks were still heathen, the fiercest of the Teutonic settlers in Gaul, and they bore an ill-repute for unfaithfulness to their plighted word and even to their oaths. Small sign as yet was there that to them would one day fall the hegemony of the Gallic nations. In the opposite corner of the country, between the Loire, the Garonne, and the bay of Biscay, the Visigoths had erected a monarchy, the most civilised and compact of all the barbarian kingdoms, and the one which seemed to have the fairest promise of a long and tri-umphant life. By the peace which their king Walia concluded with Honorius (416) after the restoration of Placidia, they had obtained legal possession of the district called Aquitania Secunda, together with the ter-ritory round Toulouse, all of which allotment went by the name of Septi-

* So Apollinaris Sidonius, *Panegyric of Avitus*, 325–6.

mania* or Gothia. For ten years (419–29) there had been firm peace between Visigoths and Romans; then, for ten years more (429–39), fierce and almost continued war, Theodoric, king of the Visigoths, endeavouring to take Arles and Narbonne; Aetius and his subordinate Litorius striving to take the Gothic capital of Toulouse, and all but succeeding. And in these wars Aetius had availed himself of his long-standing friendship with the Huns to enlist them as auxiliaries against the warriors of Theodoric, dangerous allies who plundered friends and enemies, and carried back doubtless to their dreary encampment in Hungary vivid remembrance of the sunny vineyards of Languedoc and Guienne. For the last twelve years (439–51) there had been peace, but scarcely friendship, between the courts of Ravenna and Toulouse.

North of the Visigoths, the Celtic population of Brittany, known by the name of the Armoricans, had risen in arms against their Roman rulers, and had with some degree of success maintained their independence. From this time, perhaps, we ought to date that isolation of Brittany from the politics of the rest of France, which has not entirely disappeared even at the present day. But the terrible invader from the east welded even the stubborn Breton into temporary cohesion with his neighbours, and in the pages of Jordanes we find the 'Armoritiani' fighting side by side with the Roman legions against Attila.

The same list includes a yet more familiar name, 'Saxones'. How came our fathers thither; they, whose homes were in the long sandy levels of Holstein? As has been already pointed out, the national migration of the Angles and Saxons to our own island had already commenced, perhaps in part determined by the impulse northward of Attila's own subjects. Possibly like the Northmen, their successors, the Saxons may have invaded both sides of the English channel at once, and may on this occasion have been standing in arms to defend against their old foe some newly won possessions in Normandy or Picardy.

In the south-east of Gaul, the Burgundians had after many wars and some reverses established themselves (443) with the consent of the Romans in the district then called Sapaudia and now Savoy. Their territory was somewhat more extensive than the province which was the cradle of the present royal house of Italy, since it stretched northwards beyond the lake of

* From the seven chief cities comprised therein, which were – taking them from south to north – Toulouse (the Visigothic capital), Agen, Bordeaux, Périgueux, Angoulême, Saintes, and Poitiers.

Neuchâtel, and southwards as far as Grenoble. Here the Burgundian immigrants, under their king, Gundiok, were busy settling themselves in their new possession, cultivating the lands which they had divided by lot, each one receiving half the estate of a Roman host or *hospes** (for under such gentle names the spoliation was veiled), when the news came that the terrible Hun had crossed the Rhine, and that all hosts and guests in Gaul must unite for its defence.

The Alans, who had wandered thus far westwards from the country between the Volga and the Don, had received (440) the district round Valence for a possession from the Romans, on much the same terms prob‑ ably as those by which the Burgundians held Savoy.† Of all the barbarian tribes now quartered in Gaul they were the nearest allied to the Huns, and Sangiban, their king, was strongly suspected of having some secret and treacherous understanding with Attila.

This chaos of barbarian tribes occupied perhaps one half of Gaul. Wherever chaos was not, wherever some remains of the old Imperial cos‑ mos were still left unsubmerged, there was Romania. We may conjecture that by this time very little of Roman domination remained in the Belgic Gaul. The eastern portions of Gallia Lugdunensis and Gallia Aquitan‑ ica, especially the city of Lyons and the mountains of Auvergne, seem to have been fervently loyal to the emperor. Gallia Narbonensis with its cap‑ itals of Arles and Narbonne, but excepting Toulouse and its surrounding country, had successfully beaten back the Visigothic invader, and was almost more Roman than Rome itself.

But the question of transcendent importance for Gaul, and indirectly for the whole future of western Europe, was – 'Would chaos and cosmos blend for a little space to resist the vaster and wilder chaos which was roar‑ ing for them both, fierce from its Pannonian home? Especially could Aetius and Theodoric, so lately at death‑grips for the possession of one another's capitals – Aetius who had all but lost Arles, Theodoric who had all but lost Toulouse – unite heartily enough and promptly enough to beat back Attila?'

* A later division was effected, which gave the Burgundian two‑thirds of the arable land; but the primary apportionment seems to have been in equal shares.

† Tiro says (442), *Alani, quibus terrae Galliae ulterioris cum incolis dividendae a Patritio Aetio tra‑ ditae fuerant, resistentes armis subigunt, et expulsis dominis terrae, possessionem vi adipiscuntur* [The Alans, who had been given the land of Further Gaul by patrician Aetius to share with the inhabitants, took up arms in resistance, drove out the landowners, and gained the ownership by force].

This was the doubt, and Attila thought he saw in it an opportunity to divide his foes. 'A subtle man, and one who fought by artifice before he waged his wars',* he sent ambassadors to Valentinian, representing his intended invasion as only a continuation of the old joint campaigns of Roman and Hun against the Visigoth. To Theodoric he sent other messengers, exhorting him to break off his unnatural alliance with Rome, and to remember the cruel wars which so lately had been kindled against his people by the lieutenants of the Augustus.

Happily there was a little too much statesmanship both at Ravenna and Toulouse to allow of the success of so transparent an artifice. Valentinian's ambassadors to Theodoric addressed the Visigothic nation (if we may believe their panegyrist Jordanes) in some such words as these:

'It will comport with your usual wisdom, O bravest of the nations, to confederate with us against the tyrant of the universe, who longs to fasten the chains of slavery on the whole world, who does not seek for any reasonable excuses for battle, but thinks that whatsoever crimes he may commit are lawful because he is the doer of them. He measures the frontiers of his dominions by what? By the space that his arms can ravage. He gluts his pride by licence, he spurns the ordinances of earth and of heaven, and shows himself the enemy of our common nature. Surely he deserves your hatred who proves himself the spiteful foe of all. Recollect, I pray you (what assuredly he does not forget), blood has once flowed between you, and with whatever wiles he may now cover his thirst for vengeance, it is there, and it is terrible. To say nothing of our grievances, can you any longer tolerate with patience the pride of this savage? Mighty as you are in arms, think of your own griefs' (and here, doubtless, words were used which would recall to the mind of Theodoric the cruel outrages inflicted on his daughter by Attila's Vandal ally), 'and join your hands with ours. Help the republic which has given you one of her fairest provinces for a possession. If you would know how necessary the alliance of each of us is to the other, penetrate the council-chamber of the foe, and see how he labours to divide us.'

Theodoric was probably already meditating the Roman alliance, but these words are said to have decided him, and he replied, 'Romans, you have your will. Attila is your foe; you have made him ours also. Wheresoever the sound of his ravages shall call us, thither will we follow him; and all inflated as he is with his victories over so many proud nations, yet the

* Jordanes, *De Rebus Geticis*, 36.

Goths too know how to do battle with the proud. Strong in the goodness of my cause, I deem no war laborious. No evil omen daunts me when the majesty of the emperor of Rome smiles upon me.'

There is something hollow and unreal, doubtless, in these orations. In point of fact the Goths showed no alacrity in the defence of Roman Gaul till the storm of war rolled up to their own borders, and even then, according to one account, required a special messenger to rouse them from their unreadiness.* But the foundation for an alliance between Roman and Visigoth was laid, and it saved Gaul.

Attila, foiled in his diplomacy, swept with his vast host across the Rhine, and began the congenial work of destruction. City after city of the Belgic Gaul (which comprised all France north-east of the Seine) fell before him. What help he may have received from the Bagaudae, or rendered to the young Frankish chieftain, his ally, we know not. We only hear that one city after another was broken up by his savage hordes; but no simple human voice comes out of the chaos to tell us what common men and women suffered in that breaking up of the great deep. The ecclesiastics, intent on the glorification of their own favourite saint or chapel, tell us a little of what was done, or was not done in the way of miraculous interposition on behalf of particular places, and even for their childish legends, of uncertain date, and bearing elements of fiction on the face of them, we have to be grateful, so complete is the silence of authentic history as to the earlier events of the invasion.

The bishop of Tongres in Belgium, Servatius by name, implored God, amidst fastings and watchings and constant showers of tears, that he would never permit 'the unbelieving and ever-unworthy nation of the Huns' to enter Gaul.† Feeling sure in his spirit that this prayer was not granted, he sought the tomb of the apostle Peter at Rome, and there, after three days' fasting, pressed his suit. The apostle appeared to him in a vision and told him that according to the councils of the Most High, the Huns must certainly enter Gaul and ravage it for a time. But so much was conceded to Servatius, that he should not see the misery which was coming on his flock. He was therefore to return at once to his home, choose out his grave-clothes, and set his house in order, and then should he 'migrate from this body'. He returned accordingly, set all things in order for his burial, and told his flock that they should see his face no more. 'But they following him with great

---

* Apollinaris Sidonius, *Panegyric of Avitus*, 329–51.
† Gregory of Tours, *Historia Francorum*, ii.5.

wailing and many tears, humbly prayed him – "Leave us not, O holy father; forget us not, O good shepherd!" Then, as they could not prevail upon him to stay, they received his blessing, kissed him, and departed. He went to the city of Utrecht, where he was seized with a mild fever, and his soul departed from his body. His corpse was brought back to Tongres, and buried by the city wall.' Such was the end of Servatius. Of the fate of his flock we have no further particulars.

'On the very eve of the blessed Easter, the Huns, coming forth out of Pannonia and laying waste everything on their march, arrived at Metz. They gave up the city to the flames, and slew the people with the edge of the sword, killing the priests themselves before the sacrosanct altar of the Lord. And in all that city no place remained unburnt except the oratory of the blessed Stephen, protomartyr and Levite.' Gregory of Tours then proceeds to describe at unnecessary length a vision in which someone saw the blessed Levite, Stephen, interceding for this oratory with the apostles Peter and Paul, and obtaining a promise that it should remain unharmed, 'that the nations might see that he availed somewhat with the Lord'.*

From Lorraine into Champagne rolled on the devastating flood. St Nicasius, bishop of Rheims, was hewn down before the altar of his church, while his lips were uttering the words of the psalm, 'My soul cleaveth unto the dust, quicken thou me according to thy word.' Thus he attained the crown of martyrdom, though it has been truly remarked that the bishops and priests who fell beneath the swords of the Huns perished, not strictly as confessors of a religion, but as chief citizens of their dioceses, and as guardians of sacred treasure. Attila was a plunderer, but not a persecutor. He made war on civilisation and on human nature, not on religion, for he did not understand it enough to hate it.

The inhabitants of a little town upon a clayey island in the Seine, near its junction with the Marne, were in such dread of its invasion by the Huns that they had made up their minds to flee, when a young girl of the neighbouring village of Nanterre, named Genovefa, succeeded in communicating to the wives of the inhabitants her own calm and heaven-born confidence that the place would not be assailed. The men disbelieved her mission, called her a false prophetess, would gladly have stoned her, or drowned her in the river. But the influence of the women, aided by the remembrance of the undoubted holiness of a neighbouring saint, Germanus of Auxerre, who had in former days taken the part of Genovefa,

* *Historia Francorum*, ii.5–6.

saved her from insult, and her counsels from rejection. The inhabitants remained; the prayers of the women, or the insignificance of the place, saved it from the presence of the enemy. Could the squalid Pannonian hordes have overleapt fourteen centuries of time as well as the few miles of space which intervened, how their eyes would have sparkled, and their hearts well-nigh stopped beating with the ecstasy of rapine, for the town which was then scarcely worth attacking is now known by the name of Paris. Justly, if the story be true, are Sainte Geneviève and Saint Germain among the names still held in highest honour by the beautiful city on the Seine.

In the after-growth of medieval ecclesiastical chronicles it may well be supposed that Attila's destroying hand is made responsible for even more ruin than it actually caused. Thus, 'Maistre Jacques de Guise', writing his history of Hainault in the fourteenth century, informs his readers that 'they must know that no town, fortress, or city, however strong it might be, could resist this people, so cruel was it and malevolent . . . Moreover, by this tyrant Attille were destroyed nearly all the cities of Gaul and Germany. Firstly, Reims, Cambrai, Treveres [Trier], Mectz [Metz], Arras, Tongres, Tournai, Thérouanne, Coulongne [Cologne], Amiens, Beauvais, Paris, and so many towns, cities, and fortresses that whoso should wish to put them all in writing he would too much weary the readers . . .

'Item, by him were destroyed in Germany, Mainz, a very noble city, Warmose [Worms], Argentore [Strasbourg], Nymaie [?], Langres and Nerbonne [?]. In this year, as saith Sigebert, were martyrised the eleven thousand virgins in the city of Coulongne.'

This extract does not, of course, possess any shadow of historical authority. It is certainly wrong as to Narbonne and Nîmes (if that be the city intended by Nymaie), and it is probably wrong as to Paris. But, with these exceptions, the cities named are all either in or upon the confines of Gallia Belgica, the chief scene of Attila's ravages, and the list is not an improbable one, though we can well believe that, as every defaced tomb and mutilated statue in an English church claims to have been maltreated by 'Cromwell's soldiers', so no monkish chronicler who had a reasonable opportunity of bringing 'Attille' and his malevolent Huns near to the shrine of his favourite saint would be likely to forgo the terrible fascination.

When Belgic Gaul was ravaged to his heart's content, the Hun turned his footsteps towards Aquitaine, which contained the settlements of the Visigoths, and where, as he well knew, his hardest task awaited him. The

Loire, flowing first northwards, then westwards, protects, by its broad sickle of waters, this portion of Gaul, and the Loire itself is commanded at its most northerly point by that city which, known in Caesar's day as Genabum, had taken the name Aureliani from the great emperor, the conqueror of Zenobia, and is now called Orléans. Three times has Aureliani played an eminent part in the history of Gaul. There broke out the great insurrection of 52 BC against the victorious Caesar; there Attila's host, in AD 451, received their first repulse; and there in 1429, the maid of Domrémy, by forcing the duke of Bedford to raise the siege, wrested from the English Plantagenets their last chance of ruling in France.

The hero of Orléans, in this defence of her walls, was the bishop, Anianus. He had visited Aetius at Arles, and strongly impressed upon the mind of that general the necessity of relieving Orléans before the 24th of June at the very latest. Then returning to the city he cheered his flock with words of pious hope. The battering-rams of Attila thundered against the walls, and the hearts of the people began to fail them. To Anianus himself the promised help seemed to linger. He knew not, and we cannot with certainty state the true cause of the delay which is related to us only by one doubtful authority.* Aetius, it is said, emerged from the Alpine passes with only a slender and ill-officered train of soldiers, and then found that the Goths, instead of moving eastward to join him, were thinking of awaiting the attack of the dreaded foe in their own territory behind the Loire. In this unforeseen perplexity, Aetius availed himself of the services of Avitus, a Roman noble of Auvergne, and a *persona grata* at the court of Theodoric. His visit to the Gothic king proved successful.

'He aroused their wrath, making it subservient to the purposes of Rome, and marched in the midst of the skin-clothed warriors to the sound of the trumpets of Romulus.'

Meanwhile the consternation within the city of Orléans went on increasing, as the citizens saw their walls crumbling into ruin beneath the blows of the battering-rams of Attila. One day, when they were fervently praying in the church, 'Anianus said, "Look forth from the ramparts and see if God's mercy yet succours us." They gazed forth from the wall, but

---

* Apollinaris Sidonius, *Panegyric of Avitus*, 328–56. As the whole object of this poem is to pour laudation on the head of Avitus, it is not unreasonable to suppose that the backwardness of the Visigoths has been exaggerated or even invented in order to enhance his glory. He may have simply borne to the camp of Theodoric a message from Aetius arranging the time and place of meeting for the two armies.

beheld no man. He said, "Pray in faith: the Lord will liberate you today."
They went on praying; again he bade them mount the walls, and again they
saw no help approaching. He said to them the third time, "If ye pray in
faith, the Lord will speedily be at hand to help you." Then they with weeping and loud lamentation implored the mercy of the Lord. When their
prayer was ended, a third time, at the command of that old man, they
mounted the wall, and looking forth they saw from afar, as it were, a cloud
rising out of the ground. When they brought him word of it he said, "It is
the help of God." In the meanwhile, as the walls were now trembling
under the stroke of the rams, and were already on the point of falling into
ruin, lo! Aetius and Theodoric, the king of the Goths, and Thorismund,
his son, come running up to the city, turn the ranks of the enemy, cast him
out, and drive him far away.'* It was apparently on the very day fixed
between the bishop and the general (the 24th of June) that this relief came.

Foiled in his attempt to take Orléans and to turn the line of the Loire,
Attila, with his unwieldy host, began to retreat towards the Rhine. It is the
weakness of those marauding warriors of whom he may be considered the
type, that their recoil must be as rapid as their onset. A ruined and devas-
tated country cannot be compelled to furnish the subsistence for lack of
which it is itself perishing. Everywhere along the line of march are thousands of bitter wrongs waiting for revenge. And the marauders themselves
to whom pillage, not patriotism or discipline, has been the one inspiring
motive, and the common bond of union, when the hope of further pillage
fails, are each secretly revolving the same thought, how to leave the ravaged
country as soon as possible with their plunder undiminished.

Doubtless Aetius and Theodoric were hovering on Attila's rear,
neglecting no opportunity of casual vengeance on the stragglers from the
host, and endeavouring to force him to battle at every point where, from
the nature of the country, he would be compelled to fight at a disadvantage.
But we hear no details of his retreat till he reached the city of Troyes, 114
Roman miles from Orléans. The bishop of Troyes was the venerable

* This is the account of the siege of Orléans given by Gregory of Tours about a century
and a half after the event (*Historia Francorum*, ii.7). The story given in the life of St Anianus in the *Acta Sanctorum* differs in some particulars from this. Nothing is said of the
three visits to the walls or the far-off cloud of dust; but the prayers of the saint bring a four
days' storm of rain, which greatly hinders the works of the besiegers. They have, however, made a practicable breach and are actually within the city, when the relieving army
appears. Gregory's word *ejiciunt* (cast them out) gives some probability to this part of the
narrative.

Lupus, a man who was by this time nearly seventy years of age, and who, in common with St Germanus, had greatly distinguished himself by his opposition to the Pelagian heresy, which he had combated in Britain as well as in Gaul. Troyes was an open city, undefended by walls or arsenals, and the immense swarm of the Huns and their allies who came clamouring round it were hungering for spoil and chafed with disappointment at their failure before Orléans.* Lupus, as we are told in the *Acta Sanctorum*, betook himself to his only weapon, prayer, and thereby successfully defended his city from the assaults of the enemy. The ecclesiastical biographer seems to be purposely enigmatic and obscure, but there are touches in the story which look like truth. It appears that Attila, who may have been partly swayed by the remembrance that the allies were close upon his track, and that a night of pillage would have been a bad preparation of his troops for the coming battle, was also impressed – 'fierce wild beast as he was'† – by something which seemed not altogether of this earth in the face and demeanour of Lupus, something unlike the servile and sordid diplomatists of Byzantium who had hitherto been his chief exemplars of Christianity. In granting the bishop's prayer for the immunity of his city from pillage, he made one stipulation, that, 'for the safety of himself and his own army the holy man should go with them and see the streams of the Rhine, after which he promised that he would dismiss him in peace. And so it was; as soon as they arrived at the river he offered him a free passage back, did not hinder his return, sent guides to show him the way; and even earnestly besought, by the mouth of the interpreter Hunagaisus, that the bishop would pray for him.'

This Hunagaisus is undoubtedly the same minister with whom we have made acquaintance in the Hunnish camp under the name of Onegesius or Onégesh, and the introduction of his name here in a biography probably composed about the middle of the sixth century, affords some guarantee that we are on the track of a genuine tradition. If so, the thought that a Gaulish theologian was present in the camp of Attila during the scenes which are next to follow, gives a fresh interest to the picture, some of the details of which he may himself have described.

* It is only by conjecture that the following incident is assigned to the time of Attila's retreat. The words of the *Acta Sanctorum* would be consistent with the interpretation that the Huns were still moving on into Gaul. But the expression *Rheni etiam fluenta visurum* [to see the streams of the Rhine], looks as if Attila's face was now set Rhinewards. The first life given by the Bollandists is evidently of far greater value than the second: in fact, this latter is worthless. It is curious to observe that it contains the cant phrase *flagellum Dei* [scourge of God], which is absent from the other record.   † *Acta Sanctorum*, the 29th July .

For in the interval between Attila's arrival before Troyes, and his dismissal of Lupus on the banks of the Rhine, occurred that great clash of armed nations which decided the question whether the west of Europe was to belong to Turanian or to Aryan nationalities. Posterity has chosen to call it the battle of Châlons, but there is good reason to think that it was fought fifty miles distant from Châlons-sur-Marne, and that it would be more correctly named the battle of Troyes, or, to speak with complete accuracy, the battle of Méry-sur-Seine.*

By what preceding arts of strategy the campaign was marked, whether Attila willingly offered battle or was so sorely harassed in his retreat that he was unable to decline it, we know not, except that we read of a skirmish between the Franks and Gepidae on the night preceding the general engagement.† It was probably in the early days of July that the two great armies at length came together. What followed shall be told in the (freely rendered) words of Jordanes himself, who throws all his heart into the narration, rightly feeling that this death-grapple with the enemies of Rome was in some sense the mightiest deed that his kinsmen had achieved, and sympathising, notwithstanding his own Ostrogothic descent, with Theodoric the Visigothic antagonist of Attila, rather than with Walamir his Ostrogothic feudatory.

After enumerating the various nationalities which fought under the banner of Aetius, he continues, 'All come together therefore into the Catalaunian, which are also called the Maurician plains, one hundred Gallic *leugae* in length and seventy in breadth. Now the *leuga* is equivalent to one Roman mile and a half. So then that district of the world becomes the parade ground of innumerable nationalities. Both the armies which there meet are of the mightiest; nothing is done by underhand machinations, but everything by fair and open fight. What worthy reason could be assigned for the deaths of so many thousands? What hatred had crept into so many breasts and bidden them take up arms against one another? It is surely proved that the race of man live but for the sake of kings; since the mad onset of one man's mind could cause the slaughter of so many nations, and in a moment, by the caprice of one arrogant king, the fruit of nature's toil through so many centuries could be destroyed.

---

* In contemporary language 'the battle of the Mauriac plain'. [For more information on the site of the so-called battle of Châlons see appendix ii, pp. 366–8.]

† See Jordanes, *De Rebus Geticis*, 41, quoted below.

Chapter 37

'But before relating the actual order of the fight, it seems necessary to explain some of the preliminary movements of the war, because famous as the battle was, it was no less manifold and complicated. For Sangiban, king of the Alans, foreboding future disaster, had promised to surrender himself to Attila, and to bring into obedience to him the city of Orléans where he was then quartered. When Theodoric and Aetius had knowledge of this, they built great mounds against the city and destroyed it before the coming of Attila.* Upon Sangiban himself they set a close watch, and stationed him with his own proper tribe in the very midst of their auxiliaries. Attila meanwhile, struck by this occurrence, distrusting his own powers, fearing to engage in the conflict, and secretly considering the expediency of flight, which was more grievous to him than death itself, resolved to enquire as to the future from the augurs. These men, according to their wont, first pored over the bowels of some sheep, then pondered the direction of the veins in some scraped bones, and at last gave forth their augury, "Ill fortune to the Huns." They qualified it however with this crumb of comfort, "that the chief leader on the opposite side should fall in the midst of victory, and so mar the triumph of his followers". To Attila the death of Aetius' (whom he supposed to be intended by the words "the chief leader of the enemy") 'seemed to be worth purchasing even by the defeat of his army, yet being naturally rendered anxious by such an answer, and being a man of much address in warlike matters, he determined, with some fear and trembling, to join battle about the ninth hour of the day [3 p.m.],† so that if his affairs turned out ill, impending night might come to his aid . . .

Chapter 38

'Now this was the configuration of the field of battle. It rose [on one side] into a decided undulation which might be called a hill; and as both parties wished to get the not inconsiderable advantage of the ground which this eminence conferred, the Huns took possession of the right-hand portion of it with their troops; the Romans and Visigoths of the left with their

* If the text is not corrupt here, Jordanes must have received some very distorted account of the events of the siege of Orléans.

† This note of time suits July better than October. Even for July, the interval between three o'clock and sunset seems full short for such a battle *multiplex et immane* [varied and savage].

auxiliaries.* Leaving for a while the fight for the possession of this ridge [let us describe the order of the main battle]. On the right wing stood Theodoric with the Visigoths, on the left Aetius with the Romans. In the middle they placed Sangiban, the leader of the Alans – a piece of military caution to enclose him, of whose disposition they were none too confident, in a mass of loyal soldiers. For the man in the way of whose flight you have interposed a sufficient obstacle, easily accepts the necessity of fighting.

'The line of the Huns was drawn up on a different principle, for in their centre stood Attila with all his bravest warriors. In this arrangement the king consulted his own personal safety, hoping that by taking his place in the very heart and strength of his own people he at least should be de-livered from the impending danger. Upon the wings of his army hovered the many nations and tribes whom he had subjected to his dominion. Pre-eminent among these was the host of the Ostrogoths, led by the three brothers, Walamir, Theodemir and Widemir, men of nobler birth than the king himself whom they then obeyed, since the mighty line of the Amals was represented by them. There too, at the head of the countless warriors of the Gepidae, was their king Ardaric, that man of valour and of fame who for his extraordinary fidelity towards Attila was admitted into his inmost counsels. For Attila, who had well weighed his sagacious char-acter, loved him and Walamir the Ostrogoth above all his other subject princes; Walamir, the safe keeper of a secret, the pleasant in speech, the ignorant of guile, and Ardaric, who, as we have said, was illustrious both by his loyalty and his wise advice. To these two nations Attila believed, not undeservedly, that he might safely entrust the battle against their Visigothic kindred. As for all the rest, the ruck of kings – if I may call them so – and the leaders of diverse nationalities, these, like subaltern officers, watched each nod of Attila; and, when a look of his eye summoned them, in fear and trembling they would gather round him waiting in submissive silence to receive his commands, or at any rate' (i.e. if their subservience was less abject) 'they would carry out whatever he ordered. But Attila alone, king of all the kings, was over all in command, and had the care of all upon his shoulders.

'As I before said, the fight began with a struggle for the possession of some rising ground. Attila directed his troops to occupy the summit of the hill, but he was anticipated by Thorismund and Aetius, who [from the

* Perhaps Jordanes means that the right wing of the Hunnish army and the left wing of the confederates both endeavoured to occupy this ground.

Hunnic bronze cauldrons. *Right*, a panther-shaped cup handle from a Gothic hoard found at Pietroasa, Rumania, dating from the period of the Hunnic empire. *Below, left* and *right*, *fibulae* from the hoard at Pietroasa

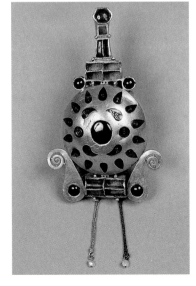

The obverse and reverse of a gold medallion, set with a multiple of Galla Placidia, from a Frankish hoard found at Velp in the Netherlands which was probably hidden at the time of Aetius' campaigns in northern Gaul. *Below*, sword fittings and other ornaments from a Gothic grave – possibly that of King Theodoric I – at Pouan, near Troyes, France

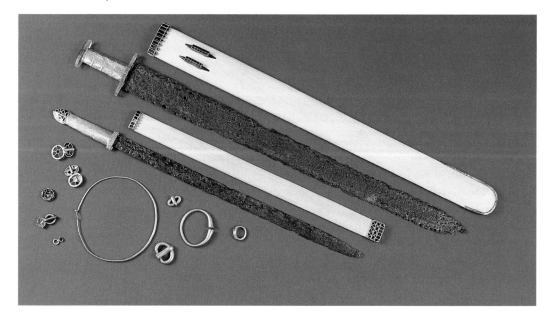

other side] struggled up to the highest point, and then, having the advantage of the hill in their favour, easily threw into confusion the advancing
Huns.

Chapter 39

'Then Attila, seeing his army somewhat disturbed by this skirmish,
thought the time a suitable one for confirming their courage by an address.

SPEECH OF ATTILA

' "After your victories over so many nations, after a whole world subdued, if
ye only stand fast this day, I should have deemed it a fond thing to whet your
spirits with words, as though ye were yet ignorant of your business. Let a
new general or an inexperienced army try that method. It were beneath my
dignity to utter, and beyond your obligation to listen to, any of the commonplaces of war. For what other occupation are you practised in, if not in
fighting? And to the strong man what is sweeter, than with his own right
hand to seek for his revenge? It is one of the greatest boons which nature
gives us to glut our souls with vengeance. Let us therefore go forward with
cheerfulness to attack the enemy, since they who strike the blow have ever
the boldest hearts. You who are united under my sway — I tell you to despise
these jarring nationalities, leagued together for the momentary purpose of
self-defence by an alliance which is in itself an index of their terror. Lo! ere
they have yet felt our onset, they are carried to and fro by their fear; they look
out for the rising ground, they are exciting themselves over the occupation
of every little hillock, and bewailing too late their own rashness; they are
clamouring for ramparts in these open plains. Known to you right well are
the flimsy arms and weak frames of the Roman soldiers; I will not say at the
first wound, at the first speck of dust on their armour they lose heart. While
they are solemnly forming their battle array and locking their shields
together into the testudo, do you rush into the conflict with that surpassing
courage which it is your wont to show, and, despising the Roman line,
charge at the Alans, press heavily on the Visigoths. It is there that we must
look for speedy victory, for they are the key of the position. Cut the sinews,
and the limbs will be at once relaxed; nor can the body stand if you have
taken away its bones.

' "O ye Huns, raise your hearts battle-high and let your wonted fury
swell your veins. Now put forth all your cunning; now use all your arms.
Let him who is wounded seek still for at least one enemy's death; let him

who is unhurt revel in the slaughter of the foe. Him who is fated to conquer, no dart will touch; him who is doomed to die, fate will find in the
midst of slothful peace. And, last of all, why should fortune have set her
mark upon the Huns as conquerors of so many nations, unless she was
preparing them for the delights of this battle too? Who opened the way
across the pool of Maeotis,* for so many centuries an impenetrable secret
from our ancestors? Who made armed men bow before them while they
were still unarmed? Yonder motley host will never endure to look upon the
faces of the Huns. The event cannot mock my hopes; this, this is the field of
victory which so many previous successes have avouched us of. I shall be
the first to hurl my weapon against the enemy, and if anyone can linger
inactive when Attila fights, he is a thing without a soul, and ought to be
buried out of hand."

'Their hearts were warmed at these words, and all rushed headlong into
the fray.

Chapter 40

'The position of their affairs was not without its suggestions of fear, but the
presence of their king removed all tendency to delay even from the most
hesitating.

'Hand to hand the two armies were soon engaged. It was a battle – ruthless, manifold, immense, obstinate – such as antiquity in all its stories of
similar encounters has nought parallel to, such as, if a man failed to see, no
other marvel that he might behold in the course of his life would compen-
sate for the omission. For if we may believe the report of our elders, a brook
which was gliding down between low banks through the aforesaid plain,
receiving the blood which gushed from thousands of wounds, was, not by
showers of rain, but by that ghastly intermingling, swollen from a brook
into a torrent. And those whom parching thirst, the consequence of their
wounds, drove to its banks, found that murder was mixed with the
draught. A miserable fate for them who drank of the gore which their own
wounds poured forth.

'Here the king Theodoric, while he was galloping backwards and forwards, cheering on his army, was thrown from his horse, and being
trampled under the feet of his own party, thus ended his life in a ripe old
age. Others however assert that he was smitten by a javelin from the hand of
Andages, of the nation of the Ostrogoths who were then following the

* The sea of Azov.

lead of Attila. This was the event which Attila's soothsayers had foretold to him in their divinations, though he understood them to speak of Aetius.

'Then the Visigoths, splitting off from the Alans, rushed upon the squadrons of the Huns, and had well-nigh slaughtered Attila himself, but he prudently fled, and straightway enclosed himself and his followers within the defences of his camp, upon which he had placed the wagons by way of rampart. It seemed a frail bulwark to be sure, still they clung to it as their last chance of life; and yet these were the men whose desperate onset a little while ago stone walls could not stand against. Meanwhile Thoris-mund, the son of King Theodoric, the same who had taken part with Aetius in the occupation of the hill, and in driving down the enemy from that higher ground, lost his way in the blind night, and thinking that he was rejoining his own men on their line of march, came unawares upon the wagons of the enemy. Here, while he was fighting bravely, his horse was killed under him by a wound in the head. He fell to the ground, but was rescued by the care of his people, and persuaded to desist from the unequal encounter. Aetius in the same way was separated from his host in the con-fusion of the night, and went wandering through the midst of the enemy,* trembling lest some untoward event should have occurred to the Goths, and ever asking the way, till at length he arrived at the camp of his allies, and passed the remainder of the night under the shelter of their shields.

'Next morning when day dawned, and the allied generals beheld the vast plains covered with corpses, but saw that the Huns did not venture to sally forth, they concluded that the victory was theirs. They knew perfectly well that it could have been no common slaughter which had compelled Attila to fly in confusion from the battlefield; and yet he did not act like one in abject prostration, but clashed his arms, sounded his trumpets, and con-tinually threatened a fresh attack. As a lion, close pressed by the hunters, ramps up and down before the entrance to his cave, and neither dares to make a spring, nor yet ceases to frighten all the neighbourhood with his roarings, so did that most warlike king, though hemmed in, trouble his conquerors. The Goths and Romans accordingly called a council of war and deliberated what was to be done with their worsted foe. As he had no store of provisions, and as he had so posted his archers within the bound-aries of his camp as to rain a shower of missiles on an advancing assailant, they decided not to attempt a storm, but to weary him out by a blockade. It

---

* Having from his youth been accustomed to intercourse with the Huns, he probably spoke their language like a native.

is said however that seeing the desperate condition of his affairs, the aforesaid king, high-minded still in the supreme crisis of his fate, had
constructed a funeral pyre of horses' saddles, determined, if the enemy
should break into his camp, to hurl himself headlong into the flames, that
none should boast himself and say, 'I have wounded Attila', nor that the
lord of so many nations should fall alive into the hands of his enemies.

Chapter 41

'During the delays of this blockade the Visigoths were looking for their old
king, and marvelling at his absence from the scene of victory. After a long
search they found him, as is wont to be the case with brave men, lying there
where the bodies were thickest; and singing their songs in his honour, they
bore away his corpse from the gaze of the enemy. Then should you have
seen the Gothic companies lifting up their untuned voices in a wild strain
of lamentation, and, while the battle still raged around them, giving all
heed to the exact observance of the rites of burial. Tears were shed, but they
were the tears which are rightly paid to brave men dead. The death had
been on our [the Gothic] side, but the Hun himself bore witness that it had
been a glorious one, and even Attila's pride might bow when he saw the
corpse of such a king borne out to burial with all his kingly ornaments
about him.

'The Goths, while still paying the last honours to Theodoric, by the
clash of their weapons hailed the majesty of a new king, and the brave and
glorious Thorismund, decked with that title, followed the funeral of his
dearly loved father as became a son. Then, when that was finished, grief for
the loss which he had sustained, and the impulse of his own fiery valour,
urged him to avenge the death of his father upon the Hunnish host. First,
however, he consulted Aetius the patrician, as the senior general and a man
of ripened experience, what step he would advise to be next taken. He,
fearing lest if the Huns were destroyed root and branch, the Roman
Empire might be still more hardly pressed by the Goths, earnestly tendered
this advice, "that he should return to his own capital and grasp the kingdom which his father had left; lest otherwise his brothers should seize on
his father's treasures, and so make the realm of the Visigoths their own,
whereupon he would have to commence a laborious campaign, and one in
which victory would be a wretched business, since it would be over his
own flesh and blood".

'Thorismund received this advice as the best thing for his own interest, without perceiving the duplicity which lurked beneath it, and leaving the Huns, he returned to his own district in Gaul. So does human frailty, if it becomes entangled in suspicion, often lose irretrievably the opportunity of achieving great results.*

'In this most famous battle, which was fought between the bravest nations in the world, it is reported that 162,000 men were slain on both sides, not including fifteen thousand of Gepidae and Franks, who, falling foul of one another the night before the battle, perished by mutually inflicted wounds, the Franks fighting on the side of the Romans, the Gepi-dae on that of the Huns.†

'When Attila learned the departure of the Goths, the event was so unexpected that he surmised it to be a stratagem of the enemy, and kept his troops within the camp for some time longer. But when he found that the absence of the enemy was followed by a long time of silence, his mind again rose with the hope of victory, future joys unfolded themselves before him, and the courage of this mighty king returned again to its old level. Meanwhile Thorismund, who had been clothed with the regal majesty on the Catalaunian plains on the very place where his father had fallen, entered Toulouse, and here, notwithstanding that his brothers had a strong party among the chiefs, he so prudently managed the commencement of his reign, that no dispute was raised as to the succession.'

So far Jordanes. The battle then was lost but not won: lost as far as Attila's invasion of Gaul was concerned, but not won for the Roman Empire by the destruction of its most dreaded foe. In reading the story of Attila's escape from Aetius, one is naturally reminded of Alaric's escape from Stilicho, forty-eight years before, and of the imputations then thrown out‡ as to the connivance of the Roman general. And the same remark which was made then may be to some extent applicable now. With troops of such uncertain temper, and, in this case, with such imperfect cohesion as the greater part of the Roman auxiliaries showed, it might be dangerous to animate the vast host of Attila with the irresistible courage of despair. In all ages, from Sphacteria to Saratoga, and from Saratoga to Sedan, the final operation of compelling the surrender of a beaten army, the landing, so to

* And thus the native hue of resolution
　　Is sicklied o'er with the pale cast of thought.
† Idatius puts the number of slain at three hundred thousand. Of course all estimates of the slain on such a battlefield are of the vaguest and most untrustworthy kind.
‡ By Orosius, vii.37.

speak, of the fisherman's prize, has been an operation requiring some nicety of generalship and a pretty high degree of confidence in the discipline of the victorious troops. Even the clash of arms and the blast of trumpets in the camp of the Huns — the lashing of the lion's tail, and the deep thunder of his roar — may have struck some terror into the hearts of his hunters. But after all, Jordanes is probably not very wide of the mark when he imputes both to Aetius and to Thorismund a want of wholeheartedness in securing the fruits of victory.

Aetius had not, most probably, such accurately wrought-out views of the balance of power as the historian imputes to him, nor such an overmastering dread of Gothic bravery as their countryman supposed. But, in the very outset of his career, his life had been passed alternately in the Hunnish camp and the Roman palace; he had been 'mingled among the heathen and learned their works'. He had used the help of his barbarian friends in the marshes of Ravenna and under the walls of Toulouse. Reasons of sentiment as well as of policy may have made him reluctant to aid in obliterating the very name of the Huns from the earth. And above all, as the events of the next few years showed, he himself was safe only so long as he was indispensable. There was a dark and rotten-hearted Augustus skulking in the palace at Ravenna, who endured the ascendancy of Aetius only because he trembled at the name of Attila.

On the Gothic side there were also good reasons for not pushing the victory too far. It scarcely needed the whisper of the Roman general to remind Thorismund how uncertain was his succession to the royalty of his father. The kingly office among the Visigoths became, in days subsequent to these, a purely elective dignity. If at this time some notion of hereditary right, or at least of hereditary preference, hovered round the family of the dead king, it was by no means clear that one son alone must succeed, nor that son the eldest. All was still vague and indeterminate in reference to these barbaric sovereignties. In point of fact Thorismund, though he now succeeded to the throne, was, only two years later (in 453), deprived of crown and life by his brother Theodoric II, who, after a peaceful and prosperous reign, succumbed in like fashion to the fratricidal hand of his successor Euric (466). Every motive therefore of individual ambition and far-seeing patriotism concurred in recommending to Thorismund and his chiefs a speedy return to Toulouse, that the same army which brought the tidings of the death of Theodoric might also announce the election of his successor.

This is all that history can say with unhesitating voice concerning the

death of the Visigothic king and the accession of his son on the Mauriac
plain. Archaeology, however, offers a contribution to our knowledge,
which, if not raised beyond the reach of all contradiction, is at least curious
and interesting. In 1842, a labourer digging for gravel near the little village
of Pouan, on the south bank of the Aube, and about ten miles from Méry-
sur-Seine, found at a depth of nearly a yard below the surface 'some human
bones, two rusted blades, and several jewels and golden ornaments of considerable weight'. Examined more in detail, the most interesting objects in
this find appeared to be

(1) A two-edged sword, two feet eight inches long, and three inches broad.
    The point is protected by a little oblong hoop of iron, to prevent it from
    penetrating into the scabbard, which was probably of wood, and
    which of course has disappeared.
(2) A cutlass, about twenty-two inches long, and an inch and a half
    broad. Both of these two weapons have the hilts richly adorned with
    gold, and at the top a sort of lattice-work of gold and purple glass.
(3) A golden necklace, serpent-shaped, weighing three ounces.
(4) A golden armlet, five ounces in weight, with the ends left open, so as to
    give it elasticity in fitting it on to the forearm.
(5) Two golden clasps (fibulae) with the same lattice-work of gold and
    purple glass which is found on the hilts of the swords.
(6) A golden signet ring, an ounce and a half in weight, with the word
    HEVA in Roman capitals on the flat surface.

Some gold buckles and other ornaments, one of which has an inlay of
garnets instead of purple glass, complete the treasure trove, which, having
been eventually purchased by the emperor Napoleon III, was presented by
him to the museum of the city of Troyes.

The question arises, 'Can we form any probable conjecture whose grave
is this in which we find a skeleton surrounded with articles of adornment,
worth even now perhaps £100 in intrinsic value, and pointing by the style
of their workmanship towards the fifth or sixth century, as the time of their
fashioning, and towards a Gothic or Frankish artificer as their maker?'

M. Peigné Delacourt, to whom we are indebted for these details,*

---

* See *Recherches sur le lieu de la Bataille d'Attila en 451 par Peigné-Delacourt, Membre correspon-
dant de la Société Impériale des Antiquaires de France*, Paris, 1860, with supplement published
at Troyes, 1866.

answers unhesitatingly, 'We can. It is probably the tomb of Theodoric I, king of the Visigoths.' But how reconcile such a theory with the narrative of Jordanes? To accomplish this, M. Delacourt imagines a few unrecorded details, which of course no one is bound to accept, but which certainly seem to bring us a little nearer to that tremendous battlefield, dim with the haze of fourteen centuries. 'When the servants of Theodoric', so his imagined story runs, 'found that their king was wounded to death, they dragged him a little aside from the "vast and manifold and ruthless conflict". They dug a shallow trench in the gravelly soil, and there they laid the bruised and trampled body of the snowy-bearded warrior. His golden-hilted sword was still by his side, his cutlass hung from the baldric, the purple robe of his royalty was fastened over his shoulders by the golden fibula. Round his neck was the golden torque, his forearm was clasped by the unclosed bracelet, on his finger was the ring of gold bearing the mysterious name Heva, perhaps a remembrance of his dead wife, perhaps a symbol of his kingship.* All these things were buried with him. The only object of his henchmen was to find a temporary resting place for their lord. When the tide of battle should have rolled away from that spot, they would come again and disinter him and carry him southwards, to be laid with proper pomp in Gothic Toulouse by the Garonne. Such was their thought, but fortune, in making void their counsel, worked a strange reprisal for the barbarity practised in the burial of Alaric. As his tomb was dug by the unwilling hands of captives, whose instant death ensured their secrecy, so the few faithful friends of Theodoric were all slain in the terrible turmoil of war which raged round the spot where he had fallen, and thus his grave remained unmarked for 1,391 years. The battle was won, and the cry was raised, "Where is the body of the king?" They found it at last, says Jordanes, after a long search, lying under a heap of dead. Who knows if they really did find it? In those hot July days it might not be an easy task to identify a body gashed with wounds and lying under a pile of slain. Thorismund's interest was obviously to get his father's funeral and his own elevation to the sovereignty accomplished as speedily as possible. Perhaps he did not insist too punctiliously on the recovery of the right corpse out of all that vast slaughterhouse, the one strangely missing body out of all those acres upon acres of dead Romans, Goths, and Huns.'

* Heva may possibly mean 'wife' or 'house'. But it seems more probable that it is a proper name. The termination *a* is frequent in Gothic names; more so, however, we must admit in those of men than of women.

And so, M. Delacourt suggests, the body round which the Visigothic warriors circled, singing their wild chorus of lamentation, may have been not that of Theodoric at all. He all the while lay in that shallow trench in the gravel-bed at Pouan, not to be disturbed there till Jacques Bonhomme, in blouse and sabots, came with his pickaxe in 1842 to break the repose of centuries. The story is well imagined, and certainly cannot be pronounced impossible. What militates most against it is that Jordanes says that the body was borne out to burial with its ornaments. In its favour is a certain peculiar silence of his concerning the actual interment of the corpse. He may have felt that it was improbable that the Goths should have left their beloved chieftain lying there in alien territory, in the cold Catalaunian plains, and yet no tradition authorised him to say that they took him back to the sepulchre of his predecessors at Toulouse, a course which Thorismund may have had sufficient reasons for emphatically prohibiting.

Finally, whether this body and these ornaments be Theodoric's, or belong to one of the *turba regum** who swarmed around the car of Attila; in either case their discovery, coupled as it appears to be with that of numerous other human remains in the not distant village of Martroy, seems to add great probability to the theory that here and not at Châlons (two days' march to the northward) was fought the great battle which decided that Europe was to belong to the German and the Roman, not to the Tartar race.

* [Crowd of kings.]

CHAPTER IV

Attila in Italy

I N THE SUMMER OF 451, ATTILA, WITH HIS BEATEN army, recrossed the Rhine, and dismissed the courageous Lupus with a safe-conduct back to Troyes, bidding his chief minister and interpreter Onégesh intercede with the holy man that he might receive the benefit of his prayers.

All that autumn and winter we may imagine him dwelling, moody and sore of heart, within his wooden stockade upon the plains of Hungary, receiving the homage of his nobles as he drank to them out of his goblet of ivy-wood, scowling while all around were laughing at the gabble and the jests of Zercon, or passing his fingers through the dark locks of Ernak, while he whispered to himself, 'This boy shall build up the house of Attila.'

With spring, the spring of 452, came back the longing for 'the joys of strife',* and the determination to wipe out the shame of the Mauriac plains on some fresh battlefield. But this time he would not try conclusions with the hardy Visigoth. Aetius, Valentinian, Italy, should bear the sole weight of his revenge.† He marched, probably through the passes of the Julian Alps and down the valley of the Frigidus, by the route already trodden by Theodosius and Alaric, and stood, perhaps before the spring had ripened into summer, before the walls of Aquileia.

This town was then, both as a fortress and a commercial emporium, second to none in northern Italy. It was situated at the northernmost point of the gulf of Hadria, about twenty miles north-west of Trieste, and the place

* Jordanes, *De Rebus Geticis*, 39.
† Possibly there had intervened some slackening of the alliance or even actual dissensions between Ravenna and Toulouse. Jordanes says that Attila watched his opportunity in the departure of the Visigoths, and seeing, what he had often hoped for, his enemies divided into two parts, with a feeling of security moved forward his array for the destruction of the Romans.

where it once stood is now in the Austrian dominions, just over the border which separates them from the kingdom of Italy. In the year 181 BC a Roman colony had been sent to this far corner of Italy to serve as an outpost against some intrusive tribes, called by the vague name of Gauls, who were pressing into the Adriatic shores over the passes of the Carnic Alps, those Alps which are so familiar to the sojourners in Venice as 'blue Friuli's mountains'. The colonists built their town about four miles from the sea by the banks of the river Aquilo* (the river of the north wind) from whence it probably derived its name. Possessing a good harbour, with which it was connected by a navigable river, Aquileia gradually became the chief entre⁄pôt for the commerce between Italy and what are now the Illyrian provinces of Austria. Under the emperors, and especially after Trajan's conquest of Dacia, these provinces, rich in mineral and agricultural wealth, and enjoy⁄ing long intervals of settled government, attained to a high degree of pros⁄perity, and had the glory of seeing many Illyrian brows bound with the Imperial diadem. Naturally Aquileia rose in importance with the coun⁄tries whose broker she was. She sent the wine, the oil, the costly woven fabrics of the Mediterranean provinces over the Julian and Carnic Alps into Pannonia and Noricum, and she received in return their cattle, their hides, amber from the shores of the Baltic, and long files of slaves taken in the border wars which were being perpetually waged with the Germanic and Slavonic tribes beyond the Danube and the Carpathians. The third century after the Christian era was probably the most flourishing period of her commercial greatness, some of the springs of which must have been dried up by the troubles with the barbarians after the loss of the province of Dacia. Still, as far as can be ascertained from the language of contemporary authors, she was, at the time at which we have now arrived, entitled to con⁄test with Milan and Ravenna the distinction of being the most important city of northern Italy. Ecclesiastical had followed commercial supremacy, and the bishop of Aquileia ruled as metropolitan over the provinces of western Illyricum and Venetia, so that, between the years 350 and 450, Silistria on the lower Danube and Verona in the heart of Lombardy, both (though not both at the same time) owned his spiritual sway.† In a military

---

* Otherwise called the Natiso, now the Isonzo.

† Probably the ecclesiastical limits would so far agree with the political, that the portion of Illyricum which was assigned to the Eastern sceptre at the accession of Theodosius ceased before long to be within the obedience of the see of Aquileia. On the other hand Verona and the whole of western Venetia were (possibly as some indemnification for this loss)

point of view the city held a yet higher place. The strength which she derived from the river, the sea, perhaps the intervening marshes, had been increased by the elaborate fortifications of successive emperors. The savage Maximin (dethroned by the senate in 238) had in vain attempted to take it, and had eventually been murdered under its walls by his mutinous soldiers. Equally vain had been the efforts of the army of Julian more than a century later, though they built huge wooden towers and floated them on rafts down the stream past the walls of the city. The inhabitants set the towers on fire, and were continuing a vigorous resistance when the news which arrived of the death of Constantius II, in whose cause they were fighting, released them from the necessity of further defence, and justified them in opening their gates to Julian, now sole and lawful emperor. Rightly there-fore might Aquileia have claimed to herself the proud title of a 'virgin fortress';* and we can now understand why it was that Aetius, who appar-ently regarded the defence of all the rest of northern Italy as hopeless, left troops – we know not how many, nor for how long a siege prepared – to hold the great fortress by the Natiso against the enemy.

The Roman soldiers of the garrison were of unusually good quality and high courage, and under their guidance the town made so long and stubborn a defence that Attila's soldiers began to weary of their work. Ominous murmurs began to be heard in the camp, and it seemed as if Aquileia was about to add another and more terrible name to the list of her unsuccessful assailants. But just then, while Attila was pacing round her walls, moodily deliberating with himself whether to go or stay, the flapping of wings and the cry of birds overhead arrested his attention. He looked up, and saw the white storks which had built their nests in the roofs of the city, rising high in the air, and inviting their callow young to follow them, evi-dently with the intention of leaving the beleaguered town, and contrary to their usual habits, betaking themselves to the open country. The mother wit of the Hunnish chieftain caught at the expressive augury. 'Lo, there!' he cried to his grumbling soldiers. 'See those birds, whose instinct tells them of futurity; they are leaving the city which they know will perish, the fortress which they know will fall. It is no mere chance, no vague uncertainty

transferred from the metropolitan jurisdiction of Milan to that of Aquileia, at the death of St Ambrose or shortly after that event.
* The sudden attack by which Theodosius wrested it from Maximus (388) was so com-pletely a surprise that the city can hardly be deemed to have lost its character of impregnability thereby (see vol. i, p. 264).

which guides their movements. They are changed from all their natural love of home and humankind by their knowledge of the coming terror.'* The wild hearts of the Huns were stirred by the speech of their king, and took courage from the fresh voice of nature on their side.† They again pushed up their engines to the walls, they plied the slings and catapults with renewed energy, and, as it were in an instant, they found themselves masters of the town.

In proportion to the stubbornness of the defence was the severity of the punishment meted out to Aquileia. The Roman soldiers were, no doubt, all slain. Attila was not a man to encumber himself with prisoners. The town was absolutely given up to the rage, the lust, and the greed of the Tartar horde who had so long chafed around its walls. The only incident of the capture which enables us to grasp more definitely these commonplaces of barbaric conquest, is the story‡ of a noble lady, named Digna, eminent for beauty and virtue, whose house was situated upon the walls of the city. Close to her house was a high tower, overlooking the glassy waters of the Natiso. When she saw that the city was taken, in order to save her honour from the scornful outrages of those filthiest of foes, she ascended the tower, and having covered her head in the old Roman fashion, plunged into the stream below.

When the barbarians could plunder no more, they probably used fire, for the very buildings of Aquileia perished, so that, as Jordanes tells us, in his time, a century later than the siege, scarcely the vestiges of it yet remained. A few houses may have been left standing, and others must have slowly gathered round them, for the patriarch of Aquileia retained all through the Middle Ages considerable remains of his old ecclesiastical jurisdiction, and a large and somewhat stately cathedral was reared there in the eleventh century. But the city of the north wind never really recovered from the blow. Her star had fallen from the firmament, and from this time she almost disappears from history. At the present day two or three mean-looking little villages cower amid the vast enclosure, which is chiefly filled with maize-fields and cherry-trees, while the high-pitched roof of the duomo, with its tall detached campanile, dominates the plain.

The terrible invaders, made more wrathful and more terrible by the resis-tance of Aquileia, streamed on through the trembling cities of Venetia.

* Jordanes, *De Rebus Geticis*, 42.
† It is important to remember the tradition that they had been guided into Europe by a hind, a somewhat similar kind of augury.   ‡ Told in the *Historia Miscella*, xiv.

Each earlier stage in the itinerary shows a town blotted out by their truly Tartar genius for destruction. At the distance of thirty-one miles from Aquileia stood the flourishing colony of Julia Concordia, so named, prob-ably, in commemoration of the universal peace which, 480 years before, Augustus had established in the world. Concordia was treated as Aquileia, and only an insignificant little village now remains to show where it once stood.* At another interval of thirty-one miles stood Altinum, with its white villas clustering round the curves of its lagoons, and rivalling Baiae in its luxurious charms. Altinum was effaced as Concordia and as Aquileia. Yet another march of thirty-two miles brought the squalid invaders to Patavium, proud of its imagined Trojan origin, and, with better reason, proud of having given birth to Livy. Patavium, too, was levelled with the ground. True it has not, like its sister towns, remained in the nothingness to which Attila reduced it. It is now 'Many domèd Padua proud', but all its great buildings date from the Middle Ages. Only a few broken friezes and a few inscriptions in its museum exist as memorials of the classical Patavium.

As the Huns marched further away from Aquileia, and the remem-brance of their detention under its ramparts became less vivid, they were less eager to spend their strength in mere blind rage of demolition. Vicenza, Verona, Brescia, Bergamo, all opened their gates at their approach, for the terror which the fate of Aquileia had inspired was on every heart. In these towns, and in Milan and Pavia (Ticinum), which followed their example, the Huns enjoyed doubtless to the full their wild revel of lust and spoli-ation, but they left the buildings unharmed, and they carried captive the inhabitants instead of murdering them.†

* In the *Academy* of the 3rd September, 1881, there is a notice by F. Barnabei of the very interesting excavations by S. Bertolini in Concordia and its neighbourhood. Especially noteworthy must have been the great sarcophagi with their heavy lids, grouped on both sides of the Roman road which led to Aquileia and the East. 'In some places we see slabs that have been completely wrenched from their sarcophagi by means of levers; and in imagination we witness the desolating invasion of the ruthless Huns, who cared not one jot for the pains and penalties with which he who should desecrate the tombs was threat-ened, but broke them open in every direction in order to rifle the valuables which had been buried with the corpse.'

† This distinction between the cities of eastern Venetia and their western neighbours, which is quite evident to anyone at the present day who is in quest of Roman remains, is very clearly brought out by the *Historia Miscella* (xiv) which is here our best authority. *Concordiam, Altinum sive [= et] Patavium vicinas Aquilejae civitates, illius instar demoliens solo coaequavit. Exinde per universas Venetiarum urbes, hoc est Vincentiam, Veronam, Brixiam, Perga-mum, seu [= et] reliquas, nullo resistente, Hunni bacchabantur, Mediolanum Ticinumque pari sorte*

At Milan a characteristic incident, which rests on fair if not contemporaneous evidence, is said to have occurred. The Hunnish king took up his quarters at the Imperial palace, the stately edifice in which Constantine signed the edict for the legalisation of Christianity, the same edifice in which, eighty years later, Theodosius expired, sick at heart for the ruin which he saw impending over the Empire. Besides other works of painting and sculpture with which the palace was no doubt liberally adorned, Attila beheld a picture representing the triumph of Rome over the barbarians. Here were the two Augusti of the East and West seated on their golden thrones, and here in the front of the picture were the figures of the vanquished Scythians, some slain, others crouching in abject submission before the feet of the emperors. Even so may the king of Prussia have looked, in the long galleries of Versailles, upon the glowing battle-pieces in which the genius of Lebrun and of Vernet commemorates the prowess of France and the humiliations of Germany. Attila took the insult as aimed at his own ancestors, though it is almost certain that the 'Scythians' whom any painter at Milan delineated would be Goths rather than Huns. With that grim humour which flashed forth now and again upon the sullen background of his character, he called for an artist whom he commissioned to paint, perhaps on the opposite wall, a rival picture. In this, King Attila sat on his throne, and the two emperors bowed low before him. One still bore upon his shoulders a large miller's sack filled with pieces of gold, the other was already pouring out the contents of a similar sack at his feet. This reference to the tributary obligations which Attila had forced upon both Rome and Constantinople harmonises with the language of Priscus, and seems to invest the story with a semblance of probability. Would that amidst the subsequent changes of fortune which have befallen the fair city of Milan, notwithstanding the despair of the Ostrogoths and the rage of Barbarossa, that picture might have survived to tell us what the great Hun looked like in his pride, the artistic Theodosius and the sensual Valentinian in their humiliation.*

---

diripiunt, ab igne tamen abstinentes et ferro [He razed the neighbouring cities of Concordia, Altinum, and Pavia to the ground, as he had Aquileia. Then the Huns stormed unopposed through all the cities of Venetia – Vicenza, Verona, Brescia, Bergamo, and the rest – and likewise plundered Milan and Pavia, but without fire and slaughter].

* This story is preserved for us in the work – half dictionary, half encyclopaedia – of Suidas. Unfortunately his own date is so uncertain, and so many additions have been made to the original work, that it is quite impossible to say from external evidence whether

The valley of the Po was now wasted to the heart's content of the invaders. Should they cross the Apennines and blot out Rome as they had blotted out Aquileia from among the cities of the world? This was the great question that was being debated in the Hunnish camp, and strange to say, the voices were not all for war. Already Italy began to strike that strange awe into the hearts of her Northern conquerors which so often in later ages has been her best defence. The remembrance of Alaric, cut off by a mysterious death immediately after his capture of Rome, was present in the mind of Attila, and was frequently insisted upon by his counsellors, who seem to have had a foreboding that only while he lived would they be great and prosperous.

While this discussion was going forward in the barbarian camp, all voices were hushed, and the attention of all was aroused, by the news of the arrival of an embassy from Rome. What had been going on in that city it is not easy to ascertain. The emperor seems to have been dwelling there, not at Ravenna. Aetius shows a strange lack of courage or of resource, and we find it difficult to recognise in him the victor of the Mauriac plains. He appears to have been even meditating flight from Italy, and to have thought of persuading Valentinian to share his exile.* But counsels a shade less timorous prevailed. Someone suggested that possibly even the Hun might be satiated with havoc, and that an embassy might assist to mitigate the remainder of his resentment. Accordingly ambassadors were sent in the once mighty name of 'the emperor and the senate and people of Rome' to crave for peace, and these were the men who were now ushered into the camp of Attila.

The envoys had been well chosen to satisfy that punctilious pride which insisted that only men of the highest dignity among the Romans should be sent to treat with the lord of Scythia and Germany.† Avienus, who had,

---

this anecdote was committed to writing in the fifth century or at a much later period. Suidas relates it twice, once under the heading Κόρυκος and once under Μεδιόλανον. The former word, which signifies 'a sack' is of very infrequent occurrence, and it has been suggested that this is probably the cause of the preservation of the story.

* This hint as to the feebleness of Aetius is to be found in Prosper of Aquitaine.

† We know, from a letter of the Ostrogothic king Theodoric, that the grandfather of his secretary Cassiodorus was sent on an embassy to Attila and obtained peace for Rome (Cassiodorus, *Variae*, i.4). Some historians have perplexed themselves by trying to reconcile that account with this of the embassy of Leo and his two colleagues. But it seems much more probable that the embassy of the grandfather of Cassiodorus was an earlier one, perhaps one of the many relating to the vases of Sirmium. He was accompanied by Carpilio, son of Aetius, who, as we learn from Priscus (p. 179, Bonn edn), had passed many years as a hostage at Attila's court.

two years before, worn the robes of consul, was one of the ambassadors. Trigetius, who had wielded the power of a prefect, and who, seventeen years before, had been despatched upon a similar mission to Gaiseric the Vandal, was another. But it was not upon these men, but upon their greater colleague that the eyes of all the barbarian warriors and statesmen were fixed. Leo, bishop of Rome, had come on behalf of his flock, to sue for peace from the idolater.

The two men who had thus at last met by the banks of the Mincio are certainly the grandest figures whom the fifth century can show to us, at any rate since Alaric vanished from the scene. Attila we by this time know well enough: adequately to describe Pope Leo I, we should have to travel too far into the region of ecclesiastical history. Chosen pope in the year 440, he was now about halfway through his long pontificate, one of the few which have nearly rivalled the twenty-five years traditionally assigned to St Peter.* A firm disciplinarian, not to say a persecutor, he had caused the Priscillianists of Spain and the Manichees of Rome to feel his heavy hand. A powerful rather than subtle theologian, he had asserted the claims of Christian common sense as against the endless refinements of oriental speculation concerning the nature of the Son of God. Like an able Roman general, he had traced in his letters on the Eutychian controversy the lines of the fortress in which the defenders of the Catholic verity were thenceforward to entrench themselves, and from which they were to repel the assaults of Monophysites on the one hand, and of Nestorians on the other. These lines had been enthusiastically accepted by the great council of Chalcedon (held in the year of Attila's Gaulish campaign), and remain from that day to this the authoritative utterance of the church concerning the mysterious union of the Godhead and the manhood in the person of Jesus Christ.

And all these gifts of will, of intellect, and of soul, were employed by Leo with undeviating constancy, with untired energy, in furthering his great aim, the exaltation of the dignity of the popedom, the conversion of the admitted primacy of the bishops of Rome into an absolute and world-wide spiritual monarchy. Whatever our opinions may be as to the influence of this spiritual monarchy on the happiness of the world, or its congruity with the character of the teacher in whose words it professed to root itself, we cannot withhold a tribute of admiration from the high temper of this

* *Non videbis annos Petri* [You will not see the years of Peter], the exhortation which is said to be addressed to each pope on his accession, and which no pope till Pius IX lived to falsify. The pontificate of Leo I lasted only twenty-one years.

Roman bishop, who in the ever-deepening degradation of his country still despaired not, but had the courage and endurance to work for a far-distant future, who, when the Roman was becoming the common drudge and footstool of all nations, still remembered the proud words, *Tu regere imperio populos, Romane, memento!** and under the very shadow of Attila and Gaiseric prepared for the city of Romulus a new and spiritual dominion, vaster and more enduring than any which had been won for her by Julius or by Hadrian.

Such were the two men who stood face to face in the summer of 452 upon the plains of Lombardy. The barbarian king had all material power in his hand, and he was working but for a twelvemonth. The pontiff had no power but in the world of intellect, and his fabric was to last fourteen centuries. They met, as has been said, by the banks of the Mincio. Jordanes tells us that it was 'where the river is crossed by many wayfarers coming and going'. Some writers think that these words point to the ground now occupied by the celebrated fortress of Peschiera, close to the point where the Mincio issues from the lake of Garda. Others place the interview at Governolo, a little village hard by the junction of the Mincio and the Po. If the latter theory be true, and it seems to fit well with the route which would probably be taken by Attila, the meeting took place in Virgil's country, and almost in sight of the very farm where Tityrus and Meliboeus chatted at evening under the beech tree.

Leo's success as an ambassador was complete. Attila laid aside all the fierceness of his anger and promised to return across the Danube, and to live thenceforward at peace with the Romans. But, in his usual style, in the midst of reconciliation he left a loophole for future wrath, for 'he insisted still on this point above all, that Honoria, the sister of the emperor, and the daughter of the Augusta Placidia, should be sent to him with the portion of the royal wealth which was her due; and he threatened that unless this was done he would lay upon Italy a far heavier punishment than any which it had yet borne'.

But, for the present, at any rate, the tide of devastation was turned, and few events more powerfully impressed the imagination of that new and blended world which was now standing at the threshold of the dying Empire than this retreat of Attila, the dreaded king of kings, before the unarmed successor of St Peter. Later ages have encrusted the history with legends of their own. The great picture in the Vatican, which represents

* [Be mindful, Roman, of your right to rule peoples!]

the abject terror of the Huns in beholding St Peter and St Paul in the air championing the faithful city, gives that version of the story which has received eternal currency from the mint mark impressed by the genius of Raphael. As mythology has added to the wonder, so criticism has sought of later days to detract from it. The troops of Marcian, the Eastern emperor, are said to have been in motion. Aetius, according to one account, had at length bestirred himself and cut off many of the Huns. But on carefully examining the best authorities we find the old impression strengthened, that neither miracle, nor pious fraud, nor military expediency determined the retreat of Attila. He was already predisposed to moderation by the counsels of his ministers. The awe of Rome was upon him and upon them, and he was forced incessantly to ponder the question, 'What if I conquer like Alaric, to die like him?' Upon these doubts and ponderings of his super-vened the stately presence of Leo, a man of holy life, firm will, dauntless courage – that, be sure, Attila perceived in the first moments of their inter-view – and, besides this, holding an office honoured and venerated through all the civilised world. The barbarian yielded to his spell as he had yielded to that of Lupus of Troyes, and, according to a tradition which, it must be admitted, is not very well authenticated, he jocularly excused his unaccus-tomed gentleness by saying that 'he knew how to conquer men, but the lion and the wolf [Leo and Lupus] had learned how to conquer him'.

The renown and the gratitude which Leo I earned by this interposition placed the papal chair many steps higher in the estimation both of Rome and of the world. In the dark days which were coming, the senate and people of Rome were not likely to forget that when the successor of Caesar had been proved useless, the successor of Peter had been a very present help. And thus it is no paradox to say that indirectly the king of the Huns con-tributed, more perhaps than any other historical personage, towards the creation of that mighty factor in the politics of medieval Italy, the pope-king of Rome.

His share in the creation of another important actor on the same stage, the republic of Venice, has yet to be noticed. The tradition which asserts that it and its neighbour cities in the lagoons were peopled by fugitives from the Hunnish invasion of 452, is so constant, and in itself so probable, that we seem bound to accept it as substantially true, though contemporary, or nearly contemporary evidence to the fact is utterly wanting.*

* For more information on the date of the foundation of Venice see appendix iii, pp. 368–73.]

The thought of 'the glorious city in the sea' so dazzles our imaginations when we turn our thoughts towards Venice, that we must take a little pains to free ourselves from the spell, and reproduce the aspect of the desolate islands and far-stretching wastes of sand and sea, to which the fear of Attila drove the delicately nurtured Roman provincials for a habitation. And as in describing the Hiong-nu at their first appearance in history we had to refer to physical geography for an account of that vast Asian upland which was their home, so now that we are about to part with the Huns for ever, we must hear what the same science has to tell us of that very different region (the north-eastern corner of Italy) in which they, who came but to destroy, unwittingly built up an empire.

If we examine on the map the well-known and deep recess of the Adriatic sea, we shall at once be struck by one marked difference between its eastern and its northern shores. For three hundred miles down the Dalmatian coast not one large river, scarcely a considerable stream, descends from the too closely towering Dinaric mountains to the sea. If we turn now to the north-western angle which formed the shore of the Roman province of Venetia, we find the coastline broken by at least seven streams, two of which are great rivers. Let us enumerate them. Past the desolate site of Aquileia flows forth that Isonzo, once called the river of the north wind, with which we have already made acquaintance. It rises in an all but waterless range of mountains on the edge of Carniola, and flows, milk-white with its Alpine deposits, through the little Austrian county of Gorizia. Tagliamento and Livenza rise in 'blue Friuli's mountains', and just before they reach the sea encircle the town of Concordia, with which we have also made acquaintance as the second Italian city which Attila destroyed. Rising among the mysterious Dolomites, and flowing through Cadore and Titian's country, then past Belluno and Treviso, comes a longer and more important river, the Piave. The shorter but lovely stream of the Brenta, rising within a few miles of Trento, and just missing the same Dolomite ancestry, washes with her green and rapid waters the walls of Bassano, full of memories of Ezzelin's tyrannies, and of a whole family of Venetian painters, and then, running within sight of Padua, empties her waters into the sea a few miles south of Venice.* Adige comes next, dear to the heart of the pedestrian traveller in South Tyrol, who has through many a mile of his pilgrimage towards Italy been cheered by the loquacious companionship of

* The mouth of the Brenta was formerly just opposite to the island of Rialto. The Venetian canal-makers took the river round to Brondolo.

its waters, who has seen its tributary, the Eisach, swirling round the por-
phyry cliffs of Bolzano, and the united stream rushing under the old battle-
mented bridge at Verona. Last and greatest of all, the Po, the Eridanus of
the poets, rising under the shadow of Monte Viso, flowing nearly three hundred miles through the rich plain of Lombardy, and receiving in its course
countless affluents from the southern gorges of the Alps and the northern
face of the Apennines, empties its wealth of waters into the Adriatic about
a dozen miles from the all but united mouths of the Brenta and the Adige.
The delta of this abundant, but comparatively sluggish river, projecting
into the Adriatic sea, makes a marked alteration in the Italian coastline,
and causes some surprise that such a delta should not yet have received its
Alexandria; that Venice to the north, and Ravenna to the south should have
risen into greatness, while scarcely a village marks the exit of the Po.

These seven streams, whose mouths are crowded into less than eighty
miles of coast, drain an area which, reckoning from Monte Viso to the
Terglou Alps (the source of the Isonzo), must be 450 miles in length, and
may average two hundred miles in breadth, and this area is bordered on
one side by the highest mountains in Europe, snow-covered, glacier-
strewn, wrinkled and twisted into a thousand valleys and narrow defiles,
each of which sends down its river or its rivulet to swell the great outpour.

For our present purpose, and as a worker-out of Venetian history, Po,
notwithstanding the far greater volume of his waters, is of less importance
than the six other smaller streams that we named before him. He, carrying
down the fine alluvial soil of Lombardy, goes on lazily adding foot by foot
to the depth of his delta, and mile by mile to its extent. They, swiftly hurrying over their shorter course from mountain to sea, scatter indeed many
fragments, detached from their native rocks, over the first meadows which
they meet with in the plain, but carry some also far out to sea, and then,
behind the bulwark which they thus have made, deposit the finer alluvial
particles with which they too are laden. Thus we get the two characteristic
features of this ever-changing coastline, the *lido* and the *laguna*. The *lido*,
founded upon the masses of rock, is a long, thin slip of terra firma which
forms a sort of advanced guard of the land. The *laguna*, occupying the
interval between the *lido* and the true shore, is a wide expanse of waters generally very few feet in depth, with a bottom of fine sand, and with a few
channels of deeper water, the representatives of the forming rivers, winding
intricately among them. In such a configuration of land and water the state
of the tide makes a striking difference in the scene. And unlike the rest of

the Mediterranean, the Adriatic does possess a tide, small it is true in comparison with the great tides of ocean, (for the whole difference between high and low water at the flood is not more than six feet, and the average flow is said not to amount to more than two feet six inches), but even this flux is sufficient to produce large tracts of sea which the reflux converts into square miles of oozy sand.*

Here, between sea and land, upon this detritus of the rivers, settled the detritus of humanity. The Gothic and the Lombard invasions contributed probably their share of fugitives, but fear of the Hunnish world-waster (whose very name, according to some, was derived from one of the mighty rivers of Russia†) was the great 'degrading' influence that carried down the fragments of Roman civilisation and strewed them over the desolate lagoons of the Adriatic.

The inhabitants of Aquileia, or at least the feeble remnant that escaped the sword of Attila, took refuge at Grado. Concordia migrated to Caprularia (now Caorle). The inhabitants of Altinum, abandoning their ruined villas, founded their new habitations upon seven islands at the mouth of the Piave, which, according to tradition, they named from the seven gates of their old city – Torcellus, Maiurbius, Boreana, Ammiana, Constantiacum, and Anianum. The representatives of some of these names, Torcello, Mazzorbo, Burano, are familiar sounds to the Venetian at the present day. From Padua came the largest stream of emigrants. They left the tomb of their mythical ancestor, Antenor, and built their humble dwellings upon the islands of Rivus Altus and Methamaucus, better known to us as Rialto and Malamocco. This Paduan settlement was one day to be known to the world by the name of Venice. But let us not suppose that the future queen of the Adriatic sprang into existence at a single bound like Constantinople or Alexandria. For 250 years, that is to say for eight generations, the refugees on the islands of the Adriatic prolonged an obscure and squalid existence, fishing, salt-manufacturing, damming out the waves with wattled vine-branches, driving piles into the sandbanks;‡

* No reader of Ruskin's *Stones of Venice* will need to be reminded of that magnificent chapter, 'The Throne', at the commencement of the second volume, in which the influence of this Adriatic tide on the history and architecture of Venice, and the whole connection between the physical configuration and political development of the city, are worked out with inimitable clearness and force.

† Etzel (= Attila) is said to have been the Tartar name of the Volga.

‡ See the well-known letter of Cassiodorus, praetorian prefect under the successors of Theodoric the Ostrogoth: written probably about 537 (*Variae*, xii.24).

and thus gradually extending the area of their villages. Still these were but fishing villages, loosely confederated together, loosely governed, poor and insignificant; so that the anonymous geographer of Ravenna, writing in the seventh century, can only say of them: 'In the country of Venetia there are some few islands which are inhabited by men.'* This seems to have been their condition, though perhaps gradually growing in commercial importance, until at the beginning of the eighth century the concentration of political authority in the hands of the first doge, and the recognition of the Rialto cluster of islands as the capital of the confederacy, started the republic on a career of success and victory, in which for seven centuries she met no lasting check.

But this lies far beyond the limits of our present subject. It must be again said that we have not to think of 'the pleasant place of all festivity', but of a few huts among the sandbanks, inhabited by Roman provincials, who mournfully recall their charred and ruined habitations by the Brenta and the Piave. The sea alone does not constitute their safety. If that were all, the pirate ships of the Vandal Gaiseric might repeat upon their poor dwellings all the terror of Attila. But it is in their amphibious life, in that strange blending of land and sea which is exhibited by the lagoons, that their safety lies. Only experienced pilots can guide a vessel of any considerable draft through the mazy channels of deep water which intersect these lagoons; and should they seem to be in imminent peril from the approach of an enemy, they will defend themselves, not like the Dutch by cutting the dykes which barricade them from the ocean, but by pulling up the poles which even those pilots need to indicate their pathway through the waters.

There, then, engaged in their humble beaverlike labours, we leave for the present the Venetian refugees from the rage of Attila. But even while protesting, it is impossible not to let into our minds some thought of what those desolate fishing villages will one day become. The dim religious light, halfrevealing the slowly gathered glories of St Mark's; the ducal palace – that history in stone; the Rialto, with its babble of many languages; the piazza, with its flocks of fearless pigeons; the brazen horses; the winged lion; the Bucentaur; all that the artists of Venice did to make her beautiful, her ambassadors to make her wise, her secret tribunals to make her terrible; memories of these things must come thronging upon the mind at the mere mention of her spelllike name. Now, with these pictures glowing vividly before you, wrench the mind away with sudden effort to the dreary plains of

* v.25.

Pannonia. Think of the moody Tartar, sitting in his log-hut, surrounded by his barbarous guests, of Zercon gabbling his uncouth mixture of Hun-nish and Latin, of the bath-man of Onégesh, and the wool-work of Kreka, and the reed candles in the village of Bleda's widow; and say if cause and effect were ever more strangely mated in history than the rude and brutal might of Attila with the stately and gorgeous and subtle republic of Venice.

One more consideration is suggested to us by that which was the noblest part of the work of Venice, the struggle which she maintained for centuries, really on behalf of all Europe, against the Turk. Attila's power was soon to pass away, but in the ages that were to come, another Turanian race was to arise, as brutal as the Huns, but with their fierceness sharp-pointed and hardened into a far more fearful weapon of offence by the fanaticism of Islam. These descendants of the kinsfolk of Attila were the Ottomans, and but for the barrier which, like their own *murazzi* [sea-walls] against the waves, the Venetians interposed against the Ottomans, it is scarcely too much to say that half Europe would have undergone the misery of subjection to the organised anarchy of the Turkish pashas. The Tartar Attila, when he gave up Aquileia and her neighbour cities to the tender mercies of his myrmidons, little thought that he was but the instrument in an unseen hand for hammering out the shield which should one day defend Europe from Tartar robbers such as he was. The Turanian poison secreted the future antidote to itself, and the name of that antidote was Venice.

Our narrative returns for a little space to the Pannonian home of Attila. Before the winter of 452 he had probably marched back thither with all his army. Jordanes tells us that he soon repented of his inactivity, as if it were a crime, and sent one of his usual blustering messages to Marcian, threaten-ing to lay waste the provinces of the East unless the money promised by Theodosius were immediately paid. Notwithstanding this message, how-ever, he really had his eyes fixed on Gaul, and burned to avenge his former defeat upon the Visigoths. The Alans, that kindred tribe now encamped on the southern bank of the Loire, seemed again to hold out some hope of facilitating his invasion. King Thorismund, however, detected the subtle schemes of Attila with equal subtlety, moved speedily towards the country of the Alans, whom he either crushed or conciliated, then met the Hun-nish king in arms once more upon the Catalaunian plains, and again compelled him to fly defeated to his own land (453). 'So did the famous

Attila, the lord of many victories, in seeking to overturn the glory of his conqueror, and to wipe out the memory of his own disgrace, bring on him-self double disaster, and return inglorious home.'

By the unanimous consent of historians, this second defeat of Attila by the Visigoths is banished from the historical domain. The silence of all contemporary chroniclers, the strange coincidence as to the site of the battle, the obvious interest of the patriotic Goth to give his countrymen one victory over the Hun, of which neither Roman nor Frank could share the credit: these are the arguments upon which the negative judgement of his-torians is based, and they are perhaps sufficient for their purpose. It may be remarked, however, that the events assigned by the chroniclers to the year 453 do not seem absolutely to preclude the possibility of a Gaulish cam-paign, and that it is somewhat unsafe to argue against positive testimony from the mere silence even of far more exhaustive narrators than the annal-ists of the fifth century.

For the next scene, however, we have far more trustworthy authority, for here the words of Jordanes – *ut Priscus refert** – assure us that we have again, though at second-hand, the safe guidance of our old friend the Byzantine ambassador.

It was in the year 453, the year that followed his Italian campaign, that Attila took to himself, in addition to all his other wives (and, as we have seen, his harem was an extensive one), the very beautiful damsel, Ildico. At the wedding feast he relaxed his usual saturnine demeanour, drank copi-ously, and gave way to abundant merriment. Then when the guests were departed, he mounted the flight of steps that led up to his couch, placed high in the banqueting hall,† and there lay down to sleep the heavy sleep of a reveller. He had long been subject to fits of violent bleeding at the nose, and this night he was attacked by one of them. But lying as he was upon his back in his deep and drunken slumber, the blood could not find its usual exit, but passed down his throat and choked him. The day dawned, the sun rose high in the heavens, the afternoon was far spent, and no sign was made from the nuptial chamber of the king. Then at length his servants, suspect-ing something wrong, after uttering loud shouts, battered in the door and entered. They found him lying dead, with no sign of a wound upon his body, the blood streaming from his mouth, and Ildico, with downcast face, silently weeping behind her veil. Such a death would, of course, excite some suspicion – suspicion which one of the Eastern chroniclers expanded

* [As Priscus reports].   † See Priscus' description quoted in the second chapter.

into certainty* – of the guilt of Ildico, who was probably regarded as the Jael by whose hand this new and more terrible Sisera had fallen. It is more probable, however, that the cause assigned by Jordanes, apparently on the authority of Priscus, is the true one, and that the mighty king died, as he says, a drunkard's death.

It seems to be a well-attested fact, and is a curious incidental evidence of the weight with which the thought of Attila lay upon the minds even of brave men, that on the same night in which he died, the stout-hearted emperor of the East, Marcian, who had gone to sleep anxious and dis-tressed at the prospect of a Hunnish invasion, had a dream in which he saw the bow of Attila broken. When he awoke he accepted the omen that the Huns, whose chief weapon was the bow, were to be no longer formidable to the Empire.

In proportion to the hope of other nations was the grief of Attila's own people when they found that their hero was taken from them. According to their savage custom they gashed their faces with deep wounds,† in order that so great a warrior might be honoured by the flowing, not of womanish tears, but of manly blood. Then in the middle of the vast Hungarian plain they erected a lofty tent with silken curtains, under which the corpse of the great chieftain was laid. A chosen band of horsemen careered round and round the tent, like the performers in the circensian games of the Romans, and as they went through their mazy evolutions they chanted a wild strain, rehearsing the high descent and great deeds of the departed. What the form of these Hunnish songs may have been, it is impossible to conjecture; but the thoughts, or at least some of the chief thoughts, have been preserved to us by Jordanes, and may perhaps, without unfitness, be clothed in metre, for in truth his prose here becomes almost metrical.

THE DIRGE OF ATTILA

Mightiest of the royal Huns,
    Son of Mundzuk, Attila!
Leader of earth's bravest ones,
    Son of Mundzuk, Attila!

---

* Marcellinus says, 'Attila, king of the Huns, despoiler of the provinces of Europe, is' (at the instigation of Aetius) 'stabbed in the night by the hand and dagger of a woman. Some, however, relate that he lost his life by a haemorrhage.'
† Compare the lines of Claudian quoted at the beginning of [chapter i].

Power was thine, unknown before.
German land and Scythia bore,
Both, thy yoke. Thy terror flew
Either Roman Empery through.
O'er their smoking towns we bore thee,
Till, to save the rest, before thee,
Humbly both the Caesars prayed.
Thy wrath was soothed, and sheathed thy blade.
Slave-like at thy feet they laid
Tribute, as their master bade,
    The son of Mundzuk, Attila.

At the height of human power
    Stood the chieftain, Attila,
All had prospered till that hour
    That was wrought by Attila.
Thou diedst not by the foeman's brand,
Thou felt'st no dark assassin's hand.
All thy landsmen, far and wide,
Were safe from fear on every side.
In the midst of thy delight,
'Mid the joys of wine and night
Painless, thou hast taken flight
    From thy brethren, Attila!

Shouldest thou thus have ended life,
With no pledge of future strife?
Thou art dead: in vain we seek
Foe on whom revenge to wreak
    For thy life-blood, Attila!

When the wild dirge was ended, the great funeral feast, which they call the *strava*,* was prepared, and the same warriors who but a few days before had been emptying great goblets of wine in honour of the marriage of Attila, now with the same outward semblance of jollity, celebrated his

* There is some doubt whether the word *strava* does not mean the heap of arms and trophies of war which was sometimes raised over the body of a dead warrior; but here the emphasis laid on the obscurity of the burial place seems to negative that interpretation.

death. Even while the feast was proceeding, the dead body was being secretly consigned to the earth. It was enclosed in three coffins; the first of gold, the second of silver, the third of iron, to typify the wealth with which he had enriched his kingdom, and the weapons wherewith he had won it. Arms won from valiant foes, quivers studded with gems, and many another royal trinket, were buried with him. Then, as in the case of Alaric, in order to elude the avarice of future generations and keep the place of his burial secret for ever, the workmen, probably captives, who had been engaged in the task of his sepulture, were immediately put to death.

As far as we know, the grave of Attila keeps its secret to this day. But his deeds had made an indelible mark on the imagination of three races of men – the Latin peoples, the Germans, and the Scandinavians; and in the ages of darkness which were to follow, a new and strangely altered Attila, if we should not rather say three Attilas, rose as it were from his mysterious Pannonian tomb, gathered around themselves all kinds of weird traditions, and hovered ghostlike before the fascinated eyes of the Middle Ages. To trace the growth of this Attila legend, however interesting the work might be as an illustration of the myth-creating faculty of half-civilised nations, is no part of my present purpose. Moreover, the task has been so well performed by M. Amedée Thierry in the last section of his *Histoire d'Attila*, that little remains for any later enquirer but simply to copy from him. It will be sufficient therefore to note as briefly as possible the chief characteristics of the different versions of the legend.

(1) The traditions of the Latin races, preserved and elaborated by ecclesiastics, naturally concerned themselves with the religious, or rather irreligious, aspect of his character. To them he is, therefore, the great persecutor of the fifth century, the murderer of the eleven thousand virgins of Cologne, but above all, he is the *flagellum Dei*, the scourge of God, divinely permitted to set forth on his devastating career for the punishment of a world that was lying in wickedness. This title, *flagellum Dei*, occurs with most wearisome frequency in the medieval stories about Attila; and wheresoever we meet with it, we have a sure indication that we are off the ground of contemporaneous and authentic history, and have entered the cloud-land of ecclesiastical mythology. Later and wilder developments in this direction, attributed to him the title of 'grandson of Nimrod, nurtured in Engedi, by the grace of God king of Huns, Goths, Danes, and Medes, the terror of the world'. There may have been a tendency, as Mr Herbert thinks, to identify him with the Antichrist of the Scriptures, but this is not

proved, and is scarcely in accordance with the theological idea of Antichrist, who is generally placed in the future or in the present rather than in the past.

(2) Very unlike the semi-Satanic Attila of ecclesiastical legend is the Teuton's representative of the same personage, the Etzel of the *Nibelungenlied*. In the five or six centuries which elapsed between the fall of the Hunnish monarchy and the writing down of this poem, the German seems to have forgotten almost everything about his mighty lord and foe, except that he dwelt by the Danube, that there was glorious feasting in his palace, and that he had relations both in peace and war with the Burgundians and the Franks. Hence, in the *Nibelungenlied* all that is distinctive in Attila's character disappears. He marries the Burgundian princess Kriemhilde, the widow of Siegfried, and at her request invites her kindred, the Nibelungs, to visit him in Hun-land. There, good-nature and hospitality are his chief characteristics; he would fain spend all day in hunting and all night at the banquet; he is emphatically the commonplace personage of the story. True, it is in his hall that the terrible fight is waged for a long summer day between the Nibelungs and the Huns, till the floor is slippery with the blood of slaughtered heroes. But this is not his doing, but the doing of his wife, that terrible figure, the Clytemnestra or the Electra of the German tragedy, 'reaping the due of hoarded vengeance' for the murder of her girlhood's husband Siegfried. Her revenge and Hagen's hardness, and the knightly loyalty of Rudiger only serve to throw the genially vapid king of the Huns yet further into the background. This round and rubicund figure, all benevolence and hospitality, is assuredly not the thunder-brooding, sallow, silent Attila of history.

(3) The Scandinavian Atli, the husband of Gudruna, is a much better copy of the original. He himself is the cause of the death of the Niblung heroes, he plots and diplomatises and kills in order to recover the buried treasure of Sigurd, just as the real Attila moved heaven and earth for the recovery of Honoria's dowry or the chalices of Sirmium. Above all, the final scene in which he with a certain grand calmness discusses, with the wife who has murdered him, the reason of her crime and appeals to her generosity to grant him a noble funeral, is not at all unlike what Attila might have said to Ildico, if the suspicion of the Byzantine courtiers had been correct, that he had met his death at her hand.

That the king of the Huns should be mentioned at all, far more that he should play so large a part in the national epic of the far-distant Iceland, is a strange fact, and suggests two interesting explanations. First: the statement of the Western ambassadors to Priscus that Attila had penetrated even to the isles of the Ocean may have been more nearly true than one is disposed, at first, to think possible, and he may have really annexed Norway and Sweden (the 'island of Scanzia', as Jordanes calls it) to his dominions. Second: throughout the early Middle Ages there was probably an extensive reciprocal influence between the literatures of the countries of western Europe, especially a borrowing of plots and scenery and characters by the minstrels of various nations from one another, and it may have been thus that the fiction of the king of the Huns and his murdered guests travelled from the Danube to the North sea. It seems a paradox, yet it is probably true that the thought of Austria had more chance of blending with the thought of Iceland in the days of the skald and the minnesingers than in the days of the railroad and the telegraph.

Another line of inventions rather than of traditions must be referred to, only to reject them as containing no valuable element for the historian or the archaeologist. The Magyars, a race of Turanian origin, and bound by certain ties of kindred to the Huns, entered Europe at the close of the ninth century, and established themselves in that country which has since been known as Hungary. As they slowly put off the habits of a mere band of marauders, as they became civilised and Christian, and as they thus awoke to historical consciousness, like a man sprung from the people who has risen to riches and honour, they looked about them for a pedigree. Such a pedigree was found for them by their ecclesiastics in an imagined descent from Attila, *flagellum Dei*. Little of course did they then foresee that their own noble deeds would furnish them with a far prouder escutcheon than any that even a genuine affinity to the great marauder could bestow upon them. So, from the eleventh to the fifteenth century a series of Magyar chroniclers, Simon Keza, Thurocz, Nicolaus Olahus, and others, made it their task to glorify the nation of the Hungarians by writing out the great deeds of Attila. There is no sufficient evidence that they were recording that which had been truly handed down, however vaguely, from their ancestors. On the contrary, there is everything to show that they were, as they supposed, embellishing, and certainly expanding the literary history of Attila by imaginations of their own. Inventions of this kind are valuable neither as fact nor as legend. They no more truly illustrate the history of Attila than the book of Mormon illustrates the history of the Jews; and they probably reflect no more light on the genuine traditions of the Asiatic and heathen Magyars than is thrown by the *Morte d'Arthur* on the thoughts of British minds in the days of Cassivellaunus and Boadicea. All this invented history should be sternly disregarded by the student who wishes to keep before his mind's eye the true lineaments of the great Hunnish warrior.

We return for a moment, in conclusion, to the true historic Attila, whose portrait, as painted by Priscus and Jordanes, has been placed, it may be with too great fullness of detail, before the reader. It is impossible not to be struck by a certain resemblance both in his character and in his career to those of the latest world-conqueror, Napoleon. Sometimes the very words used to describe the one seem as if they glanced off and hit the other. Thus a recent German historian in an eloquent passage, contrasting the Hun and his great Roman antagonist, Aetius, says—

'Conspicuous above the crowd, the two claimants to the lordship of the world stood over against one another. Attila in his wild dream of building up a universal empire in the space of one generation: opposite to him wthe general of that power which, in the course of a thousand years, had extended its dominions over three continents, and was not disposed to relin-quish them without a struggle. But in truth, the idea of a world-empire of the Huns had passed out of the sphere of practical politics even before the battle on the Catalaunian plains. Far and wide Attila enslaved the nations, but the more the mass of his subjects grew and grew, the more certain they were, in time, to burst the fetters which the hand of one single warrior, however mighty, had bound around them. With Attila's death at latest his empire must fall in ruins, whether he won or lost on the battlefield by Troyes. But the Roman would still stand, so long as its generals had the will and the power to hold it together.'*

Do we not seem to hear in these words a description of Napoleon's posi-tion, sublime but precarious, when he was at the zenith of his glory? As the Hun led Scythia and Germany against Gaul, so the Corsican led Gaul and Germany against Scythia in the fatal campaign of 1812. The kings of Sax-ony and Bavaria were his Ardaric and Walamir; Moscow his Orléans; Leipzig his *campus Mauriacensis* [Mauriac plain]. He won his Honoria from an 'emperor of the Romans', prouder and of longer lineage than Valentin-ian. Like Attila, he destroyed far more than he could rebuild; his empire, like Attila's, lasted less than two decades of years; but, unlike Attila, he out-lived his own prosperity. Of course, even greater than any such resemblance are the differences between the uncultured intellect of the Tartar chieftain,

* Professor Binding, *Geschichte des Burgundisch-Romanischen Königreichs*, p. 44.

and the highly developed brain of the great Italian-Frenchman who played with battalions as with chessmen, who thought out the new Paris, who desired 'to go down to posterity with his code in his hand'. But in their insatiable pride, in the arrogance which beat down the holders of ancient thrones and trampled them like the dust beneath their feet, in their wide-stretching schemes of empire, in the haste which forbade their conquests to endure, in the wonderful ascendancy over men which made the squalid Hun the instrument of the one, and the Jacobin of the other, and above all, in the terror which the mere sound of their names brought to fair cities and widely scattered races of men – in all these points no one so well as Napoleon explains to us the character and career of Attila.

*The Vandal Invasion and the
Herulian Mutiny*

CHAPTER V

Extinction of the Hunnish Empire and the Theodosian Dynasty

WITH DRAMATIC SUDDENNESS THE STAGE after the death of Attila is cleared of all the chief actors, and fresh performers come upon the scene, some of whom occupy it for the following twenty years. Before tracing the character and following the fortunes of the Vandal invaders of Rome, let us briefly notice these changes.

The death of Attila was followed by a dissolution of his empire, as complete and more ruinous than that which befell the Macedonian monarchy on the death of Alexander. The numerous progeny of his ill-assorted harem were not disposed to recognise any one of their number as supreme lord. Neither Ellak, the eldest son, who had sat uneasily on the edge of his chair in the paternal presence, nor Ernak, the youngest, his father's darling, and he upon whom the hopes of Attila had most confidently rested, could obtain this pre-eminence. There were besides, Emnedzar, Uzindur, Dinzio, and one knows not how many more uncouthly named brethren; in fact, as Jordanes says, 'these living memorials of the lustful disposition of Attila made a little nation themselves. All were filled with a blind desire to rule, and so between them they upset their father's kingdom. It is not the first time that a superabundance of heirs has proved more fatal to a dynasty than an absolute deficiency of them.'

To end the quarrel, it was decided that this tribe of sons should partition between them the inheritance of their father. But the great fabric which had been upheld by the sullen might of Attila was no longer a mere aggregation of nomad clans, such as the Hunnish nation had once been. If it had still been in this rudimentary condition, it might perhaps have borne division easily. But now it contained whole nations of more finely fibred brain than the Huns, astute statesmen-kings like Ardaric, sons of the gods like the three Amal brothers who led the Ostrogoths to battle. These men and their followers had been awed into subservient alliance with the great Hun. They had elected to plunder with him rather than to be plundered by him, and they had perhaps found their account in doing so. But not for that were they going to be partitioned like slaves among these loutish lads, the sons of Attila's concubines, men not one of whom possessed a tithe of their father's genius, and who, when they had thus broken up his empire into fragments, would be singly but petty princelings, each of far less importance than many of their own vassals. Should the noble nation of the Ostrogoths lose the unity which it had possessed for centuries, and be allotted part to Ellak and part to Ernak? Should the Gepidae be distributed like agricultural slaves, so many to Emnedzar, and so many to Uzindur? That was not Germania's understanding of the nature of her alliance with Scythia, as it would not have been the king of Saxony's or the king of Bavaria's understanding of the tie which bound them to Napoleon. Ardaric, king of the Gepidae, lately the chosen confidant of Attila, now (in 454) stepped forth to denounce this scheme of partition, and to uphold Teutonic independence against Attila's successors. The battle was joined near the river Nedao, a stream in Pannonia which modern geographers have not identified, but which was probably situated in that part of Hungary which is west of the Danube. 'There,' says Jordanes, whose Gothic heart seems to beat faster beneath his churchman's frock whenever he has a bloody battle to describe – 'There did all the various nations whom Attila had kept under his dominion meet and look one another in the face. Kingdoms and peoples are divided against one another, and out of one body divers limbs are made, no longer governed by one impulse, but animated by mutual rage, having lost their presiding head. Such were those most mighty nations which had never found their peers in the world if they had not been sundered the one from the other, and gashed one another with mutual wounds. I trow it was a marvellous sight to look upon. There should you have seen the Goth fighting with his pike, the Gepid raging with his sword, the Rugian breaking the darts of the enemy at the cost of his own wounds; the Sueve pressing on with nimble foot; the Hun covering his advance with a cloud of arrows; the Alan drawing up his heavy-armed troops; the Herul his lighter companies, in battle array.'* We are not distinctly told what was the share of the Ostrogoths in this great encounter, and we may reasonably doubt whether all the German tribes were arranged on one side and all the Tartars on the other with such precision as a modern ethnologist would

* *De Rebus Geticis,* 50.

have used in an ideal battle of the nationalities. But the result is not doubtful. After many desperate charges, victory, which they scarcely hoped for,
sat upon the standards of the Gepidae. Thirty thousand of the Huns and
their confederates lay dead upon the field, among them Ellak, Attila's first-
born, 'by such a glorious death that it would have done his father's heart
good to witness it'. The rest of his nation fled away across the Dacian
plains, and over the Carpathian mountains to those wide steppes of southern Russia, in which at the commencement of our history we saw the three
Gothic nations taking up their abode. Ernak, Attila's darling, ruled tranquilly under Roman protection in the district between the lower Danube
and the Black sea, which we now call the Dobruja, and which was then
'the lesser Scythia'. Others of his family maintained a precarious footing
higher up the stream, in Dacia Ripensis, on the confines of Serbia and Bulgaria. Others made a virtue of necessity, and entering 'Romania', frankly
avowed themselves subjects and servants of the Eastern Caesar, towards
whom they had lately shown themselves such contumelious foes. There is
nothing in the after-history of these fragments of the nation with which
anyone need concern himself. The Hunnish empire is from this time forward mere driftwood on its way to inevitable oblivion.

What is more interesting for us, as affecting the fortunes of the dwellers
in Italy during the succeeding century, is the allotment of the dominions of
Attila among the Teutonic tribes who had cast off the Hunnish yoke.
Dacia, that part of Hungary which lies east and north of the Danube, and
which had been the heart of Attila's domains, fell to the lot of the Gepidae,
under the wise and victorious Ardaric. Pannonia, that is the western portion of Hungary, with Slavonia, and parts of Croatia, Styria and Lower
Austria, was ruled over by the three Amal-descended kings of the Ostrogoths. What barbarous tribe took possession of Noricum in the general
anarchy does not appear to be clearly stated, but there is some reason to
think that part of it at least was occupied by the Heruli, and that the south-
eastern portion, Carinthia and Carniola, received those Slavonic settlers
(coming originally in the triumphant train of Attila) whom, to increase the
perplexity of the politicians of Vienna, it still retains.

The death of Attila and the disruption of his empire removed the counterpoise which alone had for many years enabled the Western emperor to
bear the weight of the services of Aetius. It is true that quite recently vows
of mutual friendship had been publicly exchanged and sealed with the rites
of religion between these two men, the nominal and the real rulers of Italy.

It is true that a solemn compact had been entered into for the marriage of the son of Aetius* with the daughter of Valentinian, and thus, as the emperor had no son, a safe path seemed to be indicated in the future, by which the ambition of the general might be gratified, yet the claims of the Theodosian line not sacrificed. All this might be, but nothing could avail against the persuasion which had rapidly insinuated itself into the emperor's mind that the minister, so useful and so burdensome, was now no longer needed. Just as Honorius forty-six years before had planned the ruin of Stilicho, so now did the nephew of Honorius plot the murder of the only Roman general who was worthy to rival Stilicho's renown. The part which was then played by Olympius was now played by the eunuch Heraclius. Whether, as some chroniclers say, the eunuch filled his master's mind with suspicions as to the revolutionary designs of Aetius, or whether, as others, the emperor first resolved on the murder of his general, and secured the grand chamberlain's assistance, does not greatly signify. As planet attracts planet and is itself attracted by it, so villain works on villain, and is worked upon by him, when a great crime, profitable to both, presents itself as possible.

The emperor enticed Aetius into his palace without an escort. Possibly the pretext was some further conversation as to the marriage treaty between their children. Possibly when the general had entered the presence-chamber, his master announced that he must consider this contract as at an end, for we are told that Aetius was urging with uncourtly warmth the pretensions of his son, when he was suddenly stabbed by the emperor himself. The swords of the bystanders finished the work with unnecessary circumstances of cruelty, and the chief friends of the murdered minister having been on one pretence or other allured singly into the palace, were all slain in like manner. Among them was his most intimate friend, Boethius, the praetorian prefect, and the grandfather, probably, of the celebrated author of the *Consolations of Philosophy*.

In narrating this event, the count Marcellinus (writing about a century after it had occurred) rises above his usual level as a mere chronicler, and remarks, 'With Aetius fell the whole Hesperian realm, nor has it hitherto been able to raise itself up again.' We seem, in the faded chronicle, to read almost the very words of Shakespeare—

* Probably Gaudentius, so named after his paternal grandfather. But there was at least one other son, Carpilio, who had been sent as a hostage to the Huns (see p. 43, and compare p. 96, note).

Oh, what a fall was there, my countrymen!
Then I, and you, and all of us fell down,
Whilst bloody treason flourished over us.

Another historian tells us that immediately after the murder, 'a certain Roman uttered an epigram, which made no small reputation for its author. The emperor asked him if in his opinion the death of Aetius was a good deed to have accomplished. Whereupon he replied, "Whether it was a good deed, most noble emperor, or something quite other than a good deed, I am scarcely able to say. One thing, however, I do know, that you have chopped off your right hand with your left." '*

A contemporary author, the Gaulish poet Apollinaris Sidonius, in some verses written a year or two after the event, alludes in passing to the time when

The thing, scarce man, Placidia's fatuous son,
Butchered Aetius.†

So that this deed at least had not to wait for a late posterity to be judged according to its desert.

It was probably towards the end of 454 that the murder of Aetius was perpetrated, and the scene of the crime was Rome, which for ten years previously seems to have been the chief residence of the emperor, though Ravenna was occasionally visited by him.

In the middle of the succeeding March (455) the emperor rode out of the city one day to the Campus Martius. He halted by two laurel bushes in a pleasant avenue, and there, surrounded by his court and his guards, was intently watching the games of the athletes. Suddenly two soldiers of barbarian origin, named Optila and Traustila, rushed upon him and stabbed him.‡ The eunuch Heraclius, the confidant who had planned the death of Aetius, was also slain. No other blood seems to have been shed, and apparently it must be taken as an evidence how low the emperor had fallen in the esteem of his subjects, that in all that courtly retinue, and in all that surrounding army, not a hand stirred to avenge his death. The murderers were

---

* Procopius, *De Bello Vandalico*, i.4.   † *Panegyric of Avitus*, 359.

‡ We get the names of the assassins from Marcellinus, whom Jordanes (*De Regnorum et Temporum Successione*, 334) follows. *Codex Havniensis* calls them Accila the armour-bearer of Aetius, and Trasila, son-in-law of Aetius.

well known as henchmen of Aetius, who, moved partly by resentment at his fate, and partly, no doubt, by chagrin at the interruption of their own career of promotion, had for months been dogging the steps of the heedless emperor with this black design in their hearts.

Valentinian III left no son, and thus the Imperial line of Theodosius became extinct, after it had held the Eastern throne seventy-four years (379–453),* and the Western sixty-one (394–455). The choice of the people and army fell on Petronius Maximus, an elderly senator, who assumed the purple with every prospect of a wise and perhaps even a suc-cessful reign.

The new emperor was apparently related to Probus, the eminent Roman, whose two sons were made consuls in the same year (395) amid the high-flown panegyrics of Claudian. He is said to have been also grandson of that usurping emperor Maximus, who was taken prisoner by the soldiers of Theodosius at the third milestone from Aquileia. But his own career as a member of the civil hierarchy had been so much more than merely respectable, that it seems impossible to deny to him the possession of some ability, and even of some reputation for virtue, as Roman virtue went in those days. At the age of nineteen he was admitted into the Imperial coun-cil as tribune and notary; then count of the sacred largesses, and then prefect of Rome, all before he had attained his twenty-fifth year. When he was holding this last office, the emperor Honorius, at the request of the sen-ate and people, erected a statue to his honour in the great forum of Trajan. Consul at the age of thirty-eight, prefect of Italy from the age of forty-four to forty-six, again consul at forty-eight, and again prefect, he had attained at fifty the crowning dignity of the patriciate. This was evidently a man whom both prince and people had delighted to honour, and from whom, now that he had reached his sixtieth year, a reign of calm and statesmanlike wisdom, and such prosperity as those evil days would admit of, might not unreasonably have been hoped for.

How different was the result, and how far he was from attaining, much more from bestowing, happiness during the seventy days, or thereabout, that he wore the Imperial purple, we learn from a letter addressed, some time after his death, by one† who was himself well acquainted with the inner life of courts, to Serranus, a faithful friend, who still ventured to pro-claim his attachment to an unpopular and fallen patron.

* Pulcheria died in the year 453, aged fifty-four.
† Apollinaris Sidonius, *Epistolae*, ii.13.

'I received your letter', says Sidonius, 'dedicated to the praises of your patron the emperor Petronius Maximus. I think, however, that either affection or a determination to support a foregone conclusion has carried you away from the strict truth when you call him most happy because he passed through the highest offices of the state and died an emperor. I can never agree with the opinion that those men should be called happy who cling to the steep and slippery summits of the state. For words cannot describe how many miseries are hourly endured in the lives of men who, like Sulla, claim to be called Felix [fortunate] because they have clambered over the limits of law and right assigned to the rest of their fellow citizens. They think that supreme power must be supreme happiness, and do not perceive that they have, by the very act of grasping dominion, sold themselves to the most wearisome of all servitudes: for, as kings lord it over their fellow men, so the anxiety to retain power lords it over kings.

'To pass by the proofs of this that might be drawn from the lives of preceding and succeeding emperors, your friend Maximus alone shall prove my maxims.* He, though he had climbed up with stout heart into the high places of prefect, patrician, consul, and had, with unsatisfied ambition, claimed a second turn at some of these offices, nevertheless when he arrived, still vigorous, at the top of the Imperial precipice, felt his head swim with dizziness under the diadem, and could no more endure to be master of all than he had before endured to be under a master. Then think of the popularity, the authority, the permanence of his former manner of life, and compare them with the origin, the tempestuous course, the close of his two months' sovereignty, and you will find that the least happy portion of his life was that in which he was styled *beatissimus* [most blessed].

'So it came to pass that he who had attracted universal admiration by his wellspread table, his courtly manners, his wealth, his equipages, his library, his consular dignity, his patrimonial inheritance, his following of clients – he who had arranged the various pursuits of his life so accurately that each hour marked on the waterclock brought its own allotted employment – this same man, when he had been hailed as Augustus, and with that vain show of majesty had been shut up, a virtual prisoner, within the palace walls, lamented before twilight came the fulfilment of his ambitious hopes. Now a host of cares forbade him to indulge in his former measure of repose; he had suddenly to break off all his old rules of life, and perceived when it was too late that the business of an emperor and the ease of a senator could not go

* Sidonius is an inveterate punster.

together. Moreover, the worry of the present did not blind him to the calamities which were to come, for he who had trodden the round of all his other courtly dignities with tranquil step, now found himself the powerless ruler of a turbulent court, surrounded by tumults of the legionaries, tumults of the populace, tumults of the barbarian mercenaries; and the forebodings thus engendered were but too surely justified when the end came – an end quick, bitter, and unlooked-for, the last perfidious stroke of fortune, which had long fawned upon the man, and now suddenly turned and stung him to death as with a scorpion's tail. A man of letters, who by his talents well deserved the rank which he bore of quaestor, I mean Fulgentius, used to tell me that he had often heard Maximus say, when cursing the burden of Empire, and regretting his old freedom from cares, "Ah, happy Damocles! it was only for one banquet's space that you had to endure the necessity of reigning."

Sidonius then tells in his most elaborate style the story of Damocles feasting sumptuously under the suspended sword-blade, and concludes, 'Wherefore, sir brother, I cannot say whether those who are on their way to sovereign power may be considered happy; but it is clear that those who have arrived at it are miserable.'

Let the reader store up in his mind this picture of a sorely worried emperor vainly striving to maintain his authority amid the clamours of mutinous legionaries full of fight everywhere but on the battlefield, of Roman demagogues haranguing about Regulus and Romulus, and of German *foederati* insatiable in their claims for donative and land. For this picture, or something like it, will probably suit equally well for each of the eight other weary-browed men who have yet to wear the diadem and be saluted with the name of Augustus.

As for the emperor Maximus, his mingled harshness and feebleness, both misplaced, soon earned for him the execration of his subjects. They saw with astonishment the murderers Optila and Traustila not only not punished, but received into the circle of the emperor's friends. This might be only the result of a fear of embroiling himself with the barbarians, but it was only natural that it should be attributed to a guilty participation in their counsels. Then, after a disgracefully short interval, all Rome heard with indignation that the empress Eudoxia had been commanded to cease her mourning for Valentinian, whom, notwithstanding his many infidelities, she fondly loved, and to become the wife of the sexagenarian emperor. At the same time he compelled her to bestow the hand of one of her daughters

on his son, the Caesar Palladius. The widowed empress, who was now in
the thirty-fourth year of her age, was one of the loveliest women of her
time.* The motive of Maximus may have been passion, but the double
marriage looks rather like policy, like a determination on the part of the fire-
new emperor to consolidate his dynasty by welding it with all that yet
remained on earth of the great name of Theodosius.†

If this was the object of Maximus, he signally failed, and the precau-
tions which he took to ensure his safety accelerated his ruin. Eudoxia, the
daughter, the niece, and the wife of emperors, writhed under the shame
of her alliance with the elderly official. As a still-mourning widow she
resented her forced union with the man whom some deemed an accomplice
in her husband's murder. Her aunt Pulcheria was dead, and she feared that
it was vain to hope for succour from Byzantium. In her rage and despair,
she imitated the fatal example of Honoria, and called on the barbarian
for aid. Not the Hun, but the Vandal was the champion whose aid she
invoked. Her emissary reached Carthage in safety. Gaiseric, only too
thankful for a good pretext for invading Rome, eagerly promised his aid.
He fitted out his piratical fleet, and soon from mouth to mouth in Rome flit-
ted the awful tidings, 'The Vandals are coming.' Many of the nobles fled.
The emperor, torn from his sweet clepsydra-round of duties and pleasures,
and depressed by the scorn of the beautiful avenger whose love he could
not win, devised no plan for defence, but sat trembling and helpless in
his palace, and when informed of the flight of the nobility could think of
no more statesmanlike expedient than to publish a proclamation, 'The
emperor grants to all, who desire it, liberty to depart from the city.' The fact
was that he was meditating flight himself. Better the immediate abandon-
ment of Empire than to sit any longer under that ever-impending sword of
Damocles. But then the smouldering indignation of all classes against the
man whom they deemed the author of the coming misery, burst forth. The
soldiers mutinied, the rabble rose in insurrection, the servants of the Imperial palace, faithful probably to the old Theodosian traditions, prevented the
meditated escape. Soon the tragedy, which near sixty years before had been
perpetrated at Constantinople (after the fall of Rufinus), was repeated in
Rome. The Imperial domestics tore their new master limb from limb, and

* Theophanes, *Chronographia*, p. 93 (ed. Paris, 1655).
† [For more information on Maximus' role in the murder of Valentinian III, and on his
marriage to Eudoxia, see appendix iv, 'On the Character of Petronius Maximus', pp.
373– 5.]

after dragging the ghastly fragments through the city, scattered them into the Tiber, so that not even the rites of burial might be granted by anyone to Petronius Maximus.*

This event happened on the 31st of May,† less than three months after the new emperor's accession. The sails of Gaiseric's fleet are already upon the Tyrrhene sea, and before three days are ended the third great barbarian actor, the Vandal nation, will appear upon the stage of Italy. But, before they come, we must turn back the pages of history for a while, and trace the successive steps of the migration which had led them from the forests of Pomerania to the burning shores of Africa.

* According to Jordanes, a Roman soldier named Ursus dealt the fatal blow. A passage in Apollinaris Sidonius (*Panegyric of Avitus*, 442) seems to attribute to the Burgundians some share in the tragedy.   † Anonymus Cuspiniani puts it on the 12th of June.

CHAPTER VI

The Vandals from Germany to Rome

IN THE *GERMANIA* OF TACITUS, THE BEST CONTRI-
bution made by any Roman writer to the science of ethnology, the author
says:

'My own opinion is that the Germans are the aboriginal inhabitants of
their country, with the least possible admixture of any foreign element. For
in old times all national migrations were made by sea rather than by land,
and the inhospitable ocean which washes the shores of Germany has been
seldom visited by ships from our world. Besides, putting the perils of a tempestuous sea out of the question, who would leave behind him the pleasant
shores of Asia, Africa, or Italy, and set sail for Germany, with its ugly
landscape, its rigorous climate, its barren soil; who, I mean, except a native
of that land, returning thither?

'In ancient songs, the sole kind of annals possessed by this people, they
celebrate the name of a certain Tuisco, an earth-born deity, and his son
Mannus, as the original founders of their race. To Mannus they assign three
sons, after whom are named three tribes, the Ingaevones, who live nearest to
the ocean, the Hermiones in the middle of the country, the Istaevones who
occupy the remainder. Some, however, presuming on the antiquity of their
tribes, affirm that the aforesaid god had many other sons, from whom many
gentile appellations are derived, e.g. Marsi, Gambrivii, Suevi, Vandalii.
These, they say, are the real and ancient names, that of Germans is a modern one, first given in fear by the vanquished Gauls to the warriors who
crossed the Rhine to invade them, and afterwards proudly assumed by the
conquerors.'*

This interesting passage, besides showing us the Deutsch nationality in
its earliest stage, then as now called German by the foreigner but not in its
own home; besides giving us the name of the primeval Mann, who corresponds to the Adam of the Hebrews, and suggesting some other interesting

* Tacitus, *Germania*, 2.

ethnological speculations; brings before us the Vandals as already a power-ful and long-descended tribe in the days of Tacitus, that is at the close of the first century of our era.

The slightly earlier author, Pliny, in the geographical part of his *Historia Naturalis*, mentions the Vindili as one of the five great Germanic races, and the Burgundians as one of their sub-branches.* There can be no doubt that these are the same people as the historic Vandals, who are indeed always called Bandili or Bandeli by the Greek historians.

The Vandals were nearly allied in blood to the Goths. 'The greatest names of this confraternity of nations', says Procopius, 'are Goth and Van-dal and Visigoth and Gepid. They all have fair skins and yellow hair; they are tall of stature, and goodly to look upon. They all possess the same laws, the same faith, Arian Christianity; and the same language, the Gothic. To me they appear all to have formed part of one nation in old time, and after-wards to have been distinguished from each other by the names of their leaders.' The general description therefore which has been already given of the Visigoths will apply to the Vandals; but by combining the testi-monies of various chroniclers, we may find some traits of character which belonged specially to the Vandal race. Thus, their disposition seems to have been wanting in some of the grander features of the Gothic. They were perhaps more subtle-witted,† but they were even more greedy of gain. They were confessedly less brave in war, and they were more cruel after victory. On the other hand, they were conspicuous even among the chaste Teutonic warriors for their chastity, and both in Spain and Africa their moral stan-dard was, and for some time continued to be, far above that of the uncleanly living Roman provincials.‡

The home of the Vandals, when we first meet with them in history, appears to correspond with the central and eastern part of Prussia, but a loose aggregation of restless tribes must not be too definitely assigned to any precise district on the map.§ While they were settled here they fought under

---

* *Natural History*, iv.14.   † Procopius' description of Gaiseric (*De Bello Vandalico*, i.4).
‡ Orosius (vii.38), rather spitefully, says of Stilicho that he was 'descended from the unwarlike, avaricious, perfidious, and crafty nation of the Vandals'. Salvian (*De Guberna-tione Dei*, vii.7) says that 'God, by handing over the Spanish nation to the Vandals for pun-ishment, showed in a double degree his hatred of the sins of the flesh, since the Spaniards were conspicuous for their immorality and the Vandals for their chastity, while on the other hand the latter were the weakest of all the barbarian tribes'. Their rapid decline in martial vigour after the death of Gaiseric points to the same quality in their character.
§ Jordanes (*De Rebus Geticis*, 4) speaks of the Vandals at this period of their history as

their two leaders, Ambri and Assi, a memorable battle with their neighbours, the Langobardi. The legends concerning this battle, which resulted
in the complete defeat of the Vandals, are reserved for the Lombard portion of this history.* As the Roman Empire grew weaker, the Vandals
pressed southward, and eventually they gave their name (*Vandalici montes*) to
the Riesen Gebirge (giant mountains) between Silesia and Bohemia.

The southward movement of the barbarians, of which this Vandal
migration formed part, brought on that great struggle known as the Marco-
mannic war (167–81), in which the German tribes on the middle Danube
strove, almost successfully, to pierce the gap between Pannonia and Dacia,
and to establish themselves permanently within the limits of the Empire. In
the heroic contest which Marcus Aurelius, the philosopher-emperor, waged
against these barbarians, a contest which well-nigh overtaxed both his energies and those of the Empire, he seems to have had at first the Vandals for his
foes;† but, at the conclusion of the war, we find the Asdingi, whom we
know to have been a Vandal tribe, making their peace with Rome, and
receiving from the emperor settlements in Dacia.‡ When, upon the death of
Marcus, his son Commodus made his unsatisfactory peace with the Marcomanni, the Vandals were one of the tribes taken under Roman protection,
against whom the Marcomanni were forbidden to declare war.

A generation later (in 215), the emperor Caracalla, in one of his boast-
ful letters to the senate, prided himself on the fact that whereas the Vandals
and Marcomanni had previously been friendly to one another, he had succeeded in setting them at variance.§ If we look at that curious specimen of
map-making, the *Tabula Peutingeriana* (which is thought to have been originally executed in the time of Caracalla's father Severus¶), we shall see a
striking comment on these words: for there, immediately on the other side of
the broad limitary stream of the Danube, we see in straggling letters the
name VANDVLI, and a little beyond, but almost intermingled therewith,
the name MARCOMANNI. Such close juxtaposition was very likely to
breed hostility between two barbarous tribes.

---

pressed upon by the victories of the Goths during their settlement by the Baltic.
* See Paulus Diaconus, *Historia Langobardorum*, i.7, 10.
† This is inferred from the language of Capitolinus, *Life of Marcus Antoninus the Philo-
sopher*, 17.
‡ Dion, lxxi.12. His account of the movements of the Vandals under their leaders Räus
and Raptus is very obscure, but the result is that indicated above.
§ Dion, lxxvii.20.   ¶ Or perhaps his cousin Severus Alexander.

More than half a century passes: and the emperor Aurelian, the great restorer of the Roman power in the Danubian lands, gains a signal victory over the Vandals (271). We know nothing concerning the battle; we only hear of the negotiations which followed it. The Vandals sent ambassadors to sue for peace. After hearing their lengthy harangues, on the following day Aurelian mustered his army and asked for its advice whether he should accept or reject the terms of the barbarians. With one consent the army shouted for peace, which was accordingly granted, the kings of the Vandals and several of their chief nobles, readily giving their sons as hostages for its due observance. The mass of the Vandal host returned to their Dacian home, the emperor granting them sufficient provisions to last them till they reached the Danube. Notwithstanding this concession, five hundred men, straggling from the main body of the returning host, committed cruel devastations on the plains of Moesia. For this breach of the treaty all the marauders who could be caught were put to death by their king.*

A select portion of the Vandal host remained in the Imperial camp. One of the conditions of the peace was that they should supply two thousand horsemen as *foederati* to the Roman army; and this stipulation seems to have been faithfully observed, for the army list of the Roman Empire at the commencement of the fifth century shows us 'the eighth wing of the Vandals serving in Egypt'.† It was probably in this way that in the next century Stilicho, a man of Vandalic extraction, entered the service of that Empire which he afterwards ruled.

A few years later (277) a fragment of the Vandal nation, which seems to have wandered to the Rhine in company with a troop of Burgundians, was by adroit tactics defeated by the emperor Probus. Many were slaughtered, but some were taken prisoners; Igil, the Vandal leader, being one of the latter class. These prisoners were all sent to the island of Britain, where, in some obscure insurrection against the emperor, they did good service to their recent conqueror.‡

* See Dexippus (excerpt 2) and Priscus (excerpt 11).
† *Notitia Orientis*, 25.
‡ Zosimus, i.68. Cf. Vopiscus, *Life of Probus*, 18. The statement sometimes attributed to Camden, that there was a fortress near Cambridge, on the Gogmagog hills, built by these Vandal captives and named after them Vandlebury, is not made in that form by Camden, and does not really rest on his authority, but on that of Gervase of Tilbury, from whom he quotes it; nor does it seem to be more than a piece of fantastic etymology. The words of Gervase, 'the Vandals, who made a camp here when they ravaged part of Britain and cruelly massacred the Christians', show the thoroughly unhistorical character of his

Near the end of the reign of Constantine there came a crisis in the fortunes of the Vandal nation. They were then dwelling in Moravia and the north-west of Hungary, having the Marcomanni of Bohemia as their western neighbours, and the Danube for their frontier to the south. Geberich, king of the Goths, whose territory bordered upon theirs to the east, determined to get him glory upon the Vandals, and sent a challenge to their king, Visumar. The two armies met by the Hungarian river Maros,* and fought through a long day doubtfully. At length the Goths prevailed, and Visumar, with a great part of his host, lay dead upon the field. The scanty remnant of the nation entreated Constantine to permit them to enter the limits of the Empire, and settle as his subjects in the prov-ince of Pannonia. The position was not unlike that in which the Visigoths themselves were placed forty years later when they sought the Moesian shore of the Danube, flying from the terrible Huns. The permission was granted, and for nearly seventy years the Vandals were obedient subjects of the Roman emperors.† During this time it is likely that they made some advances in civilisation; they probably often served in the Roman army, and learnt something of the legionary's discipline. It was without doubt during the same period that they embraced Christianity under that Arian form which Ulfilas was teaching to their Gothic neighbours and con-querors. At a later date, when they were invading Spain, we are told that they carried the Bible with them and consulted it as an oracle.‡ It was of course the translation of Ulfilas which thus became the Urim and the Thummim of the Vandal.

At length, in the year 406, the Vandals, or a portion of the confederacy which went by that name, left their Pannonian settlements, and linking their destinies with those of the Turanian tribe of Alans and with their High German kinsmen the Suevi, they marched north-westwards for the Rhine, intent on the plunder of Belgic Gaul. There is no need to accept the suggestion§ that 'Stilicho invited them'. After the fall of that statesman,

---

information, which, moreover, has nothing to do with the exiles under Probus.

* That is, supposing the name given by Jordanes, Marisia, to be correct. The Marus, now March, a river of Moravia, which flows into the Danube above Pressburg, would suit the rest of his geographical description better.   † Jordanes, De Rebus Geticis, 22.

‡ Salvian, De Gubernatione Dei, vii.11. This appears to be the meaning, but the good pres-byter is rhetorically obscure.

§ Made by Tiro and by Orosius (vii.38), and apparently echoed by St Jerome (Epistola ad Ageruchiam). Stilicho may, with perfect loyalty to the Empire, have invited the Vandals into Gaul, intending to use them as a counterpoise to the Franks.

everything that had gone wrong in the Empire for the last twenty years was conveniently debited to his account. But no invitation was needed to set any Germanic tribe in motion towards the Empire in the year of the nativity 406. The fountains of the great deep were broken up. Radagaisus and Alaric, with their mighty nation-armies, had crossed the Alps and poured down into Italy. One, indeed, had failed, and the other had only partially succeeded, but both had shown plainly to all 'Varbaricum' that 'Romania' was now at its last gasp, and would have enough to do to defend itself in Italy, without any hope of permanently maintaining its hold on its rich out-lying provinces, such as Gaul and Spain. The Teuton adventurer was swept across the Roman boundary by a current as strong as that which drew the Spanish adventurer across the Atlantic in the days of Cortés and Pizarro.

Of the struggles of the Vandals with the Franks we have only dim rumours. We hear, however, of a great battle, in which twenty thousand Vandals were slain, their king Godigisclus, himself of the royal lineage of the Asdings, being among the number of the dead.* It is said, indeed, that only the timely arrival of their allies, the Alans, saved them from utter destruction; but, however this may be, they crossed the Rhine frontier, and after three years of war and probably of wild ravage of the cities of Gaul, drawn southwards by the impulse which ever attracted the barbarian to the sunnier climate, and powerfully helped by the dissensions among the Romans themselves, which had arisen out of the sudden elevation of the upstart British soldier Constantine,† they stood, after three years' time, at the foot of the Pyrenees and thundered at the gates of Spain.‡ The kinsmen of Honorius, Verenianus and Didymus, who had loyally struggled to guard this rampart against usurpers and barbarians, had been, rather more than a year before, treacherously slain by Constantine, and thus but a feeble resistance, or no resistance at all, was opposed to the fierce tide of Vandals, Alans, Suevi, which swept through the Pyrenean passes and ravaged the hither and further Spain without mercy (409).

Of the twenty years which followed, some mention has already been made in describing the career of Ataulfus. It may be remembered that in 414, five years after the Vandals had entered Spain, the Visigothic chieftain followed them thither. There he and his successors carried on a long and

* We get our fullest information as to this battle from Gregory of Tours, quoting from Rena-tus Profuturus Frigeridus (*Historia Francorum*, ii.9).   † See vol. i, pp. 423–5.
‡ The leader of the united host was Guntheric or Gunderic, king of the Vandals.

bloody struggle with their fellow Teutons, during part of which time the
Goths professed to fight as champions of Rome, and for the remainder on
their own account. The provinces, lately fertile and flourishing, were so
harried by friend and foe that the Vandal soldiery were fain to buy wheat at
36s. a pint, and a mother slew and ate her own children.

At length the barbarians and the representatives of the Empire concluded some sort of peace or truce, of which a hint is given us by the
declamation of Orosius,* and a somewhat more detailed but still perplexing account in the pages of Procopius. 'Then', says he, 'Honorius made an
agreement with Godigisclus,† on condition that they [the Vandals] should
settle there, not for the devastation of the country. And whereas the
Romans have a law that if men do not keep their property in their own
hands, and an interval of time elapses which amounts to thirty years, then
they have no longer the right to proceed against those who have dispossessed
them, but their recourse to the courts is barred by prescription. The
emperor passed a law that the time during which the Vandals should
sojourn in the Roman Empire should by no means be reckoned towards
this thirty-years prescription.' Difficult as it is to see how such a law would
work out in the actual experience of Roman or Vandal land-holders, it
well illustrates the attitude of Imperial statesmen and jurists towards all the
barbarian intruders. Every peace made with them was considered to be
really only a truce. However securely the Visigoth might seem to reign at
Toulouse, the Ostrogoth at Ravenna, or the Vandal at the new or the old
Carthage, the Roman Augustus and his counsellors looked upon their
dominion as only a parenthesis, an unfortunate parenthesis, in the age-long
life of the great republic, and in their own counsels admitted no derogation
thereby to the imprescriptible rights of the sovereign Empire.

The settlement of the barbarian nations in Spain seems to have been on
this wise. The Suevi were in the north-west of the peninsula, the Visigoths
in the north-east, the Alans in Portugal, while the Vandals occupied two
widely sundered allotments. One tribe which seems to have borne the same
name as the royal clan, that of Asdingi, was settled close to the Suevi in
Galicia; the other and probably the larger tribe, that of the Silingi, took up
its quarters in Baetica, the modern Andalusia.‡

---

* See vol. i, p. 477.

† If Gregory is right this name is an error for that of Guntheric, son of Godigisclus.

‡ The derivation of Andalusia from the Vandals must now be considered more than
doubtful. Papencordt (*Geschichte der Vandalischen Herrschaft in Afrika*, 1837, p. 16, n. 1)

In the year 416 Constantius, then the accepted suitor of Placidia, by some cunning stratagem captured a king of the Vandals named Fredibal, and sent him as a captive to Honorius, before whose chariot he may possibly have walked in chains when the phantom-emperor in the following year celebrated his triumph at Rome.* But on the whole it was the hand of Wallia the Visigoth that fell most heavily on the Vandals and their allies. In 418 the Silingian Vandals in Baetica were absolutely 'extinguished' by the Goths, and the Alans were so terribly cut to pieces by the same people, that the few survivors willingly merged their nationality in that of the Galician Vandals, whose king is said to have assumed thenceforward the title 'king of the Vandals and Alans'.†

In 419 war broke out between this latter, newly united people and their neighbours the Suevi. Guntheric apparently gained a victory over the Suevic king Hermanric, and drove him and his followers into the fastnesses of the Asturias, where they were subjected to a strict blockade. In the following year, however, under pressure from Asterius, the Roman governor of Spain, Guntheric broke up this mountain siege, left Suevi and Romans alike to work their will in the north of Spain, and marched across the peninsula to Baetica. There the Asdingian Vandals settled themselves in the fair land lately occupied by their Silingian brethren (some remnants of which nation may possibly have joined them), and there gazing eastward and westward over the waters of the Mediterranean and the Atlantic, they began to dream of maritime greatness.

In the closing years of Honorius, the court of Ravenna, moved by some strange impulse of spasmodic energy, made an attempt to recover Baetica from the Vandals (in 422). Castinus, master of the soldiery (the same officer who in the following year set up the arch-notary Joannes as emperor in derogation of the claims of the son of Placidia), set sail with a large body of troops, and, having effected a junction with the Goths, invaded Baetica. But there were jealousies and divided counsels at the Imperial headquarters. We have seen how Bonifacius, the second in command, although, by the admission of all men, one of the bravest soldiers of the

quotes Casiri as his authority for the assertion that the true form of the name is Handalusia, the Arabic equivalent for Hesperia, and that it was originally given by the Moors to the whole country of Spain.

* As we hear nothing of Fredibal's relationship to Guntheric or Gaiseric he was probably king of the Silingian Vandals. It seems to me more probable that Constantius was Fredibal's captor than Wallia, though the entry in Idatius is not clear.

† Idatius, for the twenty-fourth year of Honorius.

day, unable to bear the petty jealousy and insulting arrogance of his incapable superior, hastily travelled from Ravenna to Portus, and thence set sail
for Africa, which province he afterwards held for Placidia and her children
against his rival's puppet-emperor Joannes.* Still, notwithstanding this
defection, the Imperial arms in Spain seemed likely to be victorious. The
Vandals were besieged, apparently in one of the cities of Baetica, and
suffered such severe privations that they were on the point of surrender.
Castinus, however, 'that inept commander',† rashly engaged in battle with
men made desperate by famine, was deceived by his Gothic allies, sustained
a signal defeat, and fled in disorder to Tarragona.‡

At length, after the Vandals had sojourned nearly twenty years in Spain,
came the day when Count Bonifacius, ill-requited for his loyalty to Placidia
and her children, slandered, outlawed, and driven to the brink of destruction, sent that fatal embassy, fatal for himself and for his country, by which
he invited the barbarians into Africa. The Vandals had already, without
this invitation, shown that they were not disposed to accept the frontiers of
Baetica as the fate-fixed limit of their dominion. In 425, after sacking
Cartagena and Seville, and roaming for plunder over the whole Tarraco-
nensian province, they had laid waste the Balearic isles — which came
perhaps at this time permanently under their rule — and had invaded
Mauretania, but apparently without then gaining any foothold south of the
pillars of Hercules.§ The messengers of Bonifacius found Guntheric and
his bastard brother Gaiseric at the head of the Vandal state. They proposed
(it is said) that the conquests to be effected in Africa should be considered
as made on joint account, and should eventually be divided into three parts,
one for each of the barbarian kings, and one for the Roman count.¶ The
proposal was accepted, and the Vandals began to prepare ships and men
for the great expedition. But before the enterprise was set in hand, Guntheric died. A century after the event, a rumour obtained credence that he,
like Bleda, the brother of Attila, was slain by the partner of his throne.**

* See vol. i, p. 499.   † Prosper.
‡ The account of this expedition against the Vandals, chiefly important on account of its
bearing on the after-history of Bonifacius, is given us by Idatius and Prosper.
§ Idatius, for the year 425.
¶ This story of the tripartite division rests only on the authority of Procopius, which is not
first-rate for this period.
** This rumour is mentioned by Procopius, who, however, discredits it and says that the
Vandals would not admit its truth. Procopius adds, 'I have myself heard from men of this
nation that Gontharis was taken prisoner in Spain by the Germans and crucified by them.'

But the contemporary chronicler Idatius, writing as he does in Spain, gives no hint of any such an imputation, but in some mysterious manner connects the death of the Vandal king with an act of sacrilege at Seville. 'Gunderic, king of the Wandals, having taken Hispalis [Seville], when, in his impious elation, he had stretched forth his hand against the church of that city, speedily perished, being by the judgement of God attacked by a demon.' A fever (Spain's natural revenge upon her Northern invaders), followed by raging madness and death, is perhaps the historical equivalent of this rhetorical statement.

But, whatever the cause of the death of Guntheric, the result was that the chief power in the Vandal state, and the sole conduct of the African invasion, were thereby vested in the hands of his bastard brother. For fifty years that brother was, except during the short meteoric career of Attila, the foremost figure in Europe, and we pause therefore for a moment to collect such light as the faint tapers of the chronicles afford us on the character and aspect of Gaiseric.*

Till he arose, his nation, though willing enough to join in the great plundering expeditions of the North, can scarcely be said to have prevailed in any encounter with an enemy. Defeated long ago by Geberich in Moravia, defeated more recently by the Franks on the borders of the Rhine, generally worsted in Spain by the Visigoths, the nation seemed upon the whole to be gradually losing ground, and justifying the general impression of 'Varbaricum' that the Vandals were less warlike than their neighbours. During the long lifetime of Gaiseric this imputation at any rate was never made against them. His nimble mind† and his unshaken courage proved to be the steel point needed to give penetrating power to the Vandal impact. He was cruel, not a doubt of it; his savage deeds look ghastly by the side of the knightly career of Alaric or Ataulfus. He was greedy of gain, but none of the Northern invaders was greatly superior to him in this respect. But he had that power of estimating his own resources and the resources of his foe, that faculty of inventing useful political combinations, that transcendent ability in adapting his means to his chosen ends, which denote the successful man of business in the market-place of empire. In his strong, remorseless common sense, in the awestruck tone with which, a century after his death, people

---

* His name is commonly written Genseric; but there can be little doubt that the great Vandal's real name was Gaiseric, and that is the form which I have therefore preferred to use. The incorrect form which has been accepted by history seems to have been that which was current at Byzantium.　† Procopius, *De Bello Vandalico*, i.4.

still spoke of him as the cleverest of all men,* there is something which reminds us of his fellow Teuton (we might almost say his fellow Prussian), who, like him, besieged and took the chief city of the Latin races. If Attila was the Napoleon of the fifth century, we may perhaps look upon Gaiseric as its Bismarck.

Yet the outward presentment of the Vandal king was by no means like that of the stalwart Prussian colonel of cuirassiers. 'A man of moderate stature,' says Jordanes, 'and limping in his gait, owing to a fall from his horse.' He goes on to say that this man, 'most renowned in the world by his slaughter of the Romans, was deep in mind, sparing of speech, a despiser of luxury, tempestuous in his wrath, greedy of gain, full of far-reaching schemes for harassing the nations, ever ready to sow the seeds of contention, and to play upon the animosities of mankind'.

Another Byzantine rhetorician, speaking of the change which came over the Vandal nation after the death of their mightiest king, says, 'They fell into every kind of effeminacy and had no longer the same vigour in action, nor kept together their former reserves, which Gaiseric always held in readiness for every expedition, so that he was quicker in striking than anyone else in making up his mind to strike.'†

The resources wielded by this iron will and remorseless heart were pertinaciously directed to two great objects, the humiliation of the Roman Empire and the extirpation of the Catholic faith. His hatred towards the professors of the orthodox creed was, according to the Spanish bishop, Idatius, attributed by some persons to the fact that he was himself an apostate from their ranks.‡ If this story be true (it will be seen that Idatius himself does not vouch for its accuracy), it may be owing to the fact that the Vandal prince, as the son of some Gaulish or Spanish concubine of Godigisclus, was brought up in his mother's form of faith which, on attaining manhood, he abjured in favour of the Arian creed of his martial forefathers.

Such was the man, who, in the month of May, 428,§ mustered all the families of his nation and of the Alans on the northern shore of the straits of Gibraltar in obedience to the call of Bonifacius. But before he set sail on his new enterprise, he struck one parting blow at an old enemy. Hearing

---

* Procopius, *De Bello Vandalico*, i.3.   † Malchus, excerpt 17.

‡ Idatius, for the year 428.

§ Gibbon prefers 429. [For more information on Vandal chronology see appendix v, 'Chronology of the Vandal Kings', pp. 375–82.]

that Hermigarius,* king of the Suevi, was devastating some of the provinces near to his line of march, he turned back with a troop of his
followers, pursued the pursuing marauder, and came up with him near the
city of Merida. Many of the Suevi were slain; Hermigarius fled from the
field, mounted on a steed which he trusted should carry him swifter than
the east wind, but was whelmed in the rapid waters of the Gaudiana.† He
died almost in sight of the towers of Merida, and the churchmen of that
city saw in his fall a divine judgement for an insult which he had offered to
their saintly patroness Eulalia, one of the child-martyrs in the persecution
of Diocletian.‡

The Suevi thus punished, Gaiseric again addressed himself to the invasion of Africa. Before embarking, in order doubtless to facilitate the orderly
transport of the assembled multitude, the king had all the males of his
nation numbered, 'from the feeble old men to the babe born yesterday', and
found that they amounted to eighty thousand persons. Such a number, representing at the utmost fifty thousand fighting men,§ encumbered with
women, children, and dotards, should not have been formidable to the once
well-garrisoned and well-stored provinces of Africa. But the line to be
defended was a long one, there was discord in the camp of the defenders,
and although twelve legions of infantry and nineteen vexillations of cavalry were nominally assigned to the defence of Africa,¶ in the attenuated
state of the Imperial army in the fifth century, that force, even if it were all
enlisted on the side of loyalty, probably composed a less powerful army
than two legions in the days of Caesar the dictator. It should be stated,
however, that there were certain limitary garrisons, probably composed in
great part of barbarian *foederati*, whose warriors, from the analogy of the
troops who defended the frontier walls of Britain and Germany, may well
have amounted to a very considerable number.**

Let us briefly survey the political and social condition of the vast

* Not the same as Hermanric who, having been mentioned by Idatius under the year 419,
is again met with in 430 and 433, and whose death is recorded in 438.
† This story is told, but not very clearly, by Idatius.
‡ St Eulalia's is one of the most beautiful faces in the procession of virgin-martyrs repre-
sented on the north wall of Sant'Apollinare Nuovo at Ravenna. She is said to have
miraculously prevented Theodoric II from sacking her native city in 456 (Idatius).
§ Procopius, *De Bello Vandalico*, i.5.   ¶ *Notitia Occidentis*, 7, compared with 5.
** From the *Notitia Occidentis* (23, 29 and 30) we learn that there were sixteen limitary
garrisons in proconsular Africa, eight in Mauretania Caesariensis, and fourteen in
Tripolitana.

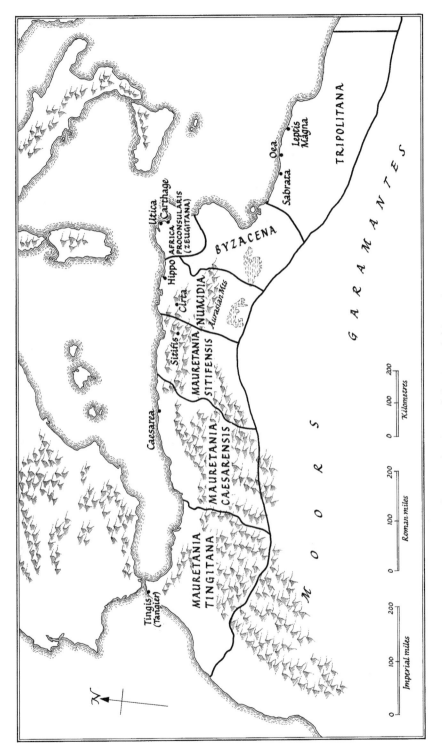

Africa at the time of the Vandal invasion, AD 428

territory for which Gaiseric and his Vandals have set sail, determined to reap from it a harvest of plunder, and possibly hoping to erect in it an enduring empire. The whole coastline from the pillars of Hercules to the borders of the Cyrenaic Pentapolis was under Diocletian divided into seven provinces.

(1) Mauretania Tingitana
(2)   do.   Caesariensis
(3)   do.   Sitifensis
(4) Numidia
(5) Africa Proconsularis or Zeugitana
(6) Byzacena
(7) Tripolitana

(1) With the westernmost province, that of which Tangier was the capital and which corresponds with the modern kingdom of Fez, we have now no concern. At the time of Diocletian's reconstitution of the Empire it was separated from the other African provinces, and assigned to the diocese of Spain and the prefecture of the Gauls.* The reason for this arrangement doubtless was that the province comprised nothing but a strip of Atlantic coastline reaching from Tangier to Sallee, separated by more than two hundred miles of roadless desert from the next province on the east, and therefore, as accessible only by sea, most naturally connected with the great and civilised country on the northern side of the straits of Gibraltar. Probably, then, from all that is about to be said touching the Vandal conquests in Africa, Tingitana may be safely excluded. We may infer that, insofar as it had any government at all and was not abandoned to mere Moorish barbarism, it still formed a part of the Roman Empire.

(2 and 3) The two next provinces, Mauretania Caesariensis and Sitifensis once belonged to the kingdom of Bocchus (who in the great civil war took the side of Caesar against the senate), and for more than seventy years after his death were governed by his descendants, but under Caligula (AD 40) they were formally annexed to the Empire, the general employed in suppressing the revolt, which was occasioned by this change, being the same Suetonius Paulinus who, twenty years later, was to lead his legions against the black-robed furies of Anglesey, and to pierce the dense masses of Britons that swarmed round the indignant Boadicea.

* See vol. i, p. 353.

These two provinces, which occupied about three-quarters of the modern territory of Algiers, had shared very imperfectly, if at all, in the civilising influence of Carthage, and though there were in them probably large breadths of cornland between the mountains and the sea, there were not many towns besides the great commercial city of Caesarea, once the capital of the Mauretanian kings. No doubt these provinces formed a part, but neither the most highly prized nor the most hardly won part of the new heritage of the Vandals.

(7) The same description would probably suit the easternmost province, which from its three chief cities* derived that name of Tripolitana by which it is still known. Fourteen limitary bodies of Imperial troops attested the difficulty with which the long and straggling frontier was guarded from the invasions of the Garamantes and the other nomadic tribes of Fezzan, who, from the ambush of their oases, poured fitfully across the desert to attack the cities of the seaborne stranger. A strange and mysterious region it is: almost unknown in history except for the fact that it gave the emperor Severus to Rome; but one of which we may possibly hear more, if ever the pressure of population or the means of subsistence should force the Italian or some other nation on the opposite shore of the Mediterranean to see what harvests may be reaped in the land of the Lotus-eaters of the *Odyssey*.

(4, 5 and 6) The three provinces which have not yet been described, Numidia, Proconsularis or Zeugitana, and Byzacena, formed the very heart and centre of the Roman dominion in Africa. On this subject I cannot do better than quote the words of the great German scholar who has written, with a fullness which no future historian is likely to surpass, the history of the Imperial provinces. 'Roman civilisation entered upon the heritage partly of the city of Carthage, partly of the kings of Numidia, and if it here attained considerable results, it should never be forgotten that it, properly speaking, merely wrote its name and inscribed its language on what was already there. Besides the towns, which were demonstrably founded by Carthage or Numidia, both states guided the Berber tribes, which had some inclination to agriculture, towards fixed settlements. Even in the time of Herodotus the Libyans westward of the bay of Gabes were no longer nomads, but peacefully cultivated the soil; and the Numidian rulers carried civilisation and agriculture still further into the interior. Nature, too, was here more favourable to husbandry than in the western part of North Africa; the middle depression between the northern and

* Leptis Magna, Oea and Sabrata.

the southern range is indeed here not quite absent, but the salt lakes and the steppe proper are less extensive than in the two Mauretanias. The military arrangements were chiefly designed to plant the troops in front of the mighty Aurasian mountain-block, the St-Gotthard of the southern frontier-range, and to check the irruption of the non-subject tribes from the latter into the pacified territory of Africa and Numidia . . . Of the details of the warfare [against these tribes of the desert] we learn little; it must have been permanent, and must have consisted in the constant repelling of the border tribes, as well as in not less constant pillaging raids into their territory.'*

The plains between the Aurasian mountains and the sea, well irrigated and rich in grain, in oil, and in wine, so far back as in the days of Agathocles, had probably increased in fruitfulness during at least the earlier centuries of the Empire. Carthage herself, indeed, lay in ruins for the greater part of the two centuries which intervened between the third Punic war and the dictatorship of Julius Caesar;† but there seems no reason to suppose that even during this interval the smaller cities (such as Utica and Hippo, which had sided with Rome against Carthage), or the bright villas which dotted the plain, and attested the long influence of the Carthaginians, were abandoned to desolation. At any rate, when the new Roman Carthage arose in all her luxury and pride, the three provinces nearest her, or so much of them as was embraced between the mountains and the sea, basked in the sunshine of her prosperity. An unfavourable element in the condition of the African provinces was probably the vast estates belonging to the Imperial exchequer. Enormous confiscations were practised in the days of Nero, and that the process had not ceased in the days of Honorius is evident from the fact that a special count was appointed to administer 'the patrimony of Gildo',‡ whose rebellion was suppressed by Stilicho in the year 398.§ These latifundia, cultivated by slaves and administered too often by corrupt and oppressive functionaries, were probably a blot upon the general prosperity of the province. And no doubt, here as elsewhere throughout the Empire, the process of the degradation of the cultivator into a serf, and the cruel impoverishment of the middle classes by ruinous taxation had been going on throughout the fourth century. Still, from the pages of Salvian and Augustine we may safely infer that there was, at any

* Mommsen, *Provinces of the Roman Empire*, ii.316 (English translation).
† The prosperity of the colony sent to Carthage by Caius Gracchus (122 BC) was of short duration.   ‡ *Notitia Occidentis*, 12.   § See vol. i, pp. 382–5.

rate relatively, a large amount of wealth, and culture, and prosperity in the three most important African provinces, up to the day when the first foot-print of the Vandal was seen on the Numidian sands.

It would be an interesting enquiry, had we sufficient evidence on which to form a judgement, how far the civilisation which prevailed in Africa in the fifth century of our era was Aryan, and how far still Semitic in its char-acter. The language of the Phoenician settlers who first founded cities and established markets on the Libyan shore, the language in which Hiram spoke to Solomon and Jezebel to Ahab, was still spoken from Tangier to Tripoli at the time of the Christian era, and was even used in the days of Tiberius by the colonies which prided themselves on their derivation from Rome. Gradually, however, Punic gave way to Latin, first in official then in social life. At the end of the fourth century the relative position of the two languages seems to have resembled that of English and Welsh in our own day in the principality. Latin was the language of the wealthy and fashion-able, but a priest who was unacquainted with Punic was in danger, at least in the country districts, of becoming isolated from his congregation. Just in the same way, too, as the representatives of the earlier race in our own land call themselves not Welsh but Cymry, so the true old national name, that name which recalled to a Hebrew the contemporaries of his forefather Abraham, the name of Canaanites was still naturally applied to themselves by the Punic contemporaries of St Augustine.

But upon the whole there can be no doubt that during the five centuries of the Empire the Latin language and literature had been striking deeper and deeper roots in the African world. It is one of the commonplaces of church history that in the early ages of Christianity the chief of the Latin-speaking champions of her cause were African provincials. Tertullian, Cyprian, Arnobius, Lactantius, all men of African birth, were conspicu-ous as Christian apologists in the third and fourth centuries, and the catalogue ends with the name of the greatest of all, Augustine of Hippo. The first translation of the Bible into Latin, the so-called Itala, is generally supposed to have been due in great part to the labours of African ecclesias-tics; and – a less enviable distinction – the first great schism, Novatianism undoubtedly originated in the church of Carthage.

A century after the Vandal invasion of Africa it was still the opinion of the men of letters at Constantinople that the Roman provincials, in that continent, spoke Latin more fluently than the citizens of Rome itself.* It is

* So says Joannes Lydus (*De Magistratibus*, iii.73).

very likely true that there was an affected prettiness, a want of spontaneity
and naturalness about this Carthaginian Latin; still, the fact that Roman
rhetoric was so extensively and successfully taught in the African provinces
– a fact which receives abundant confirmation from the *Confessions* of St
Augustine – throws an important light on the progress of Roman civilisation in that region.

Such then, in brief outline, was the state of the African provinces in the
fifth century after Christ; and their prosperity – for after making every necessary deduction we must still believe them to have been prosperous – was
all summed up and symbolised in the glory and magnificence of their capital, the 'happy Carthage' of her Roman lords.* We have already seen the
picture drawn by the stern Salvian of the seductive immorality of the great
African city,† but even through all his denunciations there runs a reluctant
acknowledgement of her surpassing beauty. Topographers dispute, and
will perhaps long dispute, as to the exact limits of the old Phoenician city,
but there cannot be much doubt as to the general position of its Roman
successor, and the main features of the landscape around it are still
unchanged. There Carthago lay upon her superb isthmus looking forth
upon her lake and her sea, even the sea landlocked and with the two-horned
mountain of the hot springs‡ rising to the south of it. Below, was her harbour the celebrated Cothon, once blocked up by the mole constructed by
Scipio during the last fatal siege, but now probably again opened to the
commerce of the world. Northwards, the long sad street of tombs stretched
up to the hill of Camart. In the city itself, besides the baths, the forum, the
amphitheatre, and all the other accustomed splendours of a Roman city,
were five temples bearing witness by the names of their tutelary gods to that
antique civilisation of the sons of Canaan which Rome might crush but
could not obliterate. These were the temples dedicated under the Empire to
Aesculapius, to Saturn, to Juno, to Hercules, and to Mercury, but which
had once borne the means of Ashmon, of Moloch, of Ashtaroth, of
Melkarth, and of Baal-Ammon. Some of these, it is true, may have been
destroyed in the outbreak of Christian zeal which marked the close of the
fourth century in Africa; but the temple of Juno Coelestis at any rate still
remained, for it was consecrated in 425 by Aurelius, bishop of Carthage, as
a temple of the newer faith which had come forth from Palestine to claim
all the shores of the Mediterranean for its heritage.

* FELIX KARTAGO is a frequent legend on the Imperial coins.
† Vol. i, p. 518.   ‡ Now Hammam Elenf.

On an eminence within the city rose the stately Byrsa, the acropolis of Carthage, bounded by a wall two miles in circumference.* Here, according to the legend transmitted by the Greeks, was the scene of Dido's famous purchase from the natives of 'a hide of land' which she interpreted to mean so much land as could be encompassed by a bull's hide† cut into strips. Modern philologists, struck with the obvious absurdity of supposing that Dido and her Phoenicians would resort to the Greek language for the name of their new city, have preferred to connect Byrsa with Bozra, a name well known to us from the Hebrew Scriptures as descriptive of the mountain fortress of the Edomites.‡ Here, at any rate, appear to have been situated the chief buildings not only of Punic Carthage, but of its Roman successor: here was the temple of Ashmon, or Aesculapius, and here in all probability the lordly *praetorium* [palace], once inhabited by the great proconsul of Africa, but soon to receive the retinue of the Vandal king.

I have said that the proconsul of Africa once dwelt in the *praetorium* of Carthage, and this was certainly his abode in the first century of the Christian era, but at the time which we have now reached, he may have been thrust out of his palace, or if still dwelling there, he may have been reduced almost to insignificance by the overshadowing might of his military rival, the count. The position of the proconsul was a somewhat peculiar one. The whole diocese of Africa, including all its six provinces, bounded by Tingitana on the west, and Cyrenaica in the east, was, as we have already seen, part of the prefecture of Italy.§ According to analogy it should have been all subject to its own *vicarius*, who should have been responsible for the whole to the *praefectus praetorio Italiae*. In fact, however, at the time of the Diocletianic reorganisation of the Empire, only five provinces (the two Mauretanias, Numidia, Byzacena, and Tripolitana) were placed under the *vicarius Africae*, while the proconsul of Zeugitana (otherwise called the proconsul of Africa, as his, though the smallest, was by far the richest and

---

* So says Orosius (iv.22), who, on account of his friendship for St Augustine, is probably a good witness at any rate as to the Carthage of the fifth century.

† Βύρσα = a hide.

‡ But בָּצְרָה (Botsrah) requires some gentle violence to press it into Bursa. I cannot help thinking that the old Greek derivation may be nearer the truth than modern scholars admit. Gesenius postulates the existence of an unused root בָּרַשׁ (barash), 'to cut' (especially to cut into slices). If the legend about Dido's bargain was, as seems probable, home-grown, Byrsa may have been derived from a kindred root to this. The similarity with the Greek βύρσα was, of course, a mere coincidence.

§ Vol. i. p. 353.

most important of all the provinces) was retained under the immediate order of the praetorian prefect of Italy. If, as seems highly probable, the *vicarius* as well as the proconsul had his residence at Carthage,* there was already some material provided for jealousies and heart-burnings between the civil governors of the diocese. But, from what we know of the course of affairs throughout the fourth and fifth centuries, and especially from the glimpses vouchsafed to us of the history of Roman Africa during that time, we may safely say that the proconsul, venerable as was the name of his office and great as his theoretical authority, was ever losing more of the substance of power, and that his losses were the gains of the military ruler of the diocese, the far-feared count of Africa.† This was the office which, in the middle of the reign of Honorius had been held by Heraclian, and which was now held by Bonifacius.

From this sketch of Roman Africa we return to trace the fortunes of its Vandal invaders. We have seen that in the month of May, and probably in the year 428, Gaiseric, with the whole body of his countrymen (the males alone of whom numbered eighty thousand souls), set sail in the ships of Bonifacius for the coast of Africa. Of the details of their first conquests we know nothing. All that we can say is that in the early part of 430, only three cities remained which had not been sacked by the barbarians, but these three were the strongly fortified towns of Hippo, Cirta,‡ and the capital of

* This is made probable, but is not actually proved by the language of Salvian (*De Gubernatione Dei*, vii.16) which is, in itself, an interesting description of the condition of Carthage on the eve of the Vandal invasion.

'I speak of Carthage, once the mightiest enemy of Rome, and now like another Rome in the world of Africa. She alone is sufficient for my purpose as an example and a witness, since she contained within herself all the resources whereby throughout the whole world the good order of the commonwealth is established or maintained. For there are all the appliances of the offices of state, the schools of the liberal arts, the lecture rooms of the philosophers, in short, all the institutions for training students either in literature or in morals. There, too, are the military forces and the authorities in command of the army, the honour of the proconsul, that daily judge and ruler, proconsul, indeed, in name but a very consul in power; there, finally, are all the distributors of wealth, the rulers, so to speak, of every street and square, who, with every imaginable variety of rank and name, govern all the regions of the city and all the members of the nation.'

‡ The official staff of the *proconsul Africae* is described in the seventeenth chapter of the *Notitia Occidentis*: that of the *vicarius Africae* in the nineteenth and that of the *comes Africae* in the twenty-third chapter.

* Possidius (the biographer of St Augustine), it is true, speaks of churches, but we may conclude that if the Vandals had ruined all the other churches, they had also taken the towns.

the province, Carthage. We know not when Cirta fell. A peculiar interest attaches to the Vandals' siege of Hippo, which was commenced about the end of the month of May, 430. This town, situated on the sea coast about 180 miles west of Carthage, and represented by the modern FrenchArabic city of Bona, was, as everyone knows, the abode of the great bishop and father, Augustine. There he was busily employed, adding a confutation of Julian of Eclana, the Pelagian heretic, to the vast library of books which already owned him as author,* when the news came of the Vandal invasion. He heard of the burnings, the massacres, the tornup fruittrees, the churches levelled to the ground, which everywhere marked the progress of the barbarian hosts through the orderly and quiet province, the beautiful land which from every side seemed smiling upon the stranger.† Bishop after bishop asked his counsel whether they should stay in their sees or fly to one of the few remaining strongholds. His first advice was, 'Remain with your flocks and share their miseries.' 'What', said one, 'is the use of our remaining, simply to see the men slain, the women ravished, the churches burned, and then to be put to the rack ourselves to make us disclose the hidingplace of treasures which we have not?' They pleaded the words of Christ, 'When they persecute you in one city, flee into another', and Augustine, reflecting on the examples of Cyprian and Athanasius, who had for a time quitted their bishoprics, with some hesitation, and with some limitations, admitted the plea. So it came to pass that Possidius, bishop of Calama, to whose pen we are indebted for this account of the last days of his master, with many other bishops from all the country round, were shut up in Hippo, sitting at the feet of the great doctor of the African church, and listening to 'that river of eloquence which had once flowed forth abundantly over all the meadows of the church, but was now almost dried up with fear, to that fountain sweeter than honey which was being turned into the bitterness of wormwood'.‡ So the good bishops sat, 'often talking together over these calamities, and reflecting on the tremendous judgements of God daily exhibited before us, saying, "Righteous art thou, O Lord, and thy judgement is just", mingling our tears, our groans, and our sighs, and praying the Father of mercies and the God of all consolation that he would see meet to deliver us from this tribulation.'§

* 'Two hundred and thirtytwo books, besides innumerable epistles, an exposition of the Psalter and the Gospels and popular *tractates*, called Homilies by the Greeks, the number of which it is impossible to ascertain' (Victor Vitensis, i.3).   † Victor Vitensis, i.1.
‡ Victor Vitensis, i.3.   § Possidius, *Life of St Augustine*, 28, 29.

But, shut up in the same town of Hippo, was one man more sad at heart and more weary of life than Augustine himself, the author of all this mis-ery, and the betrayer of his trust, Bonifacius count of Africa. It has been already told how, by the intervention of his friends, his character was cleared at Rome, and he returned to his old loyalty to Placidia.* Too late, however, for the desolated province. 'When with the most earnest entreaties and a thousand promises he besought his late allies to depart from Africa, they would not listen to his words, but thought he was making fools of them.'† A battle followed, in which he was defeated, and in consequence we find him now within the walls of the old capital of the Numidian kings (Hippo Regius) directing the defence of the beleaguered city, and listening to the tragic stories told by each fresh fugitive, of the ruin wrought in his province by his own invited guests. He had repented,

> Ay, as the libertine repents who cannot
> Make done undone, when thro' his dying sense
> Shrills 'lost through thee'.‡

It is strange to reflect that this, the most miserable man in all Africa, whose treason had brought such innumerable woes upon his people, was the same man who had sighed after a monastic life, and had scarcely been persuaded to continue to discharge the duties of a husband and a general. A con-science, this, which was always above or below the average common-sense morality of ordinary men.

The generalship of Bonifacius, or the prayers of Augustine, or the nat-ural unskilfulness of the Northern barbarians in the siege of walled cities, enabled Hippo to make a successful defence. For fourteen months the Van-dals blockaded the town, from May, 430, till July, 431. In the third month of the siege (August, 430), the great bishop of Hippo died, in the seventy-sixth year of his age and the fortieth since his ordination. He had often uttered the maxim that even the aged and experienced Christian ought not to depart out of the world except in a state of profound penitence for all sins committed after baptism;§ and acting on his own principle, he had the pen-itential psalms of David copied for him by his friends, and gazed constantly at the wall to which the sheets thus inscribed were affixed. For ten days before his death he ordered that, except when the doctor visited him, or his

* Vol. i, p. 502.   † Procopius, *De Bello Vandalico*, i.3.   ‡ Tennyson, *Harold*, iii.1.
§ Possidius, *Life of St Augustine*, 31.

meals had to be brought to his bedside, no one should enter his chamber, in order that all his waking thoughts might be given to prayer. So, amid the sorrows of the siege, in silence and contrition, passed away the spirit which, more mightily than any other since the age of the apostles ended, has moulded the thoughts of the European nations concerning the dealings of the Almighty with mankind.

In the fourteenth month of the siege the Vandals, pressed by famine, broke up from before the walls of Hippo. Soon after, Bonifacius, being joined by large reinforcements from Rome and Byzantium (the latter under the command of the veteran Aspar), tried conclusions once more with Gaiseric in the open field.* The Romans were again defeated. Aspar returned to Byzantium and Bonifacius to Rome, where (as has been before related) he received his death-wound from Aetius.†

Three years passed. It became clear to the Imperial court that the Vandals would never be forced to relinquish their prize. It had also become clear to the mind of Gaiseric that it would be wise to consolidate his conquests, that Carthage would not easily be wrested in fair fighting from a watchful foe, and that it was time for his people to desist from mere marauding ravages and to settle down as lords of the soil in such part of Africa as the emperor might be forced to surrender. Accordingly, on the 11th February, 435, peace was concluded between the emperor and the Vandal, the chief conditions being apparently that the latter was to leave unmolested the city of Carthage, and that part of the proconsular province which lay immediately around it; was to pay a yearly tribute, and to send his son Huneric to Rome as a hostage for his fidelity. On the other hand, Gaiseric's rule over the part of Africa which he had already conquered, and which probably included the remainder of the proconsular province, Byzacena and Numidia, was recognised under the formula probably in frequent use on similar occasions that 'this portion of the Empire was given to the Vandals to dwell in'.‡ The treaty was signed at Hippo, which city appears to have fallen into the hands of the Vandals, and to have been burned by them.§ Probably it may have been rebuilt, reoccupied by an Imperial garrison, and now handed over to Gaiseric, but

---

* I have assigned [this battle] to 432 (vol. i, p. 502). I do not think we can fix the date with certainty.   † See vol. i, pp. 502–3.

‡ Prosper, *Chronicon*, for the year 435. Trigetius, the negotiator of this peace, was afterwards prefect and one of the ambassadors sent in 452 with Pope Leo to the camp of Attila (see p. 97).   § Possidius, *Life of St Augustine*, 28.

as to these vicissitudes in its history we cannot speak with certainty.

Procopius greatly praises the forethought and moderation which Gais-eric showed in concluding this peace. He says that he had reflected on the possibility that Rome and Byzantium might again combine their forces against him, and that another time he might not be able to resist their united strength, that he was sobered rather than puffed up by the good fortune which he had already experienced, and remembered how often the gods delight to trip up human prosperity. No doubt this was the attitude which the Vandal wished to assume, but considering how easily the tribute might be left unpaid, the hostage enabled to escape, the promise broken, and on the other hand of what immense importance to the establishment of the Vandal rule was the recognition of its legitimacy even for a few years by the only source of legitimate authority in the Western Empire, we shall not find much difficulty in believing that the moderate and sober-minded barbarian got the best of the bargain.

In point of fact, the promise to desist from further attacks on the procon-sular province held good for rather less than five years. We have already had occasion briefly to notice those vain and futile battlings to and fro in southern Gaul between the Romans at Narbonne and the Visigoths at Toulouse,* which preceded by about twelve years the far wiser confederacy of both nations against the terrible Attila. While all the energies of Rome, and all the intellect of Aetius, who was the brain of Rome, were concen-trated on the next move in this purposeless struggle, suddenly, without warning, Gaiseric (says Prosper), 'of whose friendship no doubt was enter-tained, attacked Carthage, under cover of peace, and converted all its wealth to his own use, extorting it from the citizens by various kinds of tor-ments'. This happened on the 19th October, 439.† We may conjecture that the hostage Huneric had been before this upon some pretext or other recalled from Italy.

Now at length the great prize was won, and the Vandals were undoubted masters of Africa. Their chief, who for ten years or more had been leading them from victory to victory, seems now for the first time to have assumed the full title of king.‡ His true statesmanlike instinct is shown

---

* p. 69.   † Marcellinus puts the date four days later, on the 23rd of October.

‡ Victor Vitensis ascribes the capture of Rome (455) to the fifteenth year of Gaiseric's reign, and says that he continued in his kingship thirty-seven years and three months, evi-dently reckoning this reign, which ended in January, 477, from the date of the capture of Carthage. Prosper and Procopius also date his reign from the same event. What title,

by the fact that as soon as he touched the coast, or at least as soon as the docks and harbours of Hippo and Carthage were in his power, he, the leader of a tribe of inland barbarians, who had been indebted to the friendly offices of Bonifacius for the transport of his people across the straits of Gibraltar, turned all his energies to shipbuilding, and soon possessed incomparably the most formidable naval power in the Mediterranean. The remaining thirty-seven years of his life, especially the later ones, were made merry by perpetual piratical expeditions against Italy, against Sicily, against Illyria, against the Peloponnesus, against the rich and defenceless islands of the Aegean.* There was a joyous impartiality in these expeditions, an absence of any special malice against the victims of them, a frank renunciation of all attempts to find a pretext for making them, which is thoroughly characteristic of their author. Once when his armament was lying in the harbour of Carthage, all ready for sailing, and when the brigand-king had come limping down from the palace which had been dwelt in for centuries by the proconsuls of Africa, as soon as he set his foot on board, the pilot asked for orders to what land he should steer. The object of the expedition was the only point which the king had not yet troubled himself to determine. 'For the dwellings of the men with whom God is angry,' he said, and left the decision of that question to the winds and the waves. This was the true counterpart of the stories about 'the scourge of God', with which legend has falsely invested the history of Attila.†

then, did he now assume? In the decrees quoted by Victor Vitensis he styles himself 'king of the Vandals and Alans'; but this looks as if he may also have styled himself 'king of Carthage' or 'king of Africa'. Theophanes (*Chronographia*, for the year 449) says that he called himself 'king of the land and the sea', but he is a late writer.

* Gaiseric even rounded the pillars of Hercules and attacked the coasts of Galicia in Spain (Idatius, for the year 445).

† In the *Novellae Valentiniani III* (9) under the date 440, occurs the following interesting reference to the piratical excursions of Gaiseric: *Geisericus hostis imperii nostri non parvam classem de Karthaginensi portu nuntiatus est eduxisse, cujus repentinus excursus et fortuita depraedatio cunctis est litoribus formidanda* [Gaiseric is reported to have become the enemy of the Empire and sent out a great armada from Carthage. All our coasts are to guard against sudden attack and unpredictable plundering]. The object of the decree which was entitled *De reddito jure armorum* [The right to bear arms restored] was to convey to 'our most loving Roman people' the Imperial permission and command to use arms and band themselves together for the defence of the threatened coasts. Valentinian at the same time states that 'the army of our father, the unconquered Theodosius [II], is drawing nigh', that 'we believe the most excellent man, our patrician Aetius, to be at hand with a great power', and that 'the most illustrious master of the soldiery, Sigisvuld, ceases not to array both

So it came to pass that again after nearly six centuries of quiet submission to the rule of Rome, the name of Carthage became terrible to the
dwellers by the Tiber. The poets of the period described Gaiseric's invasions of Italy as a fourth Punic war,* and it was scarcely a licence of poetry
so to speak of them. We are reminded of the medieval superstitions about
vampire-spirits inhabiting the bodies of the dead and sucking the blood of
the living, when we find this Teutonic people entering the long-buried
corpse of the Punic nationality, and striking, from its heart, deadlier blows
at Rome than ever were delivered by Hamilcar or Hannibal. We know not
on what scale God writes his lessons for the nations, and we fear to push too
far the paradox expressed in the old proverb, 'The fathers have eaten sour
grapes, and the children's teeth are set on edge.' But, remembering the ignoble jealousy, the cruelty born of fear, with which the Romans prepared
for and consummated the 'deletion' of their fallen enemy, in the third Punic
war, we cannot but feel that there is something like a judgement of the Eternal Righteousness in the conspicuous part assigned to the city and harbour
of Carthage in harassing and embittering the dying days of Rome.

During the years immediately following the fall of Carthage, Sicily
appears to have been the main object of the Vandal expeditions. Gaiseric
was, in the year 440, moving up and down through the island, cruelly wasting her fruitful valleys, when the tidings brought to him that Sebastian, a
brave man and son-in-law to Bonifacius, had landed in Africa, caused him
to return to Carthage. Sebastian, however, as we shall hereafter see, came
not as an enemy but as a suppliant, and Gaiseric, we may presume,
returned to his career of spoliation. Next year an expedition fitted out by
the Eastern emperor under the command of Areobindus and two other
generals, came to dispute the sovereignty of the Western seas with the
Vandal king. But as was so often the case with these laboriously prepared
Byzantine armaments, the generals wrangled and procrastinated; the
favourable moment — if there were one — for striking was lost, and the
expedition failed to accomplish anything for the reconquest of Africa, and
did much to increase the miseries of the unhappy Sicilians.†

In the next year (442) the army was recalled to defend the Eastern
Empire from one of Attila's inroads, and Valentinian, feeling it hopeless to

---

milites [soldiers] and *foederati* for the defence both of the cities and the coasts'.
* Thus Apollinaris Sidonius, *Panegyric of Avitus*, 444–5.
† Prosper, *Chronicon*, for the year 441. The disputes of the generals may fairly be inferred
from what Prosper tells us of their long delays.

continue the contest single-handed, concluded another treaty with Gaiseric by which possibly Sicily or some portion of it was surrendered,* and Africa was divided by certain fixed limits between the emperor and the Vandal.† Unfortunately these 'fixed limits' have not been mentioned by the historians, and it must remain doubtful how much of Mauretania on the west and Tripolitana on the east may still have owed a precarious allegiance to the Roman Empire.

But the fate of Sicily is less doubtful. It is clear that either at this time or some years later, it became a recognised part of the Vandal dominions, and so remained till there was no longer a Western emperor to claim it. Then probably in the year 477, the greater part of it was ceded by Gaiseric to Odovacar, the barbarian ruler of Italy, on condition of his paying an annual tribute. But already, as we see, the great island is falling into that condition of partial detachment from the great peninsula, which generally marked its history under its Greek lords, and which was so frequently again to prevail in the Middle Ages, and even down to the days of our fathers.‡

As for Gaiseric, though peace was formally concluded between him and Valentinian, we need not suppose that the buccaneering exploits of the Vandal king were ended. Pretexts were doubtless still found for the visits paid with each returning spring to some 'nation with whom God was angry', and if serious war was not being waged, life was still made exciting by light-hearted piracy.

The few details which are preserved as to the internal administration of Gaiseric, and his manner of parcelling out the conquered territory among his followers, are of great value, as affording one of the earliest illustrations of that great land settlement of the victorious Teutons which was one day to form the basis of the feudal system.

'He arranged', says Procopius, 'the Vandals and Alans into regiments, over whom he set no fewer than eighty colonels, whom he called chiliarchs [captains of thousands], so creating the belief that his forces amounted to eighty thousand men. Nevertheless the number of the Vandals and Alans was said in the previous time [in the time before the invasion] not to amount to more than fifty thousand; but the natural increase of the population, together with their practice of admitting other barbarians into their confederation, had enormously added to their numbers. The names, however, of

* This is not expressly stated by Prosper.   † Prosper, *Chronicon*, for the year 442.
‡ [For more information on Sicily during this period see appendix vi, 'Vandal Dominion over the Islands of the Mediterranean', pp. 382–4.]

the Alans, and of every other barbarous tribe in the confederacy except the Moors, were all merged in the one designation of Vandals.

'Among the provincials of Africa, if he saw any man flourishing in reputation and wealth, he gave him, with his lands and other possessions, to his sons Huneric and Genzo, as servile property. From the other Africans he took away the largest and best part of their lands, and distributed them among the nation of the Vandals; and from that time these lands are called the Vandal allotments unto this day. The former possessors of these lands were for the most part left poor and free — at liberty, that is, to take them-selves off whither they would. Now all these estates which Gaiseric had bestowed upon his sons and the other Vandals were, according to his orders, free from the payment of all taxes. But all the land which seemed to him to be of poorer quality, he left in the hands of the former owners, so burdened however with taxes and public charges that nothing beyond a bare subsistence could be reaped by the nominal possessors. Many of these tried to flee, but were arrested and put to death; for sundry grievous crimes were laid to their charge, the greatest of all, according to his estimate, being the attempted concealment of treasure. Thus did the African provincials fall into every kind of misery.'*

We are able to supplement the information as to the land settlement given by Procopius by an important sentence from Victor Vitensis. 'He [Gaiseric] thus disposed of the several provinces: reserving to himself the Byzacene and Abaritan provinces, Gaetulia and a part of Numidia, he portioned out the Zeugitana or proconsular province to his army by the tie of inheritance.'† The proconsular province, as has been said, was that cor-ner of the coastline in the middle of which Carthage was situated, the smallest of all the provinces, being only about a hundred miles wide by fifty long, but doubtless also by far the richest. Numidia bordered it on the west, the Byzacene province‡ on the south. No such province as Abaritana was known to the Imperial geographers: but it was probably a small district in the proconsular province.

The historical student who considers the account thus given by Pro-copius and Victor of the Vandal land settlement will see that we have here the germs of the same state of society which prevailed in France under the Carolingian monarchs and out of the inevitable decay of which arose the feudal system.

* Procopius, *De Bello Vandalico*, i.5. (I have transposed the order of the two paragraphs.)
† Victor Vitensis, i.4.   ‡ Or Byzacium.

(1) We have first a vast royal domain, the land of *dominus noster, Gais-ericus.** If we take the expression of Victor literally, this domain included nearly the whole of the two great provinces of Numidia and Byzacena, as well as some part of Proconsularis. Probably, however, we may interpret it by the light of Procopius' explanations, and infer that Gaiseric chose for himself and his sons all the valuable estates in these provinces† leaving the poorer soils in the hands of the old cultivators. The immense domain so chosen was cultivated of course entirely by slaves, and Gaiseric chose espe-cially those who had been the richest and most influential proprietors, appropriating them and their slaves to service on his domain land. The insolence of the barbarian was gratified by thus reducing the proudest, wealthiest and most refined of the provincials to the condition of menials absolutely dependent on his will. But in course of time no doubt superior education and the old habits of command would assert themselves. These aristocratic slaves would become intendants, stewards, managers of their fellow-slaves. If the experiment had been continued for a sufficient length of time (which it was not in the case of the Vandals) these highly educated slaves would have become supple courtiers, and would have perhaps proved a formidable counterpoise to the descendants of Vandal chiefs, who once looked upon Gaiseric himself as scarcely more than first among his peers. In fact, very soon after the settlement (in 442) there was an actual conspiracy among the nobility against what they considered the overgrown power and pride of their king: but the plot was detected and the conspirators atoned for their share in it by a death of torture. The suspicions and jealousies engendered by this conspiracy were very detrimental to the Vandal state.‡

(2) The Vandal allotments (*sortes Vandalorum*) denote the next class of lands, those which are divided among the warriors of the conquering nation. Divided, surely, by lot, in a manner which suited well the ardent love of games of hazard inherent in these Teutonic nations, and in accord-ance with a custom widely diffused among them, as is testified by the occurrence of the same word, *sors*, among the Visigoths in Spain, among the Burgundians on the banks of the lake of Geneva, and among the Ripuarian Franks of the Rhine. The estates were hereditary – this we learn from Victor's express testimony – but though hereditary they doubtless carried with them some obligation of service in that 'army' to which they

* [Our Lord, Gaiseric.]
† This process is, I believe, called in Australia 'picking out the eyes' of a district.
‡ Prosper, *Chronicon*, for the year 442.

were originally 'portioned out'. Except for this implied obligation of military service they were free from all taxes. These *sortes Vandalorum* were, as
before said, chiefly to be found in the rich proconsular province, where they
must have clustered thickly, perhaps overflowing a little into the neighbouring Numidia.* Here doubtless the power of the old Vandal nobility was
greatest, and the spirit of Vandal nationality the strongest. Here, if it had
been written in the book of fate that an enduring German kingdom of
North Africa should be founded, would the speech of the Vandals have
struck the deepest root, and the songs of Vandal minstrels as to the bygone
ages spent in the forest of the Elbe and the Danube would have been the
longest preserved.

(3) There remain the poor, the unimproved, the outlying lands, abandoned half-contemptuously to the Roman provincials, who tilled, and
crouched, and paid where their fathers fought, and ruled, and robbed.
Would this kind of holding in the course of centuries have sunk down into
the 'base-tenure' whence our copyholds sprang, or would it have slowly
risen into what our ancestors called free socage? In other words, would these
downtrodden provincials have developed into villeins or freeholders? That
is an interesting question, the answer to which is drowned by the trumpets
of Belisarius. But, nevertheless, it is worthwhile noticing that we have here
in Africa, halfway through the fifth century after Christ, a division of the
nation into two distinct classes, a burdened, taxpaying, toiling common-
alty, and a lordly, untaxed, warrior class above them – that same division
which in France lasted on to the days of our grandfathers, and was shattered by the oath of the *tiers état* in the tennis-court of Versailles.

But it is not to be supposed that a majority of the subject population
were left, even in this degraded state, to enjoy the blessings of freedom. The
vast estates of the king, his sons, and the Vandal warriors, required vast
tribes of slaves to cultivate them, and to slavery accordingly, as has before
been said, the bulk of the provincial population were reduced. A story
which is told us by Procopius, and which has something in the ring of it
that reminds one of the far-distant legendary moralities of Herodotus,
brings this wholesale enslavement of the people clearly before us. 'The
Byzantine general Aspar, as was before said, brought help to the Roman
provincials of Africa, but was defeated by the barbarians [in 432]. After
the battle, Gaiseric ordered all the captives to be mustered in the courtyard
of his palace that he might allot them masters suitable to their several condi-

* Victor Vitensis, i.4.

tions. There then they were collected in the open air, and as the noonday sun' – the fierce sun of Libya – 'beat hotly on their heads, most of them sat down. But one among them, who was named Marcian, carelessly composed himself to sleep; and while he lay there an eagle, so they say, with outspread wings, hovered over him, now rising, now falling, but always contriving to shelter him, and him only, from the sun by the shadow of her wings. From the window of an upper chamber Gaiseric watched this occurrence, and being a quick-witted man, at once perceived that there was in it something of the nature of an omen. So he sent for the man, and asked him who he was, and whence he came. He replied that he was a confidential servant, or *domesticus*, as the Romans call it, of Aspar. On hearing this, and reflecting what the bird had done' (the typical eagle of Rome) 'and comparing it with the influence which Aspar possessed at the court of Byzantium, Gaiseric saw clearly that the captive before him would attain to some high career. To kill him, however, did not appear to be at all the right thing to do: for that would only show that the omen had no significance, since certainly the bird would never have taken the trouble to overshadow, as future emperor, a man who was just on the point of dying. And besides, he had no just cause for putting him to death. Nor could he do it if he was really destined to wear the purple, since what God has resolved upon, man will never be able to hinder. He therefore bound him by an oath that if he was restored to freedom he would never bear arms against the Vandals. Thus was Marcian liberated, and came to Byzantium, where, not long afterwards, upon the death of Theodosius II, he was made emperor.'* He is the same Marcian with whom we have already made acquaintance as the husband of Pulcheria, the courageous defender of the Empire against Attila, the prince who saw in his dreams the broken bow, on the night when the mighty Hun expired. 'And, though' (says Procopius) 'in all other respects he made an excellent ruler, he never seemed to take any thought for the province of Africa', mindful as he was of his vow not to bear arms against the Vandals.

The land settlement, the outlines of which are thus preserved to us, was probably completed soon after the capture of Carthage in 439. We have seen that by the peace of 442 some fragments of African dominion, probably in Tripolitana and Mauretania were still left to the Empire, but after the death of Valentinian III (455) the Vandal dominion spread unchallenged over these as well as over all the islands of the western Mediterranean.†

* Procopius, *De Bello Vandalico*, i.4.   † Victor Vitensis, i.4.

As to the administration of government in this wide territory, there are not wanting indications that here, as in so many other portions of the Empire, much was still left in the hands of the trained Roman officials. Doubtless the lawless will of the Vandal king could make itself felt wherever it pleased. Doubtless, subject to that omnipotent will, the great nobles, each in his own circle, could exercise unchecked dominion. Still there remained an infinite number of details of daily government in a community which, though half ruined was still civilised, and these details the German conquerors had neither intellect nor patience to arrange. They remained therefore in the hands of the Roman bureaucracy, and hence it is that we still, even under the Vandal kings, meet with a proconsul of Carthage,* a *primarius provinciae*,† and a *praepositus regni*,‡ though to attempt now to settle the exact functions of these governors would be a hopeless task.

With all the barbarous violence and contempt of the rights of the subject population which characterised the Vandal conquest, it deserves one praise: it was not financially oppressive. While the Imperial government, with phrases of law and right for ever on its lips, was practically sucking the lifeblood out of the people by its indictions and its superindictions, its *angaria*§ and its *chrysargyron*,¶ Gaiseric, though helping himself and his soldiers to all the fairest lands in the province, did leave to the poor provincial liberty to live on the sterile soil which he contemptuously abandoned to him. Procopius expressly assures us that when the emperor Justinian regained Africa it was no longer possible to discover in the public archives the amount of taxes which ought to be paid by each property, since Gaiseric, in the beginning of his reign, had thrown up the whole system and destroyed the registers.**

At first sight this seems contradictory to the same author's statement previously quoted, that the lands abandoned to the Romans were 'so burdened with taxes and public charges that nothing beyond a bare subsistence could be reaped by the nominal possessors'. On reflection, however, we may perhaps come to the conclusion that in that passage Procopius is speaking chiefly of the great Roman landowners, whom it was evidently part of the Vandal policy to worry out of existence. The mass of cultivators and the little burgesses in the towns, who were known under the Empire as *curiales*, were, it seems, practically untaxed. The grievous discontent which arose in the province when this operation was reversed by the Roman reconquest,

* Victor Vitensis, v.4.   † *Life of St Fulgentius*, 14.   ‡ Victor Vitensis, ii.5.
§ [Compulsory service.]   ¶ [Special levies.]   ** *De Bello Vandalico*, ii.8.

and when the people found that in their liberator they had gained a relentless taskmaster, is a striking testimony to the general lightness of the
financial yoke of the Vandal kings.

In all that has yet been said concerning the career of this people, little has
appeared to justify that charge of senseless and brutal destructiveness with
which the word 'vandalism' makes us familiar. We have heard of the pillage of towns – that, of course, is one of the commonplaces of barbaric
conquest; of populations reduced to slavery – but the slave-dealer followed
also in the track of the Roman armies; even of the fruit-trees being rooted
up – but that was consistent with the cruel logic of war, being done in
order to prevent the inhabitants from deserting the towns and prolonging a
guerrilla campaign in the country on such support as they could derive
from the produce of the orchards. We have yet, however, to see the Vandal
in his most repulsive aspect, that of a religious persecutor; and when we
have beheld him in this capacity, the kernel of truth and the large envelope
of passionate exaggeration which both together make up the common idea
of 'vandalism' will be more clearly perceived and more easily separated
from one another.

The Vandals, like almost every other Teutonic nation, had shared in
that great process of religious change of which the bishop Ulfilas was the
most conspicuous instrument. Little as their deeds savoured of Christianity, they were, by profession, Christians, holding, as a matter of course, the
Arian creed of their great apostle.

They came then with all the rancour of the Arian–Catholic feud,
which had now endured for more than a century, bitter in their hearts. And
they came into a province which was, beyond all the other provinces of the
Roman Empire, undermined by hot volcanic fires of theological passion
and bigotry. There is much in the religious controversies of Africa in the
fourth and fifth centuries which reminds us of the bloody disputes between
Episcopalian, Presbyterian and Independent at the time of our own 'Great
Rebellion'. Even the very names of men, not of one party only, have a Pur-
itan sound about them: 'What-God-wills', 'Thanks-to-God', 'Given-by-
God',* and so forth, recall the 'Praise-God Barebones' and his piously
named confederates of those stormy days. In Africa, over and above the
ordinary religious dissensions of the fourth and fifth centuries, there was a
special strife, the Donatist, which had arisen out of the cowardly conduct
of some bishops and presbyters during the persecution of the church by

* *Quod-vult-deus, Deo-gratias, A-deo-datus.*

Diocletian and his successors (303–13). A hundred and twenty years had elapsed since that time, and it might have been thought that purely personal questions, such as whether this bishop had under terror of death delivered up the sacred books to the Imperial officers, or whether that presbyter had with too great eagerness grasped the crown of martyrdom, might have been now allowed to slumber in oblivion. But sects and churches have long memories, and the Donatists, the Cameronians of Africa, were still as earnest in discussing the election of the so-called *traditor* * Caecilian to the see of Carthage, as if that event had happened yesterday instead of four generations ago. Round the Donatists, and in more or less close connection with them, were grouped the wild, fanatical Circumcelliones, savage boors, whose zeal, where it was not assumed as a cloak for rapine and lust, must have been hovering on the verge of insanity, who carried fire and sword through the villages of Africa, and whose war-cry, 'Praise be to God',† was heard in those villages with greater terror than the roar of the Numidian lion. The portrait of all these fanatics, being drawn only by their antagonists, must be received with much caution, but after making every conceivable allowance for exaggeration, we cannot avoid the conclu-sion that in this instance Christian common sense was represented by the party which successfully maintained its title to the envied designation, Catholic. But, Donatists and Catholics having both appealed to the state, and judgement having gone in favour of the latter, they, not unnaturally, according to the ideas of that age, but most unwisely according to our man-ner of thinking, brought down the iron hand of Imperial despotism with all its weight upon their foes.

It happens that the greater part of the laws against the Donatists‡ which are preserved to us belong to the reign of Honorius and the first twenty years of the fifth century, and we are thus able to see clearly mirrored in the Roman statute book the theological animosities and the petty persecutions which preceded the advent of the Vandals into Africa.§ The power of

* The name given to those who in time of persecution surrendered their Bibles to be burnt by the executioner.

† *Deo laudes*. The battle-shout of the Catholic party was *Deo gratias*.

‡ In many of the edicts the Donatists are coupled with the Manichaeans, who asserted the combined agency of two eternal principles, good and evil, in the creation. Thus one of the most special and technical of sectarian squabbles was coupled with the oldest, the strongest, and the most alluring form of unfaith.

§ See especially bk xvi of the Theodosian Code, v.37–54. By law no. 54 the scale of fines was fixed thus: a man who had filled one of the highest offices of state, proconsul,

buying, selling, and bequeathing property was denied to the Donatists, 'whom the patience of our clemency has preserved until now, but who ought to be branded with perpetual infamy, and shut out from all honourable assemblies, and from every place of public resort'. Their churches were to be taken from them and given to the Catholics. They were to pay fines, varying, according to their condition in life, from £25 to £8,000 sterling (those wild boors, the Circumcelliones, were to pay £25 a head); and these fines were to be repeated as often as the offender renewed his communion with the Donatist church. The slaves and the semi-servile agricultural labourers were 'to be prevented from audacious acts of this kind by the severest punishment'; 'to be recalled from their evil religion by more frequent blows' – if blows still proved ineffectual, to lose the third part of their accumulated savings. We have here, it is true, not a ruthless or bloodthirsty persecution, but we have a great deal of injustice of a very galling kind, perpetrated under the name of religion, just the kind of quiet, crushing, monotonous intolerance by which the Habsburgs extirpated the Protestantism of Styria and the English parliament strove to extirpate the papistry of Ireland. There can be no doubt that the Catholics had thus earned a rich legacy of hatred and revenge, which was punctually paid to them when the Vandals, heretics like the Donatists, entered Africa.*

We will now hear a little of what Victor Vitensis has to tell us of the Vandal persecutions in the reign of Gaiseric. His style is declamatory and he is full of prejudices, both national and ecclesiastical, but he is all but a contemporary – writing, as he does, 'in the sixtieth year after that cruel and savage nation reached the boundaries of our miserable Africa' – and he gives us that life and colour which we ask for in vain from the meagre and cautious annalists.

---

vicarius, or *comes*, 'if found in the Donatist flock', was to pay two hundred pounds weight of gold (about £8,000); a senator one hundred pounds weight (about £4,000); one who had held the pagan dignity of *sacerdos* [priest], the same sum; one of the leading ten men in a corporation (*decemprimi curiales*), fifty pounds of silver (about £133 sterling); a common-council-man (decurion), ten pounds of silver (a little more than £25 sterling). After one of the officials of higher rank had paid the fine five times, 'if he be not then by his losses recalled from the error of his ways, let him be referred to our clemency, that we may pass some more severe sentence concerning the capital which belongs to him, and concerning his rank in life'.

* We might naturally expect to find the Donatists, though orthodox, taking sides with the Arians against their Catholic persecutors: but [there is] some ground for believing that this was not the case either before or after the Vandal conquest.

'The wicked rage of the Vandals was especially directed against the churches and basilicas, the cemeteries and the monasteries, and they made bigger bonfires of the houses of prayer than of whole cities and towns. If by chance they found the door of the holy house fast closed, it was who should soonest force an entrance by thumping it down with his right hand; so that one might truly say, "They break down the carved work thereof at once with axes and hammers. They have cast fire into thy sanctuary; they have defiled by casting down the dwelling-place of thy name to the ground." Ah, how many illustrious bishops and noble priests were put to death by them with divers kinds of torments in the endeavour to compel them to reveal what treasures they had of gold or silver, belonging to themselves or to their churches. If, under the pressure of the torture, they easily revealed their possessions, the persecutors plied them with yet more cruel torments, declaring that part only had been surrendered, not the whole; and the more they gave up the more they were supposed to be keeping back. Some had their mouths forced open with stakes and crammed with noisome filth. Some were tortured by having strings tightly twisted round the forehead or leg-bone. Some had bladders filled with sea-water, with vinegar, with the dregs of the olive-presses, with the garbage of fishes, and other foul and cruel things laid upon their lips. The weakness of womanhood, the dignity of noble birth, the reverence due to the priesthood — none of these considerations softened those cruel hearts; nay, rather, where they saw that any were held in high honour, there was their mad rage more grievously felt. I cannot describe how many priests and illustrious functionaries had heavy loads piled upon them, as if they were camels or other beasts of burden, nor how with iron goads they urged them on their way, till some fell down under their burdens and miserably gave up the ghost. Hoary hairs enwrapping the venerable head like whitest wool won for the bearer no pity from those savage guests. Innocent little children were snatched by the barbarian from the maternal embrace and dashed to the ground. Well might our captive Zion sing, "The enemy said that he would burn my borders and slay my infants and dash my little ones to the earth." In some large and stately buildings [probably churches], where the ministry of fire had proved insufficient to destroy them, the barbarians showed their contempt of the edifice by levelling its fair walls with the ground; so that now those beautiful old cities have quite lost their former appearance, and many whole towns are now occupied by a scanty remnant of their former inhabitants, or even left altogether desolate.

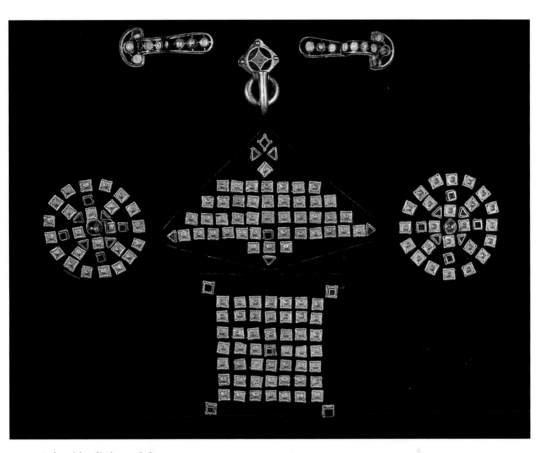

A buckle, *fibulae* and dress ornaments
from a Vandal woman's grave near
Carthage. *Right*, a silver bowl dec-
orated with pastoral scenes and
theatrical masks: one of the objects
from the Carthage treasure, which may
have belonged to a leading family of
Roman North Africa (the Cresconii)
and been hidden at the time of the
Visigothic capture of Carthage

Mosaics from North Africa. *Above*, a Vandal huntsman, dressed in Vandal departs from a fortified villa. *Below*, a villa and estate buildings

'Yea, and even today, if any buildings remain, they are continually laying them waste, as, for instance, the temple of Memory, that worthy
appendage to the theatre of Carthage, and the street called the street of
Heaven, both of which they have destroyed from top to bottom. Then too,
the large basilica, where the bones of the blessed martyrs Perpetua and
Felicitas are laid, the church of Celerina, and others which they have not
destroyed, they have, with the licence of tyrants, enslaved to their own religious rights. Did they see any strongholds which they were unable to carry
by the rush of their barbarian fury, they collected vast multitudes around
the walls and slew them with the bloody sword, leaving their carcasses to
putrefy under the ramparts, that they might slay with the stench those
whom their arms were powerless to assail.'*

This last sentence may serve as an example of the style in which the
indictment against the Vandals has been framed. It is evident that they
committed all the excesses which might be expected from a horde of triumphant barbarians, greedy beyond measure of gold, and utterly reckless
of human life, but it is also evident that the very blunders of their savage
warfare have been made to appear as parts of a diabolical machinery of
cruelty by the ecclesiastical pamphleteer.†

When we come to the details of the Vandal persecution of the
Catholics under Gaiseric (for we have no present concern with that which
happened in the next generation), we find further reason to suppose that
there has been some exaggeration in the passages already quoted. Two
bishops, Papinianus and Mansuetus, seem to have been burnt, but there
is something in the language of the historian here which leads us to conjecture that this was the work of cruel pillagers rather than a solemn state-
sanctioned martyrdom.‡ The bishop of Carthage, 'What-God-wills',§
and a great multitude of his clergy, were put on board unsound ships and
sent out to sea, but they were favoured with a prosperous wind, and arrived
in Campania, safe in body, though stripped of all their possessions. The
churches of Carthage were claimed for the Arian worship, among them
two stately and noble edifices outside the walls, which commemorated
respectively the martyrdom and burial of St Cyprian.¶ 'But who', says the

* Victor Vitensis, i.1–3.
† Gibbon sensibly remarks, '[I cannot] believe that it was a usual stratagem to slaughter
great numbers of their prisoners before the walls of a besieged city, for the sole purpose of
infecting the air and producing a pestilence, of which they themselves must have been the
first victims' (chap. xxxiii).   ‡ Victor Vitensis, i.5.   § *Quod-vult-deus.*
¶ The latter church was called Mappalia, 'the Huts', showing the humble origin from

good Victor, 'can bear to remember without tears that Gaiseric ordered us to bear the bodies of our dead, without the solemnity of hymns, in silence to the grave?' When this silent-burial grievance of the African Catholics assumes so prominent a place in the catalogue of their woes, we may perhaps conclude that the religious persecution, considered apart from the mere rapine of the barbarians, was not extremely severe.

A deputation of bishops and leading men of the provinces which the Vandals had divided among themselves, waited upon the king, when he had gone down, as his custom was, to the coast of Numidia, perhaps to inhale such freshness as might be found in the sea breezes. They pleaded with him to restore to the orthodox some places in which they might worship God. 'What? Are you here still?' he bade his interpreter say to the bishops. 'I decreed the banishment of your whole name and race: and yet you dare to ask for such things.' And so great was his anger that he would fain have drowned them all at once in the Mediterranean at his feet, had not his counsellors after long entreaty persuaded him to abandon his purpose. They departed and continued their service of God in such lowly dwellings as they could obtain, not unlike probably to those in which Paul had discoursed till break of day, and the elders of Ephesus had fed the flock of God. For some years, we infer from the language of the historian, this unobtrusive worship of the Catholics was permitted, if not expressly sanctioned. Then came denunciations and calumnies, especially against those priests who officiated 'in the regions which paid tribute to the palace'. If one of these, in his sermons to his flock, happened to mention the name of Pharaoh, or Nebuchadnezzar, or Holofernes, or any similar tyrant – and we may conjecture that these references were rather more frequent than were absolutely needful to explain the lessons for the day – he was accused of speaking against the person of the king, and banishment was his immediate sentence. For this cause a whole batch of bishops (among whom we find 'He-has-God',* bishop of Teudala) was banished at once, and the Holofernes of their denunciation would not allow the consecration of any successors to their sees.† At length, on the urgent entreaty of Valentinian, he permitted the orthodox church of Carthage to ordain for itself a bishop,

---

whence it had sprung. It is interesting to meet again this word *mappalia*, which Sallust mentions as the name of the long, hull-shaped dwellings of the Numidian rustics in the time of Jugurtha.

* *Habet-deum.*

† Victor Vitensis, i.7.

the gentle and charitable 'Thanks-to-God',* who for three years (454—7) governed the metropolitan see with general approval.† On his death there was another long interval of widowhood for the churches, till at last, about the year 475, towards the very end of the reign of Gaiseric, on the interces-sion of Zeno, emperor of the East, the surviving bishops were permitted to return from the widely scattered seats of their long banishment.

Besides the exile, and in some cases the enslavement of the bishops, other oppressions were practised upon the orthodox. The demand made in the time of Diocletian for the surrender of sacred books and vessels was repeated. The officer of the barbarians, a man with the Roman name of Proculus, who was sent to enforce this demand, finding his authority resisted, laid violent hands on all the treasures of the sacristies that he could find, and adding contumely to rapine, caused the beautiful altar-cloths which were already used in the churches to be cut up into shirts and drawers for his followers.‡ The sacrilege was remembered, and was deemed to have been divinely punished when, not long after, Proculus died of cancer in the tongue. In a town called Regia a battle took place between Catholics and Arians for the possession of the church,§ which reminds us of the last fatal fray in St Mark's chapel at Florence at the time of the downfall of Savonarola. It was Easter-time: the Catholics were celebrating the festival, and the Arians finding the doors of the church closed against them, under the guidance of a presbyter named Andiot,¶ got together a band of armed men and proceeded to hammer at the doors, to mount the roofs of the neigh-bouring houses, to shoot their arrows through the windows of the church. The people within the church loudly chanted the defiant alleluia; especially one lector, who was sitting in the pulpit, made his voice heard above the tumult. An arrow which was shot through the window transfixed his throat, still quivering with the holy hymn; the roll from which he was singing dropped at his feet, and the lector fell down dead. In rushed the assailant Arians and slew around the altar nearly all the survivors from the previous fight, the older men being especially selected as victims of their wrath.

We have seen how it fared with churches and churchmen at the hands of the Vandals; let us now see how individual laymen were dealt with. Sebastian, the before-mentioned son-in-law of Bonifacius, a keen-witted counsellor and brave warrior, had shared the ill-fortune of his kinsman, and after the fatal conflict between him and Aetius, had been driven forth from

* *Deo-gratias.*   † Victor Vitensis, i.8.   ‡ Victor Vitensis, i.12.
§ Victor Vitensis, i.13.   ¶ Or Adduit. Is this a Teutonic name?

Ravenna and wandered over the face of the earth. First Constantinople and then the Visigothic court had been his asylum, and he had won Barcelona from the Empire for Theodoric. At last in 440* he quarrelled with the Visi-goths also and sought refuge in Africa. Gaiseric, who had feared him as a foe, welcomed him as a suppliant, and would gladly have promoted him to great honour. But he was a Catholic, and for that reason formidable to the Arian king who could not reckon upon him with certainty while he belonged to the rival church. One day, in the presence of his courtiers and Arian bishops, Gaiseric said to Sebastian, 'I know that your faith is firmly pledged to me and mine, but it would make our friendship more lasting, if here, in the presence of these holy men, you would profess yourself a fol-lower of the same religion which is dear to me and to my people.' Sebastian answered, 'I beseech you, O king, order that a loaf of the finest and whitest flour be now brought hither.' The king, wondering what could be his meaning, gave the order: the bread was brought, and Sebastian said, 'O king! to prepare this white bread and make it fit for the royal table, the wheat had to be separated from the chaff, the flour to be carefully bolted from the bran, the millstone, water, and fire had each to do their work upon it before it attained this spotless purity. Even so have I been from my youth up separ-ated from all heretical contagion, the church has made me hers by the water of baptism, and the fire of the Holy Spirit has purified me. Now if by crum-bling up this bread into little pieces and baking it afresh you can increase its whiteness, then I will take up with another faith and become an Arian as you desire me. But if not I remain a Catholic.' The king saw that he had the worst of the argument for that time, 'but afterwards he tried a different sort of logic and put that brave man to death'.†

The same command 'to pass over to the sect of the Arians' was given to four men of Spanish birth, Arcadius, Probus, Paschasius, and Eutychius, who had served Gaiseric with fidelity and stood high among his counsel-lors. Their persistent refusal was punished by exile, tortures, and eventually by martyrdom. A young lad named Paulillus, brother of Paschasius and Eutychius, whose beauty and talents had gained him a high place in the royal household, was for the same reason cruelly flogged and then sent into vile bondage. The crown of martyrdom was not awarded him, that the king might be spared the disgrace of being vanquished by a boy of such tender years.‡

* Prosper gives this date: Idatius 445.   † Victor Vitensis, i.6.
‡ Prosper, *Chronicon*, for the year 437.

Eventually the order was given that none but Arians should be tolerated about the court and person of the king. A certain Armogast, who must have been a Teuton by his name, and who seems to have been a count by office, refused to conform to the courtly religion. The persecutors tried to change his resolution with the rack and the cord, but the cords, we are assured, broke like spider's webs when the saint looked towards heaven. They hung him head downward by one foot from the ceiling, and he slept as sweetly as if he had been on a feather bed. His master, Theodoric, the king's son, wished to slay him out of hand, but was wisely warned by his Arian chaplain, 'If you kill him with the sword, the Romans will preach him up as a martyr.' The former count was therefore sent into the fields to dig ditches and to keep sheep. There he soon died, but not before he had disclosed to a faithful disciple the approaching day of his death, and the place destined for his burial, a place apparently obscure and sordid, but where the obedient disciple, when he came to dig, found a sarcophagus of the most splendid marble prepared for the reception of the saint's body.*

An example of firm adherence to the faith was found where it would scarcely have been looked for, among the comic actors who performed before the new barbaric court. A certain 'arch-mime', named Masculanus, had been long pressed by the king, with flatteries and promises, to join the religion of the dominant caste. As he ever stood firm, Gaiseric gave public orders for his execution, but, with his usual hard craftiness, being deter-mined not to present the Catholic church with a single martyr more for her veneration, he gave the following secret commands to the executioner. 'If he flinches at the sight of the sword and denies his faith then kill him all the more, for then he cannot be considered a martyr. But if he remains firm, sheathe your sword again and let him go free.' Perhaps the acting of the exe-cutioner, perplexed by such intricate orders, failed to deceive the practised eye of the arch-comedian. At any rate he stood 'firm as a pillar on the solid rock of Christ', and saved both life and truth. 'And thus', says the his-torian, 'if that envious enemy refused to allow us a martyr, he could not prevent our having a confessor,† and a glorious one.'‡

In a similar manner a certain Saturus, steward over the house of Huneric, the king's son, who had made himself conspicuous in many discussions

* Victor Vitensis, i.14.
† A Christian who lived in the Imperial persecutions and remained true to his faith, but from any cause escaped the extreme penalty of death, was generally called a confessor.
‡ Victor Vitensis, i.15.

with the Arians, was ordered to change his religion. Riches and honours were promised him in the event of his compliance; tortures for himself, poverty for his children, another and apparently a hated husband for his wife, were to be the punishments of his refusal. That wife joined her entreaties to those of the persecutors, begging him not to subject her to the yoke of a base and unworthy husband, 'while the husband Saturus, of whom I have so often boasted, still lives'. 'Thou speakest as one of the foolish women speaketh,' replied the African Job. 'If thou truly lovedst thy husband, thou wouldst not seek to entice him to his second death. I am ready to give up wife and children, and house, and lands, and slaves,* that I may continue to be a disciple of Christ.' The cruel and unjust sentence was executed. 'Saturus was spoiled of all his substance, was worn down with punishment, was sent away into beggary. His wife was given to a camel-driver. He was forbidden to return to the court; they took everything from him, but they could not take away the white robe of his baptism.'†

The reader has now before him the chief evidence against the Vandals as religious persecutors during the first generation after their conquest of Africa. He may reasonably ask why there should be set before him, with so much detail, facts which have no direct bearing on the history of Italy. The answer is that our information as to the social aspects of the struggle between Romans and barbarians in Italy itself during the fifth century is so miserably meagre, we might almost say so absolutely non-existent, that we must be content to supply the deficiency to the best of our power from what we know of the mutual relations of conquerors and conquered, of Arians and orthodox, in other provinces of the Empire, especially in Africa and Gaul. And this peculiar attitude of the Teutonic nations towards their Catholic subjects in the dawn of the Middle Ages, tending as it did to sever for a time the connection of the orthodox clergy with the state, and to throw them back into somewhat of their old position as men of the people, and sympathisers with the people, is so important with reference to the subsequent growth and development of the spiritual power, that it cannot be said we are wasting time in considering it a little more closely.

Reviewing then the indictment which has been framed by Victor Vitensis against the persecutor Gaiseric, we come to the following conclusions:

(1) It is clear that the churches were as a rule either handed over to the

---

* This clause in the sentence pronounced on Saturus is important, as showing that the provincials who were attached in a servile capacity to the royal household had slaves of their own.   † Victor Vitensis, i.16.

Arians for their worship, or else destroyed. And it is this wanton demolition and desecration of ecclesiastical buildings which more than anything
else has caused the name of vandalism to be synonymous in later days with
senseless destructiveness.

(2) The bishops were for the most part banished, and their flocks were
forbidden to elect successors to them. The Vandal king, himself surrounded
by Arian bishops, knew, better probably than Decius or Diocletian, how
sore a blow, according to the prevailing theories of ecclesiastical organisation, he was thus dealing at the very existence of the church. But under the
influence of occasional solicitations from Rome and from Byzantium, he
wavered more than once in the execution of this stern policy; and even had
he been always constant to it, one cannot easily see how the mere mandate of
the king could have permanently and universally prevented the consecration
of at least some bishops, and the transmission of the episcopal prerogatives,
throughout the whole province of Africa.

(3) Individual Catholics were not as a rule persecuted on account of
their faith. Occasionally the headstrong arrogance of the king or his sons
was roused into fury by the discovery that the officers of their household, or
the menials who ministered to their amusement, would not yield servile
obedience to their nod in all things, but claimed a right in matters apper-
taining to God to act according to the dictates of their own consciences.
But even in these cases, from mere motives of expediency, Gaiseric was
intensely anxious to avoid making new martyrs for the Catholic church.
And as to the great mass of the people, the downtrodden slaves who tilled
the vast domain lands of the crown, or the hungry *coloni* [serfs] who eked
out a scanty subsistence on the edge of the desert, or even the traders and
artisans of Hippo and of Carthage, Gaiseric was too much of a statesman
to attempt to convert them wholesale, by persecution, to Arianism, and
probably too little of a theologian to care greatly whether truth, or what he
deemed to be error, was being supplied as food to the souls of all that base-
born crew. In the heart of the Teuton invader there perhaps lurked the
thought that the confession of Nicaea was good enough for slaves, and that
it was well for the freeborn warrior of the North to keep his own bolder
speculations to himself. The willingness to persecute was clearly in the
hearts of these Vandals. They did not in the slightest degree recognise the
right of the individual conscience to decide for itself how best to express its
loyalty to the Great Maker. But they had some dim perception what it was
worthwhile for the ruler to attempt, and what he had better leave to itself.

And, above all, their action in the church, as in the state, was rude, fitful and ill-sustained. The quiet, grinding oppression which the Roman Caesars practised upon the Donatist and the Arian, bore to the spasmodic outbreaks of Vandal bigotry the same relation which the pressure of a hydraulic ram bears to the random strokes of a child's hammer.*

Such then was the state of the Vandal kingdom, when, in the year 455, twenty-seven years after the passage of the barbarians into Africa, and sixteen after their conquest of Carthage, the cry of the widowed Eudoxia for help reached the court of Gaiseric.† Little stimulus did the great buccaneer need to urge him to the spoil of the capital of the world. It was clear that 'the city with which God was angry' this time was Rome, and the pilot had not to ask his master twice for sailing orders. It was in the early days of June when the sentinels at Ostia saw the Vandal fleet in the offing. The helpless consternation which prevailed at Rome has been already described — no attempt to man the walls, not even courage enough to parley with the enemy, only a blind universal *sauve qui peut* which the emperor himself would fain have joined in, had he not been arrested by the indignant people, and torn limb from limb by the Imperial domestics, a sacrifice to the *manes* [shade] of Valentinian.

On the third day‡ after the death of Maximus, Gaiseric, with his yellow-haired Vandal giants, appeared before the gates of the defenceless city. Utterly defenceless, as far as the weapons of the flesh were concerned; but the majestic bishop Leo, followed probably by a train of venerable ecclesiastics, met him outside the gates of the city, eager to discover whether the same spiritual weapons which he had wielded so well three years before against the mighty Hun by the banks of the Mincio would avail now by the banks of the Tiber against the yet more dreaded Vandal. The pope's success was not complete, yet it was something. Gaiseric's sole object was booty, not power now, nor revenge, only that simple and intelligible motive which led Pizarro and his adventurers to the capital of the Incas, and which made their eyes gleam when they gazed upon Atahualpa's room of gold. This being Gaiseric's one desire, he could well afford to concede to

---

* It is to be remarked, however, that Huneric, son of Gaiseric, copied exactly the Imperial decrees against heresy, and launched them against the Catholics. But his reign was short, and on his death the persecution was much relaxed.   † See p. 123.

‡ So says Victor Tunnunensis, not our best authority. This would be the 15th of June, according to Anonymus Cuspiniani, 3rd of June according to Prosper, 25th of May according to *Incerti Chronicon*.

the pope that there should be no putting to death, no burning of public or private buildings, and he also granted, what it must have been harder for a Vandal to yield, that no torture should be applied to compel a discovery of hidden treasure. Having framed this secular concordat with the occupant of the chair of St Peter, the Vandal king passed in, and rode slowly through the unresisting city. For fourteen days — that interval at least was distinctly fixed on the memories of the Romans, and every chronicler reports it as the same, whatever their variations on other points — for fourteen days the city was subjected to 'a leisurely and unhindered' examination and extraction of its wealth.* The gold, the silver, and the copper were carried away from the Imperial palace, and stored with businesslike thoroughness in the Vandal galleys. The churches were probably despoiled of their ornaments and plate. The temple of Jupiter Capitolinus was pillaged, and half of its roof was stripped off, 'which was made of the finest copper, with a thick coating of gold over it, magnificent and wonderful'. Why only half should have been taken we know not; such moderation is surprising and almost painful to behold. Possibly the barbarians commenced the laborious process in the belief that they were stripping off solid gold, and desisted from it when they found that their reward would be only copper gilt. Statues too, good store of them, were carried off and loaded upon one of Gaiseric's vessels. Most unhappily, this one ship, out of all the fleet, foundered on the return voyage. The marble limbs of many a nymph and faun, of many a dweller on Olympus, and many a deified dweller on the Palatine, must have been lying for these fourteen centuries, fathoms deep in the Sicilian or Carthaginian waters. If the engineers of the electric cable in spinning their marvellous web from continent to continent should come across the sunken cargo of that Vandal trireme, may it be in our own day, and may we see that harvest from the deep!

But on the whole it is clear from the accounts of all the chroniclers that Gaiseric's pillage of Rome, though insulting and impoverishing to the last degree, was in no sense destructive to the queen of cities. Whatever he may have done in Africa, in Rome he waged no war on architecture, being far too well employed in storing away gold and silver and precious stones, and all manner of costly merchandise in those insatiable hulks which were riding at anchor in the Tiber. Therefore, when you stand in the forum of Rome or look upon the grass-grown hill which was once the glorious Palatine, blame if you like the Ostrogoth, the Byzantine, the Lombard, blame

* Prosper, *Chronicon*, for the year 455.

above all, the Norman, and the Roman baron of the Middle Ages, for the heartbreaking ruin that you see there, but leave the Vandal uncensured, for, notwithstanding the stigma conveyed in the word 'vandalism', he is not guilty here.*

Among the spoils which were carried in safety from Rome to Carthage were, we are told, the sacred vessels of the Jewish Temple with the sculp-tured effigies of which, on the arch of Titus, we are all familiar. No contemporary historian refers to them, and we might have been disposed to reject the story of their capture as a romance of later writers, but that in the next century we find Procopius, the friend and companion of Belisarius, distinctly asserting that on the fall of the Vandal monarchy, these vessels with countless other treasures, golden saddles, golden carriages for the ladies of the court, hundreds of thousands of talents of silver, and all kinds of ornaments inlaid with precious stones, were found in the palace of Gelimer, great-grandson of Gaiseric. All the rest of the glittering spoil was taken to Byzantium (in 534), and having given lustre to the triumph of Belisarius, was there retained; but the vessels which had been consecrated to the service of Jehovah were carried back to Jerusalem, and placed in the Christian churches there, a Jew, who saw them among the spoil, having pointed out to a friend of the emperor's that their presence (like that of the Ark in the towns of the Philistines) had brought capture and desolation first on Rome and then on Rome's Vandal conquerors.

But the fortunes of the sacred vessels of the Jewish worship have carried us eighty years away from our present moorings. We return to Gaiseric and his treasure-laden fleet. He took back with him to Carthage Eudoxia, the widow of two emperors and the daughter of a third. It was probably a greater kindness to take her as a captive to Carthage than to leave her face to face with the exasperated people of Rome, upon whom her blind desire for revenge on Maximus had brought so much misery. In the captive train also were her two daughters, Eudocia and Placidia, and (strange companion of their adversity) the son of Aetius, Gaudentius, who had once aspired to the hand of one of them. But the match upon which Aetius had set his heart so earnestly was not to be brought about by their common captivity. Gais-eric gave the elder princess, Eudocia, in marriage to his son Huneric, being the second princess of the house of Theodosius who was wedded to a Teu-

---

* Evagrius, the ecclesiastical historian, accuses Gaiseric of setting fire to the city, but he lived more than a hundred years after the capture, and his testimony may be disregarded, the contemporary authorities so clearly speaking of pillage, not fire.

tonic prince. One would like to believe that the young Vandal, while a hostage in Rome, had won the heart of the daughter of the emperor; but as he must certainly have returned before the surprise of Carthage (439) this cannot be. His future wife was but a babe in arms when he was loitering in the palace of her father. The other princess, Placidia, with her mother, after seven years' detention at Carthage, where they were treated with all honour and courtesy, was sent (in 462) to Constantinople, on the earnest entreaty of the emperor Leo. She married the Roman senator Olybrius, whose name we shall meet with among the last emperors of Rome.

Besides the empress and her daughters, the Vandal host carried a great multitude of Roman citizens back with them into captivity. It was like one of the great transportations of unwilling multitudes which we read of in the Jewish Scriptures as practised by a Shalmaneser or a Nebuchadnezzar. The skilful craftsman, the strong labourer, the young and handsome cup-bearer, the experienced house-steward, were all swept away, all ruthlessly sundered from one another, husbands from wives, and parents from chil-dren, and distributed as bondslaves through Morocco, Algiers and Tunis.* It is a strange thought, how many drops of pure Roman blood may now be flowing through the veins of the half-civilised inhabitants of northern Africa. A Kabyle robber from Mount Atlas, with cotton burnous, such as I remember to have seen in captivity on the Ile Saint-Honorat, near Cannes, spreading his carpet, turning his face towards the setting sun, and jabbering out his long and rapid prayer from the Koran, may be a truer descendant of the Fabii and the Camilli than any living inhabitant of the Eternal City.

The sufferings of the unhappy captives from Rome were to some extent, but it could only be to a small extent, alleviated by the charity of the saintly bishop of Carthage, Deogratias. He sold all the gold and silver vessels of his church in order to ransom such captives as he could, and as much as pos-sible to prevent the disruption of the family ties of those whom he could not ransom. There were no proper warehouses for receiving all this vast human livestock which the freebooters had brought back with them. He placed two large basilicas at their disposal; he fitted them up with beds and straw; he even took upon himself the heavy charge of the daily commissariat. Sea-sickness, pining for home, the sad and awful change from the luxury of the Roman villa to the miseries of a Vandal slave-ship, had prostrated many of

* 'They took many thousands of captives, according as each by their age or their skill pleased them,' are the words of Prosper.

the captives with disease. He turned his church into an infirmary: notwith-standing his advanced age and his tottering limbs, day and night he went the round of the beds of his patients, following the doctors like a careful nurse, making himself acquainted with the state of each, seeing that each received the food and medicine which was suited to his condition. Often, while he was thus moving through the wards of his basilica-hospital, intent on his work of mercy, must the words *Deo gratias* have risen to the feeble lips of the sufferers, who, perhaps, scarcely knew themselves whether they were expressing gratitude to heaven or to heaven's fitly named representative on earth. Before his charitable work was complete, his life, which had been threatened more than once by the violence of the Arian party, who were jealous even of his goodness, came to a peaceful close; and when they heard that he was taken from them, the captive citizens of Rome felt as if they were a second time delivered into the hands of the barbarians. He was buried secretly in an unusual place, to guard his body from the pious irreverence of relic-hunters, who would have dismembered the venerable corpse in their eagerness to obtain wonder-working memorials of so great a saint.

And so we leave the many thousands of Roman captives to the unrecorded sorrows of their house of bondage.

CHAPTER VII

The Letters and Poems of Apollinaris Sidonius

EIGHT EMPERORS, AND A SPACE OF TWENTY-ONE years, separate the capture of Rome by Gaiseric (455) from the familiar date of the fall of the Empire of the West (476). Is it worthwhile to do more than enumerate the mere names of these shadowy emperors, of whom only one, Majorian, has anything of the dignity of manhood, and who might all, with that one exception, share the title of the last of them, Augustulus, 'the little emperor'? Is not Avitus as Severus, and Glycerius as Nepos? May we not take for granted all this history of monotonous feeble-ness, these sham elections and involuntary abdications, this burlesque of the awful tragedy of the earlier Caesars, and planting ourselves at once in the year 476, learn amid what accompaniments the twelve centuries of Roman dominion expired?

Such is naturally one's first thought, but it may well be modified on further reflection. If physiologists have found the study of the humblest forms of life useful, as illustrating the connection between the animal and vegetable worlds, and if some of them have descended into the lowest zones of organic existence in the hope of bringing up from thence some further light on the great problem of life itself, it may well be, in like man-ner, that from the study of these, the lowest types of an emperor which Rome has to set before us, we may learn something as to that inextin-guishable idea of the Caesar which not all the storms of the Middle Ages were able utterly to destroy. We shall observe how, even in his deepest degradation, there was something which marked off the Roman *imperator* from the barbarian king. Above all, we shall see how reluctantly even the world of the Northern invaders parted from the idea of Caesarian rule; how willingly they would have kept the pageant Augustus in his place, if he had been simply able to sit upright in his world-too-wide throne; how, notwithstanding all the rude blows of Goth, and Hun, and Vandal, the Roman Empire rather died of internal decline than was slain by the sword of an enemy.

Unfortunately the materials out of which we have to reconstruct the history of this quarter of a century are singularly meagre and unsatisfactory. Had the genius of a Tacitus, or even the clear, calm intellect of a Sallust, thrown its light over this troublous time, much more had it been possible for a de Tocqueville to have analysed the causes, and a Carlyle to have painted the scenes of this revolution, we might have learned from it many a lesson, useful even in our own day to those who labour to preserve an aged empire from falling. But what can we do when the only really trustworthy authorities for the events of the time are the annalists, that is to say, some six or seven men, who having the whole history of the world from Belus and Nimrod downwards to relate, can spare only a line or two, at the outside a paragraph of moderate length, for the occurrences of the most eventful years in their own lives. The history of modern Europe, if told by annalists of this type, would run into some such mould as this—

'AD 1851. The queen reigning in England and Louis Bonaparte being president of the French republic, there was opened in a certain park near to London, a great market-place for all the wares of the world. That was the palace of crystal. The Queen of England gave birth to a son, who was named Arthur. Bishops, in obedience to the see of the holy Peter, had been sent to England. Whom the adherents of the other church, which is called the Protestant church, being unwilling to receive, passed a law forbidding any man to say "God speed" unto them, or to salute them by the names of their dioceses. That was called the ecclesiastical titles act. In Paris, the president of the republic bade many persons to be shot.

'AD 1852. The republic of France was changed into an empire, Louis Bonaparte being declared emperor. He was nephew of the emperor Napoleon.

'AD 1853. The emperor of Russia sent a proud man, named Menschikoff, as an ambassador, to the sultan of the Ottomans. There was much dissension between the emperors of Russia and France touching a certain silver star in the sanctuary at Bethlehem.

'AD 1854. It was fought most bloodily between the nation of the Russians on the one side, and those of France, England, and Turkey on the other, in the peninsula which is called the Chersonesus Taurica.

'AD 1855. After much slaughter the august city (Sebastopolis) in the

Chersonesus Taurica was taken by the armies of France and England, whom the island of Sardinia had also joined.

'AD 1856. Peace was made in Paris between the nations which were at war. That was called the peace of Paris. The treaty was signed by all the ambassadors, using a feather which had been plucked from the wings of a certain eagle. Now the eagle is the emblem of power in France and in Russia, but not in England, for in England the lion is the national emblem. That feather had a silver handle fastened to it, beautiful and costly, and it was given to the wife of the emperor Napoleon. She was a very beautiful woman, and was named Eugenia.'

No one who has read the chronicles of Idatius, of Prosper, and of Marcellinus will consider this an unfair specimen of their mode of writing annals. After all, the most important events are there, and we are grateful to the patient scribes who have preserved even so much for us from the sea of oblivion which was rising high around them, but from such scanty chronicles as these it is impossible to deduce with certainty the true proportions of those events or their exact relation to one another. We can excuse the brevity of the annalists, but it is much harder to excuse their occasional prolixity. When we find one of the best of them (Marcellinus) devoting only four lines to the capture of Rome by Alaric, and fifty-four to an idle legend about the discovery at Emesa of the head of John the Baptist, it is difficult not to grumble at the want of appreciation of the relative importance of things which must have existed in the mind of the writer, though he was no monkish recluse but a layman and a governor of a province.

It is perhaps not surprising that in Italy itself there should have been this utter absence of the instinct which leads men to record the events which are going on around them for the benefit of posterity. When history was making itself at such breathless speed and in such terrible fashion, the leisure, the inclination, the presence of mind, necessary for writing history, might well be wanting. He who would under happier auspices have filled up the interval between the bath and the tennis-court by reclining on the couch in the winter portico of his villa, and there languidly dictating to his slave the true story of the abdication of Avitus or the death of Anthemius, was himself now a slave keeping sheep in the wilderness under the hot Numidian sun, or shrinking under the blows of one of the rough soldiers of Gaiseric.

We find it much more difficult to understand why the learned and leisurely provincials of Greece, whose country for more than a century

(396–517) escaped the horrors of hostile invasion,* and who had the grandest literary traditions in the world to inspire them, should have left the story of the downfall of Rome unwritten. But so it was. Zosimus, seeing and foreseeing the inevitable decay, commenced the lamentable history, but none of his compatriots (if we except the slight references of Procopius) seems to have had the spirit or the inclination to finish it.

The fact seems to be that at this time all that was left of literary instinct and historiographic power in the world had concentrated itself on theo-logical, we cannot call it religious, controversy. And what tons of worth-less material the ecclesiastical historians and controversialists of the time have left us! Blind, most of them,† to the meaning of the mighty drama which was being enacted on the stage of the world, without faith enough in a living God to believe that he could evolve a fairer and better order out of all the chaos round them, anticipating perhaps, the best among them, the speedy return of Christ and the end of the world, they have left us scarcely a hint as to the inner history of the vast revolution which settled the Teuton in the lands of the Latin; while they force upon us details, endless and wearisome, as to the squabbles of self-seeking monks and prelates over the decrees of the council of Chalcedon. They describe to us how with stealthy step Timothy the weasel crept into the patriarchate of Alexandria; his brawls, his banishments, and his death. They are anxious to inform us that Peter the stammerer succeeded Timothy the weasel in the Egyptian see, and that Peter the fuller, his contemporary at Antioch, obtained his episco-pate by bloodshed, and signalised it by adding four words to a hymn.‡ Who really cares now for the vulgar bickerings which the ecclesiastical his-torians relate to us with such exasperating minuteness? The weasels, the fullers, and the stammerers, are all deep in mummy-dust. To the non-Christian the subject of their controversies is imaginary; to the Christian the pretensions of these men of violence and blood to settle anything con-cerning the nature of the spotless Son of Man are a blasphemy.

To sum up then; from the annalists we get some grains of fine gold, from the literati of Greece we get nothing, from the ecclesiastical historians we get chiefly rubbish, concerning the history of these eventful years. One man alone, he whose name stands at the head of this chapter, gives us that more detailed information concerning the thoughts, characters, persons of the

---

* Except insofar as the plundering raids of Gaiseric might be termed invasions.
† I except from this condemnation Salvian, the author of the treatise *De Gubernatione Dei*.
‡ He added 'Who wast crucified for us' to the 'Holy! Holy! Holy!'

The pleasures of country life: the lord and mistress of a fortified villa are brought gifts and seasonal produce from their estate

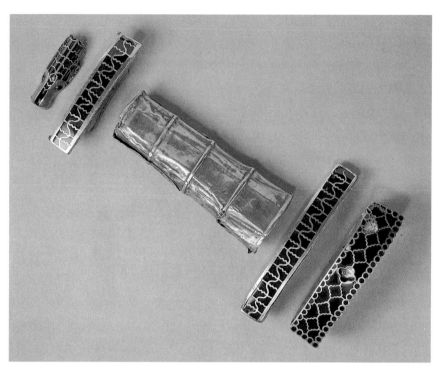

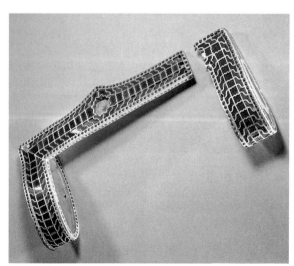

Objects from the grave of the Burgundian king Chilperic at Tournai, Belgium. *Above*, sword fittings. *Left*, scabbard fittings. *Right*, bee-shaped *fibulae*

actors in the great drama which can make the dry bones of the chronologers live. This is Caius Sollius Apollinaris Sidonius, man of letters, Imperial functionary, country gentleman and bishop, who, notwithstanding much manifest weakness of character, and a sort of epigrammatic dullness of style, is still the most interesting literary figure of the fifth century.

Sidonius was born at Lyons about the year 430. His father, grandfather, and great-grandfather had each held the high office of praetorian prefect in Gaul. Upon the whole they had been faithful to the line of Theodosius, though one of them, the grandfather, had derived his office from the usurp-er Constantine. Such high honours, enjoyed for three generations without any serious reverses, would alone have carried the family of Apollinaris high among the noble houses of Gaul at a time when the hierarchy of office, reaching from the emperor to the notary, was incomparably the most important factor in the social system of the provinces. But besides this official position, the wealth, the culture, and the respectable, if not heroic, character of most of the near ancestors of Sidonius placed him at the outset of life on a vantage-ground, from which, whatever he had of literary ability could soon make itself recognised. A man thus situated, born near the centre of the national affairs, and surrounded from his cradle with influen-tial and hereditary friends, knows nothing of that difficulty of 'emerging' which is so forcibly described in the well-known lines of a Roman poet.*

Sidonius received at Lyons as good an education probably as a young Roman noble of the fifth century could have met with anywhere in the Empire. It was an education however in words rather than things. Men had ceased to believe in the Olympian gods; so the schoolmasters taught their scholars the name of every nymph and every muse. All earnest thought about the nature of the world and the mind of man ran in Christian chan-nels; so they taught elaborately the speculations of every Greek philosopher from Thales to Chrysippus. The sword of the barbarian was carrying everything before it in the world of politics; so they went on teaching all the arts of rhetoric by which brilliant orators had won honour for themselves or exile for their adversaries from the sovereign multitude in the cities of free Greece. But though it is easy for us to see how little the teaching of these schools can have done in helping the student to face any of the real

* *Haud facile emergunt quorum virtutibus obstat*
Res angusta domi
[Those whose virtues are obstructed by their humble family do not rise up easily] (Juv-enal, iii.164–5).

difficulties of his after-life, we must, on the other hand, do justice to the vast amount of intellectual activity which still remained in the Empire and which this teaching both denoted and fostered. Sometimes we think of the hundred years between Theodosius and Theodoric as wholly filled with rapine and bloodshed. Sometimes we carry back into the fifth century the thick darkness which hung over the intellectual life of Merovingian France or Lombard Italy. In both these estimates we are mistaken. A careful perusal of the three volumes of the letters and poems of Sidonius reveals to us the fact that in Gaul at any rate the air still teemed with intellectual life, that authors were still writing, amanuenses transcribing, friends complimenting or criticising, and all the cares and pleasures of literature filling the minds of large classes of men just as though no empires were sinking and no strange nationalities were suddenly rising around them. We need not believe, upon the authority of the highly wrought panegyrics of Sidonius, that he had a score of friends all more eloquent than Cicero, more subtle than Plato, and diviner poets than Homer or Virgil; but the interesting fact for us is that such forgotten philosophers and poets did exist in that age, and that their works, produced in lavish abundance, seem to have had no lack of eager students.

The impulse towards rhetoric, which was conspicuous in every part of the career of Sidonius, may very likely have been communicated by an oratorical display which he witnessed, in early adolescence, at Arles the Roman capital of Gaul. There, at the commencement of the year 449, the general Asturius was to assume the office of consul. A crowd of Roman dignitaries assembled to witness the ceremony. In the centre, on a curule chair, sat Apollinaris, praetorian prefect of Gaul, and by his side stood his son, the young Sidonius. As one after another of the great persons of the state, *consulares, praesides*, masters of horse, and masters of foot, tribunes, bishops, notaries, advanced to kiss the purple robe of the representative of the emperor, each one doubtless spared a less formal salutation for the bright, highly cultured lad who was watching the scene with eager interest, and with a mind keenly conscious, as it ever was, of the great difference between those who have rank and position and those who have them not. The new consul was proclaimed, the slave, who was always forthcoming on these occasions, received the buffet from his hand which bestowed freedom,*

* This curious custom, which seems to have been peculiar to the last ages of the Empire, is mentioned by Claudian (*De Quarto Consulatu Honorii*, 615, and *In Eutropium*, i.310), also by Sidonius himself (*Panegyric of Anthemius*, 545).

the largesse and the ivory tablets, upon which the names of the two new magistrates had been inscribed, were distributed to the people. Then stood forth Flavius Nicetius, and in brilliant, well-chosen words, pronounced the customary panegyric on the virtues and capacities of Consul Asturius. The pompous periods, the applause which followed, the compliments paid and received by the smooth-tongued orator, produced a profound impression on the boyish imagination of Sidonius, and we may perhaps conjecture that he secretly resolved that he too would one day be a prefect like his father, an orator like Nicetius, and a consul like Asturius. The first two of his aspirations were realised, 'The rest the gods dispersed in empty air.'

Sidonius was probably about twenty-one years of age when the blast of Attila's invasion swept over Belgic Gaul. Sheltered behind the walls of Lyons he felt, in all likelihood, not even the outskirts of the storm. But he may have conversed with Lupus, Anianus, and others of the chief actors in the defence of Gaul, and no doubt his imagination was powerfully impressed by all that he saw and heard of that 'horde of many-nationed spoilers' who, according to [his *Panegyric of Avitus*],* hewed down the trees of the Thüringer Wald to bridge with their rafts the bosom of the Rhine. There was even a possibility that Sidonius might have been the historian of that eventful campaign. His friend Prosper, successor of Anianus in the see of Orléans, urged him to undertake the task. He began to write, apparently in prose, and occupied himself with the origin of the barbarians who com-posed the host of Attila. But his genius was all for epigram or pompous panegyric. Plain historical narrative wearied him, and moreover the duties of his episcopate (for the work was commenced in the later period of his life) seemed to call him to other occupations. Even the fragment which he wrote has perished, and we regret its loss, for though he was not well fitted by nature or education to be the historian of such a war, he would assuredly have preserved for us some interesting details with reference to that year of terror.

About the time of the Hunnish invasion, or soon after, Sidonius mar-ried. His wife, Papianilla, was the daughter of the most powerful citizen of Auvergne, of that Avitus whom we have already met at the court of Theodoric, cementing the alliance between the Romans and the Visigoths against Attila, and whom we are shortly to meet again in a more exalted station. Sidonius was related by descent to the family of Avitus, and this

* See p. 68.

new tie linked him very closely to the mountainous land of the Arverni (the modern Auvergne) with which henceforward his life became more nearly associated than with his own foggy city of Lyons. His marriage also brought him more decisively forward on the broad stage of Imperial poli, tics, and during the years which intervene between 455 and 469 we shall have frequently to rely on his letters and poems for our sole information as to the events which occurred at the court of the Western emperors.

In the year 469 he finally retired from public life and from the court of the Caesars, and took up his abode at the charming villa of Avitacum in Auvergne, part of his wife's dowry, a place of which he has given us, evi, dently in imitation of the younger Pliny, a description which, though prolix and too much laboured, is not devoid of interest. In this descrip, tion, notwithstanding one or two minor discrepancies, which may be easily accounted for by the changes in the configuration of land and water wrought during the course of fourteen centuries, we can still recognise the characteristic features of the shores of the Lac d'Aydat. This little lake, which is about twelve miles to the south,west of Clermont,Ferrand, lies near the junction of the two great volcanic ranges of the Monts Dôme and the Mont Dore. From two summits of the former range (the Puy de la Vache and the Puy de Lassolas) descended, in that far distant age when the volcanoes of Auvergne were still glowing against the midnight sky, a great stream of molten lava, which has left a wilderness of rock five miles long and in some places a mile wide, sprawling over the once fruitful val, ley. This stony cataract, with its significant Celtic name, La Cheyre,* though ugly and desolate itself, has been the cause of beauty to the land, scape, for the little stream of Pontava coming down from some other mountains on the west, and finding its course impeded by this barrier of lava, has formed the lovely little lake of Aydat, at the south,western corner of which (if this identification be correct) once stood the villa of Sidonius. There is, of course, no trace of that stately dwelling now. A few humble cottages cluster round the little Romanesque church, which dates from the twelfth century, and has three round buttress,towers on each side, built apparently only for strength not for ornament. Inside the church, high up on the north wall of the chancel, is a long flat stone coffer built into the wall, and bearing on its front the words

---

* Abbé Crégut (*Avitacum. Essai de Critique sur l'emplacement de la villa de Sidoine Apollinaire,* 1890), refers this name to the Celtic word *car* = stone.

HIC ST (SUNT) DVO INOCENTES ⊕ ET S. SIDONIVS.*

There is a mystery about 'the two Innocents', nor is it probable that this is the actual burying-place of the poet-bishop, but it may very probably contain some relic of the saint, to whom in fact the church appears to be dedicated. There is a deep well in an adjoining house said to be of Roman excavation, and a few strokes of the pickaxe in the soil of the little village street bring to light pieces of undoubtedly Roman cement, an evidence probably of a once existing pavement.

But leaving these faint archaeological traces of a past which almost eludes our research, it is pleasant to climb the most easterly of the two hills between which Aydat nestles, and there with the unchanged, or but slightly changed, face of nature before us, to read the description of his villa given by the Gallo-Roman nobleman. He writes to his friend Domitius, and says:†

'We are now at Avitacum: that is the name of this property, which having come to me in right of my wife, is even sweeter than a paternal inheritance. A mountain on the west, steep though not rocky, sends forth lower hills, as if from a double focus, which are about four acres apart. But while the ground broadens out sufficiently to afford a fitting vestibule for the house, the sides of the hills hold straight on their course through the valley up to the margin of the villa, which has two fronts, one to the north and the other to the south.'‡ Sidonius then goes on to describe with much detail the bath-house, the fish-pond, the women's apartment, the pillared portico overlooking the lake, the winter-parlour, the little dining-room, and the summer-parlour, looking towards the north. 'This room', he says, 'lets in the daylight, but not the sun, a narrow closet being interposed' (apparently between it and the south face) 'where the drowsy grooms of the chamber sit nodding, though they may not lie down to sleep. How pleasant it is here to let the chirp of the cicadas beat upon one's ear at noon, the croak of the frogs in the twilight, the swans and geese calling upon their mates at night, the cocks crowing in the small hours of the morning, the crows with their augural voice, three times repeated, saluting the ruddy face of rising Aurora, and at daybreak Philomela trilling among the fruit-trees, or

---

* [Here are the two Innocents and St Sidonius.]   † *Epistolae*, ii.2.

‡ This obscure sentence is one of the difficulties in the identification of Avitacum. But the real difficulty is in the Latin of Sidonius rather than in the configuration of the country round Aydat.

Progne [the swallow] twittering upon the palings. To this concert you may join the pastoral muse, goddess of the seven-holed reed, for oftentimes in their nightly rivalry of song the sleepless Tityri of our mountains make their notes heard in the meadows above the tinkling bells of their flocks. And yet, believe me, all this strife of varied sounds only plunges one into the deeper slumber.

'Below us lies the lake, winding down towards the east, and sometimes when the winds ruffle it, it moistens the stones of the villa, whose foundations are laid in its sandy shores. Its right bank is abrupt, winding and wooded, its left open, grassy, and level. By nautical measurement it is seventeen furlongs in length. A stream enters it which has foamed over the rugged rocks that seek to bar its passage, but which has a short period of tranquillity before it mingles with the lake. Its exit is through hidden subterranean channels, which afford a passage to the water, but not to the fish, and these latter, forced back into the lake's slothful tranquillity, grow fat in their prison, and daily swell out a greater extent of pink flesh under their gleaming bellies. Sometimes from the villa we see the fisherman launching forth into the deep, spreading out his nets with their corks floating on the water, or arranging his hook-armed cords at certain well-marked intervals, in order that the greedy trout in their nightly prowlings through the waters may fall into the snares which are laid for their cannibal tastes. For surely it is a fitting stratagem that fish should be tempted by fish to rush upon their own destruction. Sometimes, when the winds have fallen, the surface of the fickle deep is cloven by a whole fleet of pleasure-boats. In the middle of the lake is a little island, where, upon a natural heap of stones, rises a goal often worn by the blades of the rowers' oars in their nautical contests. For this is the point round which they must steer when they would imitate the Sicilian boat-races of our Trojan ancestors, and many a comic shipwreck takes place here as one boat dashes into another.'

Such, greatly abbreviated and freely translated (for it is hardly possible to translate Sidonius literally), is the description, the not unpleasing description, of the home of a great Gaulish noble under the Empire.

After a year or two of seclusion Sidonius re-entered public life in a new capacity. He was elected bishop of the chief city of the Arverni (now called Clermont-Ferrand), and he continued in the same see for the remaining eighteen years of his life.* This election seems to have been a voluntary tribute of respect on the part of his fellow citizens to an unstained

* His wife Papianilla was still alive at the time of his elevation to the episcopate.

private character, and to the memory of an official career which, if not signalised by any brilliant services to the state, had at least not been abused to
sordid and ignoble ends. His position in the literature of the age was both a
recommendation and a stumbling-block. It was an honour for a rural diocese in the mountains to have as its president a man who had recited amid
the applause of the multitude the panegyrics of three emperors, whose
statue in brass stood between the Greek and the Latin libraries in the forum
of Trajan, whose letters were humbly prayed for and treasured up as
invaluable literary possessions by all the rhetoricians and philosophers of
Gaul. Yet, on the other hand, his very panegyrics were crammed full of the
conceits of pagan mythology; his epithalamia, though morally pure,
turned, according to the fashion in such compositions, on the voluptuous
splendours of the dwelling of Venus, on the charms of the bride, surpassing those of all the heroines of classical antiquity, and on the success of
Cupid in piercing with his arrows the bridegroom's heart. This was not
exactly the kind of composition which it was considered safe or decorous
for a Christian bishop to indulge in, so soon after the great struggle between
the new and the old faiths, and while the religion of the Olympian gods,
though prostrate and wounded to the death, still, by a few convulsive
spasms, showed signs of a vitality not yet wholly extinct. Sidonius felt the
incongruity as strongly as anyone, and as, unlike the cardinal de Retz, he
was determined to bring his private life into conformity with the sacred
character which he had assumed,* he broke off abruptly and finally from
the service of the Muses. He could not indeed bring himself to suppress
poems which were in his view so charming as his panegyrics and epithalamia, but he wrote no more verses of this description. Invocations to the
Holy Spirit take the place of invocations to Apollo, and the names of the

---

* These are de Retz's words with reference to his appointment as coadjutor-archbishop of
Paris: 'I was not ignorant of the necessity there is for a bishop to live regularly . . . But at
the same time I found that it was not in my power to live in that manner, and that all the
reasons which conscience or honour could suggest to me against an irregular life would
prove but insignificant and weak. After six days' deliberation, I chose to act ill,
designedly, which as to God is beyond comparison the most criminal, but which is without doubt the wisest as to the world. The reason is, that when you act in that manner you
always take some previous measures that will cover part of the ill action, and that you
avoid besides the most dangerous sort of ridicule that persons of our profession can be
exposed to, which is the mixing preposterously sin with devotion . . . However, I had
fully resolved to discharge exactly all the outward duties of my profession, and to take as
much care of other people's souls as I took little of my own' (*Memoirs*, bk ii).

martyrs meet us instead of those of the Argonauts. The result is not a happy one, and to a taste formed by the Christian hymnology of subse-quent ages, the later poems of Sidonius are rather less attractive than his earlier ones.

Sidonius appears to have made an excellent bishop, according to the notions of his day, which scarcely expected every prelate to rise to the saint-liness of a Polycarp, but would not have tolerated his sinking to the infamy of a Borgia. He applied himself with earnestness to the study of the Scrip-tures, in which he had probably not been well instructed as a child. He steered through the theological controversies of a difficult time with an unimpeached reputation for orthodoxy. His experience as a Roman official helped him to govern his diocese with the right apportionment of firmness and suavity. His unfailing good-nature, joined to a certain ingredient in his character, which can only be described as fussiness, made him the willing counsellor and confidant of his people even in their business difficulties, in the lawsuit, and the family quarrel. Above all, his hearty sympathies with the Romanised population of Gaul, and his antipathies, national and reli-gious, to their Arian and barbarian conquerors, made him willing to risk life and fortune, and even his dearly loved social position, on behalf of the liberties of Auvergne. During the years while the struggle between the Arverni and the Visigoths was going on, the courtier and the rhetorician were lost in the patriot, and his life rose into real grandeur. At the close of the struggle (475) Sidonius had to feel the full weight of the displeasure of the Visigothic king, Euric, who was now undisputed master of Auvergne. He was banished from his diocese, and kept, probably for about a year, in captivity in the fortress of Livia, not far from Carcassonne.* His confine-ment was not of the most rigorous description; he was allowed to employ himself, if he wished, in literary labour, and his quarters for the night seem to have been appointed him in a private dwelling-house. But his days were occupied with harassing duties, and both study and sleep were driven away from his evening hours by the clamours of two Gothic hags, whose win-dow looked upon the courtyard of his lodging, and whose life was passed in one perpetual round of scolding, intoxication and gluttony. The fastidi-ous Roman noble, forced into hourly companionship with these scenes of

---

* His biographers seem generally to treat this as an ordinary imprisonment, but there are some indications that Sidonius was entrusted with some difficult and disagreeable com-mission at Livia, no doubt with the intention of taking him away from his faithful Arverni.

barbarian vulgarity, passed his nights in sighing for the seclusion of his mountainous Auvergne, for the baths, the lake, and the fish-ponds, the airy summer apartment, and the chorus of rural voices of his own beloved Avitacum.

At length, by the mediation of his friend Leo, a Roman, a lover of literature,* and the chief minister at the court of Euric, he was restored to his home and diocese; and the remaining years of his life were passed in comparative tranquillity, but probably with an impaired fortune, and certainly with an ever-present pang of humiliation at the enforced subjection of his high-spirited Arverni to the degrading yoke of the barbarians. He had probably not reached his sixtieth year when (about 489) he was carried off by a fever. He died with Christian calmness and hope. When he felt his end approaching he desired his attendants to carry him to the church where he had been wont to officiate, and lay him before the altar. A multitude of men, women, and children crowded into the church after his bearers, and filled it with their passionate lamentations. 'Why art thou deserting us,' they cried, 'O good shepherd? Who will take care of us, thy orphans, when thou art gone? Who will feed us with the salt of the true wisdom? Who will guide us into the fear of the Lord as thou hast done?' He gently rebuked their want of faith, and said, 'Fear not, my people. My brother Aprunculus still lives, and he will be your bishop.' Then with a prayer to his Creator he yielded up his life. His dying words were verified by the election of Aprunculus (a fugitive for the sake of the Catholic faith from the wrath of the Burgundian king) to fill the vacant see.†

The end of Sidonius was in harmony with the dignified thoughtfulness which had marked his whole episcopal life. He played his part as a Christian bishop well; and yet, without imputing to him any shade of conscious insincerity or hypocrisy, it is difficult when reading his letters and pre-eminently his letters to his brother bishops, to resist the conviction that he was, in a certain sense, playing a part throughout; that he was

---

* Partly as an act of friendship, and partly by way of ransom, Sidonius translated for Leo the *Life of Apollonius of Tyana*, the Paracelsus-Cagliostro of the first century, whose marvellous career was by some of the opponents of Christianity claimed as a counterpoise to the Gospel-history of Jesus. Sidonius does not seem to be aware of this polemical use of the biography: at least, he speaks of Apollonius in terms of unqualified praise, and pays court to Leo by drawing a very strange parallel between the philosopher and the minister.
† The particulars of the death of Sidonius are given us by Gregory of Tours, *Historia Francorum*, ii.23.

essentially an author or a courtier, and only accidentally a divine. That strong bias of the mind towards the invisible which impelled St Augus-tine, through all his immoralities, through all his years of Mani-chaeanism, to ponder continually on the relation of his soul to the God of the universe; that keen intellectual interest in the Scriptures which drew St Jerome into Palestine, and supported him through all the heroic toil of his translations and his commentaries; these are qualities which it would be absurd to mention in connection with the character of Sidonius. But though his taste probably preferred the mythology of Greece, his reason accepted the doctrines of Christianity. The career of secular office was closed to him by the hard circumstances of those stormy times. The church offered him a safe and honourable retreat from war and revolution. The voices of his fellow citizens called him to a post of dignity in that church; and he therefore accepted the retreat and the dignity, and made his life harmonise fairly well with his new vocation. If some sprays of the poet's laurel were still seen under the mitre of the bishop, if his thoughts were sometimes running on Helicon and Parnassus when he was cele-brating the divine mysteries in the basilica of Arverni, at least he kept his secret well, and made his actions congruous to his character as a shepherd of the Christian flock.

He was by the general voice of his people recognised as a saint after his death, and the church of Clermont still, upon the 21st of August, the day of his death, celebrates the festival of St Sidonius. The only reason for any hesitation about canonising him would appear to be that he had never claimed any power of working miracles, that he was not, as a biographer says, 'one of those great thaumaturgic pontiffs whose glory was made com-mon property, and whose virtues were immortalised by the generous instincts of Gaul';* but the entire absence of all pretensions of this kind will not be accounted a demerit by the present age. In his attitude towards men of other faiths than his own, he showed a tolerance of spirit more like the eighteenth century than the fifth. He could not but deplore and con-demn the fury of the Arian persecutors, but he speaks with some kindliness of the Jews. 'Gozolas is the bearer of these letters of mine, a Jew by nation, and a man for whose person I should feel a cordial regard if he did not belong to a sect which I despise.'† And again, 'This letter commends a Jew to your notice. Not that I am pleased with the error in which that nation is involved, and which leads them to perdition, but because it

* Abbé Chaix, *Saint Sidoine Apollinaire et son siècle*, ii.401.   † *Epistolae*, iii.4.

becomes us not to call any one of them sure of damnation while he yet lives, for there is still a hope that he may turn and be forgiven.'* This is the language of an orthodox Catholic, but certainly not of a man who is by nature a persecutor.

Of the literary style of Sidonius it is difficult to speak with fairness. His obscurity, his long and uncouth words, often clumsily coined from the Greek, his constantly recurring epigrams, which, when examined, generally turn out to have as much point in them as the clever things which a man utters in his dreams, his preposterous and monotonous adulation of his correspondents, evidently dictated by the desire to receive their adulation in return, his frigid conceits, his childish display of classical learning, which after all was neither deep nor thorough – all these qualities make much study of the works of this author emphatically a weariness to the flesh. But it is doubtful how far he is to be blamed individually, and how far his age is responsible for the faults of his style. Latin poetry had fallen during the fourth century into the hands of elegant triflers, of the composers of triple and quintuple acrostics,† and the manufacturers of vapid centos.‡ Claudian had snatched the Latian lyre out of the hands of these feeble poetasters, and made it give forth some manlier harmonies; but even Claudian, with his courtier-like exaggerations, and his creaking mythological machinery, was not a very safe guide to follow. Suffice it to say, without attempting further to apportion the blame of a most miserable style between the author and his age, that in his poems, Sidonius bears the same relation to Claudian that Claudian bears to Virgil, and that in his letters he is as far from attaining the purity of style of the younger Pliny as the latter is from rivalling the easy grace of Cicero. It remains to reproduce from the pages of Sidonius some of his most striking pictures of social life among the Romans and barbarians.

I ROMAN LIFE

The Church Festival, and the Game at Tennis§

'Sidonius wishes health to his friend Eriphius.

'You wish me to send you the verses which I made to please that most

---

* *Epistolae*, vi.11.

† Like Optatian's panegyrics on Constantine, things distracting even to look at.

‡ Like Faltonia Proba's, telling, after a fashion, the story of the fall and redemption of man in a poem of some 650 lines entirely drawn from the *Aeneid* of Virgil, and laboriously twisted from their original meaning.   § *Epistolae*, v.17.

respectable man your father-in-law. I will do so; but as, in order to understand this trifle, you wish to know the scene and the cause of its composition, you must not complain if the preface is more long-winded than the work itself.

'We had assembled at the sepulchre of St Justus [at Lyons]; there was a procession before dawn, to celebrate the yearly festival of the saint, and a great multitude had assembled, larger than the basilica could hold, though it was surrounded with spacious arcades. When the office of vigils was ended (chanted by monks and clergy in alternate choruses) we parted from one another, but did not go far, that we might be in readiness for tierce, when the priests should return to celebrate it. The crowd in the church, the many lights, and the closeness of the weather (for it was summer, though just passing into autumn) had made us feel as if we were being stewed, and we longed for the fresh air. So when the various ranks of citizens dispersed, we who belonged to the first families of Lyons, decided to make our rendezvous at the tomb of Syagrius, which was scarce a bowshot from the church. Here some reclined under the shade of a trellis-work covered with the leaves and clusters of a vine; others, of whom I was one, sat on the green sward, which was fragrant with flowers. The conversation was full of light fun and banter; and what was best of all, there was no talk about great people or the incidence of taxation, not a word to compromise anybody, not a person whom anybody else thought of compromising. Anyone who could tell a good story, and adorn it with proper sentiments, was listened to most eagerly. But really there was such general merriment that it was not easy to hear any story distinctly to the end. At length we got tired of idleness, and discussed what we should do. The young men voted for tennis, the elder ones for the tables [backgammon]. I was prime champion of the ball, of which, as you know, I am as fond as of my books. On the other side, my brother* Domnicius, a man full of wit and courtesy, shook the counters about in the tables, and thus, as with a sound of a trumpet, summoned his party to the dice-box. I played for a long time with a troop of students till my limbs, which had grown numb, were made supple again by the healthful exercise. Then the illustrious Philimatius, as Virgil says,

> He too adventuring to the task
> That matches younger years,†

---

* Apparently, this is a title of courtesy. Domnicius was not probably the actual brother of Sidonius.   † *Aeneid*, v.499 (Conington's translation).

boldly joined the group of tennis-players. He had once played the game well, but that was when his years were fewer. Poor man! he was often forced from the place where he was stationed, by the mid-current of eager players; then, when he had to keep the middle of the ground, he could neither ward off nor dodge the quickly flying ball. Moreover he often met with a catas-trophe and fell flat on the ground, from which he raised himself slowly and laboriously. So that the upshot of the matter was that he was the first to retire from the rush of the game, which he did with deep sighs and a fearful stitch in his side. Very soon I left off too, out of kindness to him, that he might not be mortified at so soon showing signs of distress. So, when we were seated again, the sweat running down his face obliged him to ask for a basin of water. It was brought him, and with it a thick cloth which, cleaned from yesterday's dirt, happened to be hanging on a pulley behind the door of the porter's lodge. While he was slowly drying his cheeks he said, "How I should like you to dictate four lines of poetry on the cloth which does me this service." "It shall be done," said I. "But so as to bring in my name in the metre?" "What you ask for is possible." "Dictate them, then." To which I answered, smiling, "You know the Muses will not like it if there are any bystanders when I commune with their holy band." He said, very politely, but with that jocosely passionate manner of his, "Take care, Mr Sollius, that you don't much more exasperate Apollo if you ask for secret interviews with his young ladies." Imagine the applause which greeted this sally, as sudden as it was happily conceived. Then, without more delay, I called to my side his amanuensis, who was standing near with his tablets in hand, and dictated the following epigram:

O towel! in the early morn, when the bath has made him glow,
Or when with heated brow he comes at noontide from the chase,
Into thy thirsty reservoirs let the big sweat-drops flow,
When Philimatius shall wipe on thee his handsome face.

'Scarcely had our friend Epiphanius read over what had been written, when word was brought us that the time was come for the bishop to leave his private apartment, and we all rose up. Pray pardon the verses which you asked for. Farewell.'

The Country House*

'Sidonius wishes health to his friend Donidius.

'You ask me why, though I set out for Nîmes some time ago, I have not yet returned home. I will tell you the agreeable cause of my delay, since I know that the things which please me please you too.

'The fact is that I have been spending some days in a very pleasant country with two most delightful men, my hereditary friend Tonantius Ferreolus, and my cousin Apollinaris. Their estates adjoin one another and their houses are not far apart, a long walk but a short ride. The hills which rise behind are covered with vineyards and oliveyards. The view from each house is equally charming; the one looks upon woods, and the other over a wide expanse of plain. So much for the dwellings; now for the hospitality shown to us there.

'As soon as they found out that I was on my return journey, they stationed skilful scouts to watch not only the high road but every little track and sheep-walk into which I could possibly turn aside, that I might not by any chance escape from their friendly snares. When I had fallen into their hands, not very reluctantly I must confess, they at once administered to me a solemn oath not to entertain one thought of continuing my journey till seven days were over. Then, every morning a friendly strife arose between my hosts whose kitchen should first have the honour of preparing my repast, a strife which I could not adjust by a precisely equal alternation of my visits, although I was bound to one house by friendship and to the other by relationship, because Ferre-olus, as a man who had held the office of prefect, derived from his age and dignity a claim beyond that of mere friendship to take precedence in enter-taining me. So we were hurried from pleasure to pleasure. Scarce had we entered the vestibule of either house when lo! on one side the pairs of tennis-players stood up to oppose one another in the ring;† on the other, amid the shouts of the dicers, was heard the frequent rattle of the boxes and the boards. Here too were books in plenty; you might fancy you were looking at the breast-high bookshelves of the grammarians, or the wedge-shaped cases of the Athenaeum, or the well-filled cupboards of the booksellers.‡ I observed

---

* *Epistolae*, ii.9.

† Perhaps some future researches into the tennis of the Romans may elucidate these mys-terious words.

‡ The three words used in this sentence, *plutei, cunei,* and *armaria*, were all technical terms in Roman libraries.

however that if one found a manuscript beside the chair of one of the ladies of the house, it was sure to be on a religious subject, while those which lay by the seats of the fathers of the family were full of the loftiest strains of Latin eloquence. In making this distinction, I do not forget that there are some writings of equal literary excellence in both branches, that Augustine may be paired off against Varro, and Prudentius against Horace. Among these books Origen, 'the adamantine', translated into Latin by Turranius Rufinus, was frequently perused by readers holding our faith. I cannot understand why some of our arch-divines should stigmatise him as a dangerous and heterodox author.

'While we were engaged, according to our various inclinations, in studies of this nature, punctually as the water-clock marked five [11 a.m.], there would come into the room a messenger from the chief cook to warn us that the time for refreshment had arrived. At dinner we made a full and rapid meal, after the manner of senators, whose custom it is to set forth a large banquet with few dishes, though variety is produced by sometimes cooking the meat dry and sometimes with gravy. While we were drinking we had merry stories told, which at once amused and instructed us. To be brief, the style of the repast was decorous, handsome, and abundant.

'Then rising from table, if we were at Voroangus [the estate of Apollinaris] we walked back to the inn where was our baggage, and there took our siesta;* if at Prusianum [the name of the other property] we had to turn Tonantius and his brothers — nobles as they were, and our equals in age — out of their couches, as we could not easily carry our sleeping-apparatus about with us.

'When we had shaken off our noontide torpor, we rode on horseback for a little while to sharpen our appetites for supper. Both of my hosts had baths in their houses, but neither of them happened to be in working order. However, when my attendants and the crowd of their fellow revellers, whose brains were too often under the influence of the hospitable wine-cup, had made a short pause in their potations, they would hurriedly dig a trench near to the fountain or the river. Into this they tossed a heap of burnt stones, and over it they would weave a hemisphere of hazel-twigs. Upon this framework were stretched sheets of coarse Cilician canvas, which at once shut out the light, and beat back the steam rising from the

---

* It may be observed that the very word 'siesta' (at the sixth hour) marks the permanence of Roman customs in the lands bordering on the Mediterranean. As the *prandium* [dinner] was at the fifth hour, the repose would naturally be at the sixth.

hot flints sprinkled with water. Here we often passed hours in pleasant and witty talk, while our limbs, wrapped in the fizzing steam, gave forth a wholesome sweat. When we had spent as long as we chose in this rude *sudatorium*, we plunged into the heated waters to wash away the perspiration; and, having so worked off all tendency to indigestion, we then braced our bodies with the cold waters of the well, the fountain, or the river. For I should have mentioned that midway between the two houses flows the river Vuardo,* red with its tawny gravel, except when the melting snow makes pale its waters, gliding tranquilly over its pebbly bed, and well stocked with delicate fish.

'I would also describe the luxurious suppers which we used to sit down to, if my talkative vein, which knows no check from modesty, were not summarily stopped by the end of my paper. And yet it would be pleasant to tell over again their delights if I did not blush to carry my scrawl over to the back of the sheet. But now, as we are really in act to depart, and as you, with Christ's help, are going to be good enough to pay us an immediate visit, it will be easier to talk over our friends' suppers when you and I are taking our own; only let the end of this week of feasting restore to me as soon as possible my vanished appetite, since no refinements of cookery can so effectually soothe an overcharged stomach as the remedy of abstinence. Farewell.'

The New Basilica†

The bishop Patiens, an earnest and liberal-handed man, raised in his city of Lyons a magnificent church, which was dedicated to the popular Gallic saint, Justus. Sidonius and two other poets, the most eminent of their age and nation, were requested to write three inscriptions which were to be engraved on tablets at the west end of the building. The church itself, after witnessing some interesting passages of medieval history, was destroyed in the religious wars of the sixteenth century; and these lines written by Sidonius, and by him transcribed at the request of a youthful admirer, alone remain to testify of its departed glories. The chief reason for quoting them is the proof which they afford that the use of mosaics on the walls and of golden decorations on the ceiling was not confined, as we may have been inclined to suppose, to those places where Byzantine taste was predominant. Many touches in the following description would suit some of the still surviving churches of Ravenna. The atrium or oblong porch in front

* The Gard of the celebrated Pont du Gard.　　† *Epistolae*, ii.10.

of the church, the triple doorway from the atrium into the nave, and from the outside of the building into the atrium, the 'forest of columns' within, and the slabs of marble in the windows, are all also characteristic of the ecclesiastical architecture of Constantine and his successors.*

Sidonius uses the metre called hendecasyllabic

$$- - \mid - \cup \cup \mid - \cup \mid - \cup \mid - \cup$$

to which he was very partial, and which has been employed in the follow-ing translation:

> Stranger! come and admire this temple's beauty,
> Know, 'twas reared by the zeal of Bishop Patient.
> Here put up the request that earns an answer:
> Here shall all of thy heart's desires be granted.
> See how shines from afar the lofty building
> Which, square-set, nor to left nor right deflected,
> Looks straight on to the equinoctial sunrise.
>
> Inly gleams there a light: the golden ceiling
> Glows so fair that the sunbeams love to wander
> Slowly over the sun-like burnished metal.
> Marbles varied in hue, with slabs resplendent,
> Line the vault and the floor, and frame the windows.
> And, in glass on the walls, the green of spring-tide
> Bounds the blue of the lake with winding margent.†
>
> Here a portico, three-arched, fronts the gazer,
> Reared on pillars from Aquitanian quarries.
> There its counterpart stands, an inner portal,
> At the atrium's end, three-arched and stately;
> While within, and around the floor of worship
> Rise the stems of a slender marble forest.

* All these points occur in Constantine's church of the Saviour at Jerusalem, and Justin-ian's church of St Sophia at Constantinople.

† As the meaning of these lines is not very clear, I have ventured to interpolate a memory of Ravenna. In the vaulted roof above the tomb of Galla Placidia, one sees a bright mosaic picture of two stags drinking, and the pool between them is blue, lined with emerald-green grass.

Fair it rises, between the road and river;
Here it echoes the horseman's clanging footfall
And the shout of the slave who guides the chariot.
There, the chorus of bending, hauling bargemen,
As they pace by the turgid Arar's waters
Send to heaven the joyful alleluia!

Sing thus! Wayfarers sing by land or water,
Sing at sight of the house which all may enter,
Where all learn of the road that leads to safety.

*The Family Setting Out for the Country**

Evodius had asked Sidonius to furnish him with twelve verses to be engraved on the inside of a large shell-shaped silver basin which he was about to present to Ragnahild the Visigothic queen. Sidonius replies as follows:

'Sidonius wishes health to his friend Evodius.

'When the messenger brought me your letter, informing me that you were about soon to visit Toulouse at the command of the king, we too were leaving the town for a place in the country some way off. From early morning I had been detained by one cause or another, and the arrival of your letter only just gave me an excuse to shake off the crowd of attendants and try to satisfy your request while I was either walking or riding. At the very break of day my family had gone forward, meaning to pitch the tent when they had accomplished eighteen miles of the journey. The spot which they would then reach was one which many reasons combined to make desirable for the purpose of a halt; a cool spring in a shady grove, a level lawn with plenty of grass, a river just before our eyes well stocked with fish, and a favourite haunt of water-birds; and besides all this, close to the river's bank stood the new house of an old friend, so immensely kind that neither by accepting nor by refusing can you ever get to the end of his civilities.

'Hither then my people had gone before me and here I stopped for your sake, that I might send your slave back by the shortest way from the chief town in the district. By this time it was four hours and more after sunrise; already the sun which was now high in the heavens had sucked up the night-dews with his increasing rays; we were growing hot and thirsty, and

* *Epistolae*, iv.8.

in the deep serenity of the day a cloud of dust raised by our horses' feet was our only protection against the heat. Then the length of the road stretching out before us over the green and sea-like plain made us groan when we thought how long it would be before we should get our dinner. All these things, my dear sir, I have mentioned to you that you may understand how adverse the circumstances of my body, my mind, and my time were to the fulfilment of your commission.'

Sidonius then gives the verses, twelve in number, which were to be engraved in twelve grooves, reaching from the centre to the circumference of Queen Ragnahild's silver basin. The heat and the remoteness of the prospect of dinner must have been unfavourable to his courtship of the muse, for the verses are vapid, and there is scarcely a thought in them which would survive translation.

The Fortune-Hunter*

In the early days of the episcopate of Sidonius a certain Amantius asked him for letters of introduction to Marseilles. With his usual good-nature Sidonius gave him a letter to Graecus, bishop of that city, describing him as a poor but honest man, who transacted what we should call a commission business in the purchase of cargoes arriving at the seaports of Gaul. He had been lately appointed a reader in the church – a post which was not incompatible with his transactions in business – and this gave him an additional claim on the good offices of the two bishops.† The letter concluded with the expression of a hope that Amantius might meet with splendid success as a merchant, and might not regret exchanging the cold springs of Auvergne for the fountain of wealth flowing at Marseilles.‡

Not long after, Sidonius discovered that he had been imposed upon by a swindler, that the modest young man who desired an introduction to Marseilles was in fact too well known at Marseilles already, and that the honest broker was an impudent and mendacious fortune-hunter. Having occasion to write again to Graecus, who had asked him for 'one of his long and amusing letters', he thought that he could not do better than send him the history of Amantius, though the bishop of Marseilles must have been already in good part acquainted with it, and the bishop of Arverni must

* *Epistolae*, vii.2.
† As a lector he was entitled to receive *literae formatae* from the bishop, a certificate which was given to no one who was not in some sense *clericus* [a clergyman].
‡ *Epistolae*, vi.8.

have been conscious that the part which he had played did not reflect great credit on his shrewdness. After a complimentary preface, the letter proceeds thus:

'His native country is Auvergne; his parents are persons in a somewhat humble position in life, but free and unencumbered with debt; their duties have been in connection with the service of the church rather than of the state. The father is a man of extreme frugality, more intent on saving up money for his children than on pleasing them. This lad accordingly left his home and came to your city with a very slender equipment in all respects. Notwithstanding this hindrance to his ambitious projects he made a fairly successful start among you. St Eustachius, your predecessor, welcomed him with deeds and words of kindness, and put him in the way of quickly obtaining comfortable quarters. He at once began to cultivate assiduously the acquaintance of his neighbours, and his civilities were well received. He adapted himself with great tact to their different ages, showing defer-ence to the old, making himself useful to his coevals, and always exhibiting a modesty and sobriety in his moral conduct which are as praiseworthy as they are rare in young men. At length, by well-timed and frequent calls, he became known to and familiar with the leading personages of your city, and finally even with the count himself. Thus the assiduous court which he paid to greatness was rewarded with ever-increasing success; worthy men vied in helping him with their advice and good wishes; he received presents from the wealthy, favours of one kind or another from all, and thus his for-tune and his hopes advanced "by leaps and bounds".

'It happened by chance that near the inn where he was lodging there dwelt a lady of some fortune and high character, whose daughter had passed the years of childhood, yet had scarcely reached the marriageable age. He showed himself very kind to this girl, and made, as her youth allowed him to do, trifling presents to her of toys and trash that would divert a girl, and thus, at a very trifling expense, obtained a firm hold on her affections. Years passed on; she became old enough to be a bride. To make a long story short, you have on the one side a young man, alone, poorly off, a stranger, a son who had skulked away from home not only without the con-sent, but even without the knowledge of his father; on the other, a girl not inferior to him in birth, and superior to him in fortune; and this fellow, through the introduction of the bishop because he was a reader, by favour of the count because he had danced attendance in his hall, without any investigation as to his circumstances by the mother-in-law because his person was not displeasing to her daughter, woos and wins and marries that young lady. The marriage articles are signed, and in them some beggarly little plot of ground which he happened to possess near our borough is set forth with truly comic pomposity. When the solemn swindle was accom-plished, the poor beloved one carried off his wealthy spouse, after diligently hunting up all the possessions of his late father-in-law, and converting them into money, besides adding to them a handsome gratuity drawn from the easy generosity of his credulous mother-in-law, and then, unrivalled hum-bug that he was, he beat a retreat to his own native place.

'Some time after he had gone, the girl's mother discovered the fraud, and had to mourn over the dwindling proportions of the estates comprised in her daughter's settlement, at the very time when she should have been rejoicing over the augmented number of her grandchildren. She wanted to institute a suit for recovery of her money, on the ground that he had fraudu-lently overstated his property; and it was in fact in order to soothe her wrath that our new Hippolytus* set forth for Marseilles, when he first brought you my letter of introduction.

'Now, then, you have the whole story of this excellent young man, a story, I think, worthy of the Milesian fables or an Attic comedy. It remains for you to show yourself a worthy successor of Bishop Eustachius by dis-charging the duties of patronage to the dear youth whom he took under his protection. You asked me for a lengthy letter, and therefore if it is rather wordy than eloquent you must not take it amiss. Condescend to keep me in your remembrance, my lord pope.'†

What was the issue of the quarrel between the amatory Amantius and his mother-in-law we are not informed, but as he acted twice after this as letter-carrier between Sidonius and Graecus, we may conjecture that the affair of the settlement took some time to arrange.

The Master Murdered by his Slaves‡

'Sidonius wishes health to his friend Lupus.

'I have just heard of the murder of the orator Lampridius, whose death, even if it had been in the course of nature, would have filled me with sor-row on account of our ancient friendship. Long ago he used, by way of joke, to call me Phoebus, and I gave him the name of the Odrysian bard

* Referring to the affair of Hippolytus and his stepmother Phaedra.
† *Papa* [pope] was the common form of address used towards all bishops at this time.
‡ *Epistolae*, viii.11 (much abridged in translation).

[Orpheus]. Once, when I was going to visit him at Bordeaux, I sent forward to him a poem, like a soldier's billet, claiming his hospitality for Apollo.'

Then follows the poem in hendecasyllabics. Phoebus directs his favourite muse, Thalia, to go before him to Bordeaux, to knock at the door of one Orpheus whom she will find there, charming all nature by his minstrelsy, and to tell him that Phoebus has left his home, that already his oars are splashing in the rapid Garonne, that he will soon be at the house of his friend. The remembrance of these long-past, merry days draws from Sidonius a sentence in prose, which comes nearer to poetry than anything else written by him. *O necessitas abjecta nascendi, vivendi misera, dura moriendi!** He proceeds—

'See whither the fickle wheel of fortune leads us. I confess I loved the man, though in his character there were mingled some traits unworthy of his real virtues. He was of a hasty temper, easily moved to anger by slight offences, and there was a taint of cruelty in his nature, though I used to seek to extenuate it by calling it severity . . .

'The worst and most fatal fault which he committed was in resorting to astrologers in order to learn what the end of his life should be. They were natives of some of the cities of Africa, men whose dispositions were as burning as their sun. They concurred in naming to him the year, the month, and the day which, in their jargon, would be "climacteric" for him; and when they had cast his nativity they predicted for him a bloody fate, because all the planets which had risen prosperously upon his birth set in sinister aspects and with lurid fires. However false and deceptive the predictions of these mathematicians as a rule may be, in the case of our friend they were strictly correct both as to the time and manner of his death. For having been held down in his own house, and strangled by his own slaves, he died by the same death as Lentulus, Jugurtha, Sejanus and even Scipio of Numantia. The least melancholy part of the business is that the parricidal deed was discovered as soon as morning dawned. For no one could be so dull as not to see the signs of foul play on first inspection of the corpse. The livid skin, the starting eyes, the yet lingering traces of anger and pain in the face told their own tale. The earth too was wet with his blood, because after the deed was done the villains had laid him face downwards on the pavement to make it seem as if he had died of haemorrhage. The chief agent in the crime was taken, tortured, and confessed his guilt. Would that I could

* O humiliating necessity of birth, sad necessity of living, hard necessity of dying!

say that our friend was altogether undeserving of his fate. But he who thus pries into forbidden mysteries, deviates from the safe rule of the Catholic faith, and while he is using unlawful arts must not complain if he is answered by some great calamity.'

The Oppressive Governor*

'Sidonius wishes health to his friend Pannychius.

'If you have not already heard that Seronatus is returning from Toulouse, let this letter inform you of the fact. Already Evanthius† is on his way to Clausetia, and is forcing people to clear away the rubbish from the works that have been let out on contract, and to remove the fallen leaves from his path.‡ Poor man! if there is an uneven surface anywhere, he himself, with trembling hand, brings earth to fill up the trenches, going before the beast whom he is escorting from the valley of Tarmis, like the little mussels who pioneer the mighty body of the whale through the shallow places and rocky channels of the sea.

'Seronatus, however, as quick to wrath as he is unwieldy in bulk, like a dragon just rolled forth from his cave, comes towards us from the district of Gabala, whose inhabitants he leaves half dead with fright. This population, scattered into the country from their towns, he is now exhausting with unheardof imposts; now entangling them in the winding meshes of false accusations, and scarcely permitting the labourers at length to return home, when they have paid him a year's tribute in advance. The sure and certain sign of his approaching advent is the gangs of unhappy prisoners who are dragged in chains to meet him. Their anguish is his joy, their hunger is his food, and he seems to think it an especially fine thing to degrade before he punishes them, making the men grow their hair long, and the women cut theirs. If any here and there meet with a chance pardon, it will be due to a bribe, or to his flattered vanity, but never to compassion.

'But to set forth all the proceedings of such a beast would exhaust the rhetoric of a Cicero and the poetry of a Virgil. Therefore, since it is said that this pest is approaching us (whose ravages may God guard us from!), do you forestall the disease by the counsels of prudence; compromise your lawsuits if you have any; get security for your arrears of tribute; do not let the wicked man have any opportunity of hurting the good, or of laying them under an obligation. In fine, do you wish to hear what I think of

---

* *Epistolae*, v.13.   † Some subordinate official under Seronatus.
‡ Translation doubtful.

Seronatus? Others fear his fines and his punishments: to me the so-called benefits of the robber seem even more to be dreaded.'

We do not know what was the subsequent history of this oppressive governor, nor how long the crushed provincials had to endure his yoke. In another letter Sidonius speaks of him as 'the Catiline of our age, fawning on the barbarians, trampling on the Romans, joking in church, preaching at the banquet, passing sentence in bed, sleeping on the judgement-seat; every day crowding the woods with fugitives, the villas with barbarians, the altars with criminals, the prisons with clergymen; insulting prefects, and conniving at the frauds of revenue officers, treading under foot the laws of Theodosius, and exalting those of Theodoric [the Visigoth], every day bringing forth old accusations and new exactions.'* And he states in con-clusion that if Anthemius, the then reigning emperor, affords them no assistance against the tyranny of Seronatus, 'the nobility of Auvergne have resolved to sacrifice either their country or their hair', that is, to retire either into exile or into monasteries.

The Country Magnate†

'Sidonius wishes health to his friend Industrius.

'I have just been visiting the right honourable Vectius, and have studied his actions at my leisure, and from close quarters. I think the result of my investigations is worth recording. In the first place I will mention what I consider the highest praise of all; the house and its master both exist in an atmosphere of unsullied purity. His slaves are useful; his rural labourers well-mannered, courteous, friendly, obedient, and contented with their patron.‡ His table is as ready to welcome the guest as the retainer; his civil-ity is great, and yet greater his sobriety.

'Another and less important matter is that he of whom I speak is inferior to none in the arts of breaking horses, training dogs, and managing falcons. There is the utmost neatness in his raiment, elegance in his girdles, and splendour in his accoutrements. His walk is dignified, his disposition seri-ous: the former well maintains his private dignity, the latter is set upon preserving public faith. He is equally removed from spoiling indulgence and from bloody punishments, and there is a certain austerity in his charac-ter, which is stern without being gloomy. Moreover he is a diligent reader of

---

* *Epistolae*, ii.1.   † *Epistolae*, iv.9.
‡ These are evidently the *coloni*, freeborn, yet dependent on their *patronus*, the precursors of the villeins of later centuries.

the sacred volumes, with which he often refreshes his mind while in the act of taking food for the body. He frequently peruses the Psalms, and yet more frequently chants them, and thus, in a novel fashion, acts the monk, not under the habit of a recluse, but under the uniform of a general. He abstains from game, though he consents to hunt, and thus, with a delicate and unobtrusive religiousness, he uses the processes of the chase but denies himself its produce.

'One only daughter was left to him on her mother's death as the solace of his widowerhood, and her he cherishes with the tenderness of a grand-father, the assiduity of a mother, and the kindness of a father. As to his relations towards his household, when he is giving orders he "forbeareth threatening"; when he receives their advice he does not spurn it from him as valueless; when he discovers a fault he is not too persistent in tracing it; and thus he rules the state and condition of those who are subject to him, more as a judge than as a master; you would think that he rather administered his house as a trust than owned it as an absolute possession.

'When I perceived all this industry and moderation in such a man, I thought it would be for the common good that the knowledge of it should be thoroughly and widely spread abroad. To follow such a life, and not merely to don a particular [monastic] habit, whereby the present age is often grievously imposed upon, would be a useful incitement for all the men of our profession [the clerical]. For – let me say it without offending my own order – when a private individual shows such excellent qualities as these, I admire a priest-like layman more than a priest himself. Farewell.'

The Juvenile Sexagenarian*

This letter is addressed to the subject of the preceding one.

'Sidonius wishes health to his friend Vectius.

'Lately, at the request of the hon. Germanicus, I inspected the church of Cantilla.

'He himself is certainly one of the most noteworthy men of the district, for although he has already put sixty years behind him, every day, in dress and manners, he becomes, I will not say more like a young man, but actu-ally more boyish. His robe is closely girt around him, his buskin tight-laced, his hair is cut so as to make it look like a wheel, his beard is cropped close to the chin by pincers which pierce to the bottom of each fold of his skin. Moreover, by the blessing of providence, his limbs are still

* *Epistolae*, iv.13.

strongly knit, his sight is perfect, he has a firm and rapid gait, in his gums there is an untouched array of milk-white teeth. With no weakness in his stomach, no tendency to inflammation in his veins, no perturbation of his heart, no distress in breathing, no stiffness in his loins, no congestion of his liver, no flabbiness in his hand, no bending of his spine, but endowed with all the health of youth, he claims nothing that belongs to age but reverence.

'In consideration of all these peculiar benefits which he has received from God, I beg you, as his friend and neighbour, and one whose example justly exerts a great influence over him, to persuade him not to trust too much in these uncertain possessions, nor to cherish an overweening confidence in his own immunity from disease; but rather to make a decided profession of religion, and so become strong in the might of renewed innocence. Let him thus, while old in years, be new in merit; and since there is scarcely anyone who is devoid of hidden faults, let him openly show his penitence and give satisfaction for those wrong things which he has committed in secret. For a man in his position, the father of a priest and the son of a bishop, unless he lead a holy life himself, is like a briar, rough, prickly and unlovely in the midst of roses, from which it has sprung, and which it has itself produced.'

Teachers and Pupils, Masters and Slaves*

'Sidonius wishes health to his friends Simplicius and Apollinaris.

'Good God!† how do the emotions of our minds resemble a sea strewn with shipwrecks, the tempests which sweep over them being the evil tidings which messengers sometimes bring to us. A little while ago I was, together with your son,‡ Simplicius, revelling in the delicate wit of the *Hecyra* of Terence. I sat beside the young student forgetting my clerical profession in the delight which the human nature of the play afforded me. In order that I might help him to follow the flow of the comic verses more easily, I kept before me a story with a similar plot, the *Epitrepontes* of Menander. We read at the same pace, we praised our authors, we laughed over their jokes, and,

---

* *Epistolae*, iv.12.
† *Deus bone!* Sidonius is very fond of this exclamation. If it was especially affected by the Christians of Gaul, it may help to explain the frequency of the French *Bon Dieu!*
‡ We know from one of Sidonius' letters (v.4) that the sons of Simplicius studied as pupils with him. He complains that on account of his too great kindness to them at first, they did not treat him with proper respect.

according to our respective tastes, he was captivated by the reading, and I by his intelligence.

'Suddenly there stood by my side a slave of my household, pulling a very long face. "What is the matter?" said I. "I have just seen", said he, "at the gate the reader* Constans, returning from my lords Simplicius and Apollinaris; he says that he delivered your letters to them, but has lost the replies which were entrusted to his care." When I heard this the calm, bright sky of my gladness was overspread with a cloud of sorrow, and so much was my bile stirred by the untoward intelligence thus brought me, that for many days I inexorably forbade that most stupid Mercury to venture into my presence. For I should have been vexed if he had lost any ordinary letters entrusted to him by anybody, but how much more, yours, which, so long as my mind retains its vigour, will always be deemed least common and most desirable.

'However, after my anger had gradually abated with the lapse of time, I enquired of him whether he had brought me any verbal message from you. Trembling and prostrate before me, stammering and half blind with the consciousness of his offence, he answered that all those thoughts of yours, by which I had hoped to be charmed and instructed, were committed to those unlucky letters which had disappeared on the way.

'Go back therefore, dear friends, to your tablets,† unfold your parchments and write over again what you wrote before. For I cannot bear with equanimity this unlucky failure of my hopes unless I know that you are assured that your written speech has never reached me. Fare you well.'

Husbands and Wives, Parents and Children‡

'Sidonius wishes health to his wife Papianilla.

'The quaestor Licinianus, who has just arrived from Ravenna, as soon as he had crossed the Alps and touched the soil of Gaul, sent letters forward to announce his arrival, stating that he was the bearer of an imperial ordinance, bestowing the honour of the patriciate on your brother and mine, Ecdicius, whose titles will rejoice you as much as mine.§ This

* The slave who was called *lector* [who read aloud to his master] was apparently also the letter-carrier.

† *Pugillares*, the little wax-covered tablets, meant to hold in the hand, upon which hasty memoranda were inscribed.

‡ *Epistolae*, v.16. This letter was written in 475. Sidonius was probably at Lyons; his wife at Auvergne.

§ Ecdicius had done good service in defending Auvergne against the Visigoths.

honour comes very early if you consider his age, though very late if you look to his merits. For he has long ago paid the price for his new dignity, not with gold but with steel, and though a private individual, has enriched the treasury, not with money, but with trophies of war.

'This debt, however, under which your brother, by his noble labours, laid the emperor Anthemius, has now been honourably discharged by his successor Julius Nepos, a man whose character, no less than the success of his arms, entitles us to hail him as supreme Augustus. The promptitude of the act makes it all the more praiseworthy, for one emperor has at once done what the other a hundred times promised to do. Henceforward, therefore, our best men may with joyful certainty spend their strength in the service of the commonwealth, knowing that even if the emperor dies, the Imperial dignity will faithfully perform every promise by which their devotion has been quickened.

'Meanwhile you, if I rightly read your affectionate heart, will derive, even in these gloomy times, great solace from these tidings, and will not be diverted from sharing in our common joy even by the terrors of the siege which is going on so near you. For I know right well that not even my honours, which you legally share, will bring you so much gladness as this intelligence; since though you are a good wife you are also the best of sisters. Wherefore I have made haste to inform you in this congratulatory letter, of the augmented dignity which, through the favour of Christ our God, has been bestowed upon your line, and thus I have at the same time satisfied your anxiety and your brother's modesty, to which, and not to any want of affection on his part, you must attribute his silence respecting this promotion.

'For myself, great as is my rejoicing at the added honours of your family for which you have hitherto sighed impatiently, I rejoice even more at the harmony which reigns between Ecdicius and me. And I pray that this harmony may continue as the heritage of our children, for whom I put up this prayer in common, that even as we two have, by God's favour, added the patrician dignity to the praefectorial rank which we inherited from our fathers, so they may yet further enhance it by the office of consul.*

'Roscia,† our common charge, salutes you. Favoured above most other grandchildren, she is fondled in the kindest embraces of her grandmother and aunts, while at the same time she is being strictly trained, and thereby

* This gradation of ranks, *familia praefectoria, patritia, consularis,* is worth noticing.
† His daughter.

her tender age is not rendered infirm while her mind is healthily informed. Farewell.'

Debtor and Creditor. The Courtier Turned Devout*

'Sidonius wishes health to his friend Turnus.

'Well indeed with your name, and with your present business, har-monises that passage of the Mantuan poet—

> Turnus! what never god would dare
> To promise to his suppliant's prayer,
> Lo, here, the lapse of time has brought
> E'en to your hands, unasked, unsought.†

'Long ago, if you remember, your [late] father Turpio, a man of tribun-ician rank, obtained a loan of money from an officer of the palace named Maximus. He deposited no security either in plate or in mortgage on land; but as appears by the written instrument prepared at the time, he covenanted to pay twelve per cent to the lender, by which interest, as the loan has lasted for ten years, the debt is more than doubled. But your father fell sick, and was at the point of death: in his feeble state of health the law came down upon him harshly to compel him to refund the debt: he could not bear the annoyance caused by the collectors, and therefore, as I was about to travel to Toulouse, he, being now past hope of recovery, wrote ask-ing me to obtain from the creditor, at least, some moderate delay. I gladly acceded to his request, as Maximus was not only an acquaintance of mine, but bound to me by old ties of hospitality. I therefore willingly went out of my way to my friend's villa, though it was situated several miles from the high road. As soon as I arrived he himself came to meet me. When I had known him in times past he was erect in his bearing, quick in his gait, with cheery voice and open countenance. Now how greatly was he changed from his old self! His dress, his step, his bashfulness, his colour, his speech, all had a religious cast: besides, his hair was short, his beard flowing: the furniture of his room consisted of three-legged stools, curtains of goat's hair canvas‡ hung before his doors: his couch had no feathers, his table no ornament; even his hospitality, though kind, was frugal, and there was

* *Epistolae*, iv.24. It will be seen that Sidonius plays upon the name of his correspondent, which recalls the antagonist of Aeneas.   † *Aeneid*, ix.6–7 (Conington's translation).
‡ *Cilicium*, the kind of fabric that St Paul used to manufacture.

pulse rather than meat upon his board. Certainly, if any delicacies were admitted, they were not by way of indulgence to himself, but to his guests. When he rose from table I privily enquired of his attendants what manner of life was this that he was leading, a monk's, a clergyman's or a penitent's. They said that he was filling the office of priest which had been lately laid upon him by the goodwill of his fellow citizens, notwithstanding his protests.

'When day returned, while our slaves and followers were occupied in catching our beasts of burden, I asked for an opportunity for a secret conversation with our host. He afforded it: I gave him an unexpected embrace, and congratulated him on his new dignity: then with my congratulations I blended entreaties. I set forth the petition of my friend Turpio, I urged his necessitous condition, I deplored the extremities to which he was reduced, extremities which seemed all the harder to his sorrowing friends because the chain of usury was tightening, while the hold of the body upon the soul was loosening. Then I begged him to remember his new profession and our old friendship, to moderate, at least, by a short respite the barbarous insistence of the bailiffs barking round the sick man's bed; if he died, to give his heirs one year in which to indulge their grief without molestation; but if, as I hoped, Turpio should recover his former health, to allow him to restore his exhausted energies by a period of repose.

'I was still pleading, when suddenly the kind-hearted man burst into a flood of tears, caused not by the delay in recovering his debt, but by the peril of his debtor. Then suppressing his sobs, "God forbid", said he, "that I as a clergyman should claim that from a sick man which I should scarcely have insisted upon as a soldier from a man in robust health. For his children's sake too, who are also objects of my pity, if anything should happen to our friend, I will not ask anything more from them than the character of my sacred calling allows. Write then to allay their anxiety, and that your letters may obtain the more credit, add a letter from me in which I will engage that whatever be the result of this illness (which we will still hope may turn out favourably for our brother) I will grant a year's delay for the payment of the money, and will forgo all that moiety which has accrued by right of interest, being satisfied with the simple repayment of the principal."

'Hereupon I poured out my chief thanks to God, but great thanks also to my host who showed such care for his own conscience and good name: and I assured my friend that whatsoever he relinquished to you he was sending on before him into heaven, and that by refraining from selling up your father's farms, he was buying for himself a kingdom above.

'Now, for what remains, do you bestir yourself to repay forthwith the principal at least of the loan, and thus take the best means of expressing the gratitude of those who, linked to you by the tie of brotherhood, haply by reason of their tender years, scarcely yet understand what a boon has been granted them. Do not begin to say, "I have joint heirs in the estate: the division is not yet accomplished: all the world knows that I have been more shabbily treated than they: my brother and sister are still under age: she has not yet a husband, nor he a *curator* [guardian], nor is a surety found for the acts and defaults of that *curator*." All these pretexts are alleged to all creditors, and to unreasonable creditors they are not alleged amiss. But when you have to deal with a person of this kind who forgoes the half when he might press for the whole, if you practise any of these delays you give him a right to re-demand as an injured man the concessions which he made as a good-natured one. Farewell.'

From these glimpses of the social life of the Roman provincials in the middle of the fifth century, we turn to consider what light of a similar kind the correspondence of Sidonius throws on the internal history of the barbarians with whom he was brought in contact. His first description is kindly and appreciative: so much so, that it has been conjectured that it was meant to be shown to the gratified subject of the portrait. In his other character sketches of the barbarians, as we shall find, the shallow contempt of the heir of civilisation for the untutored children of nature is more distinctly visible.

2 BARBARIAN LIFE

The Visigothic King*

'Sidonius wishes health to [his brother-in-law] Agricola.

'You have many times asked me to write to you a letter describing the bodily appearance and manner of life of Theodoric, king of the Goths,† whose love for our civilisation is justly reported by common fame. I willingly accede to your request, so far as the limits of my paper will allow, and

---

* *Epistolae*, i.2. The letter is a difficult one, and I have therefore translated it more literally than usual.

† Theodoric II, son of the veteran who fell at the battle in the Mauriac plains, ascended the throne in 453, having won the crown by the murder of his brother Thorismund, and was himself slain by order of his brother and successor Euric, 466.

I praise the noble and delicate anxiety for information which you have thus exhibited.

'Theodoric is "a noticeable man", one who would at once attract atten-tion even from those who casually beheld him, so richly have the will of God and the plan of nature endowed his person with gifts corresponding to his completed prosperity. His character is such that not even the detrac-tion which waits on kings can lessen the praises bestowed upon it.* If you enquire as to his bodily shape, he has a well-knit frame, shorter than the very tallest, but rising above men of middle stature. His head is round and dome-like, his curling hair retreats a little from the forehead towards the top. He is not bull-necked. A shaggy arch of eyebrows crowns his eyes; but if he droops his eyelids the lashes seem to fall well-nigh to the middle of his cheeks. The lobes of his ears, after the fashion of his nation, are covered by wisps of overlying hair. His nose is most beautifully curved; his lips are thin, and are not enlarged when the angles of his mouth are dilated: if by chance they open and show a regular, but rather prominent set of teeth, they at once remind you of the colour of milk. He cuts every day the hairs which grow at the bottom of his nostrils. At his temples, which are some-what hollowed out, begins a shaggy beard, which in the lower part of his face is plucked out by the roots by the assiduous care of his barber. His chin, his throat, his neck, all fleshy without obesity, are covered with a milk-white skin, which when more closely inspected, is covered with a youthful glow. For it is modesty, not anger, which so often brings this colour into his face.

'His shoulders are well turned, his arms powerful, his forearms hard, his hands widespread: he is a well set-up man, with chest prominent and stom-ach drawn in. You can trace on the surface of his back the points where the ribs terminate in the deeply recessed spine. His sides are swollen out with prominent muscles. Strength reigns in his well-girded loins. His thigh is hard as horn: the leg joints have a very masculine appearance: his knee, which shows but few wrinkles, is especially comely. The legs rest upon full round calves, and two feet of very moderate size support these mighty limbs.†

* Did Sidonius not believe in Theodoric's participation in the conspiracy against Thoris-mund, or had he forgotten, or did he deliberately ignore it?

† Gibbon points out that this curiously minute appraisement of the bodily frame of Theodoric was composed by an author and perused by readers who had probably fre-quented the markets where naked slaves were exposed for sale. It is such a singular

'You will ask, perhaps, what is the manner of his daily life in public. It is this. Before dawn he attends the celebration of divine service by his [Arian] priests, attended by a very small retinue. He shows great assiduity in this practice, though if you are admitted to his confidence you may perceive that it is with him rather a matter of habit than of religious feeling. The rest of the morning is devoted to the care of the administration of his kingdom. Armed nobles stand round his chair: the crowd of skin-clothed guards are admitted to the palace in order to ensure their being on duty; they are kept aloof from the royal presence that their noise may not disturb him, and so their growling talk goes on before the doors, shut out as they are by the curtain, though shut in by the railings.* Within the enclosure are admitted the ambassadors of foreign powers: he hears them at great length, he answers in few words. In negotiation his tendency is to delay, in action to promptitude.

'It is now the second hour after sunrise: he rises from his throne and spends his leisure in inspecting his treasury or his stables. If a hunting day is announced, he rides forth, not carrying his bow by his side – that would be beneath his kingly dignity – but if in the chase, or on the road, you point out to him beast or bird within shooting distance, his hand is at once stretched out behind him and the slave puts into it the bow with its string floating in the air, for he deems it a womanish thing to have your bow strung for you by another, and a childish thing to carry it in a case. When he has received it, sometimes he bends the two ends towards one another in his hand, sometimes he lets the unknotted end drop to his heel, and then with quickly moving finger tightens the loose knot of the wandering string. Then he takes the arrows, fits them in, sends them forth, first desiring you to tell him what mark you wish him to aim at. You choose what he has to hit, and he hits it. If there is a mistake made by either party, it is more often the sight of the chooser than the aim of the archer that is at fault.

'If you are asked to join him in the banquet, which, however, on non-festal days, is like the entertainment of a private person, you will not see there the panting servants laying on the groaning table a tasteless heap of discoloured silver. The weight then is to be found in the conversation rather than in the plate, since all the guests, if they talk of anything at all, talk of

indication of the kind of flattery which a Roman provincial thought it prudent to bring to a barbarian king, that I have not thought it desirable to curtail it.
* *Cancelli*, the lattice-work partition which marked off the royal precincts, whence *cancellarius*, the doorkeeper, and our lord high *chancellor*: also the chancel of a church.

serious matters. The tapestry and curtains are sometimes of purple [cloth], sometimes of cotton. The meats on the table please you, not by their high price, but by the skill with which they are cooked, the silver by its brightness, not by its weight. The cups and goblets are so seldom replenished that you are more likely to complain of thirst than to be accused of drunkenness. In short, you may see there Greek elegance, Gallic abundance, Italian quickness, the pomp of a public personage, the assiduity of a private citizen, the discipline of a king's household. Of the luxury which is displayed on high days and holidays I need not give you any account, because it cannot be unknown even to the most unknown persons. Let me return to my task.

'The noontide slumber, when the meal is ended, is never long, and is frequently omitted altogether. Often at this time he takes a fancy to play at backgammon: then he collects the counters quickly, views them anxiously, decides on his moves skilfully, makes them promptly, talks to the counters jocularly, waits his turn patiently. At a good throw he says nothing, at a bad one he laughs; neither good nor bad makes him lose his temper or his philosophical equanimity. He does not like a speculative game either on the part of his adversary or himself, dislikes a lucky chance offered to himself, and will not reckon on its being offered to his opponent. You get your men out of his table without unnecessary trouble, he gets his out of yours without collusion. You would fancy that even in moving his counters he was planning a campaign. His sole anxiety is to conquer.

'When a game is on hand, he drops for a little time the severity of royal etiquette, and invites his companions in play, to free and social intercourse. To tell you what I think, he fears to be feared. At the end he is delighted to see the vexation of a conquered rival, and takes credit to himself for having really won the game, when his opponent's ill-temper shows that he has not yielded out of courtesy. And here notice a strange thing: often that very complacency of his, arising from such a trifling cause, ensures the successful carriage of serious business. Then petitions, which have well-nigh been shipwrecked by the injudiciousness of those who favoured them, suddenly find a harbour of safety. In this way, I myself, when I have had somewhat to ask of him, have been fortunate enough to be beaten, and have seen my table ruined with a light heart, because I knew that my cause would triumph.

'About the ninth hour [three o'clock] comes back again all that weary turmoil of kingship. The suitors return, the guards return whose business it is to remove them. Everywhere you hear the hum of claimants, and this is protracted till nightfall, and only ceases when it is cut short by the royal supper. Then the petitioners, following their various patrons, are dispersed throughout the palace, where they keep watch till bedtime arrives. At the supper sometimes, though rarely, comic actors are introduced who utter their satiric pleasantries: in such fashion, however, that none of the guests shall be wounded by their biting tongues. At these repasts no hydraulic organs blow, no band of vocalists under the guidance of a singing master intone together their premeditated harmony. No harpist, no flute-player, no choirmaster, no female player on the tambourine or the cithara, makes melody. The king is charmed only by those instruments under whose influence virtue soothes the soul as much as sweet sounds soothe the ear. When he rises from table the royal treasury receives its sentinels for the night, and armed men stand at all the entrances to the palace, by whom the hours of his first sleep will be watched over.

'But what has all this to do with my promise, which was to tell you a little about the king, not a great deal about his manner of reigning? I really must bid my pen to stop, for you did not ask to be made acquainted with anything more than the personal appearance and favourite pursuits of Theodoric: and I sat down to write a letter, not a history. Farewell.'

Syagrius and his Germanic Neighbours*

'Sidonius wishes health to his friend Syagrius.

'As you are grandson of a consul, and that on the paternal side, as you are sprung (which is more to our present purpose) from a poetic stock, descended from men who would have earned statues by their poems if they had not earned them by their services to the state, all which is shown by those verses of your ancestors which the present generation studies with unimpaired interest – as these are your antecedents, I cannot describe my astonishment at the ease with which you have mastered the German tongue. I remember that in your boyhood you were well trained in liberal studies, and I am informed that you often declaimed before a professional orator with force and eloquence. But since this is the case, pray tell me whence your soul has suddenly imbibed the oratory of an alien race, so that

* *Epistolae*, v.5. The Syagrius, upon whose relations to his German neighbours this strange sidelight is thrown by a letter from Sidonius, is apparently the same person as the son of Aegidius, the so-called 'Roman king of Soissons', whose defeat in 486 was one of the first steps in the upward career of Clovis.

you who had the phraseology of Virgil flogged into you at school, you who sweated over the long and stately sentences of Cicero, now swoop down upon us like a young falcon from the German language as though that were your old eyrie.

'You cannot imagine how I and all your other friends laugh when we hear that even the barbarian is afraid to talk his own language before you lest he should make a slip in his grammar. When you are interpreting their letters, the old men of Germany, bent with age, stand in open-mouthed wonder, and in their transactions with one another they voluntarily choose you for arbitrator and judge. A new Solon when you have to discuss the laws of the Burgundians, a new Amphion when you have to evoke music from their three-stringed lyre, you are loved and courted, you please, you decree, you are obeyed. And though the barbarians are equally stiff and lumpish in body and mind, yet in you they learn and love the speech of their fathers, the disposition of a Roman.

'It only now remains for you, O most brilliant of wits, to bestow any spare time which may still be yours on reading [Latin], and so to retain that elegance of style which you now possess. Thus while you preserve your Latin that we may not laugh at you, you will practise your German that you may be able to laugh at us. Farewell.'

Roman Intriguers at the Burgundian Court*

A young kinsman of Sidonius, also named Apollinaris, had been brought into some danger through the calumnies of informers who represented to the Burgundian prince Chilperic that he was secretly plotting for the surrender of Vaison, a border fortress, to 'the new emperor', Julius Nepos.

Sidonius writes concerning these informers to Thaumastus, the brother of the calumniated man, with sympathetic indignation.

'These are the men, as you have often heard me say, under whose villainies our country groans, longing for the more merciful barbarians. These are the men before whom even the great tremble. These are they whose peculiar province it appears to be to bring calumnious accusations, to carry off men from their homes, to frighten them with threats, to pillage their substance. These are the men who in idleness boast of their business, in peace of their plunder, in war of their clever escapes, in their cups of victories. These are they who procrastinate your law-suit if you engage them, who get it postponed if you pass them by, who are annoyed if you

* *Epistolae*, v.7.

remind them of their engagement, and forget it — after taking your fee — if you do not . . . These are the men who envy quiet citizens their tranquillity, soldiers their pay, postmasters their tariffs, merchants their markets, ambas-sadors their functions, tax-farmers their tolls, the provincials their farms, the burgesses their guild dinners,* the cashiers their weights, the registrars their measures, the scribes their salaries, the accountants their fees, the guards their largesse, the cities their repose, the publicans their taxes, the clergy their reverence, the nobles their birth, their betters their precedence, their equals their equality, the officials their power, the ex-officials their privileges, the learners their schools, the teachers their stipends, the taught their knowledge.

'These are the men drunken with new wealth, who by the vulgar display of their possessions show how little they are accustomed to ownership, the men who go in full armour to a banquet, in white robes to a funeral, in hides to church, in black to a wedding, in beaver-skin to the litany. No set of men suits them, no time seems to hit their humour. In the market they are very Scythians, in the bedchamber they are vipers, at the banquet buffoons, in confiscations harpies, in conversation statues, in argument brute beasts, in business snails, in enforcing a contract usurers. They are stone if you want them to understand, fire if they have to judge, quick to wrath, slow to pardon, panthers in their friendship, bears in their fun, foxes in their deceit, bulls in their pride, Minotaurs in their rapacity.

'Their firmest hopes are founded on the uncertainties of the times; they love to fish in troubled waters; yet fearful both from natural cowardice and from an uneasy conscience, while they are lions at court they are hares in the camp, and are afraid of a truce lest they should be made to disgorge, of war lest they should have to fight.'

The good bishop's invective rolls on still through some sentences, which need not be inflicted on the reader. Though well-nigh out of breath with following Sidonius' headlong rhetoric, he may still have gathered from it the important fact that the chief instruments of such oppression as was practised by the barbarian invaders upon the provincials were men who were themselves of Roman origin.

* *Flaminia*, literally 'their priesthoods'. But probably these old heathen dignities were only kept up for the sake of some convivial practices connected with them.

The Physique of the Burgundians*

While our poet was residing at Lyons (apparently) he was asked by one of
his friends, an ex-consul named Catulinus, to compose an epithalamium,
perhaps for his daughter's marriage.

In a short, humorous poem of apology Sidonius incidentally touches off
some of the physical characteristics of the Burgundians, by whom he was
surrounded, and who, it is important to observe, troubled him, not by their
hostility, but by their too hearty and demonstrative friendship.

> Ah me! my friend, why bid me, e'en if I had the power,
> To write the light Fescennine verse, fit for the nuptial bower?
> Do you forget that I am set among the long-haired hordes,
> That daily I am bound to bear the stream of German words,
> That I must hear, and then must praise with sorrowful grimace
> (Disgust and approbation both contending in my face),
> Whate'er the gormandising sons of Burgundy may sing,
> While they upon their yellow hair the rancid butter fling?
>
> Now let me tell you what it is that makes my lyre be dumb:
> It cannot sound when all around barbarian lyres do hum.
> The sight of all those patrons tall (each one is seven foot high),
> From my poor muse makes every thought of six-foot metres fly.†
> Oh! happy are thine eyes, my friend: thine ears, how happy those!
> And oh! thrice happy I would call thine undisgusted nose.
> 'Tis not round thee that every morn ten talkative machines
> Exhale the smell of onions, leeks, and all their vulgar greens.
> There do not seek thy house, as mine, before the dawn of day,
> So many giants and so tall, so fond of trencher-play
> That scarce Alcinous himself, that hospitable king,
> Would find his kitchen large enough for the desires they bring.
> They do not, those effusive souls, declare they look on thee
> As father's friend or foster-sire – but, alas! they do on me.
>
> But stop, my muse! pull up! be still! or else some fool will say
> 'Sidonius writes lampoons again.'‡ Don't *you* believe them, pray!

* *Carmina*, xii.   † The metre of the original is hendecasyllabic.
‡ For the explanation of this allusion see pp. 245–8.

The tenor of these verses reminds us of an epigram of unknown author-ship, but composed probably in the fifth century:

Round me the *hails* of the Goths, their *skapjam* and *matjam* and *drinkam*,
Harshly resound: in such din who could fit verses indite?
Calliope, sweet muse, from the wine-wet embraces of Bacchus
Shrinks, lest her wavering feet bear her no longer aright.*

The Young Frankish Chief and his Retinue †

'Sidonius wishes health to his friend Domnitius.

'You are fond of inspecting armour and armed men. What a pleasure it would be for you could you see the royal youth Sigismer, decked out like a suitor or a bridegroom, in all the bravery of his tribe, visiting the palace of his father-in-law, his own horse gorgeously caparisoned, other horses, laden with blazing gems, going before or following after him; and then, with a touch of modesty which was especially suitable to his circumstances, in the midst of his outriders and rearguard, he himself walked on foot, in crimson robe with burnished golden ornaments and white silken mantle, his ruddy cheeks, his golden hair, his milk-white skin repeating in his person those three colours of his dress. Of all the petty kings and confederates who accompanied him, the appearance was terrible even in their peaceful garb; they had the lower part of the foot down to the heel bound about with boots of bristly ox-leather, while their knees and their calves were without cover-ing. Above, they had garments coming high up the neck, tight-girdled, woven of various colours, scarcely approaching their bare legs; their sleeves draped only the beginning of their arms, they had green cloaks adorned with purple fringes; their swords, depending from their shoulders by baldrics, pressed into their sides the reindeers' skins,‡ which were fastened

---

* This epigram is valuable as containing four Gothic words – *hails*, 'your health' (the drinking shout also found in 'wassail'); *skapjan*, 'to make' or 'frame'; *matjan*, 'to eat'; *drinkan*, 'to drink'.

† *Epistolae*, iv.20. The assignment of a Frankish nationality to Sigismer is only a probable conjecture. Domnitius or Domnicius, the correspondent to whom this letter is addressed, is the enthusiastic dice-player of the first letter (see p. 188).

‡ The *rheno*, or reindeer's skin, seems to have answered the same purpose as the 'water-proof' of modern civilisation, and, like it, when not actually in use, would be rolled up and slung over the shoulder.

by a round clasp. As for that part of their adornments which was also a defence, their right hands held hooked lances and battleaxes for throwing, their left sides were overshadowed by round shields whose lustre, silvery at the outer circumference and golden at the central boss, declared the wealth as well as the taste of the wearers. All was so ordered that this wedding procession suggested the thought of Mars not less emphatically than of Venus.

'But why spend so many words on the subject? All that was wanting to the show was your presence. For when I remembered that you were not looking upon a sight which it would have so delighted you to behold, I translated your feelings into my own, and longed for you as impatiently as you would have longed for the spectacle. Farewell.'

It is interesting, but somewhat perplexing, to observe that some of the details of the dress of these undoubtedly Teutonic warriors would fit equally well with the Celtic highlanders of Scotland.

The Saxon Sea-Rovers*

At the end of a long letter, written by Sidonius to his friend Nammatius, after dull compliments and duller banter, we suddenly find flashed upon us this lifelike picture, by a contemporary hand, of the brothers and cousins of the men, if not of the very men themselves who had fought at Aylesford under Hengest and Horsa, or who were slowly winning the kingdom of the South Saxons.

'Behold, when I was on the point of concluding this epistle in which I have already chattered on too long, a messenger suddenly arrived from Saintonge with whom I have spent some hours in conversing about you and your doings, and who constantly affirms that you have just sounded your trumpet on board the fleet, and that, combining the duties of a sailor and a soldier, you are roaming along the winding shores of the Ocean, looking out for the curved pinnaces of the Saxons. When you see the rowers of that nation you may at once make up your mind that every one of them is an arch-pirate; with such wonderful unanimity do all at once command, obey, teach, and learn their one chosen business of brigandage. For this reason I ought to warn you to be more than ever on your guard in this warfare. Your enemy is the most truculent of all enemies. Unexpectedly he attacks, when expected he escapes, he despises those who seek to block his path, he overthrows those who are off their guard, he always succeeds in

* *Epistolae*, viii.6. In the early part of this letter Sidonius gives that description of the inaugural oration of Nicetius which has been already quoted (see p. 179).

cutting off the enemy whom he follows, while he never fails when he desires to effect his own escape. Moreover, to these men a shipwreck is capital prac- tice rather than an object of terror. The dangers of the deep are to them, not casual acquaintances, but intimate friends. For since a tempest throws the invaded off their guard, and prevents the invaders from being descried from afar, they hail with joy the crash of waves on the rocks, which gives them their best chance of escaping from other enemies than the elements.

'Then again, before they raise the deep-biting anchor from the hostile soil, and set sail from the continent for their own country, their custom is to collect the crowd of their prisoners together, by a mockery of equity to make them cast lots which of them shall undergo the iniquitous sentence of death, and then at the moment of departure to slay every tenth man so selected by crucifixion, a practice which is the more lamentable because it arises from a superstitious notion that they will thus ensure for themselves a safe return.* Purifying themselves as they consider by such sacrifices, pol- luting themselves as we deem by such deeds of sacrilege, they think the foul murders which they thus commit are acts of worship to their gods, and they glory in extorting cries of agony instead of ransoms from these doomed victims.

'Wherefore I am on your behalf distraught with many fears and various forebodings; though on the other hand I have immense incitements to hope, first, because you are fighting under the banner of a victorious nation; sec- ondly, because I hold that the power of chance is limited over wise men, among whom you are rightly reckoned; thirdly, because it is often when our friends at a distance are the safest that our hearts are filled with the most sin- ister presentiments regarding them . . .

'I send you the *Libri Logistorici* of Varro,† and the *Chronology* of Eus- ebius, a kind of literary file with which, if you have any leisure amidst the cares of the camp, you may rub off some of the rust from your style after you have wiped the blood from your armour. Farewell.'

The Woman Wrongfully Enslaved‡

The following account of the captivity and bondage of a poor woman of Auvergne incidentally illustrates the troubled condition of Gaul, while it astonishes us by the legal doctrine contained in it. Apparently the maxim

---

* Compare with this statement the classical legend concerning the sacrifice of Iphigenia at Aulis to procure favourable winds for the Grecian fleet.

† A lost work, satirising the manners of the time.   ‡ *Epistolae*, vi.4.

with which our own courts are familiar, that 'a bona fide purchaser of stolen property, without notice of the theft, may justify his holding', even applied to the most outrageous of all thefts, that of liberty; and a woman wrongfully enslaved, but in the hands of a bona fide purchaser, could not claim her freedom.

'Sidonius wishes health to Pope Lupus.*

'After that expression of homage which is endlessly due, though it be unceasingly paid, to your incomparably eminent apostleship, I take advantage of our old friendship to set before you the new calamities of the humble bearers of this letter, who, after having undertaken a long journey, and at this time of the year, into the heart of Auvergne, have returned with no fruit of their labour. A woman who was nearly related to them was by chance carried off by an inroad of the Vargi† – a name borne by some local banditti – and was taken some years ago into your district and there sold. This they ascertained on indubitable evidence, and followed tardily but surely the indications which they had received. But in the meantime, before they arrived upon the scene, she, having been sold in market overt, was living as a household slave in the family of our friend the merchant.‡ A certain Prudens who, they say, is now living at Troyes, appeared to vouch for the contract of her sale, which was effected by men unknown to me, and his subscription, as that of a fit and proper witness,§ is now shown attached to the deed of sale. You who are present on the spot will, from your exalted position, be easily able to test each link in this chain of wrongful acts. The affair is all the more criminal because, as I am informed by the bearers of this letter, one of the woman's fellow travellers was actually killed when she was carried off.

'But since the relations, who brood over this criminal affair, desire that your judgement should apply the remedy, I think it will be befitting both to your office and your character to devise some compromise whereby you may at the same time assist the grief of one party and the peril of the other. By some wise and wellconsidered sentence you may thus make the former less distressed, the latter less guilty, and both more secure; lest otherwise, such is

* This is Lupus, bishop of Troyes, the fascinator of Attila (see p. 77).

† Apparently these were Teutonic depredators. *Vargs* is found in Old High German with the signification 'an outlaw', and *vargitha* in the Gothic translation of the Bible by Ulfilas = 'condemnation' (Romans 13 : 2).

‡ Apparently an allusion to some merchant known both to Sidonius and Lupus.

§ Or guarantor.

the disturbed state of the times and the district, the affair go on to an end as fatal as was its beginning. Condescend to remember me, my lord pope.'

The 'Levite' of Auvergne*

Another illustration of the sufferings of the poorer inhabitants from the storms of barbarian conquest, is afforded by the following letter of interces, sion on behalf of a man of 'the Levitical order'. By this term Sidonius probably means to indicate a person who, though married, and working for his livelihood, filled (like Amantius the fortune-hunter) the office of lec, tor (reader) in the church.

'Sidonius wishes health to Pope Censorius [bishop of Auxerre].

'The bearer of this letter is dignified by an office which raises him into the Levitical order. He with his family in avoiding the whirlpool of Gothic depredation, was swept, so to say, by the very weight of the stream of fugi, tives, into your territory; and there, on the possessions of the church over which your holiness presides, the hungry stranger threw into the half, ploughed sods his scanty seeds, the produce of which he now begs that he may be allowed to reap without deductions. If you should be inclined to grant him as a servant of the faith this favour, namely, that he shall not be required to pay the quota which is due to the glebe, the poor man, whose notions are as bounded as his fortune, will think himself as well-off as if he was again tilling his native fields. If, therefore, you can let him off the lawful and customary rent, payable out of his very trifling harvest, he will return from your country as thankful as if he had been splendidly entertained. If you will also by his hands bestow upon me with your wonted courtesy a reply to this letter, I and my brethren living here will receive that written page as if it had come straight down from heaven. Condescend to remem, ber me, my lord pope.'

With this notice of the poor expatriated 'Levite' we finish our study of the social life of the falling Empire as portrayed from the works of Apollinaris Sidonius. But little effort is required to draw the necessary inferences from the condition of the Gallo-Romans to that of the Italians. From the shores of Como or Maggiore, as from the mountains of Auvergne, may many a needy tiller of the soil have been 'swept away by the tide of flight from the conquering Visigoths'. Many a Neapolitan or Tarentine woman of Greek descent and Italian nationality may have been carried away like the poor

* *Epistolae*, vi.10.

Gaulish woman by wild marauders following in the track of the invading armies, sold as a slave, and not even the place of her bondage discovered for years by her friends. The habits of the Saxon freebooters may help us to understand the life of bold piratical adventure led by the Vandals, though we must not attribute the harsher features of heathen savagery to the Arian followers of Gaiseric. And in the pictures of the court and retinue of Theodoric and Sigismer we have probably some strokes which will be equally applicable to every Teuton chief who led his men over the Alpine passes into Italy, from Alaric to Alboin.

It is impossible not to think with regret of the wasted opportunities of Apollinaris Sidonius. Here is a man who evidently hungered and thirsted for literary distinction even more than for consular dignity or saintly canon-isation. Yet he has achieved nothing beyond a fifth-rate position as a 'post-classical' author, and with difficulty do a few historical enquirers, like Gibbon, Guizot, Thierry, keep his name from being absolutely forgotten by the world. Had he faced the new and strange nationalities which were swarming forth from Germany, in the simple, enquiring, childlike attitude of the father of history, he might have been the Herodotus of medieval and modern Europe. From him we might have learned the songs which were sung by the actual contemporaries of Attila and Gundahar, and which formed the kernel of the *Nibelungenlied*; from him we might have received a true and authentic picture of the laws and customs of the Goths, the Franks, and the Burgundians, a picture which would have in turn illus-trated and been illustrated by the poetry of Tacitus' *Germania*, and the prose of the black-letter commentators on English common law. He might have transmitted to us the full portraiture of the great apostle of the Germanic races, Ulfilas, the secret causes of his and their devotion to the Arian form of Christianity, the Gothic equivalents of the mythological tales of the Scandinavian *Edda*, the story of the old runes and their relation to the Moeso-Gothic alphabet. All these details and a hundred more, full of interest to science, to art, to literature, Sidonius might have preserved for us, had his mind been as open as was that of Herodotus to the manifold impressions made by picturesque and strange nationalities. But he turned away with disgust from the seven-foot-high barbarians, smelling of leeks and onions, and by preference told over again for the hundredth time and worse than any of his predecessors, the vapid and worn-out stories of Greek mythology. Most truly has our own Wordsworth said,

> We live by admiration, hope, and love,
> And even as these are well and wisely fixed
> In dignity of being we ascend.*

For want of the first two qualities and others which spring up around them, Sidonius has missed one of the grandest opportunities ever offered in literature.

* *The Excursion*, bk iv.

CHAPTER VIII

Avitus, the Client of the Visigoths

WHEN GAISERIC AND HIS VANDAL HORDE WITH-drew from the scene of their depredations, silence and prostration seem to have fallen upon the city of Rome. There was no attempt to raise a new emperor to the dignity which had been held by the murdered Valentinian and the murdered Maximus: possibly no one was found courageous enough to offer himself for so perilous a pre-eminence. So in the heart of the once arrogant queen of the world reigned for two months the apathy of despair. At length on the 14th of August (455), some two months after the capture of the city, the news arrived that the Gaulish provinces had raised to the vacant throne a nobleman of Auvergne, named Avitus, who had assumed the purple at Arles on the 10th of July. The Imperial city bowed her head and accepted her new lord without remonstrance.

Avitus had already once played a conspicuous part in Imperial politics when it had devolved upon him to cement that alliance between Rome and the Visigoths by which the power of Attila was shattered on the Mauriac plains. We are in possession of some other details of his previous life, but they come to us from the pen of a great manufacturer of indiscriminate panegyric, and it is not easy to say what are the actual events to which they correspond. He was descended from a family, several members of which had held high commands in the army and the state, and which was, by the labours of antiquaries, connected with the old patrician families of Rome.*

* This is the explanation I would suggest of the difficult lines—
> *Gentisque suae, te teste, Philagri,*
> *Patricius resplendet apex*

[As Philagrius has shown, he heads a great patrician house] (Apollinaris Sidonius, *Panegyric of Avitus*, 156–7). Philagrius was a man of letters, renowned for the magnificence of his library (Apollinaris Sidonius, *Carmina*, xxiv.93). Unless the question related to the ancient patriciate of Rome and Avitus' shadowy descent therefrom, it is difficult to see why Philagrius should be avouched as an authority. [For more information on the family of Avitus see table ii, p. 397.]

He was born, in all probability, about the time of the death of Theodosius, and would therefore be close upon his sixtieth year when he arrayed himself with the Imperial purple.* It was told of him that in early boyhood he came one day upon a she-wolf, rabid with hunger, and snatching up a fragment of rock which lay close by, hurled it at the savage creature and broke her skull. To the studies of Cicero and Caesar, which engaged his childhood, suc- ceeded in youth the delights of boar-hunting and falconry. Yet his reading had perhaps not been wholly fruitless, for he had scarcely arrived at man's estate, when, being chosen by his neighbours to head a deputation to Con- stantius, he pleaded so eloquently for some remission of taxation that the admiring governor granted all his requests.

In middle life he served with some credit under the greatest captain of the age, Aetius, in the wars which he waged in Belgic Gaul, and in Noricum, on the lower Rhine, and the middle Danube. Once at least he exposed his person to some danger in a hand-to-hand encounter. The Roman generals were at this time (about the year 439) with marvellous impolicy bringing the Hunnish hordes into Gaul to fight their battles against less barbarous bar- barians. Litorius, that rash and feather-headed general, was marching a troop of these squalid auxiliaries through Auvergne, on his way from Brit- tany, which he had conquered, to the Gothic capital Toulouse, which he hoped to conquer. The so-called auxiliaries of Rome carried fire and sword, insolence and robbery, through the province which was conspicuous above all others by its fidelity to Rome. One of these wild mercenaries happened to quarrel with a man engaged in the service of Avitus, and struck him a mortal blow. The man in dying breathed his master's name, and coupled with it a prayer for vengeance. Avitus, when informed of his servant's death, at once donned his armour and sought the Hunnish camp. We need not believe the strained language of the panegyrist, who solemnly informs us that in his rage for his murdered servant he slew as many of the Huns as Achilles slew Trojans after the death of Patroclus: but we seem bound to accept his story of the future emperor's single combat with the murderer, which ended, after the third passage of arms, in Avitus breaking the Hun's breastplate, and transfixing his breast with his spear, which being thrust vigorously home, stood out behind the back of the caitiff. 'The blood and the life together ebbed away through the double wound.'

* We get the approximate date of the birth of Avitus from the fact that he was a very young man when he was sent on a deputation to Constantius, who was not yet married to Placidia, probably therefore about 415. This points to 394 or 395 for the year of his birth.

Shortly after this event, Avitus, who had already held three commands in the army, was raised to the high civil office of praetorian prefect in Gaul, an office which may perhaps have occupied six years of his life, from 439 to 445. From these duties he retired to his estate in the heart of Auvergne, to that very villa of Avitacum overlooking the lake, and overlooked by the mountains, of which we have already heard a description from the pen of its next possessor, Sidonius. For the family of Avitus consisted of two sons, Ecdicius and Agricola, and one daughter, Papianilla. This daughter is the lady whom Sidonius married about the year 452, and most of our information about the career, as well as the dwelling-place of the Arvernian emperor, is derived from the verses or the letters of his fluent son-in-law.

The connection which most powerfully influenced the life of Avitus, and which alone gave him any chance, a small one at the best, of being remembered in history, was a friendship which, while still a boy, he formed with the Visigothic monarch at Toulouse, and which on the side of the barbarian was continued into a second generation. A brother of the young Arvernian, named Theodorus, had been sent as a hostage to the court of Theodoric I. Avitus went to Toulouse to visit Theodorus, and by some unexplained charm of manner, or beauty of character, so won upon the Gothic king that he offered him large sums of money if he would renounce his Gallo-Roman nationality, and take up his permanent residence at the court of Toulouse. This offer was rejected, scornfully rejected, says his panegyrist; but there is some reason to think that Avitus may have discharged for a time the duties of governor to the young Visigothic princes. His powerful intercession is said to have saved Narbonne (436) when sorely blockaded by the barbarian arms, and at the last stage of famine. And on a more eventful day (in 451), as has been already described, Avitus was the chosen intermediary between Rome and Toulouse, the man who, by his personal influence with Theodoric I, did more than any other single individual to mould the great Roman—Gothic alliance against Attila, which saved Europe from becoming Tartar.

That alliance had done its work, and apparently was dissolved, when the terror from the Hun was over. But the thought probably suggested itself both to the new Visigothic king, Theodoric II, and to his Gaulish friend, that it might be revived, and might serve a useful purpose for both of them in the troubled state of Roman politics after the murder of Valentinian III. Avitus had been drawn by the emperor Maximus from his retirement, and invested with the office of *magister utriusque militiae* (captain-general of horse and foot), which gave him complete control over all military matters in Gaul. The three-months' reign of Maximus had been well employed by the new general in checking the inroads of the tribes dwelling by the lower Rhine, and his credit with the soldiers and the provincials was at a high point, when tidings arrived in Gaul of the Vandal sack of Rome and the vacancy of the Empire. Possibly the young oratorical son-in-law, Sidonius, was employed to furbish up the old friendship with the Visigoth, and he may have gained a point or two for the aspirant to the purple by diplomatic-ally losing a few games on the backgammon board of Theodoric.

Four great Germanic nations were at this time supreme in western Europe: the Vandals, the Visigoths, the Burgundians, and the Suevi. A fifth, that of the Franks, one day to be the mightiest of them all, was as yet scarcely peeping over the horizon. The Vandals, as we know, ruled Africa from Carthage, the Visigoths south-western France from Toulouse, the Burgundians were settled in the valley of the Rhône, and their chief capital was Lyons; the Suevi held the greater part of southern and western Spain, and their capital was Astorga. The Vandals and Visigoths were sworn foes ever since the cruel outrage practised by Gaiseric on his Visigothic daughter-in-law. The Burgundians and Visigoths lived in a state of simmering unfriendliness, not often passing into vindictive war. The Suevi, who were now by the departure of the Vandals the only barbarian power left in the peninsula, carried on a desultory warfare with Roman Spain, but at this time were living at peace with their Visigothic neighbours from whom they were divided by the Pyrenees, and their king Rechiarius had married a sis-ter of the reigning Theodoric.

Such being the position of affairs, the transaction which suggested itself, at some time in the summer of 455, to the minds of the most powerful men at Arles and Toulouse must have been something of this nature:

'Let us join forces and form a triple alliance. To you, Avitus, shall fall the Imperial purple: we Visigoths will assert your claims against any other com-petitor, and if need be, protect you against the hated Vandal. In return for this you shall lend us the sanction of the name and the rights of the Empire for an enterprise which we are meditating against the Suevi. Though we have been settled for the last half-century chiefly on the northern side of the Pyrenees, we have never entirely renounced the hope of including Spain in our dominion. That was the vision of the great Ataulfus, brother-in-law of Alaric, that and the welding of Roman and Visigoth into one harmonious commonwealth; and if we can now make this compact with you, our nobler and firmer Attalus, his vision may yet become a reality. And lastly, if you, Burgundians, instead of harassing us by your aimless warfare, will join our great expedition, the territories in the valley of the Rhône, which you now hold by a friendly compact with the Empire, shall be enlarged – does not the new Augustus consent to this? – and it may be that you shall reach even to the Mediterranean sea.'

Such was probably the honest prose of the transaction which raised the nobleman of Auvergne to the headship of the Empire; but in diplomacy and in poetry it of course assumes a very different aspect. The Visigothic king, no doubt in collusion with Avitus, threatened an invasion of Roman Gaul. The master of the soldiery assembled his troops, but consented to assume once more the office of ambassador to Toulouse, in order to avert the horrors of war from the provincials. He sent before him Messianus, a high functionary of Gaul. At the appearance of this messenger, many a sturdy Visigoth, intent on the rapture of coming war, foreboded that the magical influence of Avitus would again prevail, and that they would be baulked of the hoped-for struggle. Soon their fears were confirmed. The master himself appeared on the scene erect and stately. Theodoric came forth to greet him, attended by his brother Frithareiks* (the king of peace). His welcome to the Roman was eager but confused; and the three, with joined hands, entered the gates of Toulouse. It was a fortunate coincidence (if it was a mere coincidence) that just as they entered the town the news arrived of the murder of the emperor Maximus, and the capture of Rome by Gaiseric – news which considerably improved the prospects of the new partnership.

On the next day a grand council of the Visigothic warriors was held. From necessity rather than choice, the veteran chiefs who assembled there did not reflect the magnificence of the sovereign. Their robes were threadbare and greasy, their scanty skin-cloaks scarcely reached down to the knee, and their boots, made of horse's hide, were hitched up around the calf by a shabbily tied knot.† So were the men attired whose 'honoured poverty' was welcomed into the councils of the nation.

The Gothic king questioned the Roman officer as to the terms of the peace which he was come to propose between the two nations. Avitus replied, dilating on the old friendship which had existed between him and the first Theodoric. 'He, I am sure, would not have denied my request. You

* Our 'Frederick'. But it may have been Euric, or another brother.

† Apollinaris Sidonius, *Panegyric of Avitus*, 454–7.

were a child then, and cannot remember how he, in compliance with my advice, withdrew his blockading army from Narbonne, when that city was already pale with famine, and was forced to feed upon the most loathsome victuals.'

> E'en thou — as well these hoary chieftains know —
> In those young days beheld'st in me no foe.
> Oft have I pressed thee, weeping, to my heart,
> When thy nurse came, refusing to depart.
> Now once again I come thy faith to prove,
> And plead the rights of that ancestral love.
> If faith, affection, filial reverence die,
> Go! hard of heart, and peace to Rome deny.

So far Avitus: a murmur of rough voices through the council testified their approbation of his pleadings for peace. The next lines in the play fell to Theodoric; and he spoke his part with great animation and correctness. He enlarged on his old friendship for Avitus, his reluctance to break off that friendship, his willingness to serve 'the venerable might of Rome and the race which, like his own, had sprung from Mars', his desire even to wipe out the memory of the guilt of Alaric by the benefits which he would confer on the Eternal City. But there was one price which must be paid for his services. If Avitus would assume the diadem, the Empire should have in the Visigoth the most faithful of allies: if not, the war once proclaimed must rage on. If the general wished to save the world, he must govern it.*

The master of the soldiery heard these words, which were ratified by the solemn oath of the royal brothers, with an appearance of profound sadness. He returned to Arles, whither the tidings preceded him, that the desired peace with the Goths could only be obtained by the elevation of Avitus to the Imperial dignity. The chief officials of Gaul were hastily summoned to the castle of Ugernum (now Beaucaire, on the Rhône, a few miles above Arles); the proposal to declare Avitus emperor was carried by acclamation, vanity perhaps concurring with policy in the scheme of giving a Gaulish ruler to Rome. On the third day after the assembly at Ugernum Avitus appeared upon a high-heaped *agger*† surrounded by the soldiery, who put

* Apollinaris Sidonius, *Panegyric of Avitus*, 517–18.
† An earthen mound. In the bas-reliefs on the column of Trajan, the emperor is generally represented as standing on such a mound when addressing his soldiers.

upon his head a military collar, to represent the true Imperial diadem, which was probably in safe custody at Ravenna. The new Augustus wore still the same melancholy countenance with which he had first listened to the flattering proposal of Theodoric; and it is possible that by this time the sadness may have been not all feigned, some conviction of his own inability to cope with the weight of the falling commonwealth having already entered his soul.

The story of Avitus' elevation to the throne has seemed worth telling, because it illustrates the manner in which the great barbarian monarchies influenced the fortunes of the dying Empire, the degrees in which force and art were still blended in order to secure obedience to its behests, and the nature of the tie which bound those later 'shadow emperors' to their by no means shadowy patrons. But of the reign of this emperor, which lasted only sixteen months, we have but a few faint details from the annalists, which leave us little more to say than that he reigned, and that he ceased to reign.

The autumn of 455 was probably employed in an expedition to the province of Pannonia, an expedition which, we are asked to believe, reunited to the Empire regions which had been lost to it for generations. It is possible that in the complete collapse of Attila's power, Rome may have successfully reclaimed some portions of her ancient dominion by the Danube; but it is difficult to conjecture the motives which could have sent the new emperor forth on so distant an expedition, while the terrible and unsubdued Vandal was still crouching at his gates ready to repeat his spring.

On the first day of the year 456 Rome witnessed the usual splendid pageant which announced that the supreme Augustus condescended to assume the historic office of consul, and to mark the year with his name.* Among the solemnities of the day, the young Sidonius recited, in the hearing of the senate and the people,† a panegyric 602 lines long, after the

* There is a puzzle here. Avitus' name does not appear in the consular *fasti* for the year 456, except in the chronicles of Idatius the Spaniard. All other chroniclers assign the year to 'Joannes and Varanes'. Tillemont suggests that Marcian, emperor of the East, refused his sanction to the elevation of Avitus; but this does not seem a probable solution of the difficulty, especially as Idatius says, 'Marcian and Avitus enjoyed the headship of the Roman Empire in concord.' Can there have been on the fall of Avitus some judicial process like the English attainder, erasing his name from the lists both of consuls and patricians? This might help to explain the difficulty as to the non-patrician rank of the family of Avitus. See note to p. 222.   † *Epistolae*, ix.16.

manner of Claudian, which he had composed in honour of his father-in-law. This panegyric is the source – the doubtful source, it must be admitted – from which have been drawn the facts previously related concerning the private life of the Arvernian senator and the manner of his elevation to the throne. The attempt to emulate Claudian's panegyrics on Honorius and Stilicho is evident, but the failure to reach even Claudian's standard of excellence is equally evident. The old, worn-out mythological machinery is as freely used, and with even less of dramatic fitness and truth. Jupiter convokes an assembly of the gods; all the Olympians of the first and second rank attend it. Thither also come all the great river-gods of the world, the Rhine, the Po, the Danube, the Nile.* And thither at last, with bent head and flagging steps, without a helmet, and scarce able to drag the weight of her heavy lance, comes unhappy Rome. She begins at first with some naturalness and spirit, longing for the happy days when she was still small, obscure, and safe, before greatness had brought its harassing penalty. She recurs with dread to the omen of the twelve vultures seen by the Etrurian augur on Mount Palatine at the foundation of the city. If those twelve vultures did truly mean, as some supposed, that she should have twelve centuries of greatness, her day is done, for the allotted time expired eight years ago (in AD 447).

Soon, however, the unhappy queen of the world wanders off into mere Roman history. She repeats to great Jove a versified compendium of Livy, and condenses the lives of the first twelve Caesars into an equal number of lines, which might have been prepared as a *memoria technica* by a Roman schoolboy.

The father of gods and men takes up the tale, and shows that he is not to be outdone in knowledge of Livy and Tacitus. Then, having vindicated his scholarship, he tells her that he has prepared a man for her deliverance, born in Auvergne, a land fertile in heroes. This destined deliverer is Avitus, whose respectable life and fortunes Jupiter describes in 460 lines of unbroken monologue. We listen in weariness to the long, level narrative, and think what a change has come over the court of Olympus since, in a few majestic words, the Thunderer granted the earnest prayer of silver-footed Thetis. Then Jupiter nodded, now his hearers.

To the taste of the Romans of the fifth century, however, the fluent hexameters of the young Gaulish poet probably appeared really meritorious.

* The last of these is happily enough described – 'The Nile whom all know for his source unknown.'

At any rate they were written by the son-in-law of Augustus, and consequently every good courtier was bound to admire them. The senate decreed that 'an everlasting statue' of brass should be raised in honour of Apollinaris Sidonius, which should stand between the Greek and Latin libraries in the forum of Trajan.*

While the new emperor was thus inaugurating his reign at Rome, his powerful patron at Toulouse was using the new alliance for his own purposes. Embassies passed to and fro between the king of the Visigoths and the king of the Suevi. The former, whose messengers were accompanied by the Gaulish count Fronto, as representative of Rome, called upon his Suevic brother-in-law to cease from the attacks which he had been lately making on Roman Spain, the Empire and the Visigothic monarchy being now united in mutual league, and the invaders of the one being the enemies of the other. To this embassy Rechiarius returned a haughty answer: 'If thou complainest of what I am doing here, I will come to Tholosa where thou dwellest; there, if thou art strong enough, resist me.' This insolent defiance hastened the warlike preparations of Theodoric. Early in the year 456 (apparently) he invaded Spain with an enormous army, to which the two kings of the Burgundians, Gundiok and Chilperic, brought their promised contingent; and he was able to assert (probably thereby commanding some assistance from wavering provincials) that he came 'with the will and by the ordinance of Avitus the emperor'.

This campaign destroyed the greatness of the Suevic kingdom.† Rechiarius was defeated in a great battle at the river Urbicus, twelve miles from Astorga (5th October). Theodoric pushed on to Braga, took that place on the 28th of October, and though that day was a Sunday, and the victory had been a bloodless one as far as his host was concerned, he used his success in a manner which horrified his contemporaries; carried off vast numbers of men, women, and children into captivity, stripped the clergy naked, filled the holy places 'with horrors of horses, cattle, and camels', and in short repeated all the judgements which the wrath of God had suffered to fall on Jerusalem. The fugitive Rechiarius was taken prisoner next year 'at a place called Portucale' (Oporto), and after some months' captivity, was put to death by his vindictive brother-in-law, who could not forget his insulting message about the visit to Toulouse.

* Apollinaris Sidonius, *Epistolae*, ix.16, and *Carmina*, viii.7–8.
† It lingered on, however, in an enfeebled condition for more than a century longer, till it was in 584 finally overthrown by Leovigild, king of the Visigoths.

While Theodoric was thus engaged with the Suevi, news was brought to him of an important victory which his Imperial ally had gained over the Vandals. Sixty of their ships had set sail from the harbour of Carthage; they had reached Corsica and cast anchor there, seeming to threaten Italy and Gaul at once. The brave and capable count Ricimer followed them thither, outmanoeuvred and surrounded them with his fleet, and slew of them a great multitude.*

So far all seemed going well with the Romano-Gothic confederation, and the moment when Hesychius, the Imperial ambassador, presented himself at the camp of Theodoric in Galicia with these tidings, with presents from the emperor, and with the further intelligence that his master had come to Arles, probably to meet his Visigothic ally – this moment was probably the apogee of the new combination. But there was a worm at the root of this apparent prosperity. Ricimer was after his late victory the idol of the army and the most powerful man in the Empire, and Ricimer had determined to shatter the new alliance. Nor was such a determination wonderful, since this strange and perplexing character who, for the next sixteen years, played the part of king-maker at Rome, was himself the son of a Suevic father, though of a Visigothic mother, and was not likely to hear well-pleased the tidings of the sack of Braga and the countless horrors which had befallen his countrymen at the hand of the ally of Avitus.

He resolved that the Arvernian senator must lay aside the purple, and he probably had the popular voice with him when he pronounced Avitus unfitted for the emergencies of the Empire. The Gaulish nobleman was a man of unspotted private character, and had once possessed some courage and capacity for war, but he was fond of ease, perhaps of luxury, and the almost childlike simplicity and openness of his nature, to say nothing of his sixty years, unfitted him to cope with the lawless intriguers, Roman and barbarian, by whom he was surrounded.† Famine broke out in Rome, and for this the people blamed Avitus (who had now returned into Italy) and the crowd of hungry dependants whom he had brought with him from Gaul. Under popular pressure he was compelled to dismiss his Visigothic bodyguard. Having no funds in his treasury wherewith to pay them, he stripped the public buildings in Rome of their copper (completing perhaps the half-finished Vandal spoliation of the temple of Jupiter Capitolinus), and turned

* Idatius, for the year 456.
† [For more information on Avitus' character see appendix vii, 'On the Alleged Immoralities of Avitus', pp. 384–6.]

the copper into gold for his Gothic friends. All this of course increased his unpopularity in Rome.* The revolt, now openly headed by Ricimer and his young comrade Majorian, spread to Ravenna. On the 17th of September, Remistus the patrician (an official who is otherwise unknown to us), was killed in the palace at Classis. The emperor fled from Rome, hoping to reach his native and friendly Gaul. But he was taken prisoner at Placentia by Ricimer, who now held the all-important office of master of the soldiery. On the 17th of October, the patrician Messianus, a Gaul, and probably the intimate friend of Avitus, the same who had acted as his *avant-courier* to the court of Theodoric the year before, was put to death. Avitus himself was spared. Even the stern Ricimer could not bring himself to take the life of the innocent old man. But he was stripped of the purple, and (strange fate for an Augustus) was consecrated bishop at Placentia. Of the name of his see and of his subsequent fate we have no certain information.† It seems probable that he died by a natural death, though possibly hastened by disappointment and alarm, within a twelvemonth after he had abdicated the Empire.‡ A tradition, recorded by Gregory of Tours (who was himself a native of Auvergne), related that the forlorn bishop-emperor, fearful for his life, left Italy by stealth to repair to the tomb of Julian the martyr, an Arvernian saint, whose protection he hoped to purchase by rich presents, the wreck it may be of his Imperial splendour; that he died on the road, but that his body was taken and buried at the feet of the martyr in the village of Brioude in Auvergne. Few things in the fitfully illuminated history of the times are stranger than the fullness of information which is given us as to the rise of this unfortunate emperor, and the barrenness of the history of his fall. And yet he was the keystone of a great and important political combination, a combina-tion which, had it endured, would certainly have changed the face of Europe, and might have anticipated the empire of Charles the Great in favour of a nobler nation than the Franks, and without the interposition of three centuries of barbarism.

---

* These particulars are derived from Joannes Antiochenus, fragment 202.

† It does not seem quite clear whether the chroniclers mean to describe him as ordained bishop at or of Placentia.

‡ According to Joannes Antiochenus he was either starved to death or strangled.

CHAPTER IX

Supremacy of Ricimer. Majorian

THERE IS DANGER IN ENDEAVOURING TO ILLUS-
trate the history of a long-past age by the vivid light of modern politics;
danger from the incompleteness of our knowledge of the present, and
danger from the heat of controversy with which every topic debated by
men struggling for place and power in the world of action around us, must
necessarily be environed.

But the correspondence between the position of old Rome at the point of
her history which we have now reached, and that of 'new Rome', or Constantinople, at the present day, is in some respects so close that we are almost
compelled to notice it. The obvious differences between the conditions of
the two empires are many, but the resemblances are more, and more striking.
The Roman, like the Turk, having been the terror of the world, had become
its pity. He had lost, like the Turk, his once pre-eminent faculty of founding
empires; he had lost the faculty of generalship, and, unlike the Turk, he
had lost the mere animal courage of the common soldier. A world of new
and alien nationalities was seething round him, nationalities which had
a prophetic instinct that to them and not to him belonged the future of
Europe; nationalities whose gentlest and most friendly touch meant ruin to
the old order of things, yet nationalities which, strange to say, did not, with
one exception, wish to destroy his Empire if by any means the breath of life
could still be preserved in it. What 'the Frank' is to the Ottoman of today,
the barbarian was to the subjects of Honorius and Valentinian.

I have said that there was one exception. The Vandal, during the last
quarter of a century of the independent life of Rome, was her one implacable enemy. He had had his hour of triumph in 455; intent on pillage rather
than on conquest he had not then sought permanently to annex Italy to his
empire, but he remained watching her death-struggles, gloating over her
feeble misery, and perhaps speculating on the day when she would fall without effort into his hands, and Rome be ruled as a dependency from Carthage.

We have seen some reasons for supposing that this result was dreaded by the other Teutonic nations in the west of Europe, and that political combinations, rude and well-nigh forgotten, were formed in order to keep Rome for the Romans, even as they have been formed in our own day to keep Stamboul [Istanbul] for the Turks. But a more undoubted point of resemblance is the career of the many Teutonic adventurers who brought their knowledge of war, their energy, their courage, and sometimes their unscrupulousness to the service of the dying Empire. Merobaudes and Bauto, Arbogast and Gainas, were the prototypes of the German and English officers who in our own day have reorganised the armies or commanded the fleets of the sultan, and led the expeditions of the khedive. Not more strange to us probably is the affix of pasha to an English surname than were, in the ears of the men of that generation, the titles of consul or patrician when borne by a full-blooded barbarian. And these alien administrators of the state and army of Rome resembled those 'Frankish' admirals and generals employed by the Ottoman porte, in the knowledge that, however great the actual power which they might possess, the appearance of sovereignty would always be denied to them. As none but a lineal descendant of Othman can sit on the throne of Suleiman, so, even in the most degenerate days of Rome, public opinion, if not positive law, forbade that anyone who was the son of a barbarian father and a barbarian mother should be robed in the Imperial purple.

Such a Romanised Teuton was Ricimer, the man who for sixteen years after the deposition of Avitus was virtually head of the Roman commonwealth. It is worthwhile to notice how intimately he was connected with two if not three of the ruling barbarian families. He was the son of a Suevic father, who probably enough was sprung from the royal family of his nation. His mother was daughter of Walia, king of the Visigoths, the successor and avenger of Ataulfus; and his sister was married to Gundiok, king of the Burgundians.* A man thus connected, and concentrating in his hand whatever yet remained of the forces and the treasure of Rome, was well placed for repelling that storm of Vandal invasion which was the most pressing danger of the Empire.

Historians are unanimous in condemning the character of Ricimer, and, as we shall see, not without reason. He raised his unhappy puppets one after another to the Imperial throne, and one by one, as he grew tired of their subservience or was irritated by their opposition, was cast aside and

* [See table iii, 'Family Connections of Ricimer', p. 398.]

broken by his hand. There is not a word in the chroniclers, not a line in the venal panegyrics of Sidonius, to suggest that he had a heart accessible to any generous or tender emotion. A cold, self-seeking player with men as with counters he appears from first to last. But let us endeavour to understand what he was and why Rome bore with him. There can be little doubt that as a general he was the greatest whom the Empire could produce. That destruction of the Vandal fleet off Corsica,* of which the chroniclers give us such scanty details, was probably a great achievement, and one which liberated Italy and Gaul for years from the fear of another regular invasion. He thus succeeded, as it were of right, to that great position in the state which had been held before him by Stilicho and Aetius. But both these generals had served the emperors only too well for their own safety. The feeble Honorius had compassed the death of Stilicho; the dissolute Valentinian had planned the assassination of Aetius. Ricimer resolved that his life should not be at the mercy of any similar palace intrigue, and as soon as any of the retainers, whom he permitted to use the name of Caesar, showed signs of acquiring an independent authority in the state which might be dangerous to his authority and life, he gave the word to some trusty barbarian henchman, and the purple robe was found to be enveloping a corpse. There is only one thing to be said in mitigation of our abhorrence for this man; and that is that he does seem to have been faithful to Rome. We do not find any trace of that disposition to make a separate bargain for himself, which so often comes out in the lives of the statesmen of a collapsing monarchy. Rome seems to have understood this, to have accepted him, with all his odious qualities, as 'the necessary man' for the situation, and she may have owed it to this acquiescence in his rule that the Vandal invasion, often threatened, never actually arrived during the sixteen years of his domination.

Ricimer† was probably already a man in middle life when he thus came to the helm of the Roman state. He was simply Count Ricimer when he achieved his Corsican victory. That exploit it was, in all likelihood, which earned for him the office of master general of the soldiery. A pause ensued

* See p. 231.

† The name is, perhaps, the same as that of Count Richomer who fought in the battles of Ad Salices and Hadrianople (see vol. i, pp. 140 and 145). The beginning seems to be the Gothic *reiks*, which terminates Alaric, Theodoric, Childeric, and many other Teutonic names. The ending syllable is that which we find in the Ostrogothic Walamir, the Frankish Sigismer, etc., and probably means 'famous' (compare the Gothic *vaila-merjan*, to proclaim glad-tidings: *meri-tha*, fame). Thus Ricimer = 'famous ruler'.

upon the deposition of Avitus, perhaps in order to allow time for communications with Byzantium, but during this interval there can be no doubt that the master of the forces wielded the whole powers of the state. In four months' time (on the 28th February, 457) Ricimer abandoned his office of master of the soldiery in favour of a young general named Majorian, while he himself assumed the proud title of patrician.* This title carried with it the right to be called the father of the emperor (as soon as an emperor should be declared) and practically a life-tenure of the office of prime minister.

The extraordinary development of the power of 'the patrician' is one of the unexplained changes in the constitutional history of the last days of the Empire. The caste of patricians had, as everyone knows, lost their exclusive civil privileges long before the close of the republic. Under the Empire most of the still surviving patrician families perished by slow decay, or fell victims to the terrible trade of the *delator* (informer). The emperor Constantine revived the name, not now as a hereditary order in the state, but as a personal dignity, conferring high honour on the wearer but probably no power. The words of Zosimus (the only historian apparently who describes this innovation) are these: 'The dignity of patrician was first introduced by Constantine, who passed a law that those who were honoured by it should take precedence of the praetorian prefects.'† This enactment is lost. Only one law in the whole Theodosian Code, which decrees that 'even the splendour of the patriciate' is to be considered subordinate in rank to the consular office, mentions the name of the new dignity,‡ which moreover does not occur from beginning to end of the *Notitia Dignitatum*. Evidently the patrician of the fifth century, like the premier and the cabinet of our own day, was a term more familiar to the mouths of ordinary men than to the written documents of the constitution.

For the last twenty years of his life the great Aetius wore the name of patrician; and we may perhaps conjecture that it was during that time that men, seeing him ever the foremost figure in the state, of which he was the real

* Anonymus Cuspiniani, for the year 457.   † Zosimus, ii.40.

‡ *Codex Theodosianus*, vi.6. The order of precedence established by Gratian in this enactment still prevailed 150 years later, when Cassiodorus compiled his *Formulae*. The gradation was still (1) consul, (2) patrician, (3) praetorian prefect. 'The great distinction of the patriciate' (King Theodoric is made to say) 'is that it is a rank held for life, like that of the priesthood from which it sprang. The patrician takes precedence of prefects and of all other dignities except the consulship, and that is one which we ourselves sometimes assume.'

ruler, came to look upon the new designation as something more than a
mere title of courtesy, and upon the holder of it as an irremovable depositary
of power above the moving, changing throng of consuls and praetorian prefects. The words of a contemporary chronicler, describing the deposition of
Avitus, 'And his patrician Messianus was killed',* seem to imply an especial connection between the patrician and the emperor, just as we should say
'a colonel and his major', but not 'a colonel and his captain'. But howsoever
and whensoever the peculiar pre-eminence of the patrician began, there can
be no doubt that it existed during the period which we are now considering,
and that citizens of Rome must have spoken of 'the patrician' with at least as
much awe as the citizens of Constantinople speak of 'the grand vizier', or
the subjects of Louis XIII spoke of 'the cardinal'.

The official 'father of the emperor' was not long in providing himself
with a son. His young comrade, Majorian, 'was raised to the Empire on the
1st of April in the camp at Columellae, at the sixth milestone' no doubt
from Ravenna.† The emperor Leo, who, two months before, upon the
death of the brave old Marcian, had been in a somewhat similar manner
raised by his barbarian patron Aspar to the Eastern throne, approved the
choice, and the two emperors, between whose characters there was no little
resemblance, reigned together with more harmony and more unity of purpose than had often marked the counsels of Ravenna and Constantinople.

The new emperor, Julius Valerius Majorianus, came of an official
stock. His maternal grandfather, Majorian, was master-general of the soldiery in 379 when Theodosius was raised to the Empire. The elevation of
that emperor took place at Sirmium (not far from Belgrade), and Majorian's headquarters were then at Acincus, well known to us under its
modern name of Buda as the western half of the capital of Hungary. The
son-in-law of the elder, and father of the younger, Majorian was a faithful
comrade of Aetius, and reached the 'respectable' office of quaestor. The
future emperor served his apprenticeship to arms under his father's friend,
and was rising high in the service when suddenly Aetius dismissed him
from his military employments. No reason was assigned for this harsh step,
but the young officer and his friends maintained that it was solely due to the
envy of the patrician's wife, who feared that the fame of her husband and

* Anonymus Cuspiniani, for the year 456.
† Anonymus Cuspiniani, for the year 457. Rubeus, the historian of Ravenna, does not
throw any light on the position of Columellae, though he unhesitatingly places it at six
miles from Ravenna.

son would suffer eclipse by Majorian's growing reputation.* He retired for the time to his estate, and to the pursuits of agriculture, but when Aetius himself fell under the dagger of the assassin, his fortunes naturally revived, and Valentinian III called him forth from his seclusion to bestow upon him one of the highest posts in the army. In this position he probably co-operated with Ricimer in the overthrow of Avitus.† What is more certain is that, as already related, he was raised on the last day of February, 457, to the dignity of master of the soldiery, and on the 1st of April in the same year was saluted as Augustus.

At once a flash of something like the old defiant spirit of Rome showed her enemies that she had again a soldier for emperor. In the short interval between February and April, Majorian had sent an expedition which suc-cessfully repelled an inroad of nine hundred Alamanni, who had forced their way over the Rhaetian Alps to the northern shore of Lake Maggiore. He was next summoned to Campania, to whose rich plains Gaiseric had this year directed his piratical fleet. The lordly Vandal, fat with luxurious living, sat lazily in his galley while the Mauretanian peasant, himself a slave, ravaged the country, dragging off captives, cattle, spoil, everything that could be carried away, and swept them into the holds of the Vandal warships. Such was the picture of arrogant and indolent rapacity when the troops of Majorian appeared on the scene. In an instant all was changed; horses were landed, suits of mail were donned, poisoned arrows were fitted to the string, and fiery darts were brandished in the hand. On both sides the trumpets sounded, and the dragon ensigns floated sinuously to the breeze. Then came the clash of opposing squadrons, soon followed by the flight of the Vandals. Horses and men crowded into the water in an agony of fear, and only the strongest swimmers succeeded in reaching the ships. When the fight was over, Majorian roamed over the battlefield examining the bodies of the slain. Among them was a well-known corpse, that of the husband of Gaiseric's sister. All the wounds of the Roman soldiers were in front; all those of the Vandals in the back. Such is the account which Sido-nius gives of the encounter. After making every deduction for rhetorical amplification, we are bound to believe that the Vandal was worsted in a skirmish, and retired from the shores of Campania.

* This is probably the prosaic kernel of Sidonius' declamation. Through 131 angry hexameters he makes the wife of Aetius rave on, recounting the exploits of the young Majorian, and urging her husband to slay both him and Ricimer, who are both too illus-trious not to arrive at supreme power.   † As we are informed by the chronicler Marius.

A campaign in Pannonia apparently followed; the obscure details of which need not be given here. But it may be observed that among the sub-ject nations who are represented as following the standards of Majorian are mentioned the Rugian and the Ostrogoth.* So invariable was the course of barbarian movement into Italy. The tribes who were to be the next con-querors of Rome always first figured as her stipendiaries.

The second year of Majorian's reign was signalised by his accepting the office of consul in conjunction with his Byzantine colleague, Leo. Scarcely since the palmy days of the Republic had two men so worthy of that famous dignity ridden behind the lictors and fasces and given their names to the year. The address of Majorian to the senate, written at Ravenna and preserved among his laws, makes a show of moderation and deference for that ancient body, which though it was probably understood by all concerned to be only a piece of acting, was yet gracious and dignified acting. He says that having been elected by the free choice of the senate, and by the will of his valiant army, he consents to assume a dignity for which he has himself no desire, in order that he may not be accused of ingratitude to the commonwealth, nor seem to wish to live only to himself. He implores the favour of heaven, and asks for their co-operation with the emperor of their choice. 'Let them take heart as to their own fortunes. As a private man he always condemned the infamy of informers, and he is not going to encourage them now that he is emperor. The military affairs of the state shall receive the ceaseless attention of himself and his father and patrician Ricimer. They two together by hard service in the field have freed the state of the Roman world from foreign foes and civil broil, and with the help of providence they will yet preserve it.

'Fare ye well, conscript fathers of the most venerable order.'

The years 458 and 459 were probably spent in war with the Visigothic king, naturally indignant at the overthrow of his candidate for Empire. It would necessarily be waged in Gaul, but we know nothing concerning it but the result, a glorious one for Majorian. In the year 459 'ambassadors were sent to the Galicians by Nepotian, master of the soldiery, and Sunieric the count, announcing that Majorian the Augustus, and Theodoric the king, have ratified with one another the firmest bonds of peace, the Goths having been overcome in a certain conflict'.†

* Apollinaris Sidonius, *Carmina*, v.474–8.
† Idatius, for the year 459. Observe the interesting Gothic name Sunieric = *Sunja-reiks*, the king of truth. So in Ulfilas' translation of John 18 : 38, *Thanuk quth imma Peilatus, 'Wa ist so sunja?'* (Then quoth Pilate to him, 'What is the truth?')

But though we know nothing else of these campaigns in Gaul, they have a certain interest for us as having been the means of bringing Majorian within the orbit of the universal panegyrist, Sidonius. That unfortunate courtier must have seen with deep chagrin all his hopes of official advance-ment blasted by the dethronement of his father-in-law. Apparently he did not accept the triumph of the party of Ricimer without a struggle. Did he actually join himself to the Visigoths, and fight under their banners against Rome? Did he stir up revolt among the Gaulish provincials, and strive to maintain the cause of some other claimant to the purple? Did the city of Lyons join the revolt, and was she only reduced to obedience by the motley army of Majorian after a stubborn resistance? Such are some of the con-clusions drawn by commentators from a few obscure passages in the works of Sidonius, who naturally describes the conversations of the Olympian deities with much greater minuteness than his own exertions on behalf of an unsuccessful cause. The provoking silence of the chroniclers prevents us from either affirming or denying these conclusions. One can only say that it is extraordinary that a civil war, and the reduction by force of so important a city of the Empire as Lyons (if these events really occurred) should have been left altogether unnoticed by the historians.

However this may have been, there is no doubt that Sidonius was in disgrace, that the triumphant emperor was at Lyons, and that a hint was given that a panegyric would be the price of the poet's restoration to favour. The broker in this transaction was the emperor's secretary, Petrus, himself a man of letters and a distinguished diplomatist. The panegyric was accordingly composed and recited, no doubt in the emperor's hearing, amidst the applause of the courtiers. It was a hard task for the son-in-law of Avitus to bring his flowing rhetoric to glorify the rival, perhaps the exe-cutioner of his relative. But the instinct of reverence for success carried Sidonius safely through his perilous undertaking. In 603 lines (one more than he had given to his father-in-law) he sang the joy of Rome in the tri-umphs of Majorian, and the very difficulty of the enterprise invigorated his muse. The personifications are decidedly less tedious, the imagery more imaginative, the flow of declamation more animated, in this work than in the panegyric on Avitus.*

---

* The poem is prefaced by two dedications, one to Petrus and one to the emperor, in which a natural comparison is made between the author's position and that of Virgil and Horace. Majorian is obviously another Augustus, Petrus another Maecenas. There is some literary interest in these dedications, if it be true that they are our sole authority for

This is the plan of the poem. Rome sits on her throne, and receives the homage and the appropriate presents of the nations from India to Spain. To her enters Africa, 'the third part of the world', her black cheeks scarred, and the ears of corn which crowned her bending forehead all broken. She complains that she is made miserable by the insolent happiness of one man (Gaiseric), the robber, the maidservant's son, who has insinuated himself into her home, and made himself master of her resources. She calls on Rome to deliver her from this hateful vassalage; on Rome, now able to strike by the strong arm of Majorian, whose parentage and past exploits she recounts at considerable length. That Rome may not think the exploit beyond her strength, she informs her that Gaiseric is now sodden and ener-vated by the life of vicious luxury which he has been leading. His pale cheeks and bilious habit show that his endless banquets have at last begun to tell upon his health. What Capua was to Hannibal, the cook-shops of Carthage have been to the Vandal.

Rome, in a few dignified words, assures Africa of coming succour. Gaul, which for nearly eighty years has been left unvisited by emperors, has now been visited by Majorian, who has corrected the disorders caused by that long absence, and who is now coming 'through these wars to thy war. Why waste we our time in speaking? He will arrive: he will conquer.'

Here ends the allegorical part of the poem. Then, in his own person, and with some poetic fire, Sidonius recounts the later exploits of the emperor; the fight by Maggiore, the defeat of the Vandal pirates, the pas-sage of the Alps by his motley armament.

> 'Twas winter. Through the marble-shining Alps
> The rocks affronting heaven, the cliffs whose brows
> Threaten incessantly the wayfarer
> With the dry deluge of the avalanche,
> Through these thy foot first passes: thou the first
> Dost plant thy pole upon the slippery slopes.
>   And now the host has reached the midmost pass:
> Their limbs begin to stiffen with the cold;
> Blocked in the narrow windings of the way,
> To walk, or e'en to creep incapable,
> So great the glassy smoothness of the ground.

the universally received tradition that it was the good offices of Maecenas, that procured the pardon of Horace after the battle of Philippi.

Then one, by chance, from out that straggling file,
Whose wheel the frozen Danube once had worn,
Exclaims, 'I choose instead the gory sword
And the chill awfulness of quiet death.
A rigid torpor binds my stiffening limbs,
With fire of frost my parchèd frame consumes.*
We follow one who labours without end,
Our stripling leader.† Now the bravest brave,
Monarch or people, safe are housed in camp,
And, e'en in camp, lie under shaggy hides.
But we — we change the order of the year.
What he commands transcends e'en nature's laws.
He bends not ever from his ruthless schemes
And grudges victory to the angry sky.
Oh, where and of what nation was he born
Whom I, the Scythian, cannot cope with? Where,
Under what rock Hyrcanian did he grow,
Sucking the milk of tigers? To this pitch
What drearier clime than mine has hardened him?
Lo, where he stands upon that topmost peak,
Urges his shivering ranks, and laughs at cold,
Hot with his spirit's ardour. When I heard,
Long since, the bugles of a Northern king,
They told me the Imperial arms of Rome
And Caesar's household dwelt in soft repose,
Lapped in perennial luxury. For me
Nought boots it to have changed my former lords
If this be Roman kingship.'
                              More he had said,
But from thy cliff thou hurlest thy words of scorn,
'Whoe'er thou art whom daunts the difficult way,
Cut with thine axe the hanging water's hide,
And make thee steps out of the frozen wave.

* So Milton—

The parching air
Burns frore, and cold performs the effect of fire.
† The picture of the young Napoleon crossing the Alps on his way to Marengo will sug-
gest itself to every reader.

Stop those unmanly murmurs. Sloth is cold,
But work will warm you. Soldiers! look on me!
Hath nature given me the centaur's limbs;
The wings of Pegasus; the plumèd heels
Of Zetes or of Calaïs? Yet I crunch
E'en now the snowy summit of the pass.
You groan beneath a winter in the Alps.
I promise you a soldier's recompense –
A summer 'neath the sun of Africa.'
Thus with thy voice thou cheerest the fainting ranks;
Thus thine example stirs them. Every toil
By thee ordained is first by thee endured.
The crowd with eagerness obey thy laws,
Seeing their author is their promptest slave.

Passing on from the story of Majorian's campaigns, the poet here inter-
weaves a little skilful panegyric on his friend Petrus, and then comes to the
practical part of his effusion. 'Look upon the ruined estate of our city of
Lyons, and lighten her load of taxation.'

And since to these o'erwearied hearts of ours,
Our only hope, thou comést, help our fall:
And while thou passest turn a pitying eye
On this thy city, Lyons's conqueror!
Broken with toil, she looks to thee for rest.
Peace hast thou given: give hope for days to come.
The ox, after short respite from the plough,
Better resumes his struggle with the soil.
Our Lyons sees herself bereft of all,
Oxen and corn, the serf, the citizen.
While still she stood she felt not all her bliss:
Captive, she knows her past prosperity.
   O emperor! when delight is ours once more,
'Tis sweet to muse on vanished misery.
Though sack, though fire have laid our glories low,
Thy coming pays for all. Ruin herself
Shall please us if she make thy triumph more.

The word 'triumph' suggests the thought of the emperor's car climbing the Capitolian slope, of the mural and civic crowns encircling his forehead, of all the spoils of the defeated Vandal borne proudly before him. 'I will go before thee through the struggling crowds. I will make my feeble note heard through all their noisy shoutings. I will say that thou hast conquered seas and mountains, the Alps, the Syrtes, and the Libyan hordes; but I will say that before and beyond all these victories, thou hast conquered my heart by thy clemency.'

Who could resist such energy of praise? Not Majorian, whose frank and hearty nature accepted the flattery with all goodwill, and who appears to have not merely pardoned the poet, but received him into the circle of his friends. Emboldened by the success of his first petition, Sidonius essayed another of a more personal kind than that which he had already preferred on behalf of his fellow citizens. He himself individually was groaning under the weight of a heavy assessment, perhaps imposed upon him as a penalty for some insurrectionary movements after the downfall of Avitus. We are not able to ascertain the precise mode of this assessment, but it is clear that it was denoted by heads (*capita*), and that a wealthy or an obnoxious citizen paid taxes upon so many more *capita* than his poorer or more loyal neighbours. Sidonius considered that he had at least three *capita* too many; that is, probably, that his taxes were fourfold what they ought to be. In a short epigrammatic poem he reminds the emperor of a certain fortunate hunting excursion of his, in which he had killed three animals on one day – a stag, a boar, and a serpent,* and hints that another day's sport of the same kind would now be acceptable. Hercules killed the three-headed monster Geryon; let Majorian, the new Hercules, knock the three *capita* from the poet's taxability, and give him a chance of unharassed life. The answer to this curious petition is not stated, but it was probably favourable, since the author included the epigram in the list of his published poems.

Majorian's war with the Visigoths detained him for more than a year in Gaul, which he afterwards revisited, and Sidonius had frequent access to the Imperial presence. To the end of his life but slight solicitation was needed to draw from him the story of the high doings which he witnessed 'in the times of Augustus Majorian'. One of these anecdotes, though trifling in itself, may serve to introduce us into the private life of a Roman emperor of the last days. The scene is laid at Arles, the capital of Roman Gaul; the time is the year 461. There had suddenly appeared in the city a

* This feat is also referred to in the panegyric (153–4).

copy of anonymous verses, bitterly satirising some of the chief persons in the Imperial court, cleverly hitting off the favourite vices of each, and all but mentioning their names. The nobles were furious, and none more so than a certain Paeonius, a demagogue turned courtier, a man who had played a little with revolutionary intrigue and then sold himself for office, a slave to money-getting till the time came when he saw an opportunity of bartering money for position, and purchasing a highly placed husband for his only daughter by a lavish and unusual dowry. This was the person who, born in obscurity though not in poverty, had clambered up, no one exactly knew how, during the troubles and anarchy at Rome, to the distinguished position of prefect of the Gauls. This was he who, having been among the courtiers most severely lashed by the anonymous satirist, was the keenest in his endeavours to find out and punish the author. That author, there can be little doubt, was Sidonius himself. He affects to consider it a great injustice that the piece should have been fathered upon him; but in the letter (written several years later) in which he tells the story,* he nowhere expressly repeats his denial, and the impression left on our minds is that though, as a noble-man and a bishop, he deemed it decorous to disavow the lampoon, as an author he was very proud of the excitement which it had occasioned.

At the time when the satire appeared, Sidonius was still at his country house in Auvergne; but public opinion, guided by Paeonius, tried him for the authorship, and found him guilty, in his absence. When he appeared at Arles shortly afterwards, and, having paid his respects to the emperor, descended into the forum, what unaccountable change had come over his former friends? One came up to salute him, bowed profoundly, so as almost to touch his knees, and passed on; another, with gloomy face, stalked past him without uttering a word; the greater number skulked behind a column or a statue, so as to avoid the disagreeable necessity of either saluting or ignoring him. Sidonius professes to have been utterly bewildered by this strange conduct, till at length one of the number, deputed by the rest, approached and saluted him. 'Do you see those men?' said he. 'Yes, I see them, and view their odd conduct with wonder, but certainly not with admiration.' 'They know that you have written a lampoon, and all either detest or fear you in consequence.' 'Who? What? Where? When? Why?' Sidonius asked in well-simulated wrath. Then, with greater composure and with a smile on his face, 'Be good enough to ask those angry gentlemen whether the base informer who dares to accuse me of such an offence

* *Epistolae*, i.11.

pretends to have seen the lampoon in my handwriting. If he does not, they will do well to retract their charge, and behave a little less offensively.' With this equivocal denial, the courtiers were, or professed themselves to be, satis-fied, and they came forward promptly and in a body to clasp his hand and kiss him on the cheek.

The next day the emperor gave a banquet in connection with the games of the amphitheatre. Among the invited guests were the consul of the year, two ex-consuls, two other men of high rank, and Paeonius and Sidonius, whose black looks at one another no doubt caused much secret amusement to their fellow-guests and to the emperor himself. Host and guests, eight in all, reclined upon the *triclinium* (triple couch) with the table in the midst. It is interesting to observe the order of precedence. The most distinguished guest, Severinus (the consul for the year), reclined at the end (or 'horn', as it was called) of the left-hand couch. Opposite to him, at the first seat of the right-hand couch, reclined the Imperial host. The other guests lay accord-ing to their order of precedence, counting from the seat of Severinus; and so it came to pass that Paeonius, as ex-prefect of Gaul, reclined in the fourth place, at the middle couch, and that Sidonius, who as yet had no official rank, was the lowest-placed among the guests, but by that very in-feriority was brought into the closest contact with the emperor.

When the banquet was nearly ended, Majorian began to talk. First, in few words, to the consul Severinus. Then ensued a more lively dialogue on literary subjects with the consular who lay next him. Camillus came next, a consular, and nephew of a consul. 'Brother Camillus,' said the emperor, 'you had an uncle, for whose sake I think I may congratulate myself on having given you a consulship.' 'Do not say *a* consulship, Lord Augustus! Call it a *first* consulship.' This clever hint, that further favours of the same kind would be welcome, was received with a tumult of applause, notwith-standing the emperor's presence. Then passing Paeonius by unnoticed, the Imperial host put some question to Athenius, the fifth in order of the guests. Paeonius rudely interposed a reply. The emperor noticed the dis-courtesy, and the peculiar smile which played upon his face (for he greatly enjoyed a joke, and had a happy way of sharing in it without compromis-ing his dignity) amply avenged Athenius. The latter, who was a wily old fellow, and who already had a grudge against Paeonius for taking prece-dence of him at the banquet, slyly said, 'I don't wonder, emperor, that my neighbour has stolen my place, since he is not ashamed to take the words out of your mouth.' 'A fine opening this for satirists!' said the sixth guest, whose turn in the conversation was now come. Thereupon the emperor turned his head round to his next-door neighbour and said, 'I hear, Count Sidonius, that you are a writer of satires.' 'I hear it, too,' he answered.

Majorian (laughing). 'Spare ourselves at any rate.'

Sidonius. 'In refraining from forbidden jests I spare myself.'

Majorian. 'And what shall we do to those who molest you?'

Sidonius. 'My lord emperor! let my accuser accuse me in public. If he makes good his charge, I am ready to pay the penalty: but if, as is probable, I succeed in refuting it, let me have the leave of your clemency to write what I like against him.'

The emperor glanced at Paeonius, to see if he consented to the conditions; but the ex-prefect sat silent, with a blush of anger and shame upon his face. 'I will grant your request,' said Majorian, 'if you will this moment put it into verse.' 'Agreed,' answered Sidonius. He turned round and looked at the servant as if asking for water to dip his fingers in. There was an instant's pause while the nimble slave ran round the *triclinium*. Then said the emperor, 'The verses are to be improvised, remember.'

> Who says I write satires? Dread sovereign! I cry,
> Let him prove his indictment, or pay for his lie,

was the immediate repartee of Sidonius. There was again a tumult of applause, and the emperor, in a tone perhaps of mock solemnity, called God and the commonwealth to witness that the poet should henceforth write whatever he chose, adding that he considered it to be the duty of the wearer of the purple to repress this kind of vague and unproven accusation, brought by malice against innocent members of the nobility. Sidonius bowed his head and modestly uttered his thanks; Paeonius turned pale, dejection succeeded to rage, and he looked like a criminal on his way to execution. Soon after, the guests rose up. When they had donned their cloaks and gone a few steps from the Imperial presence, the consul fell on the neck of the favoured courtier, the two consulars* kissed his hand, and Paeonius, with fawning and pitiable gestures, implored pardon. On the intercession of the other members of the party, Sidonius consented to grant it, and to promise that he would leave Paeonius unlashed by his satires if he would take warning by the miserable success of this attempt to blacken his character and cease to molest him for the future.

* Literally the ex-prefects, but they were consulars also, and Paeonius was not.

The story of this banquet at Arles is no doubt trivial enough, and may seem scarcely worth the telling, but it illustrates the immense social defer- ence which was still paid to the name of Augustus, and the glamour of the purple robe. When we are reading the history of far-distant times, we are sometimes disposed to marvel how men could be found willing to take prominent positions in the world, when the state of affairs was so hopeless that they must inevitably become either the pity or the laughing-stock of the universe. Perhaps the explanation is to be found in the fact that so long as power commands the reverence of the few score of persons with whom it comes into daily contact, it will have irresistible attractions for mankind. Further than its own immediate environment it need not and will not look: least of all will it trouble itself about the sort of figure that it will make in history. Here was Julius Majorianus, struggling bravely, it is true, but almost desperately, for the last tatters of the Roman inheritance that were left to him by the Rhône and the Ebro; yet his favour still gave life, a harsh word from his lips or a frown on his brow sent the unhappy object of his displeasure out of the Imperial presence, pale, trembling, half-choked with terror; the courtiers still contended for the smile of 'the purple-wearer' as eagerly as when he was the master of sixty legions, and when none could escape his wrath or stay his hand, from Cheviot to Caucasus.

The short reign of Majorian was a time of considerable legislative activ- ity. Especially was the year of his consulship (during which his headquar- ters seem to have been at the palace in Ravenna) marked by his additions (*Novellae*) to the Theodosian Code. But the laws all tell one tale; all speak, in one relation or another, of the desperate misery which was engulfing the inhabitants of Italy. Population was decreasing so fast that the emperor, notwithstanding the strong feeling of the church in favour of virginity, and against second marriage, found himself compelled to forbid women to take the veil under forty years of age, and to command all childless widows to marry a second husband within five years of the death of the first, or else to forfeit half their property to their relatives or to the exchequer.* The cost of maintaining a family was so great, the rivalry for the paternal inheritance so keen, that in many instances an unpopular son or brother was forced into the ranks of the clergy and actually ordained priest against his will. Where such an offence was proved to have been committed, the unjust parents were con- demned to forfeit a third of their property to the unwillingly consecrated son, who was permitted to return into the world, a forced ordination having

* *Novellae Majoriani, 6.*

no binding power. The archdeacon who might have wittingly co-operated in the offence, was liable to a fine of ten pounds of gold (£400). A curious provision that if a bishop had been consecrated without his consent the ordination could not be impugned,* is perhaps a concession to the harmless comedy of the *nolo episcopari*,† which was so commonly played in those days. Or possibly it may have proceeded from an uneasy consciousness of the legislator's own share in the forced consecration of his predecessor at Placentia.

Majorian's laws are remarkably outspoken as to the rapacity of the tax-collectors, especially those who were clothed with military authority, whose extortions he denounces in the strongest terms. 'Raging against the bowels of the unhappy provincials, they are safe from punishment, for none cares to accuse them before a provincial judge, too often supine and cowardly and ready to cringe and fawn at the mere sight of an officer's belt, while the expense and vexation of an appeal to the Imperial court is so great that most men will submit to any injustice rather than resort to it.'‡ A change in administration, bringing fiscal questions under the more immediate notice of the governor of the province, was meant to remedy this evil, which may have been partly relieved by another short but emphatic edict concerning the election of the *defensor*, that singular official of whose functions some account has been already given§ and who was perhaps the only functionary whom power has ever avowedly created as a safeguard against its own exorbitances. The harassed citizens were daily leaving the towns, to pick up a precarious subsistence in the remote country districts, where they were at least safe from the hated presence of the *apparitor*¶ and the *canonicarius*.** In order to check this process of depletion, Majorian ordained that in accordance with ancient usage, the magistracy and people of each considerable town should assemble and choose a *defensor*, who, when confirmed in his office by the emperor, might avail to keep the insolence of the revenue officers in check and tempt back the scattered citizens to their homes.††

The exactions of the tax-gatherers, themselves very likely (as is the custom in decaying states) often defrauded of their lawful salaries, were sometimes so extravagant as to be almost amusing. Thus continual objection was made to taking the Imperial *solidus* (twelve-shilling piece), even though it was of full weight; and some strange tricks, the nature of which we can but faintly conjecture, were played upon the popular partiality for

* *Novellae Majoriani*, 11.   † [I refuse to be bishop.]   ‡ *Novellae Majoriani*, 2.
§ See Vol. i, pp. 357–9.   ¶ Magistrate's officer.   ** Tax-collector.
†† *Novellae Majoriani*, 3.

gold pieces with the head of Faustina, coins which, if they represented the pure undepreciated currency of the Antonine period before the terrible debasements of the coinage in the third century, were not undeserving of a high place in public favour. All this elaborate machinery of injustice was destroyed, as far as mere decrees could destroy it, by Majorian, and the officers of the tribute were ordered to take all coins alike which were of full weight, except those minted of Gaulish gold, which was admitted to be of an inferior quality.

Some other unwarranted importunities of the official hierarchy were repressed by the same series of decrees.* Servants of the governors asking for New Year's gifts, presents on the first day of the month, or drink-money (literally dust-money, an indemnification for the dust which the messenger had contracted on his journey), all these were punished by a fine of £40 for each offence. Governors of provinces were not to be at liberty to half-ruin a city by taking up their quarters therein for an indefinite time, and calling upon the inhabitants to bring a constant supply of rare and costly delicacies to their table. Three days' provisions for himself and suite, on a scale of expense to be settled by the prefect, were all that the governor might require annually from each city.

These enactments, together with a remission of arrears of tribute of more than eleven years' standing,† seemed to show a generous consideration for the poverty of the exhausted people. They were however to some extent counterbalanced by a little clause in the longest edict, which stated that now that the cultivator was relieved from so many presents to governors and other illegal exactions, he could not think it burdensome if his land-tax, which now stood at two per thousand on capital (equivalent perhaps to two per cent on income‡), was increased by one quarter so as to stand thenceforward at two and a half per thousand.§

One more law must be noticed, since it shows the disintegrating influences which were already at work upon the buildings of old Rome, influences internal and domestic, which, far more than the transitory visits of Goth or Vandal, have brought about her present desolation.

'We, as rulers of the republic, are determined to remedy the detestable process which has long been going on, whereby the face of the venerable city [of Rome] is disfigured. For it is too plain that the public edifices, in which all the adornment of the city consists, are being everywhere pulled to

* *Novellae Majoriani*, 7.   † *Novellae Majoriani*, 2.
‡ Taking the average rate of interest at ten per cent.   § *Novellae Majoriani*, 7.

pieces at the suggestion of the city officials, on the pretence that stones are wanted for the public works. Thus the stately piles of our old buildings are being frittered away, and great constructions are ruined in order to effect some trifling repair. Hence, too, it arises that private individuals engaged in house-building, who are in a position to curry favour with the city judges, do not hesitate to supply themselves with materials from the public build, ings, although these which have so much to do with the splendour of the city ought to be regarded with civic affection, and repaired rather than destroyed.

'We therefore decree that no buildings or ancient monuments raised by our forefathers for use or beauty, shall be destroyed by any man; that the judge who orders their destruction shall pay a fine of fifty pounds of gold [£2,000]; and that the clerks and other subordinates who have fulfilled his orders shall be beaten with clubs and have their hands struck off – those hands that have defiled the ancient monuments which they ought to have preserved.

'The buildings which are altogether past repair shall be transferred, to adorn some other edifice of a not less public character.'*

It is interesting to observe that this decree, so purely Roman and local in its character, was like the others issued from Ravenna (10th July, 458).

But it was not for legislation, nor for administrative reform, but for war that Julius Majorianus had been robed in the mantle of the Caesars. To him all the Roman world looked with hope, to exorcise the cruel and mocking fiend that had entered the corpse of Carthage. If the Vandals could be subdued, he was surely the man to do it. He had felled the forests of the Apennines, and filled the harbours of the Upper and Lower sea with Roman triremes. His campaign in Gaul had been successful, and the haughty Visigoth was now his submissive ally. It might have been expected that he would repeat the exploit of Scipio Africanus, transport his troops to the Libyan shore, and fight another Zama within a week's march of Carthage. For some reason not clearly explained to us, possibly because he knew of disaffection among the Mauretanian and Numidian allies of Gaiseric, he adopted a different course. He determined to make Spain his base of operations, and to assemble his navy, consisting of three hundred ships,† in that magnificent bay, one of the finest natural harbours in the Mediterranean, which we call Cartagena, and which then still bore the name of 'the new Carthage'. It seemed as if history was about to repeat

* *Novellae Majoriani*, 4.   † So Priscus, excerpt 36.

itself, and as if Spain might play the same part now, in the thirteenth century of Rome, which she had played in the sixth century, when the Hasdrubals and the Scipios fought there. But while all Europe was watching the movements of the Roman triremes in that spacious bay, suddenly the enterprise collapsed. Gaiseric first laid waste with fire and sword the provinces of Mauretania which Majorian meant to make his base of operations, and poisoned the wells along his expected line of march. Then by some stratagem, of which we know nothing, the Vandals, 'warned by traitors', carried off the ships from out of the bay of Cartagena. One chronicler* places the scene of this mysterious event not at Cartagena itself, but at Elice (now Elche), a seaside town about forty miles north of Cartagena, often visited by modern travellers who wish to see the forests of palm-trees which impart to it a thoroughly oriental aspect, and have earned for it the name of 'the Palmyra of Europe'. 'No palm of victory for me,' may have been the thought of Majorian as he sadly turned his face northwards – the preparations of three years wasted, and vengeance on the Vandal indefinitely postponed.

This happened in May, 460. On the 2nd of August in the following year he was dethroned and put to death near the city of Tortona (in the south-east corner of the modern duchy of Piedmont). No cause is assigned by any of the chroniclers for his fall, except 'the jealousy of Ricimer, acted upon by the counsels of envious men'; nor is anything told us of the circumstances of his death. Probably enough, the early successes of Majorian were the real cause of his ruin, for which his final disaster furnished the pretext.

The high estimate usually formed by historians of the character of Majorian, and of what, under happier auspices, he might have accomplished for the restoration of the fortunes of Rome, is justified by nothing so much as by the impression which he produced on his most unwearied enemies, the Vandals. The Byzantine historian, Procopius, writing a century after these events, and describing the overthrow of the Vandal empire by Justinian, gives us the following paragraph about Majorian, which must surely have been derived from Vandal sources, and may possibly have formed part of some song or saga about Gaiseric. Scarcely a detail in the picture is historically true, and the chief event recorded – the visit to Carthage – is almost certainly fictitious, but the portrait, taken as a whole, and especially if drawn by enemies, is undoubtedly the likeness of a hero.

* Marius.

'I ought also to make mention of Majorian, who some time before [Anthemius] occupied the Western throne. For this Majorian, who surpassed all that had been emperors of Rome in every virtue, could not tamely endure the misery of Africa, but collected in Liguria a most potent armament against the Vandals, and determined to head the expedition himself, being a man eager to take his full share in every hardship, and especially in every danger.

'Now, thinking it would be expedient to ascertain previously the forces of the Vandals, the temper of Gaiseric, and the good or bad dispositions towards him of the Libyans and Moors, he took this duty upon himself. He therefore sent himself as his own ambassador, under a feigned name, to the court of Gaiseric; and, fearing lest he might be discovered, and so ruin both himself and his enterprise, he hit upon this plan. As all men knew that his hair was so yellow as to be likened to pure gold, he applied to it a wash invented expressly for the purpose, and was able within the appointed time to turn it into a bluish black.

'Now, when he came into the presence of Gaiseric, among other devices of that king to strike terror into the soul of the supposed ambassador, he was led as a friend into the arsenal where all the weapons were collected, which were many and extremely wonderful. At his entrance, say they, all these arms stirred of their own accord, and made such a clash and uproar that Gaiseric thought an earthquake was happening. But when he came forth and enquired about the earthquake, and could meet with no one who knew anything about it, great fear fell upon him, though he was still far from conjecturing who had been the cause of this portent.

'Majorian then, having accomplished all that he intended, departed to Liguria, and leading his army by land, marched to the pillars of Hercules, intending to cross by those straits, and so conduct his troops from thence to Carthage. Now when Gaiseric heard this, and perceived that he had been imposed upon in the matter of the embassy, great fear fell upon him, and he set everything in readiness for war. The Romans, on the other hand, relying on the proved valour of Majorian, were in good hopes that they should win back Africa for the Empire. But all these hopes were foiled by the death of Majorian, who was attacked by dysentery. He was a man in all things gentle to his subjects, but terrible to his enemies.'*

* Procopius, *De Bello Vandalico*, i.7.

CHAPTER X

Supremacy of Ricimer (Continued).
Severus II, the Lucanian, AD 461–5.
Anthemius, the Client of Byzantium,
AD 467–72

LIBIUS SEVERUS, 'A LUCANIAN BY NATION', WAS the man whom Ricimer had selected to wear the diadem snatched from the head of the murdered Majorian. He was proclaimed emperor at Ravenna, on the 19th of November, 461. He died at Rome on the 15th of August, 465. These two dates sum up in truth the whole of our knowledge respecting this faint shadow of an emperor. It should, perhaps, be added that one authority states that he 'lived religiously'.*

To one who is familiar with the name of the Lucanians, and who remembers the part which this stern Sabellian tribe, dwelling in the extreme south of Italy, played in three of Rome's greatest wars (the Pyrrhic, second Punic, and Social), it seems strangely incongruous that the only contribution which Lucania furnished to the list of Roman emperors should have been this meek inoffensive cipher Augustus, who 'lived reli⁄giously', and died quietly at Rome after four years of sovereignty, neither by his life nor by his death making a ripple on the downward stream of the Empire's fortunes.

The only question which can raise a momentary interest in connection with this emperor is as to the manner of his death. Was it due to the ordi⁄nary course of nature or to the hand of Ricimer? Cassiodorus, who is a good authority, and who wrote about half a century after these events, says cautiously, 'as some aver, by the hand of Ricimer, Severus was taken off by poison in the palace at Rome'. On the other hand, all the other chroniclers,

* Catalogus Imperatorum.

one or two of whom are yet nearer in date than Cassiodorus, tell us simply that 'Lord Severus died'; and Sidonius, in a poem recited in the presence of Ricimer and his next succeeding puppet, says,

> August Severus now by nature's law
> Hath mingled with the company of gods.*

Though it is hazardous to determine what a poet bent on praising power will *not* say, it seems probable that had the common voice of fame in the year 467 connected the death of Severus with the poison-cup in the hand of Ricimer, that subject would have been judiciously evaded by Sidonius.

The four years of the nominal reign of Severus seem to have been a time of desultory and exhausting strife. The rule of Ricimer, if accepted as a disagreeable necessity by the inhabitants of Italy, was regarded with aver-sion by their neighbours, and we may infer that the hatefulness of the man more than counterbalanced the undeniable capacity of the general and the statesman. To understand the course of events during this obscure time,† we must look at the relations existing between the court of Ravenna and those of the four following cities, Constantinople, Carthage, Soissons, and Spalato [Split].

(1) Leo, 'the emperor of the Eastern Romans', beheld, evidently with deep displeasure, the downfall and murder of Majorian, a kindred spirit to his own, and the substitution of the puppet-emperor Severus. The chron-icler, who most faithfully represents the sympathies of the Byzantine court,‡ uses such expressions as these: 'Severus invaded the place of Majorian', 'Severus, who snatched the sovereignty of the West', and refuses to insert him in his proper year in the list of consuls. When the 'Romans of the West' applied for ships to replace the three hundred destroyed at Cartagena, the loss of which left them at the mercy of Gaiseric's invasions, Constantinople coldly replied that the existing treaties with the Vandals would not allow of its rendering this assistance. It despatched indeed during this interval one or two embassies to the court of Gaiseric, exhorting him to abstain from invading Sicily and the Italian provinces; but an embassy more or less was a matter of no concern to the Vandal monarch, and he continued his depre-dations unmoved by the Byzantine rhetoric.

---

* *Panegyric of Anthemius,* 317–18.
† Obscure, but fitfully enlightened by the fragmentary information preserved by Priscus.
‡ Marcellinus.

(2) Gaiseric himself had his reasons for viewing the course of events at Rome with displeasure. He had a candidate of his own for the Imperial purple, and was deeply offended at that candidate's rejection. It will be remembered that after the sack of Rome he carried the empress Eudoxia and her two daughters as state prisoners to Carthage. Incessant embassies from Byzantium had prayed for the surrender of these royal ladies whose captivity, like that of Placidia half a century before, was felt to be an especial insult to the majesty of an Augustus.* At length, in the seventh year of their exile (462), Gaiseric sent the widowed empress with one daughter to Constantinople, and this was no doubt the occasion of that treaty of alliance between Africa and the East which Leo refused to endanger when the Romans applied to him for help. The other daughter, Eudocia, Gaiseric had already given in marriage to his son Huneric – an ill-assorted union, for the lady was a devout Catholic and her husband a most bitter Arian. Placidia, the sister who was allowed to retire to Constantinople, was the wife of a Roman senator, named Olybrius, and it was this man, bound to him by a somewhat loose tie of affinity, as being his son's brother-in-law, whom Gaiseric desired to place, and as we shall see, eventually did place for a few months on the Western throne.

Here then was one grievance of the Vandal against Ricimer. Another was the refusal to comply with his claim to have all the property of Valentinian III and Aetius given up to him. The claim to the late emperor's wealth of course rested on the alliance between his daughter and the Vandal prince. The more preposterous demand for the property of Aetius was probably in some way connected with the fact that his son Gaudentius had been also carried captive to Carthage. But, whatever the foundation for them, these two demands were urged by the Vandal king with insolent pertinacity, and were the occasion of countless embassies. As they were not complied with, and as the friendship now established between Carthage and Constantinople forbade him to molest the coasts of Greece, Gaiseric

* About the year 456, Marcian, as we are informed by Priscus, sent on this errand 'an ambassador named Bledas, a bishop of Gaiseric's own sect (for it so happens that even the Vandals adhere to the religion of the Christians). This Bledas, when he found that his embassy was not going to be successful, took a bolder tone and said, "It will not turn out to your advantage, Gaiseric! if, puffed up by your present prosperity, you challenge the Eastern emperor to war and refuse to give up the royal ladies." But neither his former blandishments nor his present threats availed to bring Gaiseric to reason, for he sent Bledas about his business and again despatched his forces to ravage Sicily and Italy' (Priscus, excerpt 31).

decided that 'the nation with whom God was angry'* was the Italian.
Every year, with the return of spring, he sailed his piratical fleet to the
coasts of Campania, or Sicily, or Apulia. He avoided the large towns, fearing to find there sufficiently large bodies of troops to check his advance, and
fell by preference on the villages and unwalled towns, carrying off all the
movable wealth, and making slaves of the inhabitants. This man's instincts
were essentially those of the robber rather than the conqueror. He was, so to
speak, the representative of that brood of pirates whom Pompey extermi-
nated, the forerunner of those countless spoilers of the sea, Saracen,
Moorish, Algerian, by whom the Mediterranean coasts have been wasted,
almost down to our own day.

(3) The romantic and mysterious career of Aegidius, comrade of
Majorian, master of the Roman soldiery, voluntarily chosen king of the
Franks during the exile of an unpopular chieftain, lies beyond our proper
limits, and some of its chief events rest on too doubtful authorities to make
it desirable here to describe it at length. But we are fully warranted in saying
that he ruled as an independent governor, possibly with the title of king, at
Soissons (in Belgic Gaul), that he bitterly resented the death of his old
companion-in-arms, Majorian, and was preparing to avenge it upon Italy –
that is, upon Ricimer – that, probably in order to further these purposes of
revenge, he sent ambassadors 'across the Ocean to the Vandals', and that
Rome remained for a considerable time in the greatest terror and distress in
anticipation of this new Gaulish invasion.† Eventually however (463) he
was 'drawn off from war with the Italians by a difference with the Visigoths
respecting frontiers, which led to a campaign, in which Aegidius performed acts of the greatest heroism'.‡ In this war Frederic, brother of the
Visigothic king, was killed (464), and apparently Aegidius himself died
(or was treacherously slain) soon after. The Visigoths annexed a large part
of his territory, but the city of Soissons and his strange ill-defined power
descended to his son Syagrius, whose acquaintance we have already made
as a correspondent of Sidonius, and with whose overthrow by Clovis every
student of French history is familiar, as one of the earliest incidents in the
career of the young Merovingian.§

* See p. 149.
† Priscus (excerpt 39) is our authority for attributing so much importance to the hostile
enterprises of Aegidius and Marcellinus.   ‡ Priscus, excerpt 39.
§ This was the event which led to the quarrel between Clovis and one of his soldiers.
'Thus didst thou serve the vase of Soissons.'

Possibly the English reader is more familiar with the name of Aegidius than he is aware of. For some unaccountable reason the French have modi/ fied that name into Gilles. Saint Gilles, the hermit of Languedoc, who lived about a hundred years after Count Aegidius, attained great renown both in France and England. The parish of St Giles in London and the name Giles, once so common, especially in the rural districts of England, are thus linked certainly, if somewhat obscurely, with the memory of the *tyrannus* [king] of Soissons and the friend of Majorian.

(4) We pass from Soissons by the Aisne to the long arcades of Spalato, among the bays and islands of the Dalmatian coast. Here,* in the vast palace of Diocletian, lived and reigned Marcellinus,† 'patrician of the East', 'ruler of Dalmatia and of the Epirote Illyrians'. The pupil of Aetius and the counsellor of Majorian, he had in the deaths of those two men a double reason for withdrawing from the bloodstained circle of Roman pol/ itics. Yet he does not seem, like Aegidius, to have broken with Ricimer immediately upon the death of his friend. He fought in Sicily at the head of the Imperial troops, and achieved some considerable successes over the Vandals. Finding however that Ricimer was endeavouring, by bribes, to steal away the hearts of his soldiers, and knowing that he could not hope to vie in wealth with the Suevic patrician, he retired to Dalmatia, and there founded an independent and hostile principality. 'A reasonable and noble man,' we are told,‡ 'learned, courageous, and statesmanlike, keeping his government free, not serving the Roman emperor, nor any prince or nation, but ruling his own subjects in righteousness.' Apparently one of the few men in high office who still clung to the old pagan religion and worshipped Jupiter Capitolinus, while all the rest of the world was ranging itself for or against the council of Chalcedon; practising divination and holding long conversations with a certain philosopher Sallust, who shared his most secret counsels and dwelt in his palace; this relic of an earlier world, deposited by the vicissitudes of the times upon the shores of Dalmatia, is one of the most unique figures of the age, and we would gladly know more of his history. What concerns our present purpose however is the settled hostility which he displayed for some years to the domination of Ricimer,

* The assignment of Spalato as the scene of the court of Marcellinus is only a conjecture, but it seems probable that a ruler of Dalmatia would make that place his headquarters.
† Not to be confounded with the chronicler of that name.
‡ By Suidas, himself a late writer, but almost certainly here preserving in his dictionary some scraps of contemporary tradition.

and the constant fear which pervaded Italy during that time of an invasion from the opposite coast of the Adriatic. At length (probably about 465) the good offices of Byzantium were asked and obtained; an ambassador was sent by the Eastern emperor to entreat Marcellinus to lay aside his plans of revenge; he complied with the request, and, as we shall soon see, even co-operated once more with Rome against the Vandals.

Neither of these two men, Aegidius and Marcellinus, founded any enduring monarchy out of the fragments of the Empire; nor did any other Roman succeed in the attempt. All the political reconstruction was the work of barbarian hands. Yet on the dissolution of Alexander's empire, states and monarchies innumerable were established throughout Asia and Africa by Greek adventurers. When the Caliphate fell, Saracen chiefs profited by the ruin. When the Mogul empire of Delhi lost its vitality, Mo-hammedan as well as Hindu rajahs founded sovereignties which endured for many generations. In the early part of this century the Ali pasha of Egypt entirely succeeded, and the Ali pasha of Albania all but succeeded, in rendering themselves virtually independent of the Ottoman porte. Rea-sons might probably be easily assigned why no such success was attainable by a Roman prefect of the *praetorium*, or master of the soldiery, but we can-not wonder that the experiment was made, nor should we have been surprised if it had been made more frequently.

Other enemies besides those whom we have enumerated were probably making Ricimer's position at the helm of the commonwealth a difficult one. In the year 464 Beorgor, king of the Alans, was routed and killed by the patrician, 'at Bergamo, at the foot of the mountains'.* We hear nothing more about this descent of the savage half-Tartar tribe into the plains of Lombardy. Possibly Beorgor was the successor of that Sangiban, king of the Alans, who fought, with doubtful fidelity, under Aetius on the Mau-riac plains, and he may have forced his way over the Splügen from Chur to Chiavenna, and thence to Bergamo. For one invasion of this kind, leading to a pitched battle, which has claimed a place in the meagre pages of the chroniclers, there were probably many lesser inroads and skirmishes of which no record has been preserved.

It was in August, 465, as was before said, that the unnoticeable Severus died. For a year and eight months from that time no man was saluted as

---

* *Bergamo ad pedem montis* (Anonymus Cuspiniani, 6th February, 464). Though Bergamo is in the district which we now call the Milanese, does not this description look like the beginning of the name Piedmont?

Augustus in the Western half of the Roman Empire. This absolute vacancy of the Imperial office tells a far more striking tale in a pure autoc- racy, such as the Roman government had become, than in a constitutional state, where the powers of the sovereign may be, so to speak, 'put in com- mission'. During all those twenty months, the patrician must have been avowedly the sole source of power, legislative, military, judicial, and the question must have forced itself on many minds, 'What is the use of wast- ing the dwindling income of the state on the household of an emperor, when all the work of ruling is done by the patrician?' Thus the interreg- num of 465–7 prepared the way for the abolition of the dignity of Augustus in 476. It is doubtful, however, whether Ricimer at this period entertained any thoughts of dispensing with the fainéant emperors. It seems more probable that he was balancing in his mind the respective advantages to be derived from an alliance with Carthage or with Constantinople, the isolated position which Italy had occupied for the last six years being obvi- ously no longer tenable. If this view be correct, there is perhaps a slightly greater probability of his innocence of the death of Severus. An inoffensive and almost useful tool would hardly have been removed by force, if his employer had not decided how he was to be replaced.

However this may be, the interregnum was terminated by a decision in favour of Constantinople. Not Olybrius, the brother-in-law of the son of Gaiseric, but Anthemius, the son-in-law of the deceased emperor Mar- cian, was selected by Ricimer to be the wearer of the purple; and great was the Vandal's rage in consequence. The equivalent which the Eastern Empire was to pay for the still coveted honour of giving an Augustus to Rome was hearty support against the African enemy, with whom it is probable that her own relations had for some months been growing less friendly. A great combined campaign of 468 against the Vandals – a cam- paign in which Leo, Marcellinus, and Ricimer all joined their forces – was the fruit of this alliance, and it will be well first to describe this campaign, postponing for the moment the merely complimentary proceedings con- nected with the new emperor's accession to the Western throne.

The court of Constantinople must have been at this time a curious study for any unprejudiced observer who could keep his head cool in the whirlpool of its contending factions. Passions and ambitions as old as humanity were there, striving side by side with special theological formulae whose very names are almost forgotten among men. While the mob of Constantinople were eagerly discussing Bishop Timothy the weasel's revolt against the council of Chalcedon, or Bishop Peter the fuller's addition of four words to the Trisagion, Basilicus, the brother of the emperor's wife, and Zeno, the husband of the emperor's daughter, were playing their stealthy, remorseless, bloody game for the succession to the throne of the emperor, Leo.

When Ricimer's proposals for an alliance reached Constantinople, power was slipping from the hands of the general who had for forty years been the most powerful man in the Eastern court – Aspar, the son of Ardaburius. An Alan by extraction, he, with his father, had been sent as long ago as 424 on the expedition to Italy, which overthrew the usurper Joannes and established the young Valentinian on the throne of his uncle Honorius.* Since then he had been a consul (434), and the father of consuls (447, 459, 465). He was called 'first of the patricians';† he stood on the very steps of the throne, and might have been emperor himself, but he was an Arian. Being therefore by his theological tenets, which he had probably inherited from his barbarian ancestors, and was too proud to forgo, disqualified from himself reigning over 'the orthodox Romans', he made it his care that the purple should at least be always worn by men subservient to his interests. The brave young soldier who stretched himself to sleep in the courtyard of Gaiseric's palace, whom the hovering eagle overshadowed, and whom the Vandal dismissed with a true presage of his future greatness, was Marcian, *domesticus* of Aspar.‡ So long as he reigned (450–7) the influence of his patron appears to have remained unshaken. On his death there seems to have been some expectation that his son-in-law, Anthemius, would succeed him,§ but the predominant influence of Aspar and his son Ardaburius again secured the election of a dependant, their *curator* [factor], Leo.

But, whatever might be the manner of a man's elevation to the supreme dignity of the state, even though, as in the cases of Marcian and Leo, something like domestic service might be the ladder of his promotion, when once he was hailed Augustus, the elaborate court ceremonial of Byzantium enveloped him in the eyes of acclaiming crowds and literally adoring courtiers with all 'the divinity that doth hedge a king'. We have an apt illustration of this in one of those anecdotes with which the chroniclers so

* See vol. i, pp. 482–3.   † Marcellinus, for the year 471.   ‡ See p. 155.
§ Sidonius represents Anthemius as refusing the diadem and as not choosing to be indebted to his wife for the purple (*Panegyric of Anthemius*, 210–19), but it is quite possible that they were never offered to him.

curiously diversify their otherwise meagre pages. A few years after Leo's accession, as we are informed by Marcellinus, he fell sick of a fever (462). Jacobus, a man of Greek nationality and pagan faith, and one in whom a great natural genius for the healing art had been enriched by a long course of study, was called in to prescribe for the Imperial patient. When he entered 'the sacred bedchamber', he presumed to take a seat by the emperor's bedside without having received any sign that he was at liberty to do so, and then proceeded to make his diagnosis of the case. When he returned at noon to 'the sacred couch', he found the possibility of such impertinence averted by the removal of the chair. He perceived the meaning of the hint, and at once, with awful 'intrepidity', sat down upon the Imperial couch itself, explaining to the sick emperor that he did so in conformity with the rules laid down by the old masters of his art, and not out of any disrespect to him.

To Leo the servility of the Byzantine court was perhaps useful, as giving him courage to resist the too imperious mandates of his old master. It happened, apparently in the first year of his reign (457), that Aspar asked him to appoint one of his brother Arians to the post of prefect of the city. Cowed by his long habit of deference Leo assented, but regretted his compliance the moment afterwards. That night he sent for an orthodox senator, and installed him, stealthily and with haste, in the vacant office. Great was Aspar's wrath when he heard of this act of disobedience on the part of his sovereign. He came blackbrowed into the purple presencechamber, and grasping the emperor's robe, said to him, 'Emperor! it is not fitting that he who is wrapped in this purple should tell lies!' To which Leo replied, 'Yea, rather, it is not fitting that the emperor should be bound to do the bidding of any of his subjects, especially when by his compliance he injures the state.'*

* This characteristic story rests directly upon nothing but the poor authority of Cedrenus (eleventh or twelfth century). But it harmonises with the circumstances of the Byzantine court at this time, and it receives, I think, quite sufficient confirmation from the following passage of the contemporary historian Candidus (quoted by Photius, *Library*, 79), 'He also speaks' (at the beginning of Leo's reign) 'concerning Tatian and Vivianus, and how there was a dispute between Aspar and the emperor concerning them, and what words they uttered to one another.' One may almost venture to assign the parts to the two rivals. Tatian, a trusted and orthodox counsellor (who presided at the council of Chalcedon), is probably the senator who was installed in the dead of night as prefect; Vivianus the disappointed competitor for this post, is soothed by being appointed consul in the year 463. The whole of this excerpt of Photius is of great value for the history of the emperor Leo.

For thirteen years the breach between the first of the patricians and his late *curator* went on widening. Yet Aspar was still a great power in the state, and it seemed not improbable that one of his three sons, Ardaburius, Patricius, or Hermenric, would succeed the sonless Leo who was already passing the prime of life. To strengthen himself against the anger of his former patron, the emperor began to cultivate the friendship of some of the Isaurian adventurers who at that time abounded in Constantinople, wild, rugged, unpopular men from the highlands of Asia Minor, but men who were not likely to fail him 'when hard came to hard'. One of these men, who was known by the barbarous appellation Tarasicodissa, son of Rusumbladeotus, changed his name to Zeno, and received the emperor's daughter Ariadne in marriage. Thenceforward it was understood that Zeno was the head of the party opposed to Aspar, and that he would, if possible, compass for himself, or at least for the younger Leo, his son by Ariadne, the succession to the Imperial throne.

On the other hand, a powerful counterpoise to the influence of Zeno was found in Basiliscus, the brother of the emperor's wife Verina. This man's craving to wear one day the Imperial diadem was so passionate and so ill-concealed, that it made him almost the laughing-stock of the court; but it was well known that he was the confidant of the still influential Aspar, and that in the fierce resentment of himself and his party against the council of Chalcedon, they were willing to accept help even from the Arians in order to annul its decrees. Basiliscus, the Monophysite, practically denied the true manhood of Jesus Christ; Aspar, the Arian, denied his true Godhead; but they were ready to co-operate in order to drive out of church and state the men who, in obedience to the council of Chalcedon, maintained the combined manhood and Godhead of the Saviour.

Such was the state of parties at Constantinople when in the spring of 468 Leo despatched his long-prepared armament against the Vandals. It was meant to deal a crushing blow. The Western Empire contributed probably some supplies both of men and money; Marcellinus left his Dalmatian palace and his independent principality to serve as a general under the orders of the Roman emperors; but the chief weight of the preparations fell, as was natural, on the comparatively unexhausted Empire of the East. Leo, who was a man of courage and capacity, was determined to spare neither trouble nor expense on this great enterprise. A thousand ships, a hundred thousand men, a hundred and thirty thousand pounds' weight of gold (£5,850,000 sterling), had been collected at Constantinople.* All seemed to promise well for the success of the armament, but all was ruined by the selection of its head. Basiliscus was appointed generalissimo: and showed such miserable weakness in his command that later generations believed that Vandal gold, or the secret orders of Aspar, anxious that his Arian fellow believers should not be too hardly pressed, caused his failure. Either hypothesis may be true, but historians are too apt to forget the infinite depths of simple human stupidity.

Marcellinus sailed to Sardinia, and expelled the Vandals from that island. Heraclius, another Byzantine general, made a successful descent on Tripolis, took the cities of the Vandals in that region, and marched from thence westwards to the city of Carthage. The proceedings of Basiliscus and the main body of the host shall be told in the very words of the historian Procopius, who is here our only authority. Though he wrote more than half a century after the event, yet as he was an Eastern Roman, and served in that very campaign against Carthage (533), in which Belisarius did what Basiliscus failed to do, we may listen to his story with some confidence in its general correctness.

'Basiliscus meanwhile, with his whole force, sailed for a town about thirty-five miles from Carthage, called Mercurion, from an old temple of Hermes there; and if he had not with evil purpose lingered at that place, but had at once commenced his march to Carthage, he would have taken the city at the first shout, annihilated the strength of the Vandals, and reduced them to slavery; so thoroughly was Gaiseric now alarmed at the irresistible might of the emperor Leo, who had taken from him Sardinia and Tripolis, and had sent against him such an armament under Basiliscus as all men said the Romans had never fitted out before. All this was now hindered by the general's procrastination, which was due either to cowardice or treachery. Profiting by the supineness of Basiliscus, Gaiseric armed all his subjects as well as he could, and put them on board troop-

---

* Joannes Lydus, who as an official had good means of ascertaining the facts, though he wrote in the following century, puts the expenditure on this expedition at sixty-five thousand pounds weight of gold and seven hundred thousand pounds of silver, say a little over £5 million sterling. He quite confirms the view taken by Procopius as to the mismanagement of the expedition, and the ruinous result of its failure (*De Magistratibus*, iii.43). Candidus, who is an even better authority than Joannes Lydus, says that the treasure collected for this expedition amounted to forty-seven thousand pounds' weight of gold and seven hundred thousand pounds of silver, and that this was partly raised from the sale of confiscated estates, partly contributed by Anthemius.

ships. Other ships, fast-sailers and carrying no soldiers, he held in reserve. Then sending ambassadors to Basiliscus he begged for a delay of five days, pretending that if this were granted him he would consider how he might best comply with the wishes of the emperor. And some say that he sent a large sum of money to Basiliscus, unknown to his soldiers, in order to pur-chase this armistice. He devised this scheme in the expectation, which was justified by the event, that in the meantime a wind would spring up which would be favourable to his purposes. Basiliscus then, either in obedience to the recommendation of Aspar, or as having been bribed to grant this truce, or because he really believed that it would be better for the army, stayed quietly in his camp waiting the convenience of the enemy. But the Vandals, as soon as ever the wind arose which they had been patiently expecting, unfurled their sails, and, taking the empty ships in tow, sailed against the enemy. As soon as they came near they set the empty ships on fire, and sent them with bellying sails full against the anchorage of the Romans. The ships of the latter, being tightly packed together in the quarter to which the fire-ships were directed, soon caught fire, and readily communicated it to one another.

'When the fire was thus kindled, great terror naturally seized the Roman host. Soon, the whistling of the wind, the roar of the fire, the shouts of the soldiers to the sailors, and of the sailors to the soldiers, the strokes of the poles with which they strove to push off the fire-ships or their own burning companions, created a wild hubbub of discordant noises. And now were the Vandals upon them, hurling javelins, sinking ships, or stripping the fugitive soldiers of their armour. Even in this crisis there were some among the Romans who played the man, most of all Joannes, second in command to Basiliscus, and quite guiltless of all his treachery. For when a great multi-tude of the enemy surrounded his ship, he from the deck killed numbers of them with his furious blows right and left; and when he saw that the ship was taken, he sprang in full armour from the quarter-deck into the sea. Then did Genzo, the son of Gaiseric, earnestly importune him to surren-der, offering him assistance and promising him safety, but he none the less committed his body to the sea, with this one cry, "Never will Joannes fall into the hands of dogs."

'With this the war was ended. Heraclius returned home. Basiliscus, when he arrived at Byzantium, seated himself as a suppliant in the temple which is dedicated to the great Christ and God, and which is called Sophia [wisdom] because the Byzantines think that epithet the most appropriate to God. On the earnest entreaty of his sister, the empress Verina, he escaped death, but his hopes of the throne, for the sake of which he had done all these things, were for the present dashed'* by the soon following fall of Aspar and Ardaburius.

Truly in reading Procopius' account of all the valour and treasure wasted in this campaign, one can heartily echo the saying of a more recent Byzantine historian,† 'Better is an army of stags led by lions than an army of lions led by a stag.'

In some mysterious manner the close of this campaign was connected with the fall of the brilliant and courageous Marcellinus. We are told that he 'perished by the treachery of one of his colleagues',‡ that he 'was killed in Sicily',§ that 'while bringing aid and succour to the Romans fighting against the Vandals near Carthage,¶ he was guilefully struck down by the very men whom he was coming to help'.** We know that the Dalmatian palace was left empty, that there were no more talks by the shore of the plashing Adriatic between the general and his philosopher friend Sallust, concerning the nature of the gods and the causes of the ruin of this perplexing world. But why or by whom Marcellinus died remains a mystery.

The unsuccessful campaign against Carthage occurred, as has been said, in the spring and summer of 468. We return to the events of the preceding spring in Italy. On the 12th of April 467, the population of Rome poured forth to meet the new emperor who was henceforth to rule over them in firm alliance with his brother Augustus of Constantinople. At the third milestone from the city†† Anthemius was solemnly proclaimed emperor of Rome in the presence probably of a brilliant escort from Byzantium, including his wife Euphemia, daughter of an emperor, and now empress herself, of his three sons, Marcian, Romulus, and Procopius, and a daughter, Alypia,‡‡ who was to play an important part in cementing the new alliance between East and West. The patrician Ricimer was there doubtless, scanning the features of the new sovereign, and endeavouring to find an answer to the question, 'To rule or to be ruled?' There too were the senate, the copious German guards, the dwindled ranks of the legionaries,

---

* Procopius, *De Bello Vandalico*, i.6.   † Cedrenus.

‡ Procopius, *De Bello Vandalico*, i.6.   § Cassiodorus, for the year 468.

¶ In August (Anonymus Cuspiniani, for the year 468).

** Marcellinus, for the year 468.

†† Presumably on the road to Ostia, and 'at a place called Brontotus', says Cassiodorus. I have not found any other passage which throws light on this name.

‡‡ The name of Alypia is mentioned by Joannes Antiochenus, fragment 209.

and the Roman populace, those jaded and dissipated sons of slaves who still called themselves Quirites, and talked of father Mars and the she-wolf's nurslings.

The new emperor was not merely son-in-law of Marcian, but in his own right a great Byzantine noble. On his father's side he was descended from that Procopius, whose revolt against Valentinian and whose short-lived sovereignty were described at the beginning of this history.* On his mother's side he traced his descent from Anthemius, praetorian prefect of the East, and virtual regent during the early years of the minority of Theodosius II.† Both this Anthemius (his maternal grandfather) and Procopius (his father) had been employed in important embassies to the Persian court.‡ He himself, aided no doubt by his fortunate marriage to Euphemia, had in early manhood attained the successive dignities of count of Illyricum, master of the soldiery, consul (455), and patrician. The expectation of some of the courtiers had marked him out as a probable successor of Marcian, but when the all-powerful voice of Aspar decreed the diadem to Leo, Anthemius sensibly took the disappointment in good part, attached himself loyally to the fortunes of the new emperor, and was soon entrusted by him with an important command on the lower Danube. Walamir the Ostrogoth, and Hormidac the Hun, were apparently both threatening the Roman inhabitants of the country which we now call Bulgaria. The populous city of Sardica (now Sofia), upon the northern slope of the Balkans, was in especial danger. Anthemius distinguished himself by the strict discipline which he maintained among his troops — often in those degenerate days more terrible to friend than foe — and in a pitched battle with Hormidac, he obtained, we are told, a decisive victory, notwithstanding the treacherous conduct of a subordinate — probably a barbarian — officer, who in the very crisis of the battle drew off all his cavalry, and left the Imperial flank exposed. After the victory the Roman general imposed one indispensable condition of peace upon the conquered Huns — the surrender of his traitorous colleague, who was put to death in the sight of both armies.§

* See vol. i, pp. 67–79.

† [For more information on the family of Anthemius see table iv, p. 398.]

‡ The embassy of Anthemius, which was before 405, is mentioned by Theodoret (*De Vita Patrum*, 8); that of Procopius by Sidonius (*Panegyric of Anthemius*, 75–88). But I confess that I doubt whether Sidonius has not made a blunder between the grandfather and the father of his hero.

§ Or perhaps slain by the Huns and his corpse delivered to the Romans (Apollinaris Sidonius, *Panegyric of Anthemius*, 298).

Such was the past history of the richly clothed Byzantine official who, in the spring of 467, rode proudly in through the gate of Rome, amidst the acclamations of soldiery and populace. 'Long live Anthemius Augustus! Long live Ricimer, the patrician! Long live the concord of the emperors!'

When the tidings of these Roman pageants reached the banks of the Rhône, one can imagine what envy they raised in the heart of Sidonius. 'An emperor acclaimed, and I not there to weave his praises into hexameters!' was a bitter reflection for the Gaulish poet. He had still some unused metaphors in his head; the necessary compliments to the Eastern Empire would give a motive entirely different from those of his two previous panegyrics; there was always the possibility of turning a few chapters of Livy into sonorous verse, and, in short, he resolved to resume the 'useful toil' of a panegyrist. A deputation of citizens of Auvergne was appointed to congratulate Anthemius on his accession, perhaps to solicit the redress of grievances, or help against the Visigoths; but it is plain from Sidonius' letters that the message entrusted to the deputation was the last thing in his thoughts; the real business to him was the panegyric.

His errand having received the sanction of 'the sacred autograph', he was entitled to travel at the public charge, by that admirably organised postal service (the *cursus*) which was probably about the last to perish of the Imperial institutions. In a letter to a friend, he describes his journey with a few lifelike touches, though some sentences reveal the rhetorician. But the friendly aspect of the wellknown villas by the Rhône, the short climb up the torrentbeds and over the snows of the Alps, the voyage from Ticinum (Pavia) down the Ticino and the Po, past cities which recalled the honoured name of Virgil, and through woods of oak and maple alive with the sweet song of birds, are all vividly brought before us. He admired the situation of Ravenna,* so strong for defence, so convenient for commerce, and was in doubt whether to say that the city and the harbour (Classis) were connected or divided by the long 'street of Caesar' which passed between them. But, though provisions of all kinds were to be had at Ravenna in abundance, he found, as other poets had found before him, that water fit for drinking was an unattainable luxury in that city, and he suffered the pangs of thirst though surrounded by streams.† Across the historic Rubicon and Metaurus, through the plains of Picenum and the valleys of Umbria, the Gaulish poet journeyed, no doubt with the lines of the fateful panegyric

* This description of Ravenna was quoted in vol. i. p. 490.
† I need not quote the parallel passage from the *Ancient Mariner*.

churning in his head. But either the sirocco blowing over the plains, or (as was probably the case) the imperfect drainage of Ravenna,* had by this time touched him with a fever. Alternately burning and shivering, he quaffed, but in vain, the waters of every stream and fountain near which his journey led him; and when the towers of Rome appeared upon the horizon, his feeling was that all the aqueducts of the city, and all the mimic seas of the amphitheatres,† would be insufficient to quench his thirst.

However, before entering the city he visited the tombs of the apostles, and after he had prostrated himself there, he felt that the languor of the fever departed from his limbs. He found the whole city in an uproar, on account of the wedding between the patrician Ricimer and the daughter of the ever-august emperor; a union which, while it reversed the relations between 'the father of the emperor' and his new father-in-law, was avowedly based on state considerations, and was looked upon as affording a new guarantee for the public tranquillity by cementing the alliance between Byzantine legitimacy and the rough strength of Ricimer's barbarians. Theatres, markets, temples, were all resounding with the Fescennine verses in which the populace, sometimes not too decorously, expressed their congratulations to the wedded pair. The bridegroom, with a crown upon his head, and the flowered robe of the consular upon his shoulders, went to fetch the bride from the house of her father. In the universal hubbub, no one had any ears for the Gallic deputation, and the transalpine poet, seeking the comparative quiet of his inn, drew, for the benefit of his correspondent at Lyons, an amusing picture of the 'earnest holiday' of the humming city.

When he next took up the pen he was able to announce a brilliant success. The great poem had been recited on New Year's day (468), and had earned for its author applause and a high office in the state. As soon as the wedding turmoil was over, and the riches of two Empires had been sufficiently displayed to public view, the affairs of the state resumed their ordinary course. The Gallic deputies met with entertainment and a courteous reception at the house of one Paulus, a venerable man and an ex-prefect. Sidonius describes with amusing naïvety how he then set to work to attach himself to a patron, Paulus being presumably too old to give him efficient assistance. The choice lay between two men, both of consular rank, and confessedly the most influential persons in the state after the

---

* Sidonius himself speaks of the *cloacalis puls fossarum discursu lintrium ventilata* [thick slime from the drains churned by the movement of boats].

† *Epistolae*, i.5.

emperor, 'always excepting the predominant power of the military party' –
a most significant exception, which probably included Ricimer and all his
immediate followers.

These two possible patrons were Gennadius Avienus and Caecina
Basilius. Avienus had obtained the consulship in 450, and had been congratulated by all his friends on his early promotion. Basilius had been
made consul in 463, and all the city had said, 'Why was not so good a
man raised to the office before?' Either nobleman saw his gate thronged
with suitors, and was followed through the forum by a crowd of obsequious clients; but the composition of the two bands of retainers was very
different, and so was the nature of their hopes. Avienus was most successful in pushing the fortunes of his sons, his sons-in-law, and his brothers:
when all this had been accomplished, there was not much court influence
left for more distant clients, whom he accordingly charmed with his
affable demeanour, but who somehow found that they were not drawing
any nearer to the goal of their wishes, notwithstanding all the hours that
they spent at their patron's vestibule. Basilius had far fewer of his own
friends to provide for, and his manner with those whom he admitted into
the circle of his dependants was much more reserved, almost haughty; but
when he did accept the homage of a client, he was almost certain to
obtain for him the fulfilment of his desires. Upon this estimate of their
respective characters, Sidonius wisely decided to attach himself to the
clientele of Basilius, while not omitting to pay frequent visits of ceremony
at the door of Avienus.

Favoured by the efficient help of Basilius, the affairs of the Arvernian
deputation were soon in good train for settlement. One day the patron said
to the poet, 'Come, my Sollius! The kalends of January are at hand, and
the name of our emperor is to be inscribed on the *fasti* of this new year.
Though I know that you are weighed down with the responsibility of your
deputation, can you not call upon your old muse to inspire you with some
lines in honour of the new consul? It is true that in so short a time they will
have to be almost the result of improvisation, but I can promise you a hearing for your verses, and at least my hands for their applause.'

It needs not to be said that the suggestion of Basilius was eagerly
accepted, and that upon the morning of the first day of 468 Sidonius was
ready with an 'impromptu' of 547 lines in praise of Anthemius. There is
no need to describe this poem with any fullness of detail, since the reader
can easily imagine its character from the two similar performances by the

same hand in praise of Avitus and Majorian. There is an eloquent passage
in praise of Constantinople,* and a graphic account of the manners of the
Huns,† very closely corresponding with the pictures drawn by Jordanes
and Ammianus. The lineage of Anthemius is described; the conventional
prodigies which marked his birth and infancy; the events of his military
and official career; and great stress is laid on his unwillingness − real or
imaginary − to accept the Western crown, till commanded to do so by Leo.
The real interest of the poem for us lies in its hints as to the course of contemporary politics, in its portraiture of Gaiseric and Ricimer.

> Each emperor that on Western soil is born
> Fails from the helm and perishes forlorn.
> Here the stern Vandal spreads his thousand sails
> And yearly for our ruin courts the gales.
> Strange fate! Upon our shores swart Afric throws
> The nations reared amid Caucasian snows.‡
> Alone, till now, with Mars his only friend,
> He on whose arm the fates of Rome depend,
> Unconquered Ricimer has held at bay
> The freebooter§ who makes our fields his prey,
> Who skulks from battle, yet can still contrive
> To reap the victor's spoils, a fugitive.
> Whose strength by such a foe would not be spent
> Who gives nor peace nor war's arbitrament?
> 'No peace with Ricimer', his watchword dire,
> And this the cause that fills his veins with fire.
> He knows himself the offspring of a slave,
> The sire he knows not who his being gave.
> Hence envy gnaws him, that his rival springs,
> Great Ricimer, on either side from kings.
> His sire a Sueve, a royal Gothic dame
> His mother, who of Walia's lineage came;
> The noble Walia, whose redoubted sword
> Drove forth from Spain the motley, mongrel horde

---

* *Panegyric of Anthemius*, 46−9.   † *Panegyric of Anthemius*, 243−69.
‡ This is mere poetic generalisation. Of course the Vandals had nothing to do with Caucasus. For their Alan confederates the reference is less incorrect.   § Gaiseric.

Of Vandals, Alans, worsted in the fray,
And with their corpses covered Calpé's bay.*

But Ricimer alone, says the poet, can no longer ward off the perils of the Empire. There is need of an emperor of the old type, one who can not only order wars, but wage them. Such an emperor the East can furnish, and, on the intercession of Rome, she does furnish, in the bronzed veteran Anthemius. He and his son-in-law have prepared fleets and armies which will surely reduce Africa to its ancient obedience. In some future year, when Anthemius shall be consul for a third, or Ricimer for a second time, Sido- nius promises himself the delight of again appearing before them to chant the fall of Gaiseric.

The florid panegyric was received, its author tells us, with rapturous applause. Shouts of *Sophos! sophos!* (the Greek equivalent of 'bravo') resounded from the benches where sat the senators conspicuous by their purple *laticlavi*,† and from the higher tiers of seats where swarmed the com- mon people, the representatives of the once omnipotent Roman tribes.‡ A more striking proof of approbation was given by the emperor, who, on the recommendation of Basilius, named Sidonius prefect of the city of Rome. Thus, as he himself piously expresses it, 'I have now, by the help of Christ and an opportune use of my pen, arrived at the prefecture.' In modern states (China and the great American republic alone excepted) it would be hard to find an instance of honours such as this conferred on the votaries of literature.

Sidonius was now in theory the third personage in the Empire, on a level with the praetorian prefects of Italy and Gaul, inferior only to the emperor and the patrician. In practice, however, it is probable that many a rude Herulian centurion or tribune counted for more than the versatile thin- minded poet. Besides his presidency over the senate,§ the aqueducts, the market-places, the foreshores, the harbour, the statues, were all under his care.¶ But his chief business – an infinitely harassing one in those dying days of the Empire – was the care of the provisioning of the city, which rested upon him and his subordinate, the commissary general (*praefectus annonae*),

---

* *Panegyric of Anthemius*, 346–65.   † [*Laticlavus*]: a broad stripe on the tunic.
‡ Apollinaris Sidonius, *Epistolae*, i.9.
§ The presidency of the senate was one of the functions of the *praefectus urbis*.
¶ See the *Notitia Occidentis*, 4, for a sketch of the duties of the *praefectus urbis*. See also vol. i, p. 346.

as the earthly providence of Rome. It is curious to read a letter from the new prefect to a Gaulish friend, in which he expresses his fear lest, when he next visits the amphitheatre, he should hear a harsh cry of rage from the assembled multitude,* imputing their hunger to his incapacity. A gleam of hope shines upon him when he is informed that five ships, laden with corn and honey, have arrived at Ostia from Brindisi, and he despatches his *praefectus annonae* with all speed, to receive and distribute the precious cargoes.

Sidonius retained his new dignity only for one year, but on laying it down he probably received the title of patrician† – a title which was in his case purely honorary, conferring no power and imposing no responsibility. The short tenure of his office does not exactly imply disgrace, but it may probably be asserted that if the Gaulish man of letters had shown any conspicuous ability in his prefectorate, his office would have been renewed to him at least for two or three years. He quitted Rome in the year 469, never to return to that scene of petty intrigues and worn-out splendours – pygmies masquerading in the armour of giants – a scene which must have filled a thoughtful man with sadness and a cynic with a rapture of scorn.

But before he went he witnessed the commencement of a process which attracted his deepest interest, and filled him with varied emotions – the trial and condemnation of Arvandus. This man, a fellow countryman of Sidonius, had for five years held the office of praetorian prefect of Gaul. The popularity which marked his earlier years of office had utterly deserted him before its close. He had become involved in debt, from which he sought to free himself by the most unjust exactions from the provincials; he had grown moody, suspicious, implacable; and finally, knowing the universal disfavour with which the Roman population regarded him, he had commenced a traitorous correspondence with the Visigothic king. Three Gaulish noblemen were sent as a deputation to Rome to impeach Arvandus before the senate on charges of extortion and high treason.

The arrival of this deputation, and of the accused governor, placed Sidonius in an awkward position. The deputies were all of them acquaintances of his, and one (Tonantius Ferreolus) was his relative and intimate friend.‡ On the other hand, Arvandus had been long known, though

---

* Like the *Pretium inpone carnis humanae* [Set a maximum price for human flesh], which was shouted by the people in the Colosseum, in 410, when Attalus was emperor.

† This is inferred by his biographers from the letter to his wife, Papianilla, quoted above (pp. 203–4), in which he speaks of himself as having achieved patrician honours.

‡ See the letter, quoted on p. 190, describing the visit to his house.

never liked by him, and he says that he would have thought it base and barbarous to desert him in the day of his calamity. This difficulty however was
soon solved by the accused himself, who, when Sidonius and a fellow noble
ventured to give him some hints as to the necessity of tact and moderation in
the conduct of his case, flamed out upon them with the words, 'Away with
you, ye degenerate sons of prefects! Who wants your fussy anxiety on my
behalf? Arvandus' conscience suffices for Arvandus. I can scarcely bring
myself even to hire an advocate to defend me from the charge of extortion.'

All the rest of his conduct was of a piece with this outburst of petu-
lance. While the Gaulish deputies were walking about in sad-coloured
garments, with downcast faces, as men who had a painful duty to perform
on behalf of the oppressed, Arvandus, in a white toga, with scented hair
and pumice-stoned face, gaily promenaded the forum, nodding to his
friends as if his salutation were still of the highest value, frequenting the
jewellers' shops, chaffering over the price of fashionable knick-knacks, and
all the while keeping up a running fire of complaints against the emperor,
the senate, and the laws, for allowing a person of his quality to be subjected
to the indignity of a trial.

The eventful day arrived. The senate-house was crowded. The defen-
dant, fresh from the hairdresser's hands, walked boldly up to the benches of
the 'prefectorians', and took his seat, as if of right, in the most honourable
place among his judges. Ferreolus, on the contrary, equally entitled to a seat
among the 'prefectorians', placed himself, along with his fellow deputies,
on one of the lowest benches of the senate-house. The deputation set forth
their case, and read the mandate which they had received from their fellow
citizens. Instead of lingering over the outworks of the indictment, the
charges of peculation and extortion, they went rapidly to the heart of the
matter, the accusation of treasonable intrigues with the barbarians. A letter
was produced, in the handwriting of the amanuensis of Arvandus,
addressed to the Visigothic king. It tended to dissuade him from making
peace with 'the Greek emperor' (Anthemius), suggested that he should
attack the Bretons, who were allies of the Empire, and recommended that
'the Visigoths and the Burgundians should divide Gaul between them,
according to the law of nations'.* There might have been some difficulty in
tracing the composition of this letter to Arvandus, but the infatuated culprit aimed the weapon against himself by at once boldly proclaiming that
he was the author. 'Then you are guilty of high treason,' said every voice in

* Apollinaris Sidonius, *Epistolae*, i.7.

the assembly. He then tried to retract and to qualify his previous admissions, for with incredible folly he had hitherto supposed that nothing short of the actual assumption of the Imperial purple would have justified a condemnation for high treason.* But it was too late; his guilt was manifest. He was stripped of all his dignities, and the delicately dressed and scented culprit was hurled, with every mark of disgrace, into a squalid dungeon on the Insula Tiberina, sentenced to be there killed by the executioner, to have his body dragged by an iron hook through the streets, and then to be cast into the Tiber.

By the wise and merciful legislation of Theodosius, due to the suggestion of Ambrose, an interval of thirty days necessarily elapsed between the utterance and the execution of a capital sentence.† This interval Sidonius employed in pleading for a mitigation of the punishment of the fallen prefect, though, as he contemptuously remarked, 'No greater calamity can befall him than that he should wish to live, after all the ignominy that has been heaped upon him.' An entry in one of the chroniclers‡ seems to justify the inference that the intervention of Sidonius was successful, and that the capital sentence was commuted into one of perpetual exile.

It is not improbable that one cause of Sidonius' departure from Rome may have been that he saw the political horizon darkening with the impending rupture between Ricimer and Anthemius. The great enterprise against Carthage, which should have united them, had failed, as was before stated (468); and thus, both Rome and the Suevic chief had humbled themselves before Byzantium for nothing. Anthemius was hot-tempered, and probably felt himself by intellect as well as by birth fitted for something better than to be the mere puppet of a barbarian. We have no hint as to the part taken by his daughter, in soothing or in exciting the combatants, but we can imagine that she let the middle-aged patrician, her husband, see too plainly how vast she considered her condescension in becoming the wife of a barbarian. In 470 another event added fuel to the fire. The emperor, who found his health failing him, believed that he was the victim of magical arts, and arrested many persons upon the charge of thus compassing his death. A certain Romanus, an adherent of Ricimer, himself bearing the title of patrician as well as that of master of the army, was among the persons put

---

* Possibly the dislocated relations of all the members of the Western Empire at this time might have afforded some precedents as a basis for this wild notion.

† See vol. i, p. 303.   ‡ Cassiodorus, for the year 469.

to death on this accusation. Thereat Ricimer, in a fury, flung out of Rome and called to his standards six thousand men who had served under him in the Vandal war.*

In the spring of the year 471† Ricimer was at Milan, surrounded, no doubt, by the Teutonic auxiliaries, and leaning perhaps somewhat on the aid of his brother-in-law, the king of the Burgundians, who held all the northern passes of the western Alps, since he ruled in Valais and Savoy, in Dauphiné and the lower valley of the Rhône. Anthemius was not at Ravenna, but in Rome, relying on the favour with which he was regarded by the populace of the city,‡ on the sympathies of the official class, and on the patriotism of whatsoever purely Roman and Italian elements might be left in the legions. Between these two men, all Italy perceived with horror that war was inevitable.

Such being the state of things, the nobles of Liguria assembled at the palace of Ricimer, and adoring the Suevic patrician with self-prostration, after the manner of the orientals, besought him to consent to an accommo-dation with his father-in-law. Ricimer was, or professed to be, mollified by their arguments. 'But whom will ye send as mediator?' said he. 'Who can bring this hot-headed Galatian§ prince to reason? If you ask him for the smallest favour he bubbles over with fury, and there is not a man living who can remain in a passion so long as he.' 'There is a person in this province', said the nobles, 'to whom you may safely entrust this commission; a man to whom even wild beasts would bow their necks; a man whom a Catholic and a Roman must venerate, and whom even the little Greek emperor can-not help loving if he is privileged to behold him.' And then they proceeded to sketch the life and recount the virtues of Epiphanius, the saintly young bishop of Pavia, in somewhat similar words possibly to those in which they

* Joannes Antiochenus, fragment 207; Cassiodorus, for the year 470.

† Or 472; but as Epiphanius returned from his embassy on the fourteenth day before Easter, as he was for the time successful and as Olybrius was raised to the throne by Ricimer in April, 472, it seems almost certain that we must refer the first outbreak of civil war and the mediation of Epiphanius to 471. Easter fell on the 16th of April in the year 472.

‡ Joannes Antiochenus expressly says that 'on the side of Anthemius were ranged those in office and the people, and on that of Ricimer the multitude of his own barbarians'.

§ There is some sting in this word 'Galatian' which we cannot explain. Possibly it is con-nected with the fact that the ancestral Procopius, who assumed the purple in the year 365, was *in Cilicia natus et educatus* [born and bred in Cilicia] (Ammianus, xxvi.6.1), Cilicia and Galatia being provinces not far distant from one another.

are now recorded for us by his admiring disciple Ennodius, from whom we derive our knowledge of this incident.

In the *Life of Epiphanius* we meet of course with many incidents and traits of character common to a saint of that period of the church. A super-natural light shone round his cradle when he was still busy with the rattle and the baby's bottle. On the strength of this omen he was at eight years old received into the ministry of the church as a reader, and before long distin-guished himself by the rapidity and accuracy with which he practised the art of an ecclesiastical shorthand writer. Ordained a deacon at twenty, priest at twenty-eight, and almost immediately afterwards elected bishop of Pavia, he was already in his early manhood marked out for the veneration of his contemporaries. 'He knew not that he was a man', says his biographer, 'except by his power of enduring toil; he forgot that he was in the flesh except when he meditated on his mortality.' No great miracles are recorded of his earlier years, but the saintly patience and dignity with which he, a young Ligurian of noble blood, endured the cudgelling administered to him by a rustic boor named Burco, who had a dispute with the church of Pavia about boundaries, endeared him to his fellow citizens, and enabled him to plead successfully for the life of his antagonist when the indignant populace clamoured for his execution. Altogether, though the robes of these ecclesiastical personages are beginning to fall stiffly, and though the fifth-century type of holiness lacks, to our thinking, the freshness of a true humanity, we cannot but feel that Epiphanius was one of those men to whom mere goodness gives a wonderful magnetic power over all who come in contact with them. His sweet and pure figure is a refreshing contrast to the wild passions and base treacheries with which his age is filled.

Such was the man who, on the invitation of the Ligurians, with the assent of Ricimer, while greatly doubting his own sufficiency for the task, undertook the mission to Anthemius. When he reached Rome, all the officers of the household went forth to meet him without the gates. They brought him into the Imperial hall of audience, where the flash of gems and the sombre magnificence of the purple still, as in the mightiest days of the Empire, attested the presence of Augustus. But all eyes were fixed, not on the emperor, but on the tall ecclesiastic, with brow of marble whiteness and delicately formed limbs,* who, sparing of words in his ordinary con-versation, was about to speak on behalf of Italy and peace.

* See the description of the personal appearance of Epiphanius in the beginning of the *Life* by Ennodius.

'Dread sovereign!' he began, 'we recognise the hand of God in calling to the highest place in this commonwealth you who have shown yourself a faithful adherent to the teaching of the Catholic faith, in permitting you to eclipse the triumphs of war by the arts of peace, and to restore the interrupted harmony of the Roman world. Be this still your glory, O emperor! Still blend gentleness with force, and thereby make your rule a copy of the heavenly kingdom.* Remember how David, by sparing King Saul when he was in his power, earned more glory than would have accrued from the most righteous vengeance. This is the request of Italy, this the message which Ricimer has entrusted to the mouth of my littleness. Earn for yourself a bloodless victory, overcome even this proud Goth by your benefits. Or, if you are still in doubt, consider all the chances of war, war in which you may be defeated, and in which even victory must lessen the resources of your Empire, while by a peaceful compact with Ricimer you might have enjoyed them undiminished.'

He ended, and Anthemius, raising his eyes, saw that the hearts of all the bystanders were won by the words of peace. With a deep sigh he said, 'Holy bishop! The causes of my anger against Ricimer are such as cannot be fully set forth in words. I have loaded him with benefits; I have not even spared my own flesh and blood, but have given my daughter to this skinclothed Goth,† an alliance which I cannot think upon without shame for myself, my family and my kingship. But the more I have distinguished him with my gifts, the more bitterly has he become mine enemy. He has stirred up foreign nations to war against the commonwealth; where he could not himself hurt, he has suggested to others schemes for hurting me. I myself believe that it is better to treat such a man as an open foe. To feel your enemy is the first step towards overcoming him, and anything is better than the machinations of secret hatred. But since you interpose your venerable office and your holy character as a pledge for his sincere desire for peace, be it so. I cannot resist anything which such a man as you pleads for. If your perceptions have been deceived, and if he still have war in his heart, on him shall rest the guilt of renewing the combat. I commit and commend myself and the commonwealth, whose pilot I am, entirely into your hands, and I grant to you the pardon which Ricimer himself should not have

---

* And earthly power doth then show likest God's
    When mercy seasons justice.

† Of course the 'skinclothed Goth' is a figure of speech. Probably the toga of Ricimer was as faultless as that of his fatherinlaw.

obtained, no, not if he had been grovelling in the dust before my feet.'

The bishop thanked God for having put these peaceful counsels into the heart of him whom he had chosen as the vicar of his supreme power among men; he then took a solemn oath from Anthemius to hold fast the newly re-cemented alliance, and departed in all haste for Liguria. He travelled so rapidly, although his strength was reduced by a rigorous Lenten fast, that he returned to Pavia on the sixth day after he had quitted it, and the joyful shouts of the people surrounding his house, and learning from his own mouth the news of the ratified treaty of peace, were the first intimation to Ricimer that his messenger had quitted Rome.

However, the peace between the two rival powers in the state was of short duration. Some expressions in the narrative would lead us to suppose that the position of Anthemius, at the time of the embassy, was slightly the stronger of the two, and that Ricimer showed his usual cunning in accepting the good offices of the bishop. Within fourteen months (possibly within two months) after the negotiations at Milan, we find the two parties again in arms against one another. Ricimer proclaimed Olybrius emperor, thereby conciliating the support of the Vandal king, and perhaps neutralising the opposition of the friends of Anthemius at Constantinople, for Olybrius was also a Byzantine, and also allied to the Imperial family.* He marched to the outskirts of Rome and pitched his camp near a bridge over the Anio, probably the Ponte Salaro. Within the walls opinion was divided, some even of the citizens ranging themselves on the side of Ricimer, though the majority no doubt adhered to Anthemius. For five months the siege lasted, Ricimer keeping a strict watch upon the upper and lower waters of the Tiber, and suffering no provisions to enter the city. The pressure of the famine was so great that (as Theophanes tells us) 'the soldiers were reduced to feed upon leather and other unusual articles of food'. Then an unexpected auxiliary appeared upon the scene.† 'Bilimer, ruler of the Gauls' (we have no clue to the true character of this mysterious personage), 'hearing of the conspiracy against Anthemius, came to Rome earnestly desiring to give

* Paulus Diaconus (*Historia Romana*, xv.3) makes Leo himself send Olybrius to Rome to wrest the crown from Anthemius. Perhaps the concurring testimonies of Theophanes and the *Chronicon Paschal* may be accepted as showing that this was the received version of the story at Constantinople.

† Paulus, whose sources of information are here unusually good, is our authority for this element in the story. He says also that from the famine which was raging in Rome two 'regions' were exempt in which Ricimer dwelt with his followers. Perhaps these were on the west of the Tiber.

him assistance. He joined battle with Ricimer by the bridge of Hadrian'
(the bridge leading to the castle of Sant'Angelo) 'and was immediately
overcome and slain. On his death Ricimer entered the city as conqueror,
and slew Anthemius with the sword.' Another authority (Joannes Antiochenus) tells us that 'the followers of Anthemius opened the gates to the
barbarians, leaving their master defenceless, that he mixed with the crowd of
mendicants, and sought refuge at the tomb of the martyr Chrysogonus,*
and being there discovered was instantly beheaded by Gundobad, the
nephew† of Ricimer. He received a royal burial at the hands of his enemies.' Anthemius perished on the 11th July, 472; and only five weeks afterwards his turbulent son-in-law followed him to the grave. On the 18th
August, Ricimer, the patrician, who had held supreme power in Italy for
sixteen years, died of a sudden haemorrhage, and thus the stage was left clear
for new actors. What they will make of the defence or extension of the
Roman Empire we shall see in the following chapter.

---

* The basilica of Chrysogonus (one of the martyrs under Diocletian) stands in the
Trastevere, about a quarter of a mile west of the Ponte Rotto.
† Joannes says 'brother', but this is an error.

CHAPTER XI

Olybrius, the Client of the Vandal, AD 472. Glycerius, the Client of the Burgundian, AD 473–4. Julius Nepos, the Client of Byzantium, AD 474–5. Romulus Augustulus, Son of Orestes, AD 475–6

THE NEW EMPEROR, ANICIUS OLYBRIUS, MIGHT possibly have procured some breathing-space for the exhausted commonwealth, if he had worn the purple for any considerable length of time.

Of the great Anician family, and probably descended from one of those brother consuls, Olybrius and Probinus, whose accession to office in the year 395 Claudian celebrated with such courtly enthusiasm; the husband of the great-granddaughter of Theodosius, and the representative, as far as there could be a representative, of the claims of that Imperial house; on good terms with the Eastern Augustus, perhaps openly supported by him; above all, the brother-in-law of the heir-apparent to the Vandal crown, the long-proposed and at last successful candidate of Gaiseric; Olybrius, as to whose personal qualities the page of history is a blank, possessed in these external circumstances exceptional advantages for a Roman emperor in the year 472.* But whether the care of ruling a troubled court, which had made Petronius Maximus sigh for the happier lot of Damocles, or the air of Rome, so often fatal to alien rulers, overpowered him, we know not. So it

* [See table v, 'Genealogy of Olybrius', p. 399.]

was that on the 23rd October, 472, little more than three months after the death of his rival, Olybrius died at Rome of dropsy. Had Ricimer been still living, this death would of course have figured in his catalogue of crimes, but the rough-handed Sueve had gone before Olybrius, as has been already stated, on the 18th of August.

During his short reign Olybrius conferred the dignity of patrician on the young Burgundian prince Gundobad, whose mother was sister to Ricimer, and who apparently had come to Italy to push his fortunes by the help of his all-powerful uncle.* It is conjectured with much probability that the barbarian element in the Roman army, which knew something of its strength, and was suspicious of any but a barbarian leader, transferred its fealty, or its attachment, or its obedience (it is difficult to find a word to express the nature of the tie which bound these troops to their leader) from Ricimer to his nephew, and that this transference brought with it, almost as a matter of course, his elevation to the rank of patrician and 'father of the emperor'.

For five months Gundobad allowed himself the luxury of an interreg-num; then, on the 5th of March, 473, he raised a certain Glycerius to the throne, at Ravenna. This election of Glycerius, though he had held the high office of *comes domesticorum* (commander of the household troops),† was not approved of, nor apparently recognised, at Byzantium. Our chief Eastern chronicler (Marcellinus) tells us that Glycerius was made Caesar at Ravenna 'more by presumption than by election'; and steps were soon taken to furnish a successor to Olybrius whom the Easterns could recognise as legitimate.

Some changes had taken place at the court of Constantinople since the councils preceding the elevation of Anthemius, and the expedition against Carthage. In the year 471, Aspar and his sons were murdered in the palace by the swords of the eunuchs of the emperor's household. 'An Arian father with his Arian offspring', is the pious comment of Marcellinus; but all the inhabitants of Constantinople were not disposed to consider the hetero-doxy of Aspar sufficient justification for the deed. They remembered that it was by Aspar's hand that Leo himself had been lifted to the throne; that something had been whispered of a secret compact, according to which

---

* It was Gundobad, who, as mentioned at the close of the last chapter, dealt the actual death-stroke to the fugitive Anthemius.

† So says Joannes Antiochenus, fragment 209.2. The *comes domesticorum* was entitled to the appellation *illustris*.

one of the sons of Aspar was to succeed in the Imperial dignity, and that, in fact, his son Patricius, who appeared susceptible of conversion to the Catholic faith, had been formally recognised as Caesar, and thereby desig- nated as next in succession to the throne. It might be convenient to cancel all these liabilities by the swords of the eunuchs of the household; it was, no doubt, a relief to know that that terrible patrician would never again shake his sovereign's purple robe and remind him of obligations which ortho- doxy would not suffer him to discharge; but, upon the whole, the popular instinct condemned the transaction, and branded the emperor Leo with the epithet Macellus (the butcher), a term derived from the meat-markets of Rome.

When the news of the 'presumptuous' elevation of Glycerius to the throne reached Constantinople, in the summer of 473, the emperor Leo was probably in failing health. (He died in January of the following year.) The rivalry for the succession between Basiliscus, with his firm persuasion that he should one day be emperor, and Tarasicodissa, the Isaurian, always addressed by his flatterers as Zeno, was, no doubt, becoming more intense than ever. But the threads of this and of every intrigue about the court of Byzantium were in the hands of her who was sister of one candidate and mother-in-law of the other, Verina, the wife of the dying Augustus. Influ- enced, no doubt, by her, the choice of a Western emperor fell upon Julius Nepos, by birth nephew of the brave Marcellinus of Dalmatia, and by marriage nephew of the empress Verina.

The new emperor was proclaimed in Constantinople in August, 473,* but, delayed apparently by the complications connected with the illness and death of his patron, did not land in Italy till the spring of the following year. Meanwhile Leo died; his grandson, the younger Leo, succeeded him, and being but a boy, associated his father, the Isaurian Zeno, with him in the Empire. The son-in-law had won, for the present at least, in the race for the Eastern throne.†

Before we start with Nepos on his quest of the Western sovereignty, let us see how matters have fared with the occupant whom he means to dis- place – with Glycerius. In 473, the year of his accession, a new enemy to

---

* This hypothesis seems best to explain the frequent abridgement by the chroniclers of the reign of Glycerius from sixteen months to five. The 'legitimist' writers know nothing of Glycerius as emperor after Leo had raised Nepos to the throne.

† [For more information on the genealogies of the Eastern and Western emperors see table vi, p. 400.]

Rome appeared upon the northern horizon. The Ostrogothic brother-kings, who served under Attila at the battle in Champagne, on the overthrow of the Hunnish empire obtained for themselves a goodly settle-ment in Pannonia, on the western bank of the Danube. For nearly twenty years they had been engaged in desultory hostilities with their barbarian neighbours, with Suevi and Rugians on the north and west, with Huns and Sarmatians on the south and east. Now, as their countryman, Jordanes, tells us with admirable frankness, 'the spoils of these neighbouring nations were dwindling, and food and clothing began to fail the Goths. Therefore to these men, who had long found their sustenance in war, peace began to be hateful.'* They clustered round their kings, and clamoured to be led forth to war – whither they cared not, but war there must be. Theudemir, the elder king, took counsel with his brother Widemir, and they resolved to commence a campaign against the Roman Empire. Theudemir, as the more powerful chieftain, was to attack the stronger Empire of the East; Widemir, with his weaker forces, was to enter Italy. He did so, but, like so many of the Northern conquerors, he soon found a grave in the beautiful but deathly land. His son, the younger Widemir, succeeded to his designs of conquest, but Glycerius approached him with presents and smooth words, and was not ashamed to suggest that he should transfer his arms to Gaul, which was still in theory, and partially in fact, a province of the Empire. The sturdy bands of Widemir's Ostrogoths descended accord-ingly into the valleys of the Rhône and the Loire; they speedily renewed the ancient alliance with the Visigothic members of their scattered nationality, and helped to ruin yet more utterly the already desperate cause of Gallo-Roman freedom.

It may be that this ignominious mode of dealing with an invader served to sink the insignificant Glycerius yet lower in the eyes of his people. He seems to have been keeping close under the skirts of Mont Blanc and Monte Rosa, that he might not be too far removed from the Burgundian country-men of his patron, Gundobad. In Pavia, we are told, his mother was so insultingly treated by the populace – perhaps in order to mark their con-tempt for her son – that he would have inflicted severe punishment upon them if he had not been dissuaded by the saintly peacemaker Epiphanius.†

Such was the state of things when Nepos, the Byzantine candidate for Empire, landed in Italy, in one of the spring months of 474. Did the bar-barian auxiliaries, headed by the young Burgundian Gundobad, the heir of

---

* De Rebus Geticis, 56.   † Ennodius, Life of Epiphanius.

the power of Ricimer, go forth to meet him, and did battle follow? The silence of the chroniclers rather seems to indicate that the affair was settled without a resort to arms.* And as we find Gundobad, shortly after this time, peaceably reigning with his brothers over their paternal kingdom on the banks of the Rhône, the inference drawn by some of the most careful enquirers into the history of the period is that, the death of his father Gundiok having occurred shortly after that of his uncle Ricimer, he had weighed the solid advantages of his Burgundian inheritance against the prestige of a Roman kingmaker, and found the former preponderate. Therefore, and as he also well knew the hostile designs of the Byzantine court, he quietly marched back across the Alps with the young warriors of his *comitatus* [retinue], leaving the luckless Glycerius to fight and lose his own battles alone. This may be accepted as the most probable explanation of Gundobad's disappearance from the scene; but it must be pointed out that it is not the only one. He may have stood by his client, have fought and lost some unrecorded battle, and only then have made his way over the unmelted April snows of the St Bernard or the Mont Genèvre to his Burgundian kingdom.

Let the causes of the non-resistance, or unsuccessful resistance of the barbarian auxiliaries have been what they may, the result is undoubted. The efforts of the Eastern candidate were crowned with complete success, but his triumph was not stained with cruelty. The fortified harbour-town at the mouth of the Tiber, opposite to the modern Ostia, which under the name of Portus Augusti et Trajani commemorated the names of two of Rome's most famous emperors,† witnessed in the summer of 474 two very different spectacles. There, on the 24th of June, Julius Nepos was solemnly raised to the dignity of emperor, the senate and the people of Rome being no doubt duly represented on the ground, and acclaiming the new Augustus. There also, a few days earlier or later, Glycerius, ex-count of the Domestics and ex-emperor, received the oil of consecration as a bishop. The merciful conqueror, who had spared his life, vouchsafed to him also a sphere for the exercise of his new functions. The church of Salona, the capital of the dominions of Marcellinus, was at this juncture in need of a head. Thither Glycerius was sent, and he who had lately held power nominally supreme in the Western world, subsided, apparently without a murmur, into the condition of bishop of a Dalmatian town. Even so, after a long and costly

* Joannes Antiochenus (fragment 209) expressly asserts that Rome was taken without resistance.   † 'Augustus' here = Nero who dedicated the port of Claudius.

contest for the heirship to a dukedom, the successful litigant might solace his beaten rival by assigning to him one of the family livings. With this consecration at Portus, Glycerius but for one doubtful allusion disappears from history. There have been many worse emperors, doubtless, than the 'not disreputable'* person whom Gundobad advised to become Augustus, and whom Nepos advised to become a bishop.

The only memorable events in the fourteen months' reign of Julius Nepos are those which relate to the affairs of Gaul, that country which gave her first province to the republic, and whose allegiance was the last jewel hacked from the fingers of the dying Empire.

The Visigothic throne at Toulouse was now no longer filled by the jovial and tolerant Theodoric II, to whom Sidonius lost so many games at 'the tables'. Eight years before the period which we have now reached, that prince was slain and replaced by his equally able, but narrower and harsher, brother Euric.† Though it is true that he employed as his chief minister of state the polished and learned GalloRoman Leo, we can trace in Euric a bitterer Arianism and a more acrid and antiRoman barbarianism than was shown by Theodoric, the inattentive listener to the ministrations of his heretical clergy, the staunch upholder of the alliance with Avitus.

Of the religious intolerance of Euric, Sidonius, who now looked at these questions with the eyes of a churchman (having been elected bishop of Clermont‡ in the year 472), draws a repulsive picture. 'I fear', he says, 'that this Gothic king, though he is truly formidable by the resources which he wields, is plotting not so much against the walls of Roman cities as against the laws of Christian churches. So sour, they say, to his lips, so hateful to his heart, is the very mention of the Catholic name, that you can hardly tell whether to consider him primarily as king of the Visigothic nation or as leader of the Arian sect. Moreover, he is a strenuous warrior, in the vigour of his intellect, in the prime of life; the only mistake which he makes is to attribute to the divine blessing on his misguided zeal, those successes which are really due to his own skill and good fortune.'§ Sidonius then goes on to describe the melancholy condition of the Catholic

---

* The character given of him by the chronicler Theophanes.

† The crime of fratricide deeply stained the annals of these early Visigothic kings. Thorismund was killed (in 453) by his brothers Theodoric and Frederic, and now again (in 466) Theodoric was killed by his brother Euric.

‡ In the language of the times Civitas Arvernorum.

§ Apollinaris Sidonius, *Epistolae*, vii.6.

churches of Aquitaine. Bordeaux, Limoges, Périgueux, and many more, whose bishops had died, were forbidden to elect their successors; the churchway paths were stopped up with thorns and briers, the gates wrenched from their hinges, the roofs left open to the sky, and cattle fed on the grass-grown steps of the altar.

Some of these touches recall similar passages in the Vandal persecutions – though those upon the whole were far more bloody and severe – and it is therefore not surprising to find that there was at this time a considerable drawing together of the courts of Carthage and Toulouse. There had been time for the old cruel outrage upon the daughter of Theodoric I to be forgotten, and accordingly, when Gaiseric found East and West Rome uniting to invade his pirate kingdom, he appealed, and not altogether in vain, to the Visigothic monarch to join hands with him in defence of their common interests as Teutons and as Arians.*

The weight of Euric's invasion, which apparently took place in the spring of 474, fell upon the two provinces which we now know as Berry and Auvergne, all that was still left to the Romans of the country south of the Loire. Of Berry they appear to have made an easy conquest; Auvergne, the mountain-land, defended by the stout hearts of the still undegenerate nation of the Arverni, made a much more stubborn resistance. There, in the midst of his diocese, was Bishop Sidonius, animating the people by his rhetoric and, yet more, encouraging them to hope in the miraculous efficacy of 'the rogations', a kind of litany or special series of prayers for times of calamity, which he adopted from the church of Vienne. There, too, was his brother-in-law, Ecdicius, the son of the emperor Avitus, a brave and noble-hearted man, though Sidonius trumpets forth his praises with so much bombastic exaggeration that we are in danger of not allowing to him the credit which he really deserves.

'How did we all gaze upon you', he says, 'from the walls of Arverni [Clermont]. All ranks and ages, and both sexes, looked at you with won-der from our half-ruined walls, and saw you in the open plain, in the middle of the day, pierce with scarce eighteen horsemen through a troop of some thousand Goths. At the sound of your name, at the rumour of your presence, a kind of stupor fell upon that highly disciplined host, so that the generals themselves in their blind wonderment perceived not how many followed their standards, how few yours. They withdrew up the brow of a

* Jordanes (*De Rebus Geticis*, 47) vouches for this rapprochement between Gaiseric and Euric.

hill and left all the plain to you, though you had scarcely as many men to post in the plain as one seats guests at a banquet.

'You came back at leisure to the city. How we all poured forth to meet you, with greetings, with plaudits, with laughter, and with tears! The courts of your vast house were filled with your welcomers. They kissed the very dust of your feet, they handled your heavy curb-chain, clotted with blood and foam, they lifted the saddles, steeped in sweat, from the horses of your warriors, they unclasped the fastenings of your hollow helmet, they vied with one another in loosening the foldings of your greaves, they counted and measured with trembling fingers the terrible dints in your coat of mail.

'Need I say how, after this, you, with your own private resources, col-lected a public army and chastised the enemy for their incursions; how in several encounters you slaughtered whole squadrons of the barbarians, and when you came to number your own troops after each battle, found but two or three missing. So heavy was the blow struck at the enemy in these unex-pected conflicts, that they concealed the number of their slain by an artifice more ghastly than the very battlefield. All whom the approach of night prevented them from burying they beheaded, that the mutilated trunk might not by its flaxen locks reveal the nationality of the slain warrior. When day dawned they perceived that even this brutal outrage had not availed to hide their losses;* so then they set about their funeral rites in haste – haste which was as useless to conceal their trick as their trick had been to conceal the slaughter. The bodies were unwashed, unceremented; no mound of earth was heaped above them. They lay here and there about the field, carried to their respective heaps on the gory wagons, till you, pressing down afresh and unceasingly on your beaten foe, compelled them to give up the thought of burial, and to light their funeral pyres with the fragments of the wagons which had been their moving homes.'†

History and romance are no doubt blended in this singular extract, in what proportions it is now impossible to determine. So much, however, seems clear, that by the brave defence of the Arverni, with Ecdicius at their head, the tide of Visigothic invasion was for that season (474) rolled back from their country. But the walls of the city were half in ruins, and the har-vests, not only of Auvergne, but of a large part of Provence, had been swept away by the enemy. Under this imminence of famine, Patiens, the

* Because of course the Romans would infer that all the headless trunks were Gothic.
† Apollinaris Sidonius, *Epistolae*, iii.3.

bishop of Lyons (the builder of the basilica commemorated in the verses of Sidonius*) with wise and noble munificence, collected vast stores of grain in the northern district of Gaul, transported them down the rivers Saône and Loire, and across the mountains of Auvergne, presented them as a free gift to the famishing provincials, and thus, out of his own episcopal rev-enues (helped probably by the contributions of the wealthy city in which he dwelt), 'like another Triptolemus or another Joseph',† saved a nation from famine.

In the following year (475) there seems to have been a change in the Gothic strategy. As determined as ever to add Auvergne to his dominions, Euric saw that the fight for its possession could best be waged in Provence, or even if need were, in the valley of the Po. He again crossed the line which had become the frontier of the Empire, again occupied or laid waste the *provincia* at the mouth of the Rhône, and threatened apparently to cross the Alps, or to march by what we now call the Riviera, into Italy. For these aggressions the rapid changes in the person of the Roman emperor sug-gested the occasion, and seem in some mysterious way to have served as a justification.‡ Perhaps a pretence was set up of vindicating against Nepos the claims of the Burgundian protégé Glycerius, whom he had dethroned. In these circumstances the 'council of Liguria', an assembly of whose pre-cise nature and constitution we are ignorant, but which was probably composed of the chief civil and ecclesiastical officials of the province, again assembled, as they had assembled four years before when civil strife seemed to be impending between Anthemius and Ricimer, to devise means for averting the storm of war from their country.

Again, as before, all eyes were turned upon the saintly Epiphanius, bishop of Pavia, the ideal peacemaker of his age. He again undertook the office, relying on heavenly assistance. The journey was one of about six hun-dred (Roman) miles, by way of Turin, Briançon, Nîmes, and involved a climb over the steep pass of the Mont Genèvre. But the saint was determined to make it yet more arduous by his austerities. For the mules' sake they tarried long at the different posting-houses (*mansiones*), and all these long halts were occupied with vigorous psalmody or with industrious reading; and when engaged in the latter employment he always stood. Then at night he would choose the chilliest nook of the forest, whither the noonday sun never

---

* See p. 193.   † Apollinaris Sidonius, *Epistolae*, vi.12.

‡ That some such argument was alleged seems clear from the testimony of Ennodius, who distinctly connects Euric's invasion with the accession of Nepos.

penetrated, and there, instead of in the comfortable *mansio*, would he spread his couch, watering the ground with the tears which accompanied his nightlong prayers, 'and so making fertile in spiritual blessings the soil which could never bring forth fruits of its own'.

There is no need to transcribe from his admiring and prolix biographer the exhortation to meekness and charity which Epiphanius delivered to King Euric in his court at Toulouse. The Visigothic king's reply, delivered by the mouth of an interpreter, contains some characteristic expressions. 'Though the coat of mail never leaves my breast, though my hand is ever at the brazen hilt of my sword, and the iron guards my side, I have found a man who, for all my armour, can vanquish me with his words. They err who say that the Roman's tongue is not worth a good sword and shield, for they can turn back the words which we send against them, while their words pierce to our very vitals. I will do therefore, holy father, all that you desire, though more from esteem for the messenger than from respect for the power of him who sends him. Promise me, therefore, that Nepos will keep unbroken concord with me – since a promise from you is equivalent to an oath – and my warlike designs shall be laid aside.' After giving the required pledge, the bishop, refusing an earnest invitation to meet the king at a banquet ('which would have been', says his biographer, 'polluted by the presence of his priests'), started at once on his homeward journey, 'attended by so great a crowd that Toulouse seemed to be almost deserted of her inhabitants'.

When we read the terms of peace as they were finally arranged between Euric and the four bishops of Provence,* we doubt whether the eloquence of Epiphanius had really been so triumphant as his biographer describes it. For it is evident that Auvergne and Berry were ceded to the Goths, and the Romans seem practically to have retained of all their magnificent Gaulish possessions only the strip of territory between the Mediterranean and the

---

* Graecus of Marseilles, Leontius of Arles, Basilius of Aix and Faustus of Riez. The history of the negotiations between Nepos and Euric is obscure, and it has not seemed necessary to trouble the reader with all their details; but it seems probable that there were three embassies: (1) that of the quaestor Licinianus described by Sidonius (*Epistolae*, iii.7). It was apparently on this occasion that he brought Ecdicius his promotion to the patriciate, upon which Sidonius congratulates his wife Papianilla (sister to Ecdicius) in *Epistolae*, v.16 (translated pp. 203–4). This embassy was probably unsuccessful. (2) The embassy of Epiphanius of Pavia, successful in laying down the general basis of an agreement. (3) That of the four bishops mentioned above, who drew out the exact terms of the accommodation.

river Durance, which, still under its well-known name of Provence, per-
petuates the remembrance of the *providentia* [providence] of the Roman
republic.

Bitterly does Sidonius lament this desertion by Rome of her brave
Arvernian subjects. In the letter which he addressed to Bishop Graecus,
after the negotiation of the treaty, his usual tone of bland deference towards
a brother prelate is replaced by something like a snort of defiance and
indignation.

'Alas!' he says, 'for this unhappy corner of the land, whose lot, if fame
speak truly, is to be made yet worse by peace than ever it was by war. Our
slavery is to be the price paid for other people's freedom. Yes, the slavery of
us the Arverni who, if the story of the past is to be retold, once dared to
claim Trojan blood in our veins, and to call ourselves brothers of Latium.
If you look at more recent days, we are the men who by our own private
efforts have held in check the public enemy, who did not use our walls as a
defence against the Goth but made him tremble in his camp, who, when
our neighbours moved their army into the field, could show as many generals as we had soldiers* . . . Are these the wages that are due to those who
have endured hunger, fire, and pestilence, to the swords that are fat with
slaughter, to the warriors who are lean with fasting? It was in prospect of
this glorious peace of yours, of course, that we lived upon the herbs that
grew in the chinks of our walls, and that some died, unable to distinguish
the poisonous from the harmless. For all these daring experiments of our
devotion our reward, as I hear, is that we are to be thrown overboard by the
Empire. Oh! blush, I pray you, for this peace which is neither expedient
nor honourable. Through you the embassies come and go. The beginnings
and the endings of the negotiations, in the emperor's absence, are in your
hands. Pardon the roughness of these words of truth; the pang with which
they are uttered should take away their sting.

'You, in the provincial council, are not really deliberating for the benefit
of the commonwealth. You are each of you thinking how you can mend
your private fortunes, and it is by this policy that the first province of Rome
has become her last . . . The ancestors whom we used to talk of so proudly
will soon, at this rate, have no descendants. Break off then, break off by
whatever device you can think of, the treaty for this shameful peace. We, if
needs be, shall be delighted still to suffer siege, still to do battle on the wall,
still to famish in our homes . . . But if not, if while other regions are

* A doubtful advantage in an army.

content with slavery, Auvergne may not have the martyrdom for which she sighs, then I can only say, keep our seed still alive on the earth, be ready with your ransoms for us as slaves, open your gates to us as pilgrims. If our cities must be open to the Goth, you must in charity open yours to the guest. Condescend to remember me, my lord pope!'* If we compare this passionate outburst with the similar utterances of the inhabitants of Nisibis, a little more than a century before, when they were abandoned by Rome to the king of Persia,† we shall be forced to conclude that notwithstanding the frightful misery brought upon the world by the rapacity and incompetence of Roman governors, the Eternal City laid a spell, not of power only, but of love, upon the vast and various populations under her sway, such as some other races, ruling far more righteously than she ever did, have been unable to exercise.

Fourteen months after Julius Nepos ascended the throne, he was pushed down from it by a Roman officer named Orestes. This revolution is one of the most obscure passages in all the obscure history of this time. Jordanes tells us that Ecdicius (whom he calls Decius) was obliged 'to leave his country, and especially the city of Arverna,‡ to the enemy and betake himself to safer quarters. Which, when the emperor Nepos heard, he ordered Decius to leave the Gauls and come to him.'§ Possibly it may have been on the elevation of Ecdicius to the patriciate that the next change occurred. 'In his room Orestes was ordained master of the soldiery, which Orestes, having taken the command of the army, and marching forth against the enemy, arrived at Ravenna from Rome, and there remaining made Augustulus his son emperor. Which being ascertained Nepos fled into Dalmatia, and there, as a private man, lived devoid of royalty' (this is not quite accurate), 'where already Glycerius the former emperor exercised the bishopric of Salona. But Augustulus was ordained emperor by his father Orestes at Ravenna.'

Other chroniclers¶ supply us with the dates of two of these transactions. The flight of Nepos took place on the 28th of August, 475, and the proclamation of Augustulus as emperor on the 31st of October in the same year. But what is the meaning of the transactions recorded, why we should hear of this mysterious appearance and disappearance of Ecdicius in Italy,

* Apollinaris Sidonius, *Epistolae*, vii.7.   † See vol. i, p. 59.
‡ Arverna is the form of the name used by Jordanes.
§ Jordanes, *De Rebus Geticis*, 45.
¶ Anonymus Cuspiniani and the continuer of Prosper.

against what enemies was Orestes leading the army (not Euric, for peace had been only just concluded with him; possibly the Burgundians or the Ostrogoths), and what was the pretext or the motive for the sudden rebel-lion against the authority of Nepos? – these are questions which can be but conjecturally answered, and unless further documentary evidence should be discovered, never settled.

A German historian suggests that the barbarian auxiliaries in the army saw in the order to march 'against the enemy' a covert design to remove them from Italy, and therefore revolted.* This seems a not improbable con-jecture, but we must remember that nothing is said here expressly about 'barbarian auxiliaries', or about 'leading them beyond the frontiers of Italy'. As Orestes himself was not of barbarian origin, but would be called at that time a Roman, it is open to us to suggest that dislike of a second *Graeculus imperator*,† and indignation at the surrender of Auvergne to the Visigoths, may have had some share in the result. But the history can here be only guessed at, not related.

Of Orestes, the chief actor in the new revolution, we have, thanks to those invaluable fragments of Priscus, a little more certain knowledge. In the great diplomatic campaign of 448, between Byzantium and Hun-land, he figured in a somewhat inferior position among the envoys of Attila.‡ Himself of Roman origin, that is to say, being an Illyrian provincial, he had taken service under Attila, and considered himself the equal of his fel-low envoy, Edecon, and other nobles of his court. But Vigilas, who knew the social code of the barbarians well, judged differently, and pronounced that Orestes as 'a secretary, a mere squire of Attila, was greatly inferior to Edecon, a mighty man of war and a Hun by extraction'.§ However, in the twenty-seven years which had elapsed since he was sitting with the By-zantine ambassadors among the ruins of Sardica, Orestes (who was by marriage, if not by birth, connected with the official hierarchy of the Empire) had succeeded in somewhat improving his position, and he now, without any hint of what may have been his intervening fortune, emerges in the full splendour of master of the soldiery, and, after his successful insurrection, virtual lord of the Western Empire.

There can have been no reason in the nature of things why Orestes should not have placed himself on the vacant throne. Unlike Stilicho and Ricimer he was a full-blooded Roman provincial, at least as eligible for the

* Pallmann, *Geschichte der Völkerwanderung*, ii.287–9.   † [Greek emperor.]
‡ See p. 35.   § Priscus, excerpt. 11. See p. 39.

Imperial dignity as Trajan or Diocletian. It must therefore be taken as an indication how much the majesty of the title of emperor had suffered by twenty years of revolution that he bestowed that title on his son, reserving for himself the rank only of patrician, nominally inferior in dignity, but more associated in men's minds with the idea of power, perhaps also somewhat less likely to injure his popularity with the army. It is possible moreover that the remembrance of the almost menial office which he had held in the court of Attila, and the apparently higher position of his son's maternal ancestors, may have conduced to the same result.

The name, and the face, and the age of the last emperor of the West are all that is memorable in his history. Everyone knows the strange turn of fate (as we call it) which gave to the last puny emperor of Rome the same name that was borne by her first and mightiest king, the she-wolf's nursling. It is interesting to observe that the poor lad's fateful name came to him in the most natural manner possible from his maternal grandfather in his home beside the Danube.* What may have been the precise origin of his epithet Augustulus cannot be stated; whether given by his loyal soldiers as a term of endearment to the fair boy clothed in the purple, or by his barbarian con-querors as a term of contempt for the new kind of *imperator* whom the Romans had raised over them. The latter suggestion however seems the most probable. Augustulus was a mere lad, probably about fourteen years of age,† and possessed great personal beauty.‡ The duration of his nomi-nal reign was about ten months. Of course his father was the real ruler of the Empire.

In this capacity Orestes concluded a treaty with Gaiseric§ the terms of which are not disclosed to us, but it seems probable that one of the chief conditions imposed on the Roman emperor was the cession of Sicily. In the same year probably in which this event occurred (475), peace, a peace which lasted for two generations, was concluded between the Vandal king-dom and the Eastern Empire. The ambassador chosen by the worn and harassed emperor, Zeno, who had only just donned his painful diadem, was a senator named Severus, a man whose justice and moderation had won him the respect of all his fellow citizens, and whom, to give greater honour to his embassy, Zeno raised to the dignity of patrician. A hostile raid which Gaiseric made on the Epirote city of Nicopolis seemed at first

---

* [For more information on the genealogy of Augustulus see table vii, p. 400.]
† The word used by Procopius generally means a lad of about that age.
‡ Anonymus Valesii, 38.   § Paulus Diaconus, *Historia Romana*, xv.7.

sight to promise ill for the success of the negotiations, but Gaiseric in reply to the complaints of Severus explained that such an attack was only a way of emphatically stating that he was still at war with the Empire. Now that an ambassador had actually reached his court he was quite willing to discuss with him the conditions of peace. And in fact the pure and simple character of Severus, his frugal manner of living, and his absolute inaccessibility to the lavishly offered bribes of the Vandal, so impressed Gaiseric that he not only concluded, as has been said, a firm and durable peace with Constantinople but consented to liberate all the Roman captives who were in bondage to him or his sons, having heard from the lips of Severus that such a concession would be more gratifying to him than any present of money or jewels. The captives who had been allotted to the warriors of the Vandal host Gaiseric declared that he could not liberate without the consent of their new lords, but he would throw no obstacle in the way of their redemption. The generous-hearted Severus not only restored to freedom without price the captives whom Gaiseric presented to him, but sold by public auction the costly vessels and magnificent robes by which he had set forth the majesty of Byzantium, and with the proceeds purchased the liberty of as many as he could of the slaves of the soldiers. Even the bitter Arianism of the old king was softened by the conversation of the friendly ambassador, and a breathing-space, though as it proved only a short breathing-space, between the persecutions of Gaiseric and of his son, was secured by the good offices of Severus.*

The treaty with Gaiseric is almost the only public act that we hear of in the short reign of Augustulus.

Before witnessing the downfall of the boy-emperor, the last act in this long series of successful rebellions, let us follow the dethroned Nepos across the Adriatic to his Dalmatian capital Salona. No doubt he there possessed, *de facto*, the same petty sovereignty which his uncle Marcellinus had held before him. It seems probable also that he still claimed to be *de jure* emperor of the Western world, still wore the diadem, the purple mantle, the jewelled sandals. Strange turn of fortune, which thus brought two dethroned emperors of Rome (Nepos and Glycerius) to end their lives in the same Dalmatian city, one as its civil, the other as its religious ruler! In the modern town of Spalato, the temple which Diocletian erected to Jupiter has been converted, with as little change as the Pantheon at Rome, from a heathen fane into a Christian cathedral. If we may assume that this change

* Malchus, excerpt 5, and Victor Vitensis, i.17.

took place before the end of the fifth century, we have here a subject which might be worthy of an artist's embodiment – the classic edifice reared by the great persecutor, crowded with priests and worshippers on the day of some high 'function'; two successors of Diocletian within its walls; two heads which had worn the wreath of the *imperator* bowing in prayer to the Nazarene; two men who had once been engaged in what was like to have been the death-grapple for a throne, imparting and receiving 'the kiss of peace' at the celebration of the supper of the Lord.

Notwithstanding a report of a different kind which once obtained general credence, it is probable that the two rivals ended their days in mutual charity. Nepos outlived the Western Empire four years, and perished by the hands of assassins on the 15th of May, 480. Two of his counts, Viator and Ovida, killed him 'at his villa' (probably a part of Diocletian's palace) 'not far from Salona'.* As we find Odiva (or Ovida) next year in Dalmatia, waging war with, and conquered by the ruler of Italy, it is reasonable to suppose that he murdered Nepos in order to succeed to his power. There is, however, an obscure sentence in the notebook of Photius the patriarch, which seems to throw the burden of the crime upon Glycerius. He describes his reading of the *Byzantine History* of the sophist Malchus, who lived at the time of the fall of the Western Empire. 'Malchus finishes the last book', says Photius, 'with the death of Nepos, who, driving Glycerius from the kingdom, assumed to himself the Roman power, and having cut his hair like a cleric's, made him high priest instead of emperor, by whom also, being conspired against, he was slain.'† The accusation seems distinct enough: but (1) Malchus may have erred. (2) The erudite patriarch who records in this notebook (the *Bibliotheca* [*Library*]) his remembrances of 280 books – all read during his embassy to Assyria – may have misunderstood or forgotten his author's meaning. (3) The amanuensis, in his intensely concise telegrammatic style, may have given a wrong idea of what his master dictated to him. Any one of these suppositions seems more likely than that the other chroniclers should have omitted to notice so flagrant an instance of ingratitude as the murder of Nepos by the rival whose life he had spared; that a bishop, in that age of the church, should have perpetrated so great a crime without calling forth a shout of execration from every chronicler of the period; and that Theophanes (a late writer, but not quite so late as Photius) having the proof of this terrible accusation before him, should still call Glycerius 'a not disreputable person'.

* Marcellinus.   † *Library*, 78.

CHAPTER XII

Odovacar, the Soldier of Fortune

'WHILE EPIPHANIUS, WITH THIS SEVERE SELF-discipline, was approving himself a workman of Jesus Christ that needed not to be ashamed, the old enemy of our race, that restless schemer of evil, was busy adding affliction to affliction, and devising new sufferings wherewith to torment the soul of the saint. With this view he stirred up the army against the patrician Orestes, and sowed the seeds of discord and suspicion between him and them. He excited the minds of abandoned men with the wild hope of revolution; he breathed the desire for sovereign power into the soul of Odovacer. And then, in order that the calamity might fall upon the city of Ticinum [Pavia], he allured Orestes thither to take shelter under its strong fortifications.'

So writes the episcopal biographer of the bishop of Pavia. We may not share his intimate acquaintance with the counsels of the prince of darkness, but we are bound to express our gratitude for the information which he, all but a contemporary, has given us in this paragraph concerning the immediate cause of the final catastrophe of the Western Empire. Fortified by this authority, we can unhesitatingly assert that Rome fell at last, not by an invasion of the Herulians or any other transalpine nation, but by a mutiny of the troops who were serving under her own eagles, and were paid out of her own military chest. We are thus carried back to the remembrance of the time, a century before that which we have now reached, when the Goths on a large scale entered the Roman armies as *foederati*,* and at the risk of a little repetition we may again consider the same subject.

Few things in the upward career of Rome are more wonderful than the skill with which she made her last-vanquished enemies the instruments of achieving yet another conquest. By the help of the Latins she subdues the Samnites; with Italian soldiers she conquers Spain; the dwellers around the Mediterranean shore carry her standards through Gaul; the Romanised

* See vol. i, pp. 169–70.

Gaul beats off the German. In our own country, on the desolate moorlands between the Solway and the Tyne, were encamped Batavians from Holland, Asturians from Spain, Tungrians from the Rhine, and many another representative of far-distant lands, from which, even in these days of quickened intercourse between nations, not one in a century now sets foot beside 'the barrier of the lower isthmus'. From the point of view of the subjugated and tamed provincial, this constant interchange of military service throughout that enormous Empire had much to recommend it, as bringing many widely scattered nationalities face to face with one another, as breaking down the barriers of race and creed, and as enabling one thought to vibrate unchecked from the Euphrates to the Atlantic. But viewed from the standpoint of a nationality not yet subdued, and still fighting hard for liberty, the use which Rome made of the arms of her conquered foes may well have seemed the device of some malign deity, bent on darkening the whole heaven and on destroying the happiness of the human race. Especially must this thought have forced itself on the mind of the barbarian patriot when he heard that the people of Rome itself, the men who pre-eminently styled themselves Quirites, and who shouted for wars and triumphs, no longer served in the legions themselves, but passed their useless lives between the bath and the amphitheatre, leaving all the toil of the ceaseless campaigns with which Rome vexed the universe, to men who knew the seven hills of Rome but as some cloud-built city in a dream.

Amply would such a barbarian patriot – an Arminius, a Caractacus, or a Decebalus – have been avenged, could he have foreseen the part which these same auxiliaries were to play in completing the ruin of Rome. We have seen the young Alaric learning his first lessons in the invasion of Italy as an irregular in the army of Theodosius. We have seen the Hunnish forerunners of the host of Attila introduced as auxiliaries into the heart of Gaul by Aetius – the same Aetius who was afterwards to behold them in their myriads arrayed against him on the Catalaunian plains. We are now to see the death-blow dealt at the doting Empire by men of Teutonic speech and origin, who had taken the *sacramentum*, the military oath of allegiance, and had been enlisted as defenders of Rome.

The meagre annals of the fifth century do not enable us to state what were the relative proportions of native Italians and of barbarians in the armies of Valentinian III and his successors. We may conjecture however that the former had become a very slight ingredient in the mass, and that the Germans no longer served merely as auxiliaries in the wings of the army,

but were now the backbone of the legion itself. We have a few slight indications of the progress of this change. The reader may remember that one
of the vexations which made the short-lived emperor Maximus sigh for the
fate of the happier Damocles was 'the turbulence of the *foederati*'.* When
war broke out between Anthemius and Ricimer, the men in authority and
the mob of Rome clave to the former, but 'the multitude of fellow barbarians'† (evidently soldiers) to the latter. And now, in the passage quoted at
the beginning of this chapter, we find 'the army' spoken of as rising collec-
tively against Orestes, though, as we shall soon see, the ground of quarrel
was that they as barbarians made a demand which he as a Roman could not
grant. As before said, therefore, it may be conjectured, if it cannot be
absolutely proved, that in the year 476 a very small number of true Roman
citizens was serving in the dwindled armies of the Western Empire.

The chief recruiting ground for auxiliaries during the quarter of a century after the death of Attila, seems to have been the lands on the further side
of the middle Danube, including parts of Bohemia, Moravia, the arch-
duchy of Austria, and the kingdom of Hungary. Here dwelt (in positions
which are approximately indicated on the accompanying map [p. 300])
four nations with the uncouth and harsh-sounding names of the Rugii, the
Scyri, the Turcilingi, and the Heruli.‡ The antecedent history of these
tribes, even during the second and third centuries of the Christian era, is not
clearly ascertained. According to some ethnologists the island of Rügen in
the Baltic still preserves the name of the first. A more certain memorial of
the second tribe is furnished by an inscription found at Olbia (in the south
of Russia, near Odessa), which shows that as early as the second century
before the Christian era, the inroads of the Scyri were formidable to the Hellenic settlers round the shores of the Black sea. Though a comparatively
unimportant tribe, they are thus brought into contact with the world of classical antiquity considerably earlier than the Goths themselves. Of the Turcilingi we really know nothing. The Heruli were the most widely extended
of the four nations. In the latter part of the third century, we are told, they
sailed with 500 ships forth from the sea of Azov to the shore of Pontus, and
thence through Bosporus and the Dardanelles to the coasts of Attica, when

* See p. 122.

† Literally 'barbarians who belonged to him', i.e. his barbarian followers; or 'who
belonged to him by race', i.e. those who were barbarians like himself (Joannes Antiochenus, fragment 209).

‡ The position assigned to the Turcilingi on the map is purely conjectural.

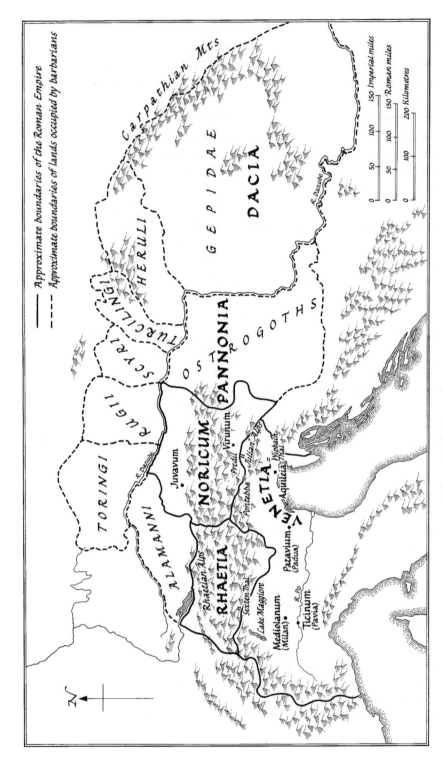

The middle Danube, AD 454–76

Athens itself suffered conflagration at their hands.* At the time of the fall of the Western Empire they appear to have been settled on the southern slopes of the Carpathian mountains, the most easterly in position, and the most powerful of the four tribes.

Whatever may have been the previous fortunes of these races, they were probably for a time subject to the loosely jointed dominion of the Huns; and in fact, we met with the names of some of them among the invaders of Gaul under the banner of Attila. After his death they may very likely have taken part in the great war of independence which culminated in the battle of Nedao; at any rate, they shared in its reward, the breaking of the Hun-nish yoke from off their necks. The Gepidae, whose king Ardaric had been the leader in the work of liberation, occupied the wide expanse of Dacia; the Ostrogoths took Pannonia; to the north and north-west of these two great nations stretched the domains which, as has been already said, were occupied by the four tribes with whose fortunes we are now concerned. On their southern frontier their strong Teutonic neighbours interposed an invincible obstacle to the wandering and predatory impulses which were partly instinctive, partly the result of contact with and subjection to the Huns. But on the south-western horizon no such barrier presented itself. There, at a distance of perhaps a week's march, lay Venetian Italy; the fortress of Aquileia which had once been its defence, was still the ruined heap to which Attila had reduced it; and thither stretched the still undes-troyed Roman roads over the passes of the Wipbach Thal, the Predil, Pontebba, and the Sexten Thal. To reach this land of promise the Rugian or Herulian mercenary had but to cross the province of Noricum (Styria, Salzburg, Carinthia); and that unhappy province, not wholly cast off by the Empire nor regularly appropriated by the barbarians, was in the same relation to them which unpartitioned Poland occupied towards Russia in the days of the empress Catherine, 'My doormat upon which I tread when-ever I wish to visit Europe.'

We may therefore imagine, during all the sixteen years of Ricimer's ascendancy, bands of the strongest and most restless-spirited of the warriors of the four tribes, streaming south-westwards through Noricum, under the shadow of the high rock of Juvavum† or over the fair plain of Virunum,‡ and so on out of the last defiles of the Julian Alps into the broad valley of the Po, their final goal being Ravenna, Rome, or Milan; any place where

* Georgius Syncellus (fl. about 800), i.717 (Bonn edn).   † Salzburg.
‡ Now the Zoll Feld near Klagenfurt.

the great patrician had set up his standard, and where the tribune or the centurion – himself perhaps a barbarian kinsman – would be in readiness to receive the young Teuton's *sacramentum*. It seems pretty clear that what ever differences of costume or of arms may have separated these four tribes from one another, they all bore a general resemblance to the great Gothic nation, and spoke the Gothic language, for which reason some of the Byzantine historians call their leader a Goth, and confuse the heterogeneous kingdom which they established, with the purely and truly Gothic monar chy which succeeded it.

It was not then an invasion in the strict sense of the word, this slow infil tration of the Heruli and their neighbours into the Italian peninsula. They came ostensibly to succour and to serve Rome. But so did the Swedes and the French come to help Germany in the two last decades of the Thirty Years War; and we may well imagine that, unwelcome as the troopers of Turenne and Wrangel were in Germany in the year 1648, even more unwelcome to the Italian citizen (when he could speak his mind freely without fear of being overheard by the myrmidons of Ricimer) was the continuous advent of these many nationed deliverers from beyond the Danube. It was not an invasion in form, but in substance perhaps it was not greatly different.

We return for an instant to the half ruined province of Noricum, through which these swarms of Rugian and other adventurers were yearly pouring. The long continued suffering of the inhabitants during thirty years of anarchy (from about 453 to 482) was somewhat soothed by the beneficent activity of St Severinus, a holy man who suddenly appeared amongst them, none knew from whence, and who, by his gentle wisdom and by the ascendancy which the simple earnestness of his nature obtained for him over the minds of the barbarians, was often able to interpose for the help of the plundered provincials. In his little cell on the banks of the Danube, round which, in the course of time, other hermits, his disciples and imitators, built their lowly dwellings, he practised all the regular aus terities of a monk of the fifth century, fasting till he had reached the utmost limits of emaciation, and walking barefoot when even the Danube was a mass of ice. Here, in his lonely meditations, the saint was believed to be sometimes filled with

> The spirit of the fervent days of old
> When words were things that came to pass, and thought

Flashed o'er the future, bidding men behold
Their children's children's doom already brought
Forth from the abyss of things that were to be*

and amid the visible wreck and ruin of the kingdoms of the world, Sever-inus, it was thought, could foretell something of the form and fashion of those which were to succeed them.

A band of young soldiers of fortune from across the Danube, on their way to Italy, came one day to the cell of this holy man to receive his blessing. They were Christians, though of the Arian type, and the candidates for enlistment in the Imperial army evidently did not fear the saint's condem-nation of their enterprise. Among them was a young man, with thick yellow moustache,† in sordid garb, but of commanding height, and, it may be, with something in his mien which marked him out as a born leader of men. As soon as this young man stepped inside the cell (the lowly roof of which obliged him to bow his head in the presence of the saint), Severinus, it is said, perceived by an inward intimation that the youth was destined to achieve high renown. The blessing was given and the young Teuton said 'Farewell.' 'Fare forward,'‡ answered the saint, 'fare forward into Italy; thou who art now covered with a mean raiment of skins, but who shalt soon bestow on many men the costliest gifts.'

The name of the tall recruit who received and fulfilled this benediction was Odovacar, commonly called Odoacer, the son of Edecon. The name has a Teutonic ring about it, and is thought by the great German philolo-gist Grimm to signify 'rich in watchfulness', or 'a good watcher'.§ He suggests that it may have been a favourite name for a watchdog, and thence transferred to a man-child in whom vigilance in war was looked for by his barbarian parents. It seems better to retain, as the German historians gener-ally do, the 'Odovacar' of the contemporary authorities in all its primeval ruggedness, instead of softening it down with later historians (chiefly the Byzantine annalists) into the smooth and slippery 'Odoacer'.

The origin and ancestry of the young soldier, who stalked into the cave of Severinus, are among the unsolved riddles of history. He is called by the annalists and by Jordanes a Goth, a Rugian, and a Scyrian, and his name is

* Byron, 'The Vision of Dante'.
† The shape of the moustache, infrequent on purely Roman faces, is portrayed on Odo-vacar's coins. The colour is of course the conventional *flavus* [golden yellow] of the Goths.
‡ *Vade* for *vale*.   § *Audags*, Gothic for 'rich' or 'blessed'; *vakir*, Gothic for 'watcher'.

also sometimes coupled both with the Turcilingi* and the Heruli,† as if he were their especial leader. The conclusion which it seems best to draw from all these conflicting testimonies is that he was a Teuton (and that fact alone, according to Byzantine usage, would entitle him to be called a Goth); that he was not of royal descent (and here the story of the mean appearance which he presented in the cave of Severinus comes in as an additional confirmation), and that, for this reason, after he had by an unexpected stroke of fortune attained to one of the foremost positions in the world, each of the four tribes which formed his motley host claimed him as of its own especial kindred.

This view does not absolutely preclude the commonly received opinion that Odovacar was the son of the same Edecon who was associated with Orestes in the embassy to Constantinople, and who listened, or seemed to listen, with too favourable an ear to the scheme for the assassination of Attila. It is true that in the wrangle about precedence between the two ambassadors, the interpreter Vigilas said that the secretary Orestes was 'not to be compared in social position with Edecon, a mighty man of war and a Hun by birth'. But these last words need not, perhaps, be interpreted with ethnological precision. Priscus himself speaks of the discontented Roman who had turned Hun, and in the same way probably any of the Teutonic warriors – Gepidae, Ostrogoths, Rugians, Herulians – whose fathers or grandfathers had accepted the rule of that 'anarch old', the Hunnish king and generalissimo, would, by comparison with a Roman provincial, be spoken of as 'a Hun by birth'. And if this be the true account of Odovacar's parentage, the breakingup of the Hunnish power after Attila's death might easily cause such a change in the position of the courtier, Edecon, as to account for the humble garb in which his son presented himself before the saint of Noricum. It must be confessed that there is a touch of dramatic completeness in the working out of the squabble for precedence between Edecon and Orestes in the persons of their sons, the first barbarian king and the last Roman emperor in Italy, which, until the theory can be actually proved to be untrue, will always commend it to the artistic instincts of the historian.‡

* Jordanes, *De Rebus Geticis*, 46.
† Prosper's continuer calls him *rex Erulorum* [king of the Heruli].
‡ The point is that no one author mentions the Edecon of the embassy and the Edecon, father of Odovacar, and says or implies that they are the same person. Priscus gives us the first, Anonymus Valesii the second, and they may be speaking of two different persons.

Top, a bronze coin of Libius Severus: *left*, the head of this inconspicuous emperor; *right*, the monogram of the patrician Ricimer. *Centre*, a gold *solidus* of Anthemius: *left*, the emperor; *right*, Anthemius and Leo I. *Bottom left*, Romulus Augustulus, the last Roman emperor of the West. *Bottom right*, Odovacar

The rival capitals of the Empire personified: *left*, Rome; *right*, Constantinople

Odovacar was born in the year 433,* but we are not able to fix the pre-cise date of his first appearance in Italy and entrance into the Imperial service. It was probably, however, between 460 and 470, since by the year 472 he had risen so high that his adhesion to the party of Ricimer against Anthemius is considered worthy of special mention by the historian Joannes Antiochenus.† For four years from that time we hear no more of him, but his name evidently became a word of power with his countrymen in the Imperial army.

Soon – we know not precisely how soon – after Orestes had placed the handsome boy, his son Romulus, upon the throne of the exiled Nepos, his own troubles began with the army, whose discontent he had so skilfully fomented. The *foederati* presented themselves before the patrician at Ravenna, with a startling demand. 'Assign to us', said they, 'one-third of the land of Italy for our inheritance.' The proportion claimed was, no doubt, suggested by the Imperial system of billeting, according to which the citizen upon whom a soldier was quartered was bound to divide his house into three compartments, of which he kept one himself, his unbid-den guest was then entitled to select another, and the third portion as well as the first remained in the occupation of the owner. It may be said also that the four tribes were more reasonable in their demands than some of their Teutonic kinsfolk, since the Visigoths had claimed two-thirds of the lands of Gaul; the Vandals had not limited themselves even to that portion, and even the Burgundians, although the mildest and most civilised of the invaders of the Empire, had taken half of the moorland, orchards, and forests, and two-thirds of the arable land.‡

But whatever arguments may be urged to give a certain plausibility to the demand of the *foederati*, it was none the less a demand which no Roman statesman with a shadow of self-respect could possibly grant. Analogies drawn from the conduct of the Visigoths in Gaul and the Vandals in

* This we know from Joannes Antiochenus (fragment 214), who tells us that he was sixty at the time of his death in 493.   † Fragment 209.

‡ This important fact, of the barbarian soldiers' demand for a division of the lands of Italy, is made known to us by Procopius (*De Bello Gothico*, i.1): 'In proportion as the bar-barians increased in consideration, did the credit of the Roman soldiers decline; and under the specious name of alliance the state fell under the tyrannical sway of the in-truders. Thus many acts of unrestrained violence were perpetrated by the latter on their unresisting entertainers, and at length they demanded a settlement upon the soil of Italy. Of this they ordered Orestes to give them one-third, and when he asserted that he would do nothing of the kind, they straightway slew him.'

Africa, only proved what every emperor since Honorius had tried to turn away his eyes from seeing, that the so-called Roman army was in fact a collection of aliens and enemies to Rome, trained, it might be, with some of the old legionary discipline, and armed from the Italian arsenals, but only so much the more dangerous to the country which it professed to defend.

Orestes, who ended his career with more dignity than he had displayed in any previous portion of it, utterly refused to despoil the subjects of his son in order to enrich the mercenaries. Possibly he placed some dependence on old habits of military obedience in the army and on the mutual jealousies of the foremost officers, the result of which might be that the mutineers would remain without a head. But in this calculation he was mistaken. Odovacar came forward and offered, if he were made leader, to obtain for the soldiers the land for which they hungered. The bargain was at once struck. On the 23rd of August, 476, Odovacar was raised upon the shield, as Alaric had been raised eighty-one years before, and from that day the allegiance to Augustulus of the barbarians, the backbone of the Roman army, was at an end.

Events marched rapidly. In twelve days the whole campaign — if campaign it could be called — was over. Orestes took refuge within the strongly fortified city of Pavia (or, as it was then called, Ticinum), the city of which the saintly Epiphanius was bishop. The defence must have been an extremely short one, but the biographer of Epiphanius (our sole authority here) gives us no details concerning it. Everything, however, seems to indicate that the army, when the barbarian adherents of Odovacar were subtracted from it, was a miserably feeble remnant, utterly unable to cope with the revolters. The barbarians burst into the city, plundering, ravishing, burning. Both churches and many houses of Pavia were consumed in the conflagration. The sister of Epiphanius, a nun, whose reputation for holiness was almost equal to his own, was dragged off by the soldiers into captivity. The chiefs of many noble families shared the same fate. At first there seems to have been some disposition to treat Epiphanius himself with harshness, on account of the insufficiency of the sum which he offered for his ransom. The soldiery could not understand that a bishop of Ticinum could be so poor as his continual almsgiving had made him. 'Oh, wickedness! that crude barbarity sought the treasures upon earth which he had sent forward to the recesses of heaven.' Soon, however, the transparent holiness of his character exerted its wonted influence even upon these infuriated plunderers. 'He rescued his venerable sister before the fatal light of that day glided into evening'; and he also procured by his earnest intercessions the liberation of many of the citizens, exerting himself especially to lessen the horrors of that terrible time for the women who were about to become mothers.

An interval of just two generations had elapsed since Pavia saw a somewhat similar scene of mutinous riot, robbery, and murder. That was in the year 408, when the intrigues of the party of Olympius against Stilicho burst forth into a flame. Then the cry was 'Down with the barbarians! Down with the Vandal, Stilicho! Slay the *foederati*!' And so the best bulwark of the Empire was sacrificed to the unworthy jealousy of the Roman party who were utterly unable to replace him by any tolerable substitute. In a certain sense it might be said that the evil deed of 408 brought about the punishment of 476, and that Odovacar avenged the blood of Stilicho.

For part of two days, apparently, the work of devastation went on in Pavia, and all the time the perpetual enquiry of the enraged soldiery was, 'Where is Orestes?' At length news was brought that the patrician, who had escaped from the city, had been discovered at Placentia, and with that the tumult subsided, and something like peace was restored to the plundered city.

It was upon the 28th August, 476, only five days after the elevation of Odovacar, that Orestes was taken at Placentia, and being taken was at once beheaded with a sword. His brother Paulus for a few days longer defended the lost cause at Ravenna, but apparently had too few men under his command to hold even that almost impregnable fortress. On the 4th of September, Paulus, who was perhaps trying to make his escape by sea, was slain by order of Odovacar, 'at the Pineta outside Classis by Ravenna'.* Within the walls of that city Odovacar found his helpless boy-rival Augustulus. Pitying his tender years, and touched with admiration of the beautiful face of the purple-clad suppliant, the successful Teuton, who was now strong enough to be merciful, spared the 'little Augustus', and assigned to him a palace and a revenue for the remainder of his life. The splendid villa which, at a lavish cost, Lucius Lucullus, the conqueror of Mithridates, had erected for himself near the city of Naples, was allotted as the residence of Romulus, with the members of his family whom the war had spared; and an annual pension of six thousand *solidi* (equal to £3,600 sterling, and perhaps corresponding to about twice that amount in our own day) was granted for his maintenance. How long this pension was drawn,

* Anonymus Valesii, 37.

how many years the son of Orestes lived among the woods and fish-ponds of the Lucullanum, whether he saw the downfall of his conqueror, or even, as he may very possibly have done, survived that conqueror's conqueror, Theodoric,* on all these points history is silent,† and her silence is an eloquent testimony to the utter insignificance of the deposed emperor.

The details, few and imperfect as they are, which we possess respecting the seventeen years' reign of Odovacar in Italy will be best given in connection with the history of that Ostrogothic invasion which brought it to a premature and bloody close. But a few words remain to be said as to transactions which happened at Carthage and Constantinople at the time or soon after the time when these events were occurring in Italy.

Early in the year 477, only half a year after the dethronement of Augustulus, died the king of the Vandals, Gaiseric. For more than fifty years had he been warring against Rome, and as if the energy of his hate had sustained him under the infirmities of age, now that the Western Empire was dead he died also. It was soon seen how largely the might of the Vandal name had been due to his destructive genius and tenacity of purpose. The strength of the kingdom rapidly declined under his son and grandson, and little more than half a century after his death it fell an easy prey to the arms of the emperor Justinian. Gaiseric had destroyed the fortifications of all the cities in his dominions, in order to prevent their giving harbourage to rebellious Africans or invading Byzantines; 'a measure', says Procopius, 'which was greatly praised at the time, and which seemed in the safest way possible to have promoted the tranquillity of the Vandals. Afterwards, however, when the absence of walled towns so greatly facilitated the invasion of Belisarius, Gaiseric was the subject of much ridicule, and his vaunted prudence was accounted foolishness. For men are perpetually changing their minds as to the wisdom of any given course, according to the light which fortune throws upon it.' These words of Procopius would have been fittingly spoken of some of the fluctuations of European opinion in our own century, veering wildly round from the extravagance of glorification to the extravagance of contempt.

The years which witnessed the elevation and the fall of Augustulus in the West saw also the climax of the long struggle between Zeno and Basiliscus in the East. Aided by the stratagems of the ever-intriguing empress Verina, his sister, Basiliscus succeeded (475) in dethroning his rival

* Odovacar was slain in 493 by Theodoric, who died in 526.
† But for one doubtful allusion in the letters of Cassiodorus (*Variae*, iii.35).

who fled to his native Isauria, among the mountains of Asia Minor. Two years after, by the treachery of the general Harmatius, who was sent to destroy him, Zeno succeeded in turning the tables on his antagonist, and found himself again reigning, as undisputed Augustus, in the palace by the Bosporus. The promise which he had given to save the life of the deposed Basiliscus was fulfilled by sending him, his wife, and children, in the depth of winter, to banishment in Cappadocia, where, deprived of every comfort and almost of necessary sustenance, they soon perished miserably of cold and hunger.

Soon after the return of Zeno to his palace two embassies waited upon him to express their congratulations on his restoration to the throne. First of all appeared the deputies of the Roman senate, sent by the command of Augustulus, which evidently was in truth the command of Odovacar, to say 'that they did not need a separate royalty, but that Zeno himself as sole emperor would suffice for both ends of the earth. That Odovacar, however, a prudent statesman and brave warrior, had been chosen by them to defend their interests, and they therefore requested Zeno to bestow on him the dignity of patrician, and entrust to his care the diocese of Italy.' In confirmation of their message and as a visible proof that the sovereignty was to be henceforth lodged at Constantinople, these Western deputies brought with them the ensigns of Imperial dignity.*

A few days after arrived from Salona the ambassadors of the titular emperor Nepos (these events happened two years before his assassination), and they, while also congratulating Zeno on his restoration, besought him to sympathise with their master, like him expelled from his lawful sovereignty, and to grant him supplies of men and money to enable him to reconquer the Empire of the West.

It would seem that each embassy touched a responsive chord in the soul of the Eastern potentate. The thought that the world needed no other emperor but him gratified his vanity, but the fugitive's appeal to his brother fugitive excited his sympathy. He therefore, in true diplomatic style, gave an answer which was no answer, lecturing the weak, flattering the strong, and leaving the whole question in the same uncertainty in which he found it.

To the messengers from the senate he replied, 'You have received two emperors from the East, Anthemius and Nepos, one of whom you have killed and the other you have driven into banishment. What your duty

* Anonymus Valesii, 64.

prescribes you know very well. While Nepos lives there cannot be two opinions about the matter; you ought to welcome his return.'

The precise nature of the reply to Nepos is not stated, but a message was sent to Odovacar, praising him for his judicious subservience to the wish of the Roman emperor, exhorting him to seek the much-desired title of patrician from Nepos, and to work for the return of that sovereign, but expressing, at the same time, the willingness of Zeno to grant him the title if Nepos should persist in withholding it. And, after giving all this admirable advice, he sent by the ambassadors a private letter with the super-scription, 'To the patrician Odovacar'. An extraordinary mystification truly, and a piece either of great vacillation or of great duplicity, but which is perhaps susceptible of explanation when we remember that Ariadne the wife, and Verina the mother-in-law of Zeno, were related to the wife of Nepos and zealous on his behalf. The admirable legitimist sentiments, and the exhortations to everybody to co-operate for the return of the Dalmatian, were probably uttered aloud in presence of those Imperial ladies. The private note with the all-important superscription, which was meant to mitigate the hostility of the terrible barbarian, was no doubt delivered to his ambassadors at some secret interview in the final moments before their departure.*

It would be a mistake to see in this curious scene at the court of Byzantium only a solemn farce enacted by Odovacar and Zeno, to amuse the people of Italy, and soothe them with the thought that they still remained under Roman dominion. The minds of men were really unable to grasp the fact that so vast and perdurable a structure as the Roman Empire could utterly perish. If it seemed to have suffered ruin in the West it still lived in the East, and might, as in fact it did under Justinian, one day send forth its armies from the Bosporus to reclaim the provinces which the city by the Tiber had lost. This belief in the practical indestructibility of the Empire, and the consequences which flowed from it, three centuries after the deposition of Augustulus, in the elevation of Charles the Great, have been re-established in their proper place, one might almost say, have been rediscovered, by the historical students of our own times, and the whole history of the Middle Ages has been made marvellously clearer by this one central fact.

But we must not allow ourselves to consider Odovacar, even after this

* We owe our information concerning this curious diplomatic encounter to Malchus, excerpt 14.

Byzantine embassy, as the mere lieutenant of Zeno, ruling with an authority delegated from Byzantium. It was well pointed out by Guizot* that in
medieval Europe we scarcely ever find one theory of life or of government
worked out to its logical end, and allowed to dominate uncontrolled, like
the eighteenth-century theories of the rights of man, or the nineteenth-
century theories of the rights of nationalities. In the Middle Ages, upon
which, after the year 476, we may consider ourselves to be entering, fragments of political theories, which are opposed to one another, and which
should be mutually destructive, subsist side by side, neither subduing nor
subdued, and often in apparent unconsciousness of their irreconcilable discord. So it was with the position of Odovacar, so, in part at least, with his
far greater successor, Theodoric. Among the barbarians, the warrior who
had conquered Orestes and deposed his son would be known as *thiudans*,
'the king', simply. If any further definition were asked for he would perhaps be called the king of the Rugians, or the king of the Herulians, the
king of the Turcilingi, or the king of the Scyri, according to the nationality
which happened to be most largely represented in the camp of the mercenaries when the discussion was going forward. But it is more likely that all
would contentedly acquiesce in an appellation which would be understood
by all, though it might not be consistent with strict ethnological accuracy,
thiudans Gut-thiudos, 'the king of the Gothic people'.† It is not certain that
the title 'king of Italy' was ever assumed by him. On the other hand,
among the Latin-speaking inhabitants of Italy, the vast majority of his new
subjects, Odovacar probably preferred to be known as 'the patrician', and
it would be in this capacity that he would control the organisation and
wield the powers of the still undestroyed bureaucracy of Imperial Rome.

Looking back, as we now do, over an interval of fourteen centuries at
Odovacar's position in history, we find it impossible to assign him a place
exclusively in the old order of things, or exclusively in the new; to say
whether he was in truth the successor of Aetius and Ricimer, or the forerunner of the kings of Italy, Pepin, Boso, and Victor Emmanuel. And if
this be our doubt now, we may be sure that at least an equal doubt existed in
the minds of his contemporaries, not lessened by the fact that there was
always, for the space of at least one generation, a chance that the old order of
things might after all be restored, and that the rule of the Teuton king

* Lectures ii and iii in the *History of Civilisation in Europe*.
† Of the annalists, Bishop Marius and Marcellinus call Odovacar *rex Gothorum* [king of
the Goths]. The reader will remember that both are nearly contemporary authorities.

might turn out to have been only an interregnum between two emperors, such as had occurred more than once under the ascendancy of Ricimer. At the time of the embassy to Zeno there were still in the world three men who had worn the Imperial purple, and coined money as emperors of Rome. We have reason to believe that one at least of these deposed emperors lived through the whole reign of Odovacar, perhaps to a much later period. Let us transfer now to the subjects of the new Teutonic king some of the same feelings of unsettlement and of half-acquiescence in change, with which a large part of the English nation regarded the Protestant succession during the reigns of Anne and the first George, or the feelings with which we ourselves have witnessed the establishment of a new French republic with three hostile dynasties sitting as angry watchers by its cradle; and we shall a little understand the mental attitude, partly of perplexity, partly of listless unconcern, which contemporary statesmen assumed towards an event which seems to us so momentous as the fall of the Western Empire.

For, in truth, the facts of the final struggle had little in them to attract the attention of bystanders. The sack of Rome by Alaric in 410 sent a shudder through the whole civilised world, and the echo of her dirge was heard even from the caves of Bethlehem. The nations held their breath with affright when in 452 Attila wreaked his terrible revenge upon Aquileia. In comparison with these events, what was the short flurry of the citizens of Pavia, or the death of Paulus in the pine-wood by Ravenna? Indisputably we ourselves have witnessed catastrophes of far greater dramatic complete-ness than this, far better calculated, according to the old definition of tragedy, 'to purify the emotions by means of pity and terror'. It is not a storm, or an earthquake, or a fire, this end of the Roman rule over Italy: it is more like the gentle fluttering down to earth of the last leaf from a withered tree.

And yet the event of 476 was, in its indirect consequences, a revolution, which affected most powerfully the life of every inhabitant of medieval and even of modern Europe. For by it the political centre of gravity was changed from the Palatine to the Lateran, and the bishop of Rome, now beyond comparison the most important personage of Roman descent left in Italy, was irresistibly invited to ascend the throne, and to wrap himself in the purple, of the vanished Augustus.

CHAPTER XIII

Causes of the Fall of the
Western Empire

WE HAVE NOW FOLLOWED THE FORTUNES OF
Italy from the days when it was the stronghold of an apparently
resistless Empire to the time when there was no longer an *imperator* in Italy,
and when the highest representative of law and government was the leader
of the Herulian mercenaries, Odovacar.

Why did the Roman Empire fall? An adequate answer to that question
would fill many volumes, and would need to spring from a deep and
minute knowledge of the Roman mind, the Roman laws, and the Roman
armaments, to which no pretension is here made. The answer suggested in
the following pages will be confessedly imperfect and inadequate, but even
the fragments of a reply to such a question can hardly be quite devoid of
interest.

The Roman Empire of the West fell because it had completed its work,
and the time had come for it to be cut down, and to cumber the ground no
longer. Its rise, its extension over nearly the whole civilised world, had been
a vast blessing to humanity; its prolonged existence, even had it been governed by an endless succession of emperors like Trajan and Marcus, would
have been a bane as great as the blessing. To all the nations around the
Mediterranean sea it had brought peace, discipline, the reign of law, the
preparation for Christianity; but it had robbed them of liberty, and as century was added to century, the virtues of the free man were being more and
more effaced by the habit of blind submission to authority. It was time for
the Teutonic nations to rejuvenate the world, to bring their noisy energy
into those silent and melancholy countries, peopled only by slaves and
despots. It was time to exhibit on the arena of the world the ruder virtues
and the more vigorous vices of a people who, even in their vices, showed
that they were still young and strong; it was time that the sickly odour of

incense offered to imbecile emperors and lying prefects should be scattered before the fresh moorland air of liberty. In short, both as to the building up, and as to the pulling down of the world-Empire of Rome, we have a right to say, 'It was, because the Lord God willed it so.'

Of course, this manner of stating the problem cannot hope for acceptance from an influential school of thinkers at the present day. 'What!' they will at once exclaim, 'would you bring back into historical science those theological terms and those teleological arguments from which we have just successfully purified it? Are you not aware that history, like astronomy, like physics, like every other science, spends its infancy in the religious stage, its adolescence in the metaphysical, and when it has reached its full maturity and become thoroughly conscious of its powers and of its aims, passes into the positive, or materialistic stage – that stage from which the will of God, the free will of man, final causes, and every other metaphysical or theological conception is excluded, and in which law, fixed and immutable, however hard to discover, must reign supreme?'

Such, it may be admitted, is the utterance of the *Zeitgeist*, of that convergence of many minds towards a single thought, which we call by the less forcible English equivalent, 'the spirit of the age'. But, looking back over many past ages, and seeing the utter death and decay of many a *Zeitgeist*, once deemed omnipotent and everlasting, the *Zeitgeist* of Egyptian hierophants, of Spanish inquisitors, of the schoolman, of the alchemist, of the Jacobin, one is disposed to look the present time-spirit boldly in the face and ask why it, any more than its predecessors, must be infallible and eternal.

There was a time when final causes were the bane of all the sciences, when men attempted to deduce from their crude notions of what God ought to have done, a statement of what he has done, and thus easily evaded the toil of true scientific enquiry. Our great master, Bacon, recalled the mind of man from these fruitless wanderings, and vindicated, for the collection of facts and the observation of law, their true place in all philosophy. But he did not share that spirit of agnosticism, that serene indifference to the existence of an ordering mind in the universe, which is professed by many of his followers in the present day. It could not have been said of him, as it may, perhaps, hereafter be said of some of his greatest disciples, 'Blindness in part has fallen upon the physical philosopher. While groping eagerly after the how of this visible universe, he has missed the clue to the vaster and more momentous questions of its why and its by whom.'

The present writer belongs to the old-fashioned school, which still dares and delights to speak of God in nature and of God in history. To declare, as we venture to do, with all reverence and confession of our dim sightedness, that we believe we can trace the finger of the Creator and Lord of the world in events like the rise and fall of the Roman Empire, is by no means to assert that we can explain the ways of providence in all the occurrences either of the present or of the past; it by no means commits us to the proposition that 'all things have happened for the best in the best of all possible worlds'. For one who believes in the God of whom the Christian revelation speaks, or even in the God whom Socrates felt after and found, neither optimism nor pessimism would seem to be the rational frame of mind. We look back over our own lives; we see faults and blunders in them past counting. Assuredly it would have been better for us and for our little fragment of the world that these should not have been committed – so much the pessimist truly urges. But then, we can also see, as we think – but here each individual of the race must speak for himself – traces of a higher power contending with us in our blindness, sometimes bringing good out of our follies and mistakes, always seeking to educate us and to raise us

> On stepping stones
> Of our dead selves to higher things.

In all this we do but ratify the statement of one who had meditated on human nature at least as deeply as any modern sociologist:

> There's a divinity that shapes our ends
> Rough hew them as we will.

So much the optimist may claim. Why the divinity has not shaped the whole world's career to naught but a good end is confessedly inexplicable, and will perhaps be for ever unintelligible to us. Meantime, therefore, we hold the two unreconciled beliefs, in the almightiness of God and in the existence of evil which is his enemy. To discard either of these beliefs, or to harmonise them, we find equally impossible, and therefore we desist from the attempt, and let both grow together till the harvest. If this be true in the universal, of the whole 'scheme and constitution of things', we may reasonably expect to find in the particular – for instance, in the course of European history – some events of which we may confidently say, 'God brought them to pass in order to promote the welfare of humanity', and others of which we can only say, 'Why this irretrievable ruin, in which apparently there lurked no germ of benefit to the human race, was permit-ted, is a mystery.' To apply these general principles to the case before us, we assert with confidence that both the arising and the fall of the Roman Empire were blessings to the human race, and that we are justified in regarding them as the handiwork of an unseen power, the maker and the friend of man. But that every step in the upward career of Rome was bene-ficial to man, or was accomplished with the smallest possible amount of human suffering, we do not believe. Nor, conversely, would we assert that the foundation of the new Teutonic kingdoms might not conceivably have come to pass at a time and in a way which would have been more beneficial to humanity. It is impossible to read the history of the early Middle Ages without feeling that, for the first six centuries after the fall of the Western Empire, there is little or no progress. The night grows darker and darker, and we seem to get ever deeper into the mire. Not till we are quite clear of the wrecks of the Carolingian fabric, not till the days of William the Nor-man and Hildebrand, do we seem to be making any satisfactory progress out of chaos into cosmos. It is possible to imagine many circumstances which might have prevented the waste of these six centuries, and perhaps have started Europe on her new career with the faith of the thirteenth cen-tury joined to the culture of the age of the Renaissance. Had the sons of Theodosius possessed half the vigour of their father; had Stilicho and Aetius not been stabbed in the back by the monarchs whom they were labouring to defend; had the Arian controversy not made its ineffaceable rift between conquerors and conquered; had the Ostrogothic kingdom of Italy and the Visigothic kingdom of Aquitaine not been overthrown by Justinian and by Clovis; had a very slight change in the obscure politics of the Arabian tribes cut short the preaching of Mohammed son of Abdal-lah; it is possible that centuries of human suffering might have been mitigated, and that the freshness of heart which so many of the European nations seem to have lost in the ages since the Renaissance might still be theirs.

But our business is with the events that were, not with those that might have been. Let us, therefore, proceed to consider some of the secondary causes which in the ordering of the providence of God, brought about the transfer of the sceptre of Rome into the hands of the barbarians.

1. THE FOUNDATION OF CONSTANTINOPLE

There is perhaps no more striking illustration of a nation's powerlessness to discern the dangers that are really most menacing to its future, than the Persophobia (if we may coin a word for history from politics), which, down to the very days of the Visigothic invasion, and even beyond them, seems to have haunted the minds of Roman statesmen. True, the Parthian or Persian monarchy was the only other civilised or semi-civilised state which rose above the horizon of Roman consciousness. The defeats of Crassus and Valerian, the ignominious peace concluded by the successor of Julian in the plains beyond the Tigris, no doubt alarmed as well as humbled every Roman. Still, after making full allowance for the impressions produced by these events, it is difficult to understand why, when Hun and Vandal and Visigoth were actually streaming into the very heart of the Empire, the Persian should still have been the favourite bugbear of poets and orators. But Claudian, for example, continually speaks of 'the Mede' as Rome's most terrible foe; and when he rises into his highest heaven of prophetic rapture over the glories of Honorius, he always predicts the conquest of Babylon or Ecbatana.

Thus, at the end of his poem *On the Third Consulship of Honorius*, he says to the Imperial brothers,

> E'en now great Babylon despoiled I see,
> In fear unfeigned the Parthian horsemen flee;
> The Bactrian cons the Roman legist's lore,
> Ganges grows pale between each subject shore,
> And Persia spreads her gems your feet before.

And so, in many similar passages, involuntary homage is rendered to the Sassanian monarchs of Persia, by representing them as the most formidable of the antagonists of Rome.

It was this fear of the Persian monarchy which doubtless partly induced Constantine to plant his new capital at the meeting-point of Europe and Asia. In a certain sense it may be said that the measure was justified by its consequences. Except for the disastrous retreat of Julian's army – and even his expedition was a triumph, only converted into a defeat by the overeagerness of the general – Persia won no considerable victories over Eastern Rome, and in the seventh century she was utterly overthrown by the emperor Heraclius. Moreover, the wonderful political prescience of the founder of Constantinople was clearly shown by the tenacity with which, through the greater part of eleven stormy centuries, the Empire, which had that city for its brain, clung to life. Avars, Bulgarians, Saracens, Russians, Seljuk Turks, Latin crusaders, foamed over the surrounding provinces and dashed themselves to pieces against its walls, but none except the crusaders effected an entrance, and none effected a durable conquest till the terrible day when the dynasty of Palaeologus succumbed to the dynasty of Othman. And the fact that Stamboul is to this day a spell of such portentous power in the incantations of modern diplomatists, is the most powerful of all testimonies to the genius of the young prince who was hailed *imperator* by the legionaries at York.

But if the question be asked, 'What was the effect of the building of Constantinople on Italy and old Rome?' if it be considered that the true object of a statesman of the lower Empire should have been, not to protract the existence of a semi-Greek, semi-Asiatic dominion, a kind of bastard Rome, but to keep the true Rome, the city of the seven hills, in her high place at the forefront of humanity, or, if she must needs fall, to make her fall as honourable and her transformed spirit as mighty as possible – then our answer will be widely different, and we shall have to rank the founder of Constantinople foremost among the destroyers of the Empire.

We have seen in the course of this history the infinite mischief wrought by the rivalry between the ministers of the Eastern and Western Empires. At the critical moment of Alaric's preparations for his invasion Stilicho alone might probably have crushed him; but the subtle Goth 'sold his alternate oaths to either throne'. Each Empire trusted that the blow was about to fall on the other – a blow which the sister realm would have witnessed with Christian resignation – and thus the time for anticipating it and for destroying the destroyer passed away.

The sort of jealousy which had sprung up between the two capitals is well illustrated by the following lines of Claudian. The passage also gives us a picture of the populace of the new Rome, which, though no doubt charged with hostile feeling, connects itself sufficiently with the Athens of Alcibiades, and the Nika rioters of the days of Justinian, to justify us in accepting its main features as correct.

In consequence of Tribigild's revolt (in 399), Eutropius, then chief minister of Arcadius, convenes a sort of council of war.

Pert youths came there and greybeards lecherous,
Whose glory was in trencher-combats won.
A menu subtly changed from yesterday's
Is a most noble exploit in their eyes.
By costly fare they tickle appetite
And give to those insatiate maws of theirs
The starry birds that drew great Juno's car,
And India's emerald prattlers of the woods.
Far realms supply their dainties: their deep greed
The Aegean sea and blue Propontis' lake
And Azov's straits with all their denizens
Soothe for an hour, but fail to satisfy.
Then with what art they wear their scented robes
Silken, but heavy for those delicate limbs!
The highest praise is his whose vapid jokes
Move loudest laughter. See their ornaments,
Fitter for girls than men, their shaven cheeks,
And mark them on the days of spectacle.
The Hun, the Goth may thunder at the gates,
The dancers will not have one gazer less.
Rome's name they ever scorn, and can admire
Only the mansions which the Bosporus laves.
Yet there are arts in which e'en these excel:
Deftly they dance and drive a chariot well.*

Of course there is spite in this description, but the fact that such a picture of the Byzantine court was acceptable to the dwellers by the Tiber shows the estrangement which had sprung up between the old Rome and the new.

Had the mistress of the world, when she found herself on all sides begirt by the 'bark† of savage nations', deliberately withdrawn to her own ancient citadel, put her fleets in order at Classis and Misenum, so as to command the Upper and the Lower seas, and sent her hardiest troops to garrison the difficult passes of the Alps, she might have lost many fair provinces, but the heart of the Empire could hardly have been pierced. It was the diffusion of her vital force over several nerve-centres, Carthage, Alexandria, Antioch, but above all, Constantinople, that ruined her. Some of the suckers lived on, but the old tree perished.

* Claudian, *In Eutropium*, ii.325–41.   † See Claudian's words as quoted on p. 347.

2. CHRISTIANITY

It was not by an accidental coincidence that the great historian of the *Decline and Fall of the Roman Empire* was also one of the ablest opponents of the Christian revelation to whom the last century gave birth. The sound of the vesper-song of barefooted friars in the temple of Jupiter Capitolinus, which seemed to call him to his great enterprise, suggested to him, not untruly, that an irreconcilable antagonism between the genius of the emperors and the genius of Christianity had caused the ruins which were piled around him. And what seems to call for particular notice here is the fact that both the good and the evil in Christianity contributed to this result; both those great spiritual truths which made the essence of the new religion when it came forth from the hands of its divine founder, and those foreign elements which it borrowed from philosophies and idolatries in the act of battling with them – all fought against the Rome of the Caesars.

First, as to the essential opposition between the uncorrupted spirit of Christianity and the continuance of the Roman state. The religious ideas of the Latin and Sabine tribes among whom the great republic was born, were poor and homely enough, without the Hellenic grace, or the Jewish sublimity, or the Teutonic tenderness; but, such as they were, they absolutely moulded the character and institutions of the Roman people. The church did not encroach upon the province of the state, it simply was the state. No order of priests contended for power or privilege with the officers of the republic; those officers themselves, as they reached certain stages in their upward progress, became ministers of the gods, and, without any question as to spiritual fitness, only with so much pretension to morality as an originally moral people naturally required in its chief magistrates, they were clothed, *ex officio*, with a certain sacred character. The word *religio* itself, whatever be its precise etymological significance, was understood to express the binding, cementing force which a constant reference to unseen supernatural powers exerts upon a commonwealth. Hence the same myth-making faculty which in the brain of

> The lively Grecian, in a land of hills,
> Rivers, and fertile plains, and sounding shores,*

created nymphs and naiads and oreads, was employed by the more prosaic

* Wordsworth, *The Excursion*, bk iv.

Evidence of the continuing vitality of pagan culture: Dido offers a sacrifice in a scene
from bk iv of the *Aeneid* taken from a manuscript of the period

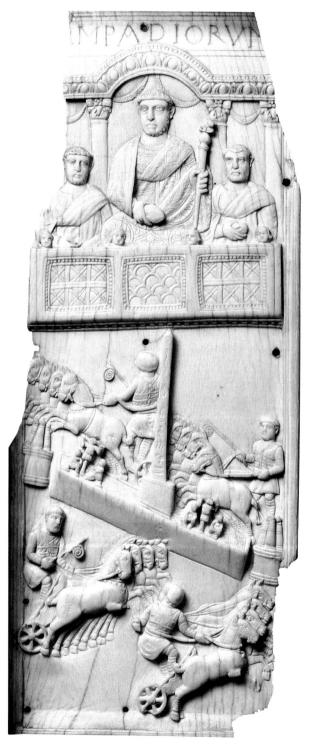

'The Imperial majesty, of which flatterers had made a kind of god upon earth': an emperor in triumphal costume presides over a chariot-race

Roman to invent fresh gods for every fresh development of the social, the political, even the financial life of man the citizen. Thus, according to the curious catalogue of St Augustine, 'they commended children in the act of birth to the goddess Ops, children crying to the god Vaticanus, lying in their cradles to Cunina, sucking to Rumina, standing to Statilinus, arriving to Adeona, departing to Abeona. They commended them to goddess Mens that they might have a good mind, to Volumnus and Volumna, god and goddess, that they might have a good volition, to the nuptial gods that they might marry well, to the rurals, and especially to goddess Fructesca, that they might receive plenteous fruits, to Mars and Bellona that they might wage war well, to Victoria that they might conquer, to the god Honor that they might be honoured, to the goddess Pecunia that they might have plenty of money, to the god Aesculanus and his son Argentinus that that money might be both of bronze and silver. For Aesculanus was made the father because bronze money was coined before silver; and, in truth, I cannot understand why Argentinus did not beget Aurinus, since the silver coinage has been followed by one of gold.'*

Such a religious system as this subjects itself easily to ridicule, as easily as the faith of a modern Italian peasant in his own particular Madonna or Bambino, in the San Cristoforo of one village, or the San Lorenzo of another. Like this latter development, too, it probably glanced lightly over the minds of the upper classes of society, and was tenaciously held in all its grotesque minuteness only by the lower. Still this was substantially the religious system under which the great republic had grown from youth to manhood; by its pontiffs had been declared the days for the assembly of the people in the forum, by its augurs had the omens been taken in every one of its battlefields. The deification of Julius and Augustus was the national expression of the feeling that the greatness of Rome was the peculiar care of the eternal gods, and that the spirits which had wrought conspicuously at this grand task during their earthly career, must still survive in the society of the immortals, to watch over the work of their own hands. It was with this faith – for faith we must surely call it – in their hearts that the legions of Rome had marched on from victory to victory. Their anticipations of reward or punishment in a future life might be vague and varying, but at least they felt that the great city with which they had linked their fortunes was eternal, and the confidence that she would survive all shocks of adverse fortune, and would treasure the names of her defenders with undying reverence, gave

* Augustine, *De Civitate Dei*, iv.21.

strength, doubtless, not only to a Decius or a Curtius, but also to many a simple Roman legionary at the moment of facing death for her sake.

The whole of this fabric of national faith, with whatsoever in it was noble, and whatsoever in it was puerile, had to fall before the apostolic proclamation, 'To us there is but one God, the Father, of whom are all things, and we in him, and one Lord Jesus Christ, by whom are all things, and we by him.' If there was any hint in the Christian Scriptures of one nation favoured above all others, that nation was the Jewish, if any notion of a city chosen by the Eternal 'to put his name there', that city was Jerusalem. But the latest and prevailing utterance of the new religion was, 'All nationalities are on the same level before God. He has made of one blood all nations of men, to dwell on all the face of the earth. Your citizen-ship, the true *civitas*, which is the highest condition that man can attain to, is in heaven. This *civitas* is within reach of all men, barbarian, Scythian, bond or free, and makes brothers of us all.'

There was an incurable opposition between teaching such as this, and the root-idea of the Roman commonwealth. The rulers of the state felt it, and were forced into persecution, almost against their will. Gladly would they have consigned Christianity to the peaceful pantheon of the tolerated religions, in which already the worship of Astarte and Mithras, of Isis and the Dea Syria, flourished happily, side by side. But they perceived – the wis-est emperors the most clearly – that this was a religion which would have all or nothing, and they hunted it into the catacombs to bar it from the throne.

The persecutions failed: they enlisted pity, generosity, love of justice, all the nobler feelings of our nature, on the side of the votaries of the new reli-gion, and to these latter they gave a drill, a discipline, we must also in truth add a bitterness of temper, which they had not possessed before. A time came when the Christians found that they were the majority in the Empire, a time when the young emperor Constantine, with his foot upon the ladder of fortune, was half-convinced of the truth of Christianity, and wholly convinced of the policy of embracing it. For three generations the em-perors, with the exception of the short reign of Julian, were the Christian masters of a household whose traditions were still pagan. Some of the anomalies which resulted from this position of theirs have been glanced at in previous pages. We have seen that no emperor till the accession of Gratian dared to refuse the title of *pontifex maximus*, which marked him as head of the state church of heathenism. We have also noticed the incon-gruity between the acts of Theodosius as defender of the Catholic faith and the conventional language of the court poet, who makes him the favourite of Mars and Jupiter during his life, and turns him into a star after his death.

That this strange medley of contending faiths had no effect in enfeebling the resolution of Rome, and making her stroke uncertain, that the regiment which had fought so long under one flag would fight just as well when that flag was replaced by another, as hostile to it as the lilies to the tricolour, is what no one would conjecture beforehand. And that the substitution of Christianity for the worship of the deities of the Capitol had something to do with the crumbling away of the Empire in the fifth century, is a conviction which forces itself on our minds, and never so irresistibly as when we are listening to the most eloquent and the most subtle apologist for Christianity, Augustine, endeavouring to prove to us in his book on the *City of God* that the thing was not so. One turns over page after page of that immortal treatise – that encyclopaedia of the whole religious thought of the age; one feels the absurdity of the pagan theory, the grandeur of the Christian conception of the vast unseen city of God, but, through it all, the antagonism between the true Roman ideas and the ideas of Christianity rises more and more definitely before the mind, and when we are called upon finally to adjudicate on the question 'Would the Rome of the Fabii and the Scipios, the Rome which heartily believed in and worshipped Jupiter and Quirinus, Mavors, Ops, and Saturnus, have fallen as the Christian Rome fell before the hordes of Alaric?' we are bound in our historical conscience to answer, 'No.'

Secondly. In the course of its three hundred years' struggle for existence the new religion had assimilated some elements, foreign as I venture to think, to its original essence; and by these also it made war on Rome. The spirit of intolerance was one of these extraneous elements, at any rate insofar as it relied on the sword of the civil magistrate to carry its sentences into effect. The words of St Paul about heretics, 'With such an one, no, not to eat', and of St John, 'Receive him not into your house, neither bid him God speed', were aimed apparently at men whose immorality was bringing the new society into reproach, and contemplated exclusion from that society as the heaviest punishment to be inflicted. The general attitude towards the heathen or the unbelieving Jew was 'What have I to do with them that are without?'; and the proposal to arrange the worldly affairs, even of Christians, authoritatively, was met by 'Man, who made me a judge or a divider over you?' 'Whiles it remained was it not thine own, and after it was sold, was it not in thine own power?' In practice, the relation of the professors of the new faith to 'them that were without' during the second century seems to have been reasonable and friendly. Justin Martyr and Quadratus still wore the philosopher's cloak after their conversion to Christianity, and endeav/ oured to persuade their fellow countrymen by an appeal to 'the voice of the soul, who is herself naturally Christian',* that the glad tidings which they had to proclaim, though marvellous, were not incredible, and were in har/ mony with the truest presentiments of man's own moral nature. Would that the new religion had always thus calmly addressed herself to the consciences of mankind, that she had never shouted nor shrieked, nor tortured, in order to enforce the acceptance of her message! Earth would be by many degrees more like heaven at this day, if she had thus remained true to her first gentle instincts.

But the persecutions came and went, and they changed, though they should not have changed, the temper of the Christian champions. So was rendered possible that utterance of Tertullian's (destined to an evil immor/ tality), in which he consoled his brethren for their conscientious abstinence from the pleasures of the hippodrome by promising them far greater spec/ tacular pleasures in the life to come, when from the safe security of heaven they should behold so many proud prefects, so many jeering philosophers, writhing in agony under the tortures of the never/dying fires of hell. It may be admitted that the stern, almost morose, temperament of Tertullian is answerable for some of this bitterness, but it would not be difficult to quote passages of a similar tendency from Lactantius and other fathers of the ante/Nicene church. In truth, it was not in human nature (though it should have been in the divine that was intermingled with it) to see parents, broth/ ers, sisters, dragged off to an insulting and cruel death, for refusing to sacrifice to the genius of the emperor, without some scowl of hatred becom/ ing fixed above the eyes which witnessed these things. And so persecution did not, as was once alleged, always and entirely fail of its end. 'The blood of the martyrs was the seed of the church'; but it was a church of different habit of growth, and producing more acrid fruit than that which it replaced.

For seventy years, however, after Constantine's edicts in favour of Chris/ tianity, the new religion showed herself but little as a persecutor, at least of heathens. The tolerant spirit of Constantine had something to do with this; the internal divisions of the Christian church, especially the long and fierce

* The phrase belongs to the following century, but the line of argument indicated by it to this.

Arian debate, still more. The Caesars of Rome, with the exception of Julian, settled down comfortably into their anomalous position, each being at once *pontifex maximus* of the old religion, and moderator in the doctrinal controversies of the new. It was as if the Ottoman sultan, still retaining his claim to the caliphate, were to become a member of the Greek church, and to throw himself earnestly into the discussions about the procession of the Holy Spirit.

We have heard Theodosius, at the council of Constantinople in the year 381, pronouncing the final triumph of the Trinitarian party within the church, and we have seen something of the increased stringency of his determination to secure for that church, by the power of the state, the victory over her external foes, whether heathens or heretics. True, these persecutions lacked the ferocity of those which were set on foot by Decius and by Galerius; still they *were*; and for some generations, with quiet, earnest deliberateness, the whole power of the emperors was employed in making all Christians think alike, and in preventing non-Christians from thinking at all.

Constantius (in 353) had said, 'We will that all men should abstain from sacrifices, and if any shall hereafter offend against this law, let him be punished by the avenging sword.'* But the decree seems to have remained a dead letter, and the heathen sacrifices went on nearly as before. Theodosius enacted new laws against heathen worship, and by such acts as the demolition of the temple of Serapis at Alexandria, gave them practical effect. At the same time appeared upon the statute book a cloud of edicts (some of which have been already quoted) against 'the noxious Manichaeans and their execrable meetings', against 'the heretics of the Donatist superstition', against 'the teachers and leaders of the crime of the Eunomians, especially their clergy whose madness has brought about this great aberration', against 'all who are tormented by the error of divers heresies, viz. the Eunomians, the Arians, the Macedonian deniers of the Holy Ghost, the Manichaeans, the Encratites, the Apotactites, the Saccofori, the Hydroparastatae'. Fine, imprisonment, loss of office, prohibition to assemble in the town or to give to their places of meeting the appearance of churches, restriction of their testamentary power – these are the penalties thundered forth in many an edict against men who had committed no crime against the state, but whose theology was different from the emperor's. The ferocity and the terror of Diocletian's persecutions have passed away, but we find ourselves breathing the

* *Codex Theodosianus*, xvi.10.4.

same atmosphere of petty ecclesiastical tyranny which produced the five mile act and conventicle act of Charles II, the penal laws against the Irish Catholics of William III and Anne. If there were nothing more to be said against it, this attempt to harass men into uniformity of religious opinion was an enormous waste of power, at a time when the energies of the state were scarcely sufficient for its own proper work of administration. But what made the matter worse, from the point of view of a Roman statesman, was that the religion which was being maintained in domination at the cost of all this legislative combat, was itself in no way essential to, nay, rather as has been before said, was of necessity antagonistic to, the root-idea of the Roman commonwealth. A Mohammedan sultan pressing heavily on the *giaour*, an Israelitish monarch slaying the priests of Baal, a most Catholic king of Spain burning Jews or expelling Moriscos, were all acting more or less in accordance with the spirit of which their royalty was the expression. But a Roman *imperator* harassing the Encratites or the Apotactites because the building in which they assembled for divine worship too closely resembled a church of the orthodox, was an utterly un-Roman Roman, an anomaly not only vexatious but ridiculous.*

Yet it is probable that to the somewhat narrow, martinet mind of Theodosius, and still more to the dazed intellects of his sons, these measures of religious persecution appeared solemn duties; nay more, that they regarded them as peace-offerings, which would ensure the secular safety of the Empire. The increasing calamities which befell the state were taken as manifestations of the wrath of God; and no more obvious means of conjuring away that wrath suggested themselves than the enactment of a new and sharper law against the Manichaean pravity or the Arian madness.

In the mist and darkness which have gathered over the history of the fifth century, a mist and a darkness through which only the bare forms of events are discernible, while thoughts and feelings are utterly hidden, we know little indeed of the mood of mind in which these successive acts of uniformity were received by the objects of them. Heathenism and heresy, like wounded creatures, crept back to their caves and died there, but after what conflicts or with what struggles we know not. The name *paganus* (villager), for the worshipper of the old gods, is one among many indications that Christianity conquered first the great cities, the centres of intellectual

* The story of Generidus the heathen, and his refusal to continue in the emperor's service unless the edict against his fellow heathens were repealed, well illustrates the baneful effect of this persecuting legislation in the defence of the Empire (see vol. i, pp. 436–7).

and commercial activity, and then gradually, and we can hardly say how slowly, pushed her way into lonely glens or wide, unfrequented pasture, lands, and made the dwellers there bow before the cross. Yet even in the cities and at the Imperial courts the victory was not fully won in the reign of Theodosius. It is a noteworthy fact how many of the small band of literary men, who flourished in the latter days of the Empire, remained faithful to the old superstitions. Ammianus Marcellinus, Zosimus, Priscus, the chief historians of this period, are all pagans, one at least of them a bitter pagan. Nor is it by any means certain that Procopius, the great historian of the reign of Justinian, ought not to be added to the list.

Two other elements of the Christianity of the third and fourth centuries co-operated in a subordinate degree towards the decay of the Empire. These were the priestly hierarchy and the monastic self-seclusion.

The fires of Roman persecution had, doubtless, much to do with hardening and shaping, as into a point of tempered steel, that marvellous episcopal organisation which was one day to penetrate the world. As the soldiers who survive on a well-fought battlefield look towards the officers who have been with them in the thickest of the fray, so we may imagine the hearts of the believers to have glowed with fresh loyalty towards the rulers of the church, when the rage of the Decian or the Galerian persecution was at length abated, and they had leisure to count their losses. Thus, here also to the repressive measures of the emperors must be attributed some involuntary share in the change which came over the spirit of the church between the first century and the fourth, and which separates the simple and scarcely differentiated overseers and elders of the Acts of the Apostles from the full-grown bishops and priests of the time of Constantine. It is not likely that such a well-disciplined and compact organisation as the Christian hierarchy can have grown up within and yet outside of the Empire without impairing somewhat of its strength. And such victories as were won by Athanasius over Constantius, or by Ambrose over Theodosius, though they command our fullest sympathy as noble triumphs of the moral over the material, had probably some effect in lessening the reverence which men felt for the Augustus as a kind of 'present divinity',* and so in loosening the fabric of the Empire. Yet possibly we ought not to attribute large results to this cause. The great strifes between bishop and sovereign belong to a later age, to the barbarian monarchies or to the Eastern Empire. Except

* According to the often-quoted words of Horace, *praesens divus habebitur Augustus* [Augustus will be thought a god among us on earth].

indirectly, insofar as it may have favoured the persecution of heathens and heretics, the Christian hierarchy need not be held responsible for a large share in the pulling down of Imperial Rome.

Probably we may come to a similar conclusion with reference to that other great phenomenon of the religious life of the fourth and fifth centuries, the rise and progress of the monastic system. It is interesting to see how this was viewed by an educated, though certainly not unbiased pagan. Zosimus, speaking of the riots at Constantinople in connection with the exile of Chrysostom (401), says (v.23), 'The city was filled with uproar, and the Christian church was occupied by the men who are called monks. Now these men renounce lawful wedlock, and fill large colleges in the cities and villages with unmarried persons, profitless for war and for any other of the state's necessities. Yet have they, in the interval between that time and the present' (perhaps half a century), 'made great advances, so that they have now appropriated a large part of the land, and under pretence of distributing all their substance to the poor, have, in a manner, made all poor alike.'

The withdrawal of so many men in the prime of life from the pursuits of industry and the defence of the state, must undoubtedly have lessened the resources of the Empire, especially as these monks were not, like their successors in the Middle Ages, the restorers of the waste places, the doctors, engineers, and journalists of the community. At a time when the manliest virtue was required to stem the torrent of corruption within and barbarism without, men of noble soul and cultured intellect, like St Jerome, retired into the caves of Bethlehem, leaving the world a prey to hypocrites and rogues, such as Olympius and Eutropius. As the latter class of men, despairing of the Roman state, sought to build up their own fortunes on the general ruin, so the former class, with the same despair of the republic in their hearts, determined at least to secure their own soul's salvation, and to live for this alone. The selfishness was of a higher kind, but it would be hard to deny that it was selfishness, and that the true Christian impulse would have been to struggle on undaunted, and persist in the endeavour to leave the world better than they found it.

But, having admitted this negative charge against monkery, we cannot assign to it, in the Western Empire at least, any great active influence for ruin. In the East, during the fifth century, the power of the monks was no doubt far more hurtful to the state. 'Armies of mad monks rushing through the streets of Alexandria',* and their brethren in Constantinople stirring

* Kingsley, *Roman and Teuton.*

up the people to shout for the deposition of the 'Manichaean tyrant', when-
ever an emperor swerved by a hair's breadth from the razor-bridge of orthodoxy as defined in the council of Chalcedon – these were undoubtedly
disintegrating and dangerous forces; and when they were predominant, the
government of the Empire might truly be styled a government by lunatics.
In the West we see no such spectacles at the time which we are now discussing, and it would be a scandalous injustice to class the calm Paulinus of
Nola and the learned Claudianus Mamertus of Vienne with the turbulent
Eutyches, or the bloodstained Barsumas of Constantinople.

3 SLAVERY

It was no accidental catastrophe which patriotism and genius
might have warded off: it was old social evils – at the bottom of
all, the ruin of the middle class by the slave proletariat – that
brought destruction on the Roman commonwealth.

MOMMSEN, *History of Rome*, bk iv, chap. 11

The men of our generation, who have read the story of General Sherman's
march through Georgia, are in a better position than their ancestors for estimating the part played by slavery in bringing about the ruin of Rome. The
short-lived southern confederacy in America had many points of resemblance to the Roman republic. It was administered by wealthy cultivators
of the soil, born warriors, born orators, a proud and courageous people.
All that mere fighting could do to preserve its existence was ably and, at
first, successfully done; but slavery, that rock of offence which the planters
had made the cornerstone of their new edifice, proved its ruin. The truth
had been suspected for some little time before, but was fully proved when
Sherman's scarcely resisted march through three hundred miles of the
enemy's country showed the hollowness of a political organisation which
had been massing its armies, by hundreds of thousands at a time, on the
banks of the Potomac, but which could not reckon on its own inhabitants
to resist or seriously to harass an invader who had once broken through the
wall of steel on the frontier. It could not reckon upon them, because the
majority of them were themselves a hostile nation, made so by the institution of slavery. True, in America as in Italy, the oppressed class waited long
before they dared to show on which side their sympathies lay. This is, for a
time, that which turns the scale in favour of the slave-holder, that his chat-
tels are too debased to be capable of self-organisation, too ignorant to

understand the great movements in the world of politics and war, too servile-hearted to dare to embrace what may not prove the winning side. But if there comes at length such a time as came in Georgia lately, and in Etruria long ago, when the slave sees with his own eyes a man, mightier than his master, come to overthrow all that existing order which has weighed on him so heavily, and saying, 'Help me, and I will give you freedom', then is seen the strange magic which lies in that word 'freedom' for even the heaviest clods of humanity; then the comfortable persuasion of the self-deceived slave-owner, that his chattel will fight for the luxury of continuing to be a chattel, vanishes like snow in summer.

We have had to record one instance – many more have probably been left unrecorded – of the readiness of the Roman slaves to turn against their masters. In the interval between the first and second sieges of Rome by Alaric, the slaves, to the number of forty thousand, fled to the barbarian camp. In his usual tantalising way Zosimus forgets to tell us the denouement of the story, but it may be conjectured that the greater part of these slaves, if they ever returned to Rome, returned with the army of Alaric through the blazing Salarian gate to guide their new friends to the plunder of their old oppressors.*

It would have been interesting to know what was the total number of slaves in existence at any particular period of the Empire, but a complete census of the whole population of the Roman world, free and servile, if it ever existed, has not survived to our day. Gibbon guesses the number of the slaves all over the Empire at the time of Claudius at sixty millions; and it seems to be impossible either to prove or disprove his conjecture. We are told, in round numbers, that some citizens possessed ten thousand or twenty thousand slaves apiece, and with more apparent accuracy that a certain freedman under Augustus, although he had been impoverished by the civil wars, left at his death 4,116 slaves.† From other sources we learn that in the days of Augustus, two hundred slaves were not considered at all an exorbitantly large establishment, and that he who had only five or ten was looked upon as either very poor or very mean. In view of these facts, forty thousand seems a very small number for even the mere house-slaves in Rome at the time of its siege by Alaric. Possibly the removal of the court to Ravenna, and the troublous character of the times, had led to the with-

* Zosimus, v.42. See vol. i, p. 455.
† Athenaeus (vi.104) is the authority for the first of these statements, Pliny (*Natural History*, xxxiii.10.47) for the second.

drawal of most of the wealthy slave-owners from Rome; or the crowds of freedmen and paupers supported by the public distribution of wheat may, in Rome itself, have thinned, by a kind of competition, the number of actual bondsmen. Or, which is perhaps the most likely supposition of all, Zosimus, the writer from whom the story of the fugitive slaves is extracted, is speaking in his usual somewhat inaccurate style when he says, that 'nearly all' the slaves in Rome deserted to the camp of Alaric.

As mention has been made of slavery as it existed down to our own days in the United States of North America, and as this is that type of the 'peculiar institution' which most readily suggests itself to our minds, it may be well to remind the reader of a few obvious points of dissimilarity between the two forms of servitude, the Roman and the American.

(1) It seems probable that the condition of a slave under a Roman master was harder than that of the negro in the southern states of America. Cruel men of course abused their dangerous power in both countries, while, under men of exceptional gentleness, the lot of the slave may have lost almost all that made it to differ from that of a hired labourer. But the great mass of masters, the men of average character, had in the United States a conception of duty towards their fellow men which was, at least in some degree, influenced by the spirit of Christianity, while the Roman derived his notions of duty from such teachers as Cato the Censor, who, in a well-known passage, uttered his opinion that whenever a slave was not asleep he ought to be at work, and that a master should always sell off his aged slaves as well as his broken-down horses. Certainly this cannot have been either the theory or the practice in Virginia or Tennessee, hardly even, one would hope, in Mississippi or Alabama. It is true that the tendency of legislation under the emperors had been towards greater mildness in the treatment of slaves. The master's absolute power of life and death was taken away; in cases where he had practised extreme cruelty he might be compelled to sell the victim of it; and the huge gloomy *ergastula*, the prisons in which the slaves had been locked up at night after their labour in the fields (which, if not subterraneous, were always lighted by windows high up in the walls, from which there was no chance of escape), were legally abolished, and perhaps practically disused. Still, the life of the Roman's slave, especially of him who was engaged in agriculture, seems to have been hard and dismal beyond even the hardness and dismalness of ordinary Negro slavery.

(2) Yet in two aspects, more important perhaps than all beside, the condition of the Italian bondsman was better than that of the American. Love

and hope were left to him. The breeding of slaves for sale was an unusual though not unknown practice; and consequently though families must sometimes have been separated, even as they are now by the ordinary economic laws of supply and demand, that great blot on the American system, the systematic tearing away of the wife from her husband and the mother from her child, did not disgrace the Roman slave-owners. Manumission also must have been a far more frequent incident of servile life among the ancients, and when it came it opened up a far happier and more unhindered career.

This difference between the two systems is chiefly due to the obvious and fundamental distinction, that in Rome there did not, as in America, yawn the wide chasm of absolute diversity of race between bond and free. All nations, even the noblest of antiquity, were represented in the slave market at Rome. The Greek doctor, or pedagogue, or scribe, the lusty Cappadocian who bore the litter, the Hebrew of whose nation Titus sold ninety-seven thousand into bondage, the Syrian, the Celt, the Dacian, the German, were all in their various ways ministering to the luxury or providing for the wants of the Roman master. From such a motley throng combination was little to be dreaded, and on the other hand there was in them no great inferiority of race to prevent the slave, once liberated, from standing side by side with his old master. Hence, and from motives of pride and profit which made the freedman often a more desirable appendage to the family of the Roman noble than the slave himself, arose the great frequency of manumission, which was indeed slightly checked in the time of Augustus,* on account of the number of debased citizens with whom it was flooding the commonwealth, but which remained a sufficiently common practice sensibly to ameliorate the condition of the Roman slave by introducing into it the vast medicament of hope.

We turn to American slavery, and we see at once a mighty contrast. There every member of the servile caste belonged to one race, and that race one separated by wide ethnological interspaces from the dominant one, and far below it in intellectual energy. It is said that a proposition once made in the Roman senate, to order all the slaves to wear a distinctive dress, was rejected, on the ground that it would be dangerous thus to reveal to them their superiority in numbers. What the senate had denied in that case, nature had done ineffaceably in the case of 'persons held to bondage' under the American laws, by clothing them all with one sable livery.

* By the *lex Aelia Sentia*.

Hence arose, on the one hand, the pride of race which placed the meanest of 'the mean whites' above the most honest and capable man of African descent, and which denied to the latter, however large his share of European blood, *ex parte paterna*,* any share in the duties and rewards of civil life. Hence, on the other hand, arose the fear of race, causing the state to throw the whole weight of its influence into the scale against manumission, and imposing upon every man, whose skin bore witness to the servile condition of his ancestors, the burden of proof that he was not himself a slave. This state of the law and of public feeling was of course utterly absent in old Rome.

(3) And, yet again, there was a difference which probably made the position of the Negro, when he began to reason and to reflect, more intolerable than that of the Dacian or the Syrian in a Roman villa or on an Italian farm. In the fifth century the conscience of the whole civilised world acquiesced in the fact of slavery; in the nineteenth it protested against it. The Roman legislator said that this abrogation of the natural rights of man was an institution of the universal law of nations,† and his saying was confirmed by the fact that there was in all probability not one nation then existing, civilised or barbarian, wherein slavery, in one form or another, did not exist. And so the bondsman of those days submitted to his servile condition, as men now submit to poverty or disease, grumbling indeed that they have drawn a bad number in the lottery of life, but without any intolerable feeling of injustice, without any indignant questioning, 'Why was this horrible fate ever placed for me or for anyone among the possible conditions of existence?'

In America we all know what far different thoughts rankled in the breast of a high-spirited and intelligent slave. Great nations were living and flourishing without this institution which made his life hateful to him. Wide sections of the Christian church condemned it as a crime against God and man. A week perhaps, or two weeks of nightly journeying towards the north star, would take him to a land where no slaves toiled; a few weeks more would set him beyond the possibility of recapture. Assuredly this ever-present thought that liberty was in the world, was near, but was not for him, must have made the chains of many an American slave more galling, must have raised, sometimes almost to madness, his exasperation against the social system which was his foe.

(4) Upon a review therefore of the main points of likeness and unlikeness

* [On the father's side.]   † Justinian, *Institutes*, i.3.

between these two conditions of society, it seems reasonable to conjecture that the men who were owned by Roman masters were less dissatisfied with their lot than those who belonged to the American planters, and that slavery as a disruptive force was more fatal to the southern confederacy than to the Western Empire.

But in Rome it had been working through twelve centuries, in the United States for less than three, and therefore its evil effects were less lasting, one may venture to hope, in the latter instance than in the former. Slavery had aided in the massing together of those 'wide farms' [*latifundia*] which were the ruin of Italy. Slavery had emptied the fields and villages of the hardy rustics who had once been the backbone of Roman power. Slavery had filled the cities with idle and profligate babblers. Slavery had indoctrinated these men, themselves often freedmen or the sons of freedmen, with the pestilent notion that manual labour was beneath the dignity of a citizen. And lastly, slavery had surrounded the thrones of the emperors with men like Eutropius and Chrysaphius, who, by the favour of a fatuous master, crept from the position of a menial to that of a prime minister, and who, when their turn came, bitterly revenged upon society the wrongs which they had suffered at its hands.

A new and happier world was to arise out of the ruins of the old. Slavery was to be softened into serfdom, and serfdom was slowly to disappear, both changes being largely attributable to the benign influence of the Christian church. The fine old medieval motto,

> By hammer and hand
> All arts do stand,

was to drive out, at any rate from the cities, the old, irrational, scorn of handicraft; and the *ergastulum* and the scourge were to vanish like an evil dream. And so if slavery was a cause, the abolition of slavery was to be a result, though by no means an immediate result, of the fall of the Empire.

4 'PANEM ET CIRCENSES', OR THE PAUPERISATION OF THE ROMAN PROLETARIAT

The Roman state at the beginning and the end of its career pursued towards its poorer classes two opposite lines of policy, both unjust, one of which might reasonably have been expected to strangle the rising nationality in its childhood, while the other certainly hastened the ruin of its old age.

In the first ages of the republic the plebeian soldier was expected to leave his farm or his business to serve for a short campaign against the Aequians or Volscians, and to return to a home which had in many instances suffered from the depredations of the enemy, enriched only by a precarious portion of the booty, which, by the fortune of war or the unfairness of the dividing general, might turn out to be worth little or nothing. The real gain of the most successful wars, the public land, was farmed out often at little more than a nominal rent to the senators or a few wealthy plebeians. Thus the whole tendency of the incessant wars of the republic was to make the rich richer and the poor poorer, a tendency aggravated by the high rates charged for interest and by the stern attitude of the Roman law towards the defaulting debtor. The well-known picture drawn in the second book of Livy of the brave old centurion, whose farm had been plundered during his absence with the army, and who, under the crushing load of debt and taxation, had been obliged first to part with the inheritance of his ancestors and then to surrender his person into the hands of his cruel creditor, and who at length escaped from his place of torment into the forum, where his squalid garb, his long unkempt hair, his old and honourable scars received in battle with the enemy, and the new and shameful scourge-marks upon his back inflicted by the slave of a Roman senator, stirred the people to fury: this picture may not be precisely and historically true of the 259th year of the city, yet doubtless it is a type of many a similar occurrence in those early days of the tyranny of wealth.

The characteristic of Roman legislation at this period is its contempt for the rights of the individual, its frightfully unfair notion of the partnership between him and the state – a partnership in which he gave his time, his blood, his heroism, to promote the glory of Rome, and received in return nothing, not even permission to live on the land of his fathers.

In the later phases of the Roman commonwealth the opposite error was committed. After the second Punic war the state really asked nothing of the poor citizen of Rome, and gave him everything that was necessary for life, and, in so giving, deprived him of 'man's first, noblest, birthright, Toil'. The pauperising legislation of Rome first wore the insidious form of a gentle intervention to lower the price of corn. When Spain, Sicily, and Africa were pouring in their tributes of corn or money to the exchequer of the republic, it was not an unnatural suggestion that the wealth thus acquired might fairly be expended in easing the material condition of the Roman citizens, of the men on whom had fallen the heaviest weight of all the blows from Regillus to Cannae, by which the Roman state had been fashioned into greatness. Not an unnatural thought; and yet if the remembrance of the scourged veteran in the forum, and of all the cruel wrongs of the early plebeians, had anything to do with ripening it into action, we have here an instance of that strange nemesis of unrighteousness, which sometimes leads statesmen in the very excess of their penitence for an injustice in the past to prepare a new and greater injustice for the future. It had been a cruel wrong to send forth the Roman plebeian to fight the Volscian or Aequian, and not even to keep his homestead free from the exactions of the creditor, who would not have been a creditor but for the military service of the bread-winner. It was not less a wrong to make the Spaniard or the Sicilian toil, in order to enable the descendants of that same plebeian to prolong a life of idleness and dissipation in the Roman forum.

And, indirectly, this interference with true economic laws injured Italy no less than the provinces. How was the Etrurian or Sabine farmer to grow his corn to a profit, when the whole machinery of the administration of the republic was being employed to sell corn from beyond the seas at far less than cost price in the Roman capital? This was not free trade; it was, if we may use the expression, protection turned inside out; it was a systematic exclusion of the Italian corn-grower from his own natural market. Of course the Italian farmer, already sorely harassed by the necessity of competition with slave labour, succumbed, and virtually disappeared from the scene. The latifundia, the vast domains worked by celibate slaves, took the place of the small yeomen's holdings; the horrible *ergastulum* replaced the free and happy homestead; sheep-walks, vineyards, and oliveyards occupied the ground once employed in the growth of corn, and, more important by far than even the disappearance of her waving cornfields, Italy ceased to produce men as she had once done, just when the need of men to bear the worldwide burden of her Empire was the greatest.

There were great fluctuations in the market price of corn under the republic. In the second Punic war it rose as high as 51s. the quarter; in the wars between Marius and Sulla as high as 102s., during a great famine under Augustus to 115s. But these were simply famine prices. On the other hand, during a year of great plenty near the close of the second Punic war, the price was as low as 2s. and 8d. a quarter. A little later, according to Polybius, it was frequently sold in the valley of the Po for a 2s. and 11d. a quarter.* As between these wide fluctuations it appears to be admitted that about 21s. a quarter was the ordinary market price. Now, by the legislation of Caius Gracchus, each citizen had the right to claim every month a bushel and a quarter of corn from the public stores for 17d., that is to say at the rate of 9s. a quarter, or less than half the average market price.† The rest of the legislation of the younger Gracchus died with him, but this, its worse feature, remained. When supreme power passed from the senate and the assembly of the people to the Caesars, these latter rulers, though in many respects the champions of the provincials against Rome, did not dare to withdraw the supplies of cheap corn from the citizens, though they did limit — eventually to two hundred thousand — the number of persons who were entitled thus to purchase it. Gradually the form of sale and purchase was done away with, and the distribution became simply gratuitous. By the middle of the second century of our era, the monthly supplies of corn had been changed for the far more convenient and even more pauperising distri-bution of wheaten loaves, baked perhaps two or three times a week.

When Aurelian ascended the throne (270), the loaf which the Roman citizen was thus entitled to receive (we know not for how many days' con-sumption), weighed one *uncia* (that is one-twelfth) less than two pounds.‡ As he went forth from the gates of the city on his expedition against the queen of Palmyra, he announced to the people that if he should return vic-torious he would present each one of them with a crown of two pounds' weight. The citizens expected that these crowns would be of gold (worth more than £80 apiece), a donative which was beyond the power and the inclination of Aurelian. Yet were they not altogether disappointed, for when he had been drawn in triumph up the sacred hill, preceded by the weeping Zenobia, he commanded that wheaten loaves, shaped like crowns and weighing each two pounds, should be distributed to the people. Through the remainder of his life and apparently during the reigns of his successors, these larger loaves were given to those who possessed the needful *tessera* or outdoor relief ticket, and this *uncia* added to the civic rations seems to have been seriously regarded by the patriotic but ill-advised emperor as

---

* Four obols (6¼d.) for the Sicilian *medimnus*. The Attic *medimnus* was a bushel and a half. We cannot be quite certain that the Sicilian *medimnus* was the same quantity, and therefore this calculation is liable to some doubt.

† More precisely, the citizen was entitled to claim five *modii* at the rate of 6½ *asses* per *mod-ius*, the *modius* being equivalent to the quarter of a bushel, and the *as* to 0.53 of a penny.

‡ The Roman pound weighed a little less than three-quarters of our pound avoirdupois.

one of his chief titles to greatness. In writing to Arabianus the public commissary-general (*praefectus annonae*), he says, 'Of all the good deeds which by the favour of the immortal gods I have wrought for the common-wealth none is more splendid than this, that I have increased the distribution of corn to every citizen by one *uncia*. To ensure the perpetuity of this benefit I have appointed more shipmasters for the Nile and for the river traffic of Rome. I have raised the banks of the Tiber and deepened the channel of its headstrong current. I have paid my vows to Perennity and the other gods, I have consecrated a statue of the gracious Ceres. Now be it thy task, my dearest Arabianus, to see that these arrangements of mine be not unfruitful. For there is nothing in the world more cheerful than the Roman people when they have well eaten.'* This same emperor, though fond of repressing what he considered inordinate luxury (forbidding his wife to wear a silken dress because silk was then worth its weight in gold, and pro-scribing the use of gold threads and gilded ceilings, whereby he considered that a metal which ought to be as plentiful as silver was unnecessarily wasted), nevertheless added to the rations of the Roman people articles which can hardly be considered as of prime necessity. He gave them pork and oil and wine; at least as to the last gift he had taken measures for plant-ing extensive vineyards in Etruria, and cultivating them with slave labour for the sake of a gratuitous distribution of wine to the citizens, but accord-ing to one story the scheme was frustrated by the intervention of the praetorian prefect who told the generous emperor that if he gave them wine he would have to supplement his gifts with roast ducks and chickens. He also gave them white tunics with long sleeves imported from various prov-inces of the Empire, and linen garments from Africa and Egypt. A generous and popular emperor doubtless, but communism thus robed in the purple is an excellent destroyer of commonwealths.

Let us now traverse an interval of a hundred years, and see what shape this system of outdoor relief had assumed under the dynasty of the Valen-tinians. A long 'title' of the Theodosian Code is devoted to the subject.† It contains fifteen laws, chiefly the handiwork of the emperors Valentinian and Valens, partly of Theodosius I and his sons. The first point which strikes us is, that Rome no longer enjoys a monopoly of the often lauded 'Imperial munificence'. Constantine in founding his new capital by the Bosporus has conferred upon it also the doubtful boon of the *annona* or free largesse of corn; and in order to meet the requirements of this largesse, the

* *Life of Aurelian*, by Flavius Vopiscus, 47.   † *Codex Theodosianus*, xiv.17.

corn-ships of Alexandria – as was remarked on a previous occasion – are now diverted from Rome to Byzantium. The city by the Tiber has now practically only the cornfields of that province of which her ancient rival, Carthage, is the capital, to look to for her supplies. Antioch and Alexandria seem also to have shared in the public distributions, but the edicts relating to these cities do not appear in the code, possibly because their largesses were left to be regulated by the local authorities.

In Rome and Constantinople the Theodosian Code presents us with a lively but strange picture of this organisation of pauperism. Three great classes are the recipients of that which is called by a courtly fiction 'the bounty of the emperors'. These classes are the *palatini*, the *militares*, and the *populares*, that is to say, the servants of the palace, the soldiers, and the mass of the people. The last class receive their rations strictly as householders. The law is very decided on this point, *Aedes sequantur annonae* (The rations must follow the houses); that is to say, if a citizen who has been receiving the ration alienates his house, he loses the right to his daily loaf. At Constantinople special stress is laid on the great founder's desire to encourage house-building in his new city, and an attempt is made (apparently not a successful one) to limit even the soldiers' share in the *annona* to those who possess houses in the capital.

The three classes seem to have received their rations seated on some of the great public staircases in which the city of the seven hills abounded, and yet abounds. Some have thought that they were all collected for this purpose in the Colosseum, but it seems more probable that each of the fourteen regions of the city had its own flight of steps on which the applicants seated themselves, as well as its own bakery, from which they were supplied. Each class of recipients is mustered apart; the *palatini*, the *militares*, the *populares*, have each their own tiers of seats. The bread which is distributed to them is called 'the step-bread' (*panis gradilis*), and the separate classes are known as 'steps'. Stringent laws forbid the transference of the *panis gradilis* from one 'step' to another, and the public commissary-general is warned that the severest penalties hang over him, if he suffers this regulation to be infringed. The prohibition can hardly relate to the mere physical transportation of a loaf of bread from one stone stair to another. It probably means that each class of recipients was to be considered as complete in itself, and that in case of death or removal, the lapsed ration of a *palatinus* was to be transferred only to another *palatinus*, that of a *popularis* to another *popularis*.

But from such an inversion of the great industrial laws upon which society is founded, abuse was inseparable. The holders of the *tessera*, or relief-ticket, eager to accept the alms of the state, but anxious to escape from the ignominy of asking for them, used to present themselves at the great public bakeries, and there, probably by bribery, obtain the loaves to which they were entitled. This practice was forbidden, and it was ordained 'that all men should receive their step-bread from the steps, and that none should be handed out by the shopkeepers, lest thereby any fraud should arise concerning the *panis gradilis*'.

A brazen tablet was to be affixed to the wall, near to the steps of distribution, and on it the name of the receiver and the measure of bread due to him were to be engraved. 'And if anyone's impertinence should carry him so far that he shall usurp for himself or his family the right of that bread, and get his name wrongfully inserted in the brazen tablet, he shall receive chastisement according to his condition.'

The meaning of these last words is made more clear by a savage decree of the emperor Valentinian (370). It seems that some of the senators and great men of Rome were guilty of the meanness of sending members of their households to receive this public bread, which was of course intended only for the poorer class of free citizens. Thereupon the edict runs: 'Should the steward or slave of any senator wrongfully obtain the *panis gradilis* by direct purchase from the clerk of distribution, or by bribery, or even by his mere connivance, let such steward or slave be subjected to the torture of the *equuleus*.* If it appears that he was prompted to this illegality by his own impudence, without the knowledge of his master, let him serve in chains in that bakery which he has been defrauding. Should, however, complicity in the offence be traced to his master, let the house of that senator be confiscated for the use of the treasury.

'In other ranks of life, if anyone who is possessed of private resources shall confess the aforesaid crime, let him and all that he has be bound over to the service of the bakery.

'If he shall be of the very poorest classes' – a provision which shows that this demoralising largesse did not even answer the purpose of a poor-law since 'the very poorest' were not all entitled to it – 'he shall be forced to labour as if he were a slave.

'As for the clerks of distribution who shall be proved to have perpetrated this forbidden wickedness, the sword which is the vindicator of the laws shall be drawn against them.'

* An instrument of torture shaped like a horse.

It would weary the reader were we to trace in further detail the intrica‐ cies of the legislation concerning the *annonae*. There are arrangements for changing stale loaves for new, edicts granting a certain supply of oil to per‐ sons designated by the prefect of the city 'for the refreshment of their frames', edicts forbidding the soldiers of the Imperial guard to transmit their right to the ration as a hereditary claim to their children, and again, other edicts repealing these.* It is a labyrinth of Imperial legislation, and all leading to what end? To the maintenance in idleness of the worthless population of four great cities, a population which every wise legislator would have sought by every means in his power to divert from the cities, to lead back into the country, to marry to the land, to raise to something of the dignity of manhood by that wrestling with nature for her blessings, which makes up the daily life of agriculture. But no: the old legal fiction of the sovereignty of the Roman people still survived, and therefore the so‐ called citizen of Rome – the descendant in all probability of a Syrian or Cappadocian slave – must be allowed to spend his days in lordly idleness, seeing the charioteers drive, and the gladiators die, and then presenting himself at the appointed time at the steps of his *regio* to receive his *panis gradilis* from the bounty of the emperor. And, to accomplish this desirable end, the administrative energies of the declining Empire must be weighted with the duties of a vast and complicated commissariat alike in peace and in war.

5 DESTRUCTION OF THE MIDDLE CLASS BY THE FISCAL OPPRESSION OF THE CURIALES

We have seen how the social and political system of Rome tended to destroy the free labourers in the country, and to degrade them in the great cities. We have now to consider that system of fiscal oppression by which the Empire crushed out the life of the middle classes in the provincial towns. A great French statesman, who has treated of this subject with a fullness of know‐ ledge drawn both from books and from practical politics, considers that this cause was more powerful than all others in bringing about the ruin of Rome.†

* Some of this legislation has reference to Constantinople, but similar arrangements would probably be in force at Rome.
† Guizot in his *Essais sur l'histoire de France*, 'Du régime municipal dans l'Empire Romain au Ve siècle de l'ère chrétienne'.

The civilisation of the great republic was essentially a municipal civilisation. An urban community herself, she naturally associated herself with
other urban communities, and wherever her influence has profoundly and
permanently modified the life of any modern people, it will be found that
that people is, by choice and not from the mere force of economic laws,
urban in its tastes and its habits. The towns of Italy and of the provinces
possessed, during the ages of the republic, very various privileges, and
stood in very various relations to the sovereign city. Some were *coloniae*, own
children of Rome, some were *municipia*, stranger towns, gathered within the
circle of 'the Roman friendship or subjection'. But as the power of the
emperors grew, and as the forms of popular government by assemblies of
the citizens at Rome faded into insignificance, the diversities of privilege
between the various cities of the Empire faded also. Political power was
now all gathered up into one centre, and lodged in the hands of one single
man, the Augustus at Rome, who might delegate it to prefect or vicar, as he
chose. But municipal freedom still existed – that is to say, during the first
three centuries after the Christian era – and municipal power was lodged in
the hands of magistrates, freely chosen by the persons who owned as much
as fifteen acres (twenty-five *jugera*) in the borough or district round it. The
affairs of the little republic were managed by an assembly modelled upon
the senate of Rome itself. It was called sometimes the senate, sometimes the
curia, and its members, who obtained a seat as the Roman senators did, by
filling some office in the state, were called *decuriones*, possibly because there
were originally ten minor *curiae* of ten members each, thus furnishing a total
of one hundred members to the senate. In the large towns, however, this
number was often exceeded. Marquardt points out that at Antioch the
number of *decuriones* varied from 1,200 at its best estate to sixty at its worst.
The sepulchral inscriptions, which we now see in such numbers in the Italian museums, recording that the dead man was a *decurio* of his native town,
show that the title was, for several centuries, one which conferred a certain
amount of social distinction on the holder, and we may perhaps say that the
DEC of these Latin epigraphs corresponds to the ESQ. of an English
churchyard.

Thus, during these early centuries of the Empire, the local government
of the towns was both in name and in fact republican. We need only recur
to some familiar examples in the Acts of the Apostles, to understand how
these municipal liberties existed side by side with the great machine of the
Imperial administration, independent in their own sphere, yet trembling

lest by any unauthorised proceeding they should be brought within its far-reaching and heavy stroke. The praetors of Philippi are afraid when their lictors bring them word that the men whom they have scourged and thrust into prison are Roman citizens. The seven 'politarchs' of Thessalonica are troubled when the mob of lewd fellows of the baser sort come surging round them, accusing the inmates of Jason's house of acting contrary to the decrees of Caesar, and teaching that there is another king, one Jesus. The recorder of Ephesus is anxious that the dispute between Paul and the silver-smiths should be determined in a legal manner before the tribunal of the proconsul of Asia, and that the authorities of the city should not have to answer difficult interrogatories as to the cause of the tumultuary assembly in the theatre. Continually we find ourselves in presence of real and living, though somewhat precarious, forms of local self-government.

The first two centuries and a half of the Empire may be perhaps considered as the golden age of the *municipia*, and the large amount of prosperity and happiness thus secured to the middle classes of society was probably the chief cause of the admitted success of the Imperial administration during the greater part of that period. Numerous laws were passed in favour of the municipalities. They were permitted to receive, and probably did receive, large gifts and bequests of property from their members. Fraud practised upon them by one of their officials was made equivalent, not to simple theft, but to the heavier offence of peculation. The decurions were exempted from capital punishment for every crime but that of parricide. Finally, the municipal treasury, devoted to the construction and mainte-nance of great public works, roads, bridges, temples and theatres, and to the celebration of the solemn public sacrifices, was easily kept full, and had not as yet attracted the avaricious regards of the emperors, who 'found the treasures of Rome and the ordinary contributions of the provinces suffice for the needs, and even for the follies, of the central power'.* From the brightness of this picture some abatement must doubtless be made, as regards the seventy years of anarchy and confusion which intervened between the death of Caracalla and the accession of Diocletian (217–84). It is not possible that when mutiny, rebellion, and civil war were the chronic condition of the Empire, the municipalities can have enjoyed the full measure of their former prosperity. But whatever they may have suffered in this way was probably irregular and exceptional. It could scarcely yet be

* Guizot, *Essais sur l'histoire de France*, 'Du régime municipal dans l'Empire Romain au Ve siècle de l'ère chrétienne'.

said, as far as the *curiales* were concerned, that the throne of the emperors was 'a throne of iniquity framing mischief by a law'.

This last and fatal phase in the history of the municipalities was prob-ably, in great measure, the result of the remodelling of the Empire by Dio-cletian. That great statesman saw that some change was needed if the Empire was not to be rent asunder by the hands of its own children. The changes which he accordingly introduced have been already briefly described.* These changes answered their immediate purpose. The Roman Empire was held together for another century and a half, but it gained life at the cost of the means of living. According to the old fable, Phaethon, when entrusted with the chariot of the sun-god, drove it too near to the earth and began rapidly to dry up all the pools and fountains of waters. Even so now, the Imperial majesty, of which flatterers had made a kind of god upon earth, appearing in all the vigour of its new administrative powers close to every portion of the Empire, began at once to dry up many a reservoir of wealth which had escaped the rapacity of former emperors. Especially was this true of the funds hitherto devoted to the purposes of local self-government. These, which the *curiae* had hitherto not only raised, but ad-ministered, were now diverted to the Imperial exchequer to provide for the pomp of the palace, the salaries of the swarms of new officials, and the dona-tives to the legions, while the strictly useful and reproductive expenditure on roads and bridges, and other local needs, fell day by day into abeyance.†

In the happier days of the municipalities, plenty of citizens had generally been found ready and anxious to discharge, even at some cost to themselves, the civic functions of their little republics. The example of England, and still more that of America, proves that where there exists a large and flour-ishing middle class, endowed with local self-government, money is for the most part freely forthcoming for the wants of the community. When the state is at peace, that healthy emulation which exists between citizens, and that desire to emerge from the ranks, which is natural to men, leads one to build a bridge, another to establish a library, a third to endow a school, a fourth to spend lavishly on the duties of his mayoralty, and so on. The same disposition had, no doubt, existed in the *curiae* throughout the Roman Empire. But now a new competitor for the generosity of the citizens appeared in the shape of the Christian church, perpetually increasing the

* See vol. i, pp. 9–10.

† This must be taken as an inference from the general course of legislation rather than as an established fact.

sumptuousness of her worship, perpetually widening the sphere of her duties as public almoner, and, for both objects, claiming and receiving large oblations from the wealthy. The parish now competed with the *curia*, and the benevolent citizen who would have built an aqueduct in the second century, founded a church in the third.

And simultaneously with this new diversion of the funds of the charitable, the great Imperial mendicant drew nigh to the impoverished *curia*, but speaking now with an altered tone, and saying no longer 'If you like', but 'You must'. We see the results of the pressure which now began to be put upon the municipalities, but the exact manner of its working does not seem to be disclosed to us. An impost called the *aurum coronarium* [golden wreath], which had once been purely a free-will offering occasionally given by the cities to the Roman generals, was now a regular tax paid by the decurions as such, and by them only. The other taxes, which were assessed afresh every fifteen years throughout the whole Empire, were levied upon the *curia* in its collective capacity, and if any member made default, his fellow decurions must make good the deficiency. Under the pressure of this continually increasing taxation, some lands went out of cultivation altogether, since there was no profit left for the proprietor after the claims of the state were satisfied. So much the more taxes must the surrounding proprietors pay, to make up for the loss to the treasury from those unsown acres.* It is evident that when once this process had reached a certain stage, the load of taxation on the proprietors who still endeavoured to bear it would increase, not in arithmetical, but in geometrical proportion, and life would become nothing but a cruel race between the tax-collector and his victim.

The inevitable result followed. The *curiae*, which had once been honoured and envied communities, easily bearing the weight of their public duties, and dispensing comfort and happiness to the district round them, were now mere gaols in which the middle classes were shut up from birth till death, to toil for the Imperial treasury. The dignity of decurion, or *curialis* as he was now often called, was no longer bestowed on the most worthy by the suffrages of his fellow citizens. It was a charge descending from the

* Possibly, as far as each particular district was concerned, this burden might be to some extent relieved at the next assessment at which, theoretically at least, account was taken of the productive capacities of every province in the Empire. But as the taxes were not diminishing, but increasing, if this process of throwing lands out of cultivation on account of the rapacity of the tax-gatherer was going on extensively throughout the Empire, it is evident that the landholders who remained must have had to bear a rapidly accumulating burden.

father to the son, which the son, however anxious to be freed from it, could not renounce.* The longest 'title' (as it is called) in the Theodosian Code, is that which contains the 188 laws, passed during 150 years, concerning the rights and duties of the decurions. Of their rights perhaps eight laws speak, of their duties the remaining 180, and that in tones of inflexible severity. The perpetually recurring expression, 'the son of a curial must be bound to the *curia*', formulated as it is with the word *mancipetur*, which we know so well by its opposite, emancipation, shows sufficiently how griev⁄ous a burden the service of the municipalities was considered. It is true that more than once we meet with a proviso that no one is to be condemned to enter the ranks of the decurions as a punishment.† 'The splendour of the *curiae*' is said to be dear to the Imperial heart, and 'a criminal should be visited with punishment, not with an accession of dignity'; but this hypo⁄critical pretence can deceive no one who reads the laws by which this enactment is preceded and followed, and who sees therein the perpetual struggle of the middle classes to escape from their connection with the *curiae*, and the ruthless determination with which emperors and prefects force them back into that hateful prison⁄house.

No provincial governor on his own authority might excuse a decurion from his municipal obligations on the score of poverty.‡ The emperor reserved to himself alone the exercise of this prerogative. Small, certainly, was the probability that a citizen, too poor to pay his curial dues, would be able to defray the expense of a journey to Rome in order to obtain this exemption. And yet their chronic misery may have urged many to under⁄take this painful pilgrimage, for we find another edict whereby they were forbidden to visit the emperor on public or private business without the leave of the governor of the province in which they dwelt.§ The prohibi⁄tion went further: they were forbidden to take any kind of journey, lest they should defraud the *curia* of their services, and for the same reason they were forbidden to leave the cities and take up their residence in the country.¶ That free circulation of the citizens, which makes the life of modern states,

---

* It would seem probable that with this degradation in the rank of the decurions, the body which they formed lost the position of a local senate which it had previously occu⁄pied. This, however, we cannot prove from the language of the laws. Only, a new class among the decurions, the *principales*, seems to hold something like the same position towards the rest of the community which the decurions held formerly.
† *Codex Theodosianus*, xii.1.66 and 108.   ‡ *Codex Theodosianus*, xii.1.1.
§ *Codex Theodosianus*, xii.1.9.   ¶ *Codex Theodosianus*, xii.1.143, 144; xii.18.

was a crime in the eyes of the Imperial legislator, because it interfered with his machinery of fiscal extortion.

Nothing gives us a more convincing proof of the utterly unbearable condition of the *curiales* than the continual efforts which they made to divest themselves of their status, and the storm of Imperial edicts by which they were constantly met and driven back into their *curiae*. In truth, the whole series of this legislation seems like an attempt to compress an incompressible fluid, or in some similar way to violate the fundamental laws of physics.

The decurion was not to be allowed to rise into the profession of an advocate, lest he should thereby obtain exemption from his curial obligations; for the same reason he was not to be allowed to descend into the guild of the *centonarii*;* nor should he be permitted to farm the taxes of the province, lest in case of his default, the emperor and the *curia* might find themselves opposing creditors of a bankrupt estate. If a decurion married a female slave, as the offspring of such a marriage would be incapable of representing him in the *curia*, he himself was to be banished to a distant island, his slave-wife to be sent to work in the mines, and his property to pass to his next of kin, upon whom would devolve his obligations to the *curia*.

It might have been thought that when every Teutonic and Scythian nationality from the Caspian to the Scheldt was pouring down upon the Empire, when the Romans were 'ringed around with barking dogs of war',† the mustering of men for the battlefield would have been an object of primary importance with their rulers, and that if an oppressive conscription were not resorted to, at least every volunteer would be eagerly welcomed. By no means: the maintenance of the *curia*, as a taxing-machine in a state of efficiency, was the first consideration, for upon this depended the splendour of the Imperial household, and the rapid fortunes of prefects and counts.

To escape from the misery of their lot as bondslaves of a bankrupt municipality, the decurions, who were legally bound to serve in a kind of local force, the *militia cohortalis*, thronged in multitudes into the regular army, the *militia armata*. Law after law was passed with tedious reiteration, forbidding the officers to enlist any man who is under curial obligations, prescribing the form in which each recruit is to declare his freedom from

---

* The *collegia* [guilds] of *centonarii* were fire-brigades. The firemen were called *centonarii* from the *centones* or coverings made of rags, which were steeped in water and used for extinguishing fires or protecting neighbouring buildings.
† Claudian, *In Eutropium*, ii.486.

such liability, and insisting on the dragging back into the *curia* of such decurions as might after all have crept through all this mesh-work of opposing edicts into the army. True, if any had already served for fifteen years in the army, he was to be safe from further pursuit; but then, on the other hand, look at this provision: 'If any man of military descent shall enlist in the *militia cohortalis*, and if, with strength yet unbroken, he shall put forward the plea of advanced age, or by reason of weakness shall be judged unfit for the work of war, he shall be drawn forth from the lurking-place of his cowardice, and bound over to the duties of the *curiae*.'* The bondage of the *curia* – that was the Chelsea Hospital which Rome provided for her broken-down soldiers in the year 380 under the auspices of Theodosius.

The church as well as the army offered a door of escape from curial obligations. We are not surprised at finding the pagan emperor Julian closing this door and decreeing that 'decurions, who as Christians' (whereby clergymen are probably intended) 'decline the offices of their township, are to be recalled'.† But if any different strain of legislation was hoped for from a pious emperor like Theodosius, the convener of the second council, the glory and defence of the Catholic church, such hopes were doomed to disappointment. 'Those *curiales*', says he, 'who prefer to serve the churches rather than their *curiae*, if they wish to be that which they simulate, let them scorn to withdraw their property from the service of their country. For we will certainly not liberate them on any other condition than this, that they renounce their patrimonies. Since it is not becoming that souls which are devoted to the contemplation of God should feel any regret at the loss of their ancestral property' (383).‡

It is true that some years later (390) an exemption is made on behalf of those who have already entered the ranks of the clergy. 'He who before the second consulship of my mildness'§ (the mildness of him who in that very year ordered the massacre at Thessalonica) 'has reached the eminence of presbyter, or undertaken the ministry of deacon, or the office of exorcist, may keep all his patrimony safe and free from curial bonds. But he who, under whatever name, shall have betaken himself to the religious ministrations of divine worship after the date of my aforesaid consulship, let him know that he must give up the whole of his patrimony.'¶

Other laws, of an earlier as well as a later date than those which have been quoted, enacted that the curial cleric should be withdrawn from his

* *Codex Theodosianus*, xii.1.83.   † *Codex Theodosianus*, xii.1.50.
‡ *Codex Theodosianus*, xii.1.104.   § AD 388.   ¶ *Codex Theodosianus*, xii.1.121.

sacred profession and restored to the civic duties from which he had absconded. Such a provision, which shows that the ecclesiastical hierarchy, however powerful, was still far from occupying the position which she held in the days of Hildebrand, must surely have clashed against even the then existing canons of the church. No instances however seem to be forthcoming, to show in what way this conflict of laws was settled.

The monks, if *curiales*, were handled by the state even more roughly than the clergy. It should be stated however that the decree which is next to follow was issued by the emperor Valens, who, as an Arian, had special reasons for hating the enthusiastically Athanasian monks of Egypt at whom it is principally aimed (365).

'Certain lovers of idleness, deserting their civic duties, affect solitary and secret places, and under the guise of religion are collected together with the assemblies of the lonely-livers. We have therefore, on deliberation, commanded that all these, and men like them, if taken in Egypt, shall be drawn forth from their hiding-places by the count of the East, and shall be recalled to undergo the charges of their native districts, or else, by virtue of this law, shall be deprived of the delights of their possessions, which, it is our pleasure, shall be claimed by those who have to undertake the charge of the public functions.'*

Besides the church and the army another career, if he only could succeed in entering it, seemed to promise to the aspiring curial an exemption from the crushing load of municipal liability. This was service in the vast Imperial households, for the *palatinus* of whatever rank was not only entitled, as has been already seen, to share in the corn-largesses; he was also, as the servant of the emperor, free from 'mancipation' to any other master. And in this way, no doubt, many thousands of decurions managed to evade the onerous obligations of local self-government. There is a long series of vacillating decrees bearing on the case of these men. According to one edict thirty years' prescription was necessary, according to others, five years sufficed, to prevent the dreaded sentence, 'Let him be dragged back to his *curia*.' The general impression left on the mind by these decrees is that they soon became waste parchment, the theory of government requiring that the rights of the *curia* should be insisted upon, while in practice the favour of the sovereign was powerful enough to shield from curial pursuit the members of his household. Theodosius (or Valentinian II), however, once breaks forth into a strain of sublime indignation against those who

* *Codex Theodosianus*, xii.1.63.

trusted to this means of deliverance (386). 'Let the *curiales* who have supposed that they could be defended by the privilege of our household be
dragged back to their *curia*, so that they may be "mancipated" to their
proper functions and may repair the public losses. Nevertheless if any of
these shall be proved to owe anything to our divine household, let him pay
it.'* This noble sacrifice by the emperor of everybody else to the necessities
of the country, coupled with the sharpest attention to the interests of his
own 'divine household', is characteristic of the legislation of that period.

From this general survey of the laws relating to the decurions it will be
seen that we have here a state of things not altogether unlike that which
existed in France before the revolution. A court and a *noblesse* above,†
exempt from the heaviest part of the national taxation, and with their
hands forever in the national exchequer: below, a people robbed and
spoiled, *taillable et corvéable à merci*, that is, without mercy and without fore-
sight, and consequently some of the most fertile countries in the world
brought by the tax-gatherer to the verge of starvation. The difference
between the two cases is that in France *taille* and corvée reached down to the
very lowest of the people: in the Roman Empire, the slaves and the plebeians (as the class of freemen who lacked the curial qualification were
called) were not shut up in the taxing-pen of the *curia*. It was essentially an
oppression of the middle classes that was thus carried on; but a century and
a half of this steady, persevering tyranny had so ground down the once
prosperous and thriving decurions, that it may be doubted whether they
were not, when the Western Empire fell, practically lower than the lowest
of the proletariat.

M. Guizot mentions two privileges which were left to the *curiales*, and
which, he thinks, may have been some slight compensation for their many
miseries.

(1) Freedom from corporal punishment. We find certainly several laws
which appear to concede this privilege to the decurions. Especially is it forbidden to chastise them with the *plumbatae*, the scourge with lumps of metal
knotted into its thongs, which was ordinarily used for the chastisement of
slaves. One remarkable law, passed in the year 381, says, 'Let all judges and
governors of provinces abstain from usurping a power which does not
belong to them, and let them know that absolutely no *principalis* nor decurion, whatever fault or error he may have committed, is to be submitted to

* *Codex Theodosianus*, xii.1.114.
† Official, it is true, rather than, as in France, hereditary.

the torments of the *plumbatae*. Should perchance any judge hereafter break forth into such pertinacity of forbidden madness as to dare to subject a *principalis* and a decurion, a man who is, so to speak, the senator of his *curia*, to the strokes of the *plumbatae*, let him be condemned to pay a fine of twenty pounds of gold [£800], and branded with perpetual infamy so that not even a special rescript of our own shall suffice to remove the stigma. The officer who has administered the chastisement shall be forced to pay a fine of fifty pounds of gold [£2,000] inasmuch as, the command of the judge being unlawful, we give him full liberty to disobey it.'* This lawgiver seems to be in earnest, and the provision for inflicting a heavier fine on the actual wielder of the lash than on his master seems cleverly contrived to prevent the perpetration of the outrage. But one may doubt, from the frequent reappearance of similar provisions in the [Theodosian] Code, whether the immunity from stripes – which was, after all, theoretically the privilege of every Roman citizen – was practically enjoyed by 'the decurion, the senator of his *curia*'. For by later edicts (387 and 392) Theodosius expressly enacts that decurions, who have been guilty of malversation in respect of the public moneys,† or 'who owe anything'‡ – a category which would of course include those whose taxes were in arrear – may be punished with the *plumbatae*. As in Egypt at the present day§ the bastinado, applied to the elders of the village, extracts the intolerable tax from the unfortunate fellah, so doubtless, many a time, in the last century of the Empire, did the cruel blows of the *plumbatae* wring the last denarius out of the coffers of the decurion.

(2) A more substantial privilege doubtless, though from its nature attainable by few, was the prospect of entering the senate, and so passing from the class of the oppressed into that of the oppressors. An inhabitant of one of the more important municipalities,¶ who was possessed of large means, and had steadily climbed the ladder of official dignities in his native town, having finally attained the rank of presiding duumvir, was to be considered free from all further curial obligations, to hold the rank of an ex-count, and with the title of *clarissimus*, had the right of a seat in the innermost circle at the public games, and the governor of the province was

---

* *Codex Theodosianus*, xii.1.85.   † *Codex Theodosianus*, xii.1.117.
‡ *Codex Theodosianus*, xii.1.126.   § Written in 1879: happily no longer true in 1892.
¶ This qualification is not expressed in the [Theodosian] Code, but we can hardly suppose that the presiding magistrate of a mere village would be entitled to claim rank as an ex-comes.

bound to salute him with a kiss. Last and most important, an entrance was permitted him into the Roman senate, 'the noblest *curia* of all', but apparently on condition of his leaving a son, or some other substitute, to represent him in the *curia* from which he emerged.

Often it would occur that a wealthy and popular curial, by official favour or by bribing his fellow townsmen, would succeed in missing some steps of the slow ascent, and would present himself in the senate-house at Rome before he was duly qualified. In such a case, said the emperor Constantius (361) —

'The decurions who shirk their own duties and betake themselves to the fellowship of our senate shall be struck off the roll of that body, and "mancipated" to their own cities. Those, however, who have served the office of praetor' (which involved heavy expenses in connection with the praetorian games exhibited to the people) 'may remain in the senate, but must restore any moneys which they may have abstracted from our Imperial exchequer, or from the bowels of the municipalities.'* Many similar laws follow, some of which ingeniously fasten on such premature senators a double pecuniary obligation, first as curial, and, second, as senator. A yet harsher tone is observable in the following law, passed in the year 398 by Arcadius, emperor of the East.†

'All the *curiales* are to abide in their original *curiae*, their duties to which are of perpetual obligation. Those who by fraud or popular canvassing have clambered up into the place of high administrators and rulers of provinces, are to be at once deprived of the honours which they have obtained, and not only with swift and strong hand drawn back to their own *curia*, and made to serve all its offices from the very beginning, but shall also be mulcted in half their patrimony.' But, by an edict which was published shortly after, these stringent provisions were somewhat modified in the case of a curial who had obtained senatorial rank 'before the ides of November, in the fourth consulship of Lord Honorius Augustus, brother of my eternity, and his colleague Eutychianus'.

'Brother of my eternity': such was the pompous style in which the imbecile Arcadius spoke of the imbecile Honorius. It was time for our Teutonic kinsman, Alaric, to tear down the purple hangings of Empire, and let in the fresh air of reality upon those chambers reeking with flattery and falsehood.

One last exemption must be noticed, which points to the dwindling

* *Codex Theodosianus*, xii.1.48.   † *Codex Theodosianus*, xii.1.159 and 160.

state of the population of the provinces, but which rests on a basis of humanity and good sense. It was enacted by the emperor Julian (363), 'He who is the father of thirteen children not only shall not be summoned to the *curia*, but even though he be a decurion, shall be left in an honoured rest' (undisturbed by the summons to undertake any curial duty).*

From the sketch, necessarily brief and imperfect, which has been here given of the decline and fall of the municipalities of the Empire, the reader can in some degree estimate for himself the share which their altered condition had in bringing about the ruin of the Empire itself. In Gaul, in Spain, in Italy, the exhaustion and impoverishment of the middle classes was, in the fifth century, so great that it had become a matter almost of indifference who ruled over them, a grandson of Theodosius, the Suevic count Ricimer, the Herulian Odovacar, or Theodoric the Ostrogoth. Their condition could not be worse under the barbarian than under the crushing, organised, relentless tyranny of the Roman bureaucracy. It might be, and as far as Odovacar and Theodoric were concerned it probably was, better.

In the East no doubt the same process of exhaustion went on, but the fortunate push from without was wanting. In Egypt and in Syria the Arabs, fresh from the desert, easily overturned, amid shouts of *Lo Ellah il Allah!*† the pallid resemblances of GraecoRoman municipalities. In the other provinces of the Byzantine Empire they still cumbered the ground with the spectacle of their decay until the close of the ninth century, when Leo VI, surnamed 'the philosopher', removed from the theory of the constitution both the senate of the Empire and the *curiae* of the towns. Of the latter he said, 'The ancient laws passed as to the *curiae* and decurions impose on the decurions intolerable burdens, and confer on the *curiae* the right to nominate certain magistrates, and to govern the cities by their own authority. Now that civil affairs have taken another form, and that all things depend entirely on the care and government of the Imperial majesty, these laws wander, so to speak, vainly and without object, around the soil of legality. We therefore abolish them by the present decree.'‡

In the West, the agony of the *municipia* had been shorter, and the remembrance of the days of their prosperity and usefulness was therefore less easily effaced. It would be an interesting task, but one outside of our present field, to show how, under the barbarian kings, aided in many cases by the influence of the church, the *curiae* rose again, as it were, from the tomb, until, in

* *Codex Theodosianus*, xii.1.55.   † [There is no God but God!]
‡ *Novellae Leonis*, 46.

the twelfth, thirteenth, and fourteenth centuries, local self-government, as set forth in the Italian commune, reached, perhaps, the noblest elevation at which the world has seen, or is likely to see it. An almost equally note-worthy tribute to the memory of the old municipal organisation is paid from a different quarter. To this day the mightiest ecclesiastical organisa-tion in the world, that which gives birth to popes, and defies or bargains with emperors, calls itself the Roman curia.

6 BARBAROUS FINANCE

The local taxation of the Empire has been dwelt upon at considerable length, because its history can be easily traced from the statute book, and because in tracing that history we can clearly see a powerful degrading influence at work upon an important class of the community.

The history of the Imperial taxation is in some respects more obscure, and to give a detailed description of it would require more space than can here be afforded. But, tried by its results, it may without hesitation be con-demned as wasteful, oppressive, and, in one word, barbarous. The more one examines into the subject the more one is convinced that great as the Romans were in legislation, and great in war, in finance their genius was below mediocrity. To violently wrest the whole or a large part of the lands of a conquered people from their former owners and appropriate them to the Roman state, to destroy great seats of industry and commerce like Corinth or Carthage, and bring their gold and silver and works of art home to figure in a Roman triumph, this easy system of momentary self-enrichment the senate and its officers were able to put in practice. But to develop, as some of the Ptolemies and some of the Tudors developed, the commercial wealth of their people, to plant wisely and water diligently the tree of manufacturing or agricultural prosperity, from which the state itself might in the time of fruit-bearing pluck a golden reward, this was a kind of enterprise for which the genius of the Roman nation was little suited, and though it cannot be said to have been never attempted, it certainly seldom succeeded in Roman hands.

It is unfortunately quite impossible to determine with any approach to accuracy the amount of the revenue of the Empire, but the conjectures of scholars who have examined carefully into the subject point to a sum of between £20 million and £30 million sterling as the probable total under the emperors. It is true that we cannot say what amount of local taxation may have existed side by side with this. But in itself the amount does not seem a crushing weight for a population of perhaps ninety million, inhabit/ ing such countries as France, Spain, and Italy are now, as Turkey in Europe, Asia Minor, Syria, Egypt, and the northern shore of Africa were before the domination of the Mussulman had blasted them. It is difficult to resist the conclusion that a modern scientific financier, keeping a wise equipoise between direct and indirect taxation, and carefully arranging his duties so as to take only a reasonable toll from the vast commerce of the Mediterranean countries, could have easily provided for the state a revenue twice as large as she seems to have actually received, without crushing out the happiness of her subjects.

But the Roman financiers seem to have relied most on the worst kind of taxation, and to have levied it in the most wasteful and oppressive manner. Unfortunately we have no specimen of the budget of a count of the sacred largesses which we can submit to a modern chancellor of the exchequer for his criticisms. But it is almost certain that the *portoria* or customs duties, varying from two to five per cent, and ultimately reaching as high as twelve and a half per cent, did not contribute an important part of the revenues of the Empire. The *vicesima hereditatum*, a succession duty of five per cent, seems to have been enforced with some hesitation, and to have been finally abandoned in the sixth century on account of its unpopularity. Yet as the duty was not paid when the property devolved upon very near relations, few taxes, one would think, could have been more easily justified, or should have been more inflexibly demanded. The *vicesima libertatis*, a tax of five per cent on the value of every liberated slave, was probably, in the existing state of Roman society, a wise impost, as tending to prevent the dilution of the ranks of Roman citizens by too large an accession of freedmen, and it brought in a considerable revenue to the state. It was, moreover, essentially a tax on luxuries, for to be surrounded by a troop of obsequious freedmen was one of the most common forms of ostentation among the Roman nobility. But when we read in the pages of Juvenal, Athenaeus, and Taci/ tus, of the portentous and childish expenditure of that nobility on other luxuries, we see that here was a field from which a modern financier would have reaped an abundant harvest. He would not have issued sumptuary edicts nor attempted by legislation to check the torrent of extravagance, but he would have said in fact to these men, the owners of half a province and the lords of an army of slaves, 'Since it pleases you to spend such vast sums on all sorts of ridiculous fantasies, spend them by all means, but give the state a share of your superfluity.' The licences and assessed taxes which an English minister of finance would have imposed upon the Roman senators would have fed many legions.

But the sheet-anchor of the Imperial financiers was evidently the share, the oppressive share, of produce which they wrested from the cultivator of the soil. In some countries this had been originally looked upon as land-tax properly so called, in others it had been treated as rent for land appropriated by the Roman people but suffered to remain in the possession of the former owners as their tenants. In some it had been originally a tithe, in others it had been spoken of as tribute. But it will probably be safe to say that these differences had now, in the fourth and fifth centuries, become mere matters of antiquarian interest. The various populations of the Empire, Italian and provincial, Greek and Sicilian, Asiatic and African, were all now theoret-ically free and practically miserable. Every fifteen years, that great revision of taxable value, called the indiction, took place throughout the Empire. Then the few who had prospered found themselves assessed on the higher value which their lands had acquired, while the many who were sinking down into poverty, obtained, it is to be feared, but little relief from taxation on account of the higher rate which was charged to all. They might be assessed on fewer *capita*, but each *caput* was larger on account of the increas-ing needs of the Imperial exchequer. This periodical reassessment was evidently one of the most important features of the inner life of the Empire, and was aptly expressed by the habit of dating each year from its place in the indiction.*

In the breathless race between the taxpayer and the tax-gatherer which financial administration became during the decay of the Empire, the inher-ent vices of the Roman system of collecting the revenue grew more and more apparent. Whether because the republic despaired of finding absolutely honest collectors among her own citizens, because she deemed it impossible for anything but the keen self-interest of a contractor to cope with the self-interest of the cultivator of the land, or because the simplicity of an auction of the taxes commended itself to the rude fiscal notions of her statesmen – whatever may have been the cause, certain it is that the tithes

---

* The indictions began under Constantine in the year 312. According to the usage then prevalent, 313 would be called the first indiction, 314 the second indiction, and so on. It was not till the twelfth century that the obvious plan of numbering the periods (according to which 312–27 would be the first indiction, 327–42 the second indiction, and so on) was introduced.

and all other forms of land-tax seem to have been, from the beginning to the end of the Roman domination, farmed out to men who bore the well-known and hated name of *publicani*. Many familiar passages in the New Testament show the aversion with which the subordinate ranks of this great corporation were regarded by the provincials. An often-quoted passage in Livy shows that the senate itself, at a comparatively early period, had perceived that the vast powers for extortion wielded by the publicans were quite incompatible with the existence of real liberty among the subject-allies of Rome.* Finlay, the historian of Greece, has traced in many pages of his history the disastrous effect of the system of tithes and tithe-farming upon both Greece and Turkey, and speaks of this system as an undoubted legacy, and a fatal one, from the Roman Empire.† If we had the materials in

* [This] was the opinion expressed by the senate when the organisation of the province of Macedonia was under discussion, 167 BC (Livy xlv.18.5).

† Compare particularly vi.13. 'From the moment that the crops began to ripen, the property of the cultivator in nine-tenths of it was treated as a matter subsidiary to the arrangement relative to the disposal of the remaining tenth which belonged to the sovereign. An industrious peasant could rarely make any profit by raising an early crop or by improving the quality of his produce ... No superiority of skill or increase of labour could under such circumstances secure a higher price ... The effects of this system of taxation on the condition of Greek agriculture may still be studied in the dominions of the Turkish sultan or the Greek king, for they rival one another in the disastrous effects of their fiscal administration [AD 1859].'

The wastefulness, though not the oppression, of a system of *publicani* is further shown by the following extract from a letter to *The Times*. It appears from this letter that the system is still the curse of Italy:

Let me mention one more reason for Italian poverty – the oppressive and absurd fiscal laws and the pernicious system of farming the taxes, a system which wrenches from the most necessitous classes from thirty to fifty per cent more taxation than is necessary. I will give one example of this, in the ruinous system of *octroi* taxes. I know a small town of about two thousand inhabitants, the taxes (*octroi*) of which are let for sixteen thousand francs the year. The farmer annually makes a profit of from five thousand to six thousand francs. The town is miserably poor, yet the wretched inhabitants have to pay this heavy sum more than is needful if the taxes were collected in a proper manner. Most of the other taxes are farmed in a similar fashion. The drain upon the community, and especially the poor, can be easily imagined.

I am, sir, your obedient servant,

SOUTHERN ITALY.

27th September, 1879.

And a letter from Angora [Ankara] (28th September, 1879) describes in the old familiar

our possession for a complete picture of the financial administration of Con‑
stantine or Theodosius, we should no doubt find that the wasteful oppression
of the *publicanus* was the main cause why so large an amount of suffering
among the peasantry produced, comparatively, so small a revenue to the state.

The phenomena of commercial life in classical antiquity are not easy to
understand. We are told that banking business had reached a high develop‑
ment both in Greece and Italy; that bills of exchange were constantly drawn
and remitted from one part of the Empire to another; that the bankers
(τραπεζῖται in Greece, *argentarii* at Rome) were in the habit of receiving
money on deposit, and relending it on overdrawn account. And yet, on the
other hand, we hear constantly of exorbitant sums being paid for interest.
Twelve and a half per cent is mentioned as a frequent rate in Rome, and
twenty‑four per cent as charged in Sicily. The latter rate, it is true, was
exacted by the tyrannical Verres, but it is far surpassed by the righteous
Brutus, who exacted forty‑eight per cent from the provincials of Cyprus. At
all times of the republic and Empire *aes alienum* (borrowed money) is spoken
of as a fruitful source of danger to the state, and the debtor never seems to
have a fair chance of emancipating himself from the yoke of the creditor.
These are all indications of a state of things in which the usurer rather than
the banker is the chief loan‑monger,* and they almost entitle us to say
(whatever indications to the contrary may be afforded by scattered passages
in the classics) that the true business of a banker – the acting as a broker
between those classes of the community which desire to lend and those
classes which desire to borrow – cannot have been understood, or if under‑
stood, cannot have been widely practised in the Roman Empire.

---

language the odious occupation of the publican and the horrible wastefulness of the tithe‑
farming system as practised in Asia Minor (*The Times*, 18th October, 1879).

* Thus distinguished. The usurer, as such, lends from his own capital; the banker, as
such, from the deposits of his customers. The usurer, therefore, if he wishes to make fif‑
teen per cent on his capital, can only do it by charging fifteen per cent to his customers.
The banker may make the same percentage while only charging three per cent to his cus‑
tomers, if a sum of money equivalent to fifteen times his capital be deposited with him at
two per cent. The usurer's best chance of profit is in being able to foreclose on oppressive
terms his debtor's mortgage. The banker, who has ever before his eyes the necessity of a
prompt repayment of his deposits, dreads few things more than the necessity of foreclos‑
ing a mortgage and so 'locking up' part of the funds entrusted to him. Thus, without
supposing the latter to be a bit more generous or less selfish than the former, he is led by
mere self‑interest into a course of dealing which gives the borrower a chance of recovering
himself from the burden of *aes alienum*.

It would be an interesting speculation to enquire what would have been the effect of a national debt – that distinguishing feature of modern political finance – in retarding or accelerating the ruin of the Empire. The first and second Punic wars seem to have been fought out to a successful issue by the senate chiefly by means of a loan, disguised under a gigantic debasement of the currency. The *as*, which was then the unit of monetary value, and which was coined out of a pound of copper when the quarrel with Carthage commenced, consisted of only one *uncia* (the twelfth part of a pound), when the dispute was settled, sixty-three years later, on the field of Zama. The disastrous effect of such a sweeping alteration in the standard of value was perhaps mitigated by the partial substitution of a silver currency for one of copper. But though the state had thus made a disguised loan from its subjects, and though at times it may have borrowed inconsiderable sums of money for short periods from the *publicani*, no such institution as a permanent national debt ever existed, or perhaps ever suggested itself as possible to the state financiers. On some great emergencies, such as the reception of the Visigothic refugees within the limits of the Empire in 376, a loan on a large scale might have been a prudent and statesmanlike measure. The secure investment thus offered to those provincials who were shut out from the great money markets of Rome and Alexandria, might have stimulated thrift. And it is almost certain that the rulers of the Empire, had they periodically appeared before their subjects as borrowers, would have been more amenable to the legitimate influence of public opinion. Flatterers might persuade a frantic debauchee that he was pious, and unconquered, and fortunate, up to the very moment when he was ripe for assassination; but a decline in the Imperial funds of ten per cent would have been an unmistakable proof that he was losing the confidence of his subjects.

Arguments like these might be advanced to show that the existence of the Empire would have been prolonged by the device of national indebtedness. On the other hand, we see, by abundant evidence in the history of our own times, that the creation of bonds and stock certificates is like dram-drinking to imperfectly organised states. The brief military usurpers of the third century would probably have raised loans on the national credit as furiously and as foolishly as the presidents of any South American republic. And even as to the great and stable states of modern times whose acknowledgements of debt command, and rightly command, for the present, as high a price as the land itself, the substratum of all national wealth, we must remember that we have as yet traced their orbit through a very small part of the world's history. We and our immediate forefathers have seen the beginning of England's borrowing, but we know not in what spirit our remote descendants may look upon its end.

7 CAUSES, OR SYMPTOMS, OF DECAY

It is time to bring to a conclusion this examination of the causes of the fall of the Roman Empire, which might range over the whole field of private and public life during the first four Christian centuries.

Some readers may be surprised at not finding a prominent place among those causes given to the autocratic power of the Caesars. Many instances have been noticed, even in the course of this history, in which a fatuous or vicious emperor accelerated the ruin of Rome. But, upon a survey of the whole history of the commonwealth before and after the consolidation of the supreme power in the hands of an *imperator*, it does not seem possible to look upon that measure as anything else than preservative of the life of the state. We have to compare the Imperial system, not with some ideal republic of Plato or More, not even with a modern European monarchy of average excellence, but with the Roman republic during the last century and a half of its existence, at a time when the government of the fairest portion of the earth was in the hands of a combination of aristocrats the most selfish, and of democrats the most senseless, that the world has perhaps ever seen, and was being jobbed and plundered for their apparent benefit with such blind rapacity that, had Caesar not arrested the process of destruction, the provin-cial population must have perished in the grasp of its oppressors.

But though, upon the whole, the power of the emperors was exerted beneficially for the Empire, the same cannot be said of the frequent and dis-astrous interference of the Imperial household in state affairs. While, on the one hand, there were long intervals, notably the reigns of the adoptive emperors, perhaps also those of Diocletian and Constantine, during which a wise and well-organised bureaucracy (to use a modern term) gave effect to the mandates of the supreme power, there were other periods, especially the reigns of Claudius, of Constantius, of the sons and grandsons of Theodo-sius, during which the personal attendants of the monarch, his freedmen, or even his eunuchs, succeeded in grasping the helm of the state, and their steering was uniformly disastrous.* The confusion between the menial ser-

* An exception should be made for the great deeds of the eunuch Narses, but they lie beyond the range of the present history.

vants of the monarch and the ministers of the Empire, though obvious in a constitutionally governed country, generally tends to efface itself under a despotism, where the sovereign, daily fed upon such flatteries as those which Claudian offered to Honorius, comes in time to believe that the triv- ialities of his daily life are matters of profound interest to his subjects, and as important to the world as the welfare of provinces. Thus it was, by play- ing upon the weakness of a master whom in their hearts they despised, that such men as Eutropius became the chief depositaries of power under such sovereigns as Arcadius; thus it was that they could sell the highest offices in the Empire,* and bitterly revenge the wrongs which they themselves had suffered in their former bondage. Whatever may be the drawbacks of a constitutional system, and they are many, it at least nullifies, if it does not destroy, the baneful influence of 'the household' in politics. A vigorous and hard-working bureaucrat, who finds himself eclipsed or thwarted by a showy and pretentious speaker in a popular assembly, may reflect that even this is less humiliating than the necessity of courting the favour of an un- educated domestic, who has risen into power by the performance of menial offices in the bedchamber of the sovereign.

The rapid and terrible decline in the efficiency of the army was without doubt another potent cause of the dissolution of the Empire. When we hear the military essayist, Vegetius, lamenting the effeminate habits of the soldiers in his day, who were no longer able to bear the weight of helmet and coat of mail, and petitioned the emperor, with success, that they might be allowed to lay aside these wearisome defences,† we feel how vast a change has come over the spirit of the legionary since the hardy Sabine and Marsian followed Cae- sar to victory. This demoralisation may be partly due, as Zosimus says it was, to the truckling policy of Constantine, who withdrew many of the legions from the arduous and unpopular duty of defending the frontiers and quar- tered them in the large cities of the Empire, where they spent their days at the amphitheatre, and their nights in debauchery, a burden on the peaceful provincials, but no longer a terror to the enemies of Rome.‡

But the true causes of the ruin of that wonderful machine of conquest, the Roman army, lay deeper doubtless than in any such special mistake of military administration as this of Constantine's. Its mainspring for centuries had been the patient strength and courage, the capacity for en- during hardness, the instinctive submission to military discipline, of the

* Compare Claudian, *In Eutropium*, i.196–221.   † *Epitoma Rei Militaris*, i.20.
‡ Zosimus, ii.34.

populations which lined the ranges of the Apennines. Taught by their example, other races in the Empire, especially the Gauls and the friendly Germans, could do good service as *foederati* or even as actual legionaries. But after all, when the old Italian population itself was gone – and we have seen some of the economic changes which led to its disappearance before the slave-gangs of the great proprietors of Italy – there was no more reason left why the Roman army should continue to conquer. The wolves of Romulus were changed into the timid sheep of Honorius and the younger Theo-dosius. What had been the hammer of the nations became now their anvil.

Simple depopulation is often assigned as a cause of the fall of the Empire. And with great truth, especially so far as the terrible plagues and earthquakes of the second and third centuries contributed to that depopula-tion. It is abundantly clear, and must have been observed by the attentive reader of this history, that there were vast solitary spaces within the borders of the Empire when the barbarians streamed across it, and that their move-ment was one of colonisation almost as much as of conquest. Still, when one looks at the whole course of affairs after the Romans had made them-selves masters of the countries bordering on the Mediterranean, depopula-tion seems to present itself to the mind as a symptom rather than a cause of the malady which was in time to prove fatal, and one is inclined to fix upon some of the vices of the Roman polity mentioned above, the slave-system, the latifundia, the extortion of the tax-gatherer, as the reasons for that ter-rible failure of 'the human harvest'.

The ruin of such a mighty fabric as the world-Empire of Rome can hardly be contemplated by the citizen of any state such as our own, which has extended its dominion over alien peoples and far-distant lands, without stirring some foreboding fears that of our country too it may one day be said, 'How art thou fallen from heaven, O Lucifer, son of the morning!' Even so, according to the well-known story, the younger Africanus, in the very midst of the ruined city of Carthage, which he had himself destroyed, shed prophetic tears over the fate of his own country, and repeated those verses of the *Iliad* —

"Εσσεται ἦμαρ, ὅτ᾽ ἄν ποτ᾽ ὀλώλῃ "Ιλιος ἱρή,
Καὶ Πρίαμος καὶ λαὸς ἐϋμμελίω Πριάμοιο.*

* Surely a day shall come for the fall of Ilion the holy,
Priam, the stout-speared king, and all the people of Priam.

But an Englishman, though his presumption may rightly be chastened by the thought of the mortality of Rome, may derive some comfort from the reflection that she was tempted, as his country is not, by absolutely unbounded success. It was not till after the destruction of Carthage that the worst qualities of the Roman conqueror, his rapacity, his cruelty, his contempt for the rights of others, began to develop themselves. The other powerful nations, both in the old and the new world, which act as a counterpoise to our own, and sometimes administer a severe rebuke to our national pride, are in truth our best friends, preserving us from that overweening arrogance which is unendurable by God and man.

Of the causes enumerated above, which conspired for the ruin of the Empire, some clearly affect us not. The Christian religion is with us no explosive force threatening the disruption of our most cherished institutions. On the contrary it has been said, not as a mere figure of speech, that 'Christianity is part of the common law of England'. And even the bitterest enemies of our religion will scarcely deny that, upon the whole, a nation imbued with the teaching of the New Testament is more easy to govern than one which derived its notions of divine morality from the stories of the dwellers on Olympus.

The partition of the Empire, the erection of a co-equal seat of authority in its Asiatic dependencies, can hardly be considered a danger for us in practical politics.

Slavery is not eating as a canker into the heart of the English state. Yet perhaps there may be something analogous to slavery in the condition of 'the dangerous classes' in our great cities, men leading a sunless and squalid existence from the cradle to the grave, serfs *adscripti* [bound] to the gaol and the workhouse. And this thought may quicken the zeal, already so earnest, of statesmen and philanthropists to remove from us this reproach.

To the eye of an inexperienced observer there appear to be symptoms in the British administration of India, especially in the preponderating importance of land-tax as a source of revenue, and in our manner of employing the native *foederati*, which suggest some anxious comparisons with the Roman Imperial system. May it prove that the resemblance is only in appearance, not in reality!

The pulverisation of the burgher-class by the fiscal oppressions practised upon the decurions may possibly contain some warnings for benevolent administrators who, in their very zeal for the improvement of the condition of the people, may allow local taxation to attain proportions which, were any pause to occur in the onward march of the country, might be found well-nigh intolerable.

But of all the forces which were at work for the destruction of the prosperity of the Roman world none is more deserving of the careful study of an English statesman than the grain-largesses to the populace of Rome. Whatever occasional ebbings there may be in the current, there can be little doubt that the tide of affairs, in England and in all the countries of western Europe, as well as in the United States of America, sets permanently towards democracy. Will the great democracies of the twentieth century resist the temptation to use political power as a means of material self-enrichment? With a higher ideal of public duty than has been shown by some of the governing classes which preceded them, will they refrain from jobbing the commonwealth? Warned by the experience of Rome, will they shrink from reproducing directly, or indirectly, the political heresy of Caius Gracchus, that he who votes in the forum must be fed by the state? If they do, perhaps the world may see democracies as long-lived as the dynasties of Egypt or of China. If they do not, assuredly now as in the days of our Saxon forefathers, it will be found that he who is 'giver of bread' is also lord.* The old weary round will recommence, democracy leading to anarchy, and anarchy to despotism, and the national workshops of some future Gracchus will build the palaces in which British or American despots, as incapable to rule as Arcadius or Honorius, will guide mighty empires to ruin, amidst the acclamations of flatterers as eloquent and as hollow as the courtly Claudian.

* Lord = *hlaford*, the loaf-giver. The derivation is questioned by some scholars.

APPENDICES

I On the Identification of the Hiong-nu with the Huns

I quote from Mr Howorth's 'Introduction to the Translation of the Han Annals' (by Mr Wylie), contributed to the *Journal of the Anthropological Institute* (iii.398), the following criticism of the theory adopted in my first edition.

'Deguignes, than whom no one has done more for the elucidation of the ethnology of Asia in ancient times, propounded the doctrine that the European Huns were descended from the Hiong-nu of the Chinese writers, and he consequently in his history of the Huns worked out in some detail the account of the Hiong-nu, so far as it could be collected from the narratives of Matuanlin and the other epitomisers of the Chinese annals. Minute ethnology was then in its infancy. The distinctions between Mongols, Turks, Ugrians, etc., etc. were hardly recognised because hardly known. Since the days of Deguignes the subject has received immense illustration from various quarters, and now no European scholar of any repute – save perhaps Dr Latham – connects the Huns with the Hiong-nu. The Huns, as I have elsewhere argued, were a race of Ugrians, led by a caste of another race now represented by some of the Lesghian tribes of the Caucasus. The Hiong-nu were not Ugrians. It was Klaproth who first proved that the Hiong-nu were Turks, and his conclusions were endorsed by the very competent authority of Abel Remusat, and since by other scholars.' The argument thus divides itself into two parts.

PROOF THAT THE HUNS WERE UGRIANS

This rests on the existence of some 'Lesghian' tribes in the eastern Caucasus who bear names which appear to be corrupted from 'Hun' and 'Avar'. Among these tribes, names closely corresponding with those of Attila and his family are still, it is said, in common use. The dialect of the 'Andi', whom Howorth takes to be the representatives of the Huns, 'approximates very closely to the Ugrian or Finnic dialects proper, while the Avar has many idiosyncrasies related to the Samoyedic class of Siberian languages.'

PROOF THAT THE HIONG-NU WERE A TURKIC TRIBE

This rests chiefly on the Turkic character of the vocabulary of the Thiu-Khiu, a fragment of the dispersed Hiong-nu who, in the fifth century, settled in the Altai mountains. Fifteen or sixteen words in use among the Thiu-Khiu, including those for house, meat, horse, wolf, black, white, old, camp, and warrior, are shown to be identical with or closely analogous to words in the Turkish or Mongol languages. Hence it is argued, the Hiong-nu must have been closely related to the Turks.

The question is one which must be decided by experts in ethnology. To me, knowing scarcely anything of that science, there seem one or two weak links in the chain of argument; but then, on the other hand, we must not forget that the equation

$$\text{Hun} = \text{Hiong-nu}$$

rests on nothing more than one, perhaps accidental, similarity of names. It is difficult not to be attracted by the theory of Deguignes, because of the almost ludicrous similarity between the treatment of the Chinese emperors by the *tan-jou* and that of the Roman emperors by Attila and his progenitors. But of course there is nothing in this similarity which can weigh against any well-settled conclusion of ethnological science.

II On the Site of the So-called Battle of Châlons

As recent historians place the site of the great battle at Châlons-sur-Marne, it may be well to show how little there is to support this view in the earliest authorities.

The place which we now call Châlons was probably under the Romans named Duro-Catalaunum. It was the chief place of the Catalauni, a tribe who dwelt next to the Suessiones. As in so many other parts of Gaul, the old tribal name has finally prevailed, and Duro-Catalaunum has become Châlons, as Lutetia Parisiorum is Paris, Augusta Suessionum, Soissons, and so on. In Roman miles (ten of which are about equal to nine English), and by the Roman roads, Châlons was 170 miles distant from Metz, and fifty-one from Troyes. Fanum Minervae, now La Cheppe, where the so-called 'camp of Attila' is to be found, is about ten miles to the north-east of Châlons 'as the crow flies', but owing to the interposition of the river Vêle, seems to have been fifty-five miles by road (which went northwards to Rheims, and then returned on the other bank of the river to Châlons. This camp is square, of Roman origin, and was therefore certainly not con-structed by Attila even if he encamped inside it.

We may now consider the words of the original authorities.

Jordanes says, 'They come together therefore at the Catalaunian plains, which are also called the Maurician plains, one hundred Gaulish leagues in length and seventy in breadth.' These measurements would cover the whole space between 48° and 50° N latitude, and 3° and 5° E longitude, or a district at least equal to the old French province of Cham-pagne.

Gregory of Tours says (*Historia Francorum*, ii.7), 'Aetius and Theodore put Attila to flight [from Orléans], and he, going to the Mauriac plain, arrays his troops for battle.' Here we have no mention of the Catalaunian, but only of the Mauriac plain.

Idatius (twenty-eighth year of Theodosius II) puts the battle 'in the Catalaunian plains not far from the city of Metz which the Huns had broken up'. This statement is evidently quite wide of the mark, and shows that the Galician bishop had such vague notions of the geography of north-eastern Gaul that we cannot safely accept his guidance.

The continuer of Prosper gives the most precise details: 'The battle was fought at the fifth milestone from Troyes, at a place called Maurica in Champagne.'

Now when we look (1) at the exceedingly wide range which, as we see from Jordanes, was given to the term *campi Catalaunici* [Catalaunian plains]; (2) at the persistent reference to the *campus Mauriacus* [Mauriac plain] or some similar name as the field of battle; (3) at the fact that there is still existing a place called Méry-sur-Seine, which may fairly be supposed to represent the ancient Mauriacum; (4) at the situation of this place, not indeed at the fifth milestone from Troyes, apparently about twenty miles distant from it, but situated in a plain which may very probably have been called the *campus Mauriacensis*, and may have extended to the fifth milestone from Troyes; (5) at the great strategical importance of Troyes, placed at the centre of a perfect cobweb of roads, in the Roman time as well as now, and commanding apparently the passage of at least one important river; consid-ering all these facts and comparing them with the authorities, we must, as it appears to me, accept the conclusion that the battle was fought near to Méry-sur-Seine, but upon widely extended lines, and that it may easily have rolled over into what were properly called the Catalaunian plains (the Catalauni being the next tribe to the Tricasses), though it cannot have extended as far as the modern Châlons-sur-Marne, which was two days' march from the field of battle.

III On the Date of the Foundation of Venice

The assertion in the text, that the story of Venice having been founded by fugitives at the time of Attila's invasion rests on mere tradition, may surprise some readers. Others, with the popular histories of Venice in their hands, may think that an earlier date ought to have been assigned to that event. Daru (*Histoire de Venise*, i.27), after asserting that the invasions of Alaric sent some fugitives across the lagoons (a very probable hypothesis, though one entirely unsupported by proof), goes on to state that twenty-four houses on the Rialto having been destroyed by fire, a church to St James was dedicated there in the year 421. *La ville de Padoue y envoya des magistrats annuels, avec le titre de Consuls. On trouve dans un vieux manuscrit le plus ancien monument de l'histoire de Venise; c'est un décret du sénat de Padoue, sous la date de 421, qui ordonne la construction d'une ville à Rialte, pour y rassembler, en une seule communauté, les habitants répandus sur les îles environnantes, afin qu'ils puissent y tenir une flotte armée, parcourir la mer avec plus de sûreté, et se défendre avec plus d'avantage dans leur asyle. Tels furent les commencements de la superbe Venise.* *

This seems circumstantial enough, and has been copied in good faith by the writers of popular manuals who have to deal with the early history of Venice, though they are evidently puzzled by finding the foundation of the city thus assigned to the year 421, thirty-one years, as they well know, before the invasion of Attila, which they have also to represent to their readers as the main cause of the settlement of Venice.

The fact is, and it cannot be stated too clearly in order to relieve this useful class of writers from an unnecessary dilemma, that the whole story of the foundation of the city or the building of the church of St James in 421,

* [The city of Padua sent magistrates bearing the title of consul there every year. In an old manuscript we find the most ancient monument of the history of Venice, the decree of the senate of Padua under the date of 421, which orders the construction of a city at Rialto, in order to gather together in a single community the people inhabiting the surrounding islands so that they might be able to keep an armed fleet there to provide security for sea traffic and more effective defence for their haven. Such were the beginnings of proud Venice.]

is a mere fable (the result of ignorance rather than of dishonesty), and that the alleged 'decree of the senate of Padua', is as valuable a contribution to history as the forgeries of Ireland or Chatterton, but no more so.

(1) The earliest historian of Venice is Andrea Dandolo, who was born in 1307, was doge from 1343 to 1354, and was the immediate predecessor of Marino Faliero. His history (*Chronicon Venetum*) is very uncritical, but in his account of the events of the fifth century he builds a good deal on Jordanes and the *Historia Miscella*, though also to some extent on the Hungarian romancers (historians they cannot be called) who wrote about Attila. He appears to be under the impression that Attila began to reign over the Huns about 415, since he places his accession before the election of Pope Zosimus in 417; and he describes a battle which took place between him and Macrinus, 'Tetrarch of Pannonia, Dalmatia, Macedonia, Phrygia, and Pamphylia', in which forty thousand Huns were slain, but Macrinus also fell, and the Roman army was routed.* The title attributed to Macrinus is sufficient to show that Dandolo is here working with absolutely unhistorical materials.

He then proceeds in the next part to relate how the chiefs and people of the cities of Venetia, exhausted by the incursions of the barbarians, decided to construct certain maritime cities of refuge. 'First of all, Gallianus de Fontana, Simeon de Glauconibus, and Antonius Calvus de Limianis, consuls of Patavium [Padua], not unmindful of the past invasion, went to the maritime regions, and there near the mouth of the river Realtis, having found an island suitable for their purposes, laid the foundations of the city of Rivoaltus on the 25th March in the year of our Lord 421.' The fire (issuing from the house of a Greek shipmaster named Eutinopus), by which twenty-four mansions were consumed, and the building of a church dedicated to St James are then recorded. This is the first and best authority for the statement quoted above from Daru, and it is hardly necessary to say that it has not the slightest claim to be regarded as authentic history. The three consuls of Padua, with such names as 'de Fontana', 'de Glauconibus' and 'de Limianis', in the early part of the fifth century, are alone quite enough to condemn it.

But Dandolo, though he was quite at fault as to the date of the commencement of Attila's reign, knew, with something like accuracy, the date of the fall of Aquileia, which he puts about 454. He knew very little however as to the circumstances of that disaster. We have the story of the storks,

* *Chronicon Venetum*, v.1.9.

of course, and of the matron Digna, who threw herself headlong into the Natiso. But he says that after nine thousand of Attila's men and two thousand of the citizens of Aquileia had been slain, the latter, 'being no longer able to resist so great a multitude, put statues as sentinels on the walls, and thus, by distracting Attila's attention, almost all escaped to Grado.' Soon after, however, Attila let fly his hawk, which settled on the hand of one of the statues. The boldness of the bird and the immobility of the man revealed the trick to Attila, and in his anger he rased the city to the ground (v. 5). Attila then presses on to Concordia, whose inhabitants fly to Caprulae (Caorle), to Altino (whose inhabitants colonise Torcello and the five neighbouring islands, and name them after the six gates of their city), and lastly to Padua (which Dandolo here calls by its modern name and not Patavium). 'The king of the city of Padua sent his queen with his sons, their wives and little ones, and all his treasure to Rialto and Malamocco. Attila attacked the city, was first defeated, then he gained a victory and destroyed Padua.' Again we have here a narrative which is absolutely unhistorical, and which, even as an invention, must have belonged to a period long subsequent to the fifth century.

(2) Andrea Nogier, a Venetian noble, who lived about 1500, is the reputed author of a history of Venice. It would be an insult to Dandolo to put Nogier's work for a moment in comparison with his. It is full of fables and anachronisms in the early part, and the man who can read it through must have plenty of spare time on his hands. It is only worth noticing here as showing the growth of the legend about the foundation in 421 and its utter historic worthlessness.

Attila, according to this account, was the grandson of a king of Hungary named Osdrubald. His invasion of Italy is placed in the years 420–8. His sieges of Aquileia, Concordia, Altino, and Pafagonia (Padua) are described at great length, and with no regard to truth. The name of the king of Padua is Janus, his queen is *Andriana ovvero Vitaliana*.* The siege of Padua is said to have lasted seven years. In the second year of Attila's invasion, i.e. 421, 'on the 15th of March, which was a Saturday, it was determined by the nobles and tribunes of the kingdom of Padua, to build a city on the island of Rivoalto. And three consuls were set over this work whose names were Julius Falier, Thomas Candianus and Cosmas Paulus.' By some mistake the author represents the design to build the city as formed on the 15th of March, though the first stone is laid three days earlier, on the 12th of March,

* [Andriana or Vitaliana.]

421, 'in which year, month, and day the arrangement of the heavens was by the divine will and ordering of such favourable aspect as verily to promise that the aforesaid city should be noble and powerful, as is seen at this day'.

Then follows a good deal more atrociously disjointed history, in which for instance Totila the Ostrogoth* (who really reigned from 541 to 552) is represented as invading Italy and persecuting the Christians in 440. Soon after, the mendacious scribe, who must surely be laughing at his readers, says, 'From 442 to 648 the history of Venice is lost, and none of it can be written.' There need not have been any blank spaces in a history written on such principles.

(3) Marino Sanuto, who flourished towards the end of the fifteenth century, and was still alive in the year 1522, admits that there are various opinions about the time of the *principio* [foundation] of Venice, one author putting it 'in the year 456 [453], so indicating the time in which, at the death of Attila, reigned Pope Leo I, Marcian, Gaiseric, Meroveus, and Valentinian Junior'.

'But the truth is that in the year 421, as I have said, on the 25th of March, Friday, was laid the first stone, as many writers tell, of the church of San Jacopo di Rivoalto. On which day, as holy Scripture testifies, our first father Adam was formed at the beginning of the creation of the world. On the same day was the annunciation of the angel Gabriel to the blessed Virgin Mary, and the Son of God was conceived in her womb. And on the same day, according to some theologians, Jesus Christ, our redeemer, was crucified by the Hebrews on Mount Calvary. So this day is a very memorable one.' An astrological diagram is appended, to show the aspect of the heavens at that day and hour. It is of course a great matter, from this point of view, to get for the foundation of the city a day which corresponds according to the days of the week as well as according to those of the year with the supposed day of the crucifixion. (Not however an ecclesiastical Good Friday which fell in 421 a week later, on the 1st April.)

(4) It is scarcely necessary to quote the passage in which Marco Antonio Sabellico, another great Venetian historian (who died in 1504), gives his opinion concerning *la vera origine Veneta*.† He is slightly heterodox about the

---

* Totila and Attila seem to have been generally confounded by the Italians of the Middle Ages. Dante (*Inferno*, xiii.149) makes Attila instead of Totila the destroyer of Florence. And the *Ottimo Commento*, in its note on that passage, says, 'Some say that Attila and Totila were two different persons, and others that they were the same.'

† [The true origin of Venice.]

year, which according to him is 422, but he is quite certain about the day. 'Almost all agree in this that on the 25th of March began the origin of this city.' And then he proceeds, like Sanuto (who perhaps copied from him), to enumerate the wonderful events which according to Scripture and tradi-tion happened on this most auspicious day.

For all the statements which have been quoted from these four historians, it is abundantly clear that there is not the slightest true historical founda-tion. They are mere fancies of medieval Venetian patriotism, which may be revered or smiled at according to the mood of the reader, but which, having no relation to fact, should be carted away out of the domain of history with the least possible delay.

Whether the mistake under which the early Venetian historians evi-dently laboured as to the accession of Attila, and which led them to ante-date his operations against Italy by nearly thirty years, or the astrological and ecclesiastical back-reckonings which led them up to the 25th of March, 421, as a very choice day on which their city should have been built, were the original cause of the error, it is not likely that we can now ascer-tain. Perhaps the historical error and the chronological conceit grew together and each strengthened the other.

The student however will expect, before the subject is dismissed, to hear something of that which Daru calls 'the most ancient monument of the history of Venice, the decree of the senate of Padua under the date of 421, which orders the construction of a city at Rialto'. Daru quotes this docu-ment. It begins, *Anno a nativitate Christi ccccxxi in ultimo anno papae Innocentii primi . . . Aponencis, regno Pataviencium feliciter et copiose florenti, regentibus rem-publicam Galiano de Fontana, Simeone de Glausonibus, et Antonio Calvo dominis consulibus . . . decretum est . . . aedificari urbem circa Rivolatum,** etc.; and he con-cludes, *Nam Gothorum multitudinem et instantiam verebantur et recordabantur quod anno Christi ccccxiii [sic] ipsi Gothi cum rege eorum Alarico venerant in Italiam, et ipsam provinciam igne et ferro vastatam reliquerant et ad urbem processerunt eam spoliantes.*†

---

* [In year 421 from the birth of Christ, the last year of Pope Innocent I . . . of Aponus, a time of great fortune and prosperity for the citizens of Padua, in the consulate of Gal-lianus de Fontana, Simeon de Glauconibus, and Antonius Calvus . . . the decision was taken . . . to build a city around Rivolatus.]
† [For they feared the numbers and proximity of the Goths and remembered that in the year of Christ 413 (*sic*) these very Goths had entered Italy with Alaric their king, had left that same province ravaged with fire and sword, and had come plundering to their city.]

According to Daru, '*Le bibliographe ajoute* "*Reliquum legere non potui*'".* It was really not worthwhile his reading so far. Every scholar must at once perceive that this document, the so-called 'most ancient monument of the history of Venice', is an absurd and clumsy fabrication. The misdating of Alaric's invasion by at least three years is a comparatively trifling error. The use of the date *anno Christi*, in the year 421, a century before Dionysius Exiguus, and the ridiculously unclassical names of the three consuls of Padua, at once stamp the document as a forgery, and give one a very low idea of the attainments of the historian who could be imposed upon by it.†

The real 'most ancient monument of the history of Venice' is the celebrated letter of Cassiodorus to the Venetians in the early part of the sixth century. This letter proves that already among the Venetian islands, though very likely not precisely at the Rialto, there was collected such a population of fishermen, salt-manufacturers, and hardy mariners as those whom we find thriving there when in 697 the first doge is elected and the continuous history of Venice commences.

IV On the Character of Petronius Maximus

The account of the character and actions of this emperor, given in the text, is drawn almost exclusively from the writings of his contemporaries – Apollinaris Sidonius (430–88) and Prosper of Aquitaine (about 400–60). In some respects it is less unfavourable than that which is usually given and which is derived from later authorities.

The chief difference is in the degree of culpability which has to be assigned to him for the death of his predecessor. Some suspicion undoubtedly rested upon him in the minds of his contemporaries, but I have endeavoured not to treat this suspicion as more of a certainty than it actually was. The obvious, patent cause of Valentinian's murder was the two barbarians' desire to revenge the death of Aetius; and, to a certain extent, the whole people and army of Rome, by witnessing it unmoved, made the

* [The bibliographer adds 'I could not read the rest'.]

† Endeavouring to follow up at Venice the reference which Daru gives as to this MS, I was unable to discover where it is at present. The Camaldulensian convent in whose library it was placed is, as I understood, dispersed. But I was informed that the Tomaselli collection, of which this MS formed part, consisted chiefly of *copie di copie di copie*, and was of extremely slight archaeological value.

crime their own. It was the extraordinary conduct of Maximus after the murder, in admitting the assassins to his most intimate counsels, which naturally raised a suspicion that he was their accomplice, but this suspicion does not appear ever to have reached the stage of proof. The following words of Prosper no doubt express all that the immediate contemporaries of the two emperors knew about the chief actors in the tragedy.

'As soon as this parricide' (the murder of Valentinian by the friends of Aetius) 'had been perpetrated, Maximus, a man who had twice filled the office of consul, and was of patrician rank, assumed the Imperial dignity. It had been supposed that he would be in all ways serviceable to the imperilled commonwealth, but he very soon showed what disposition he was of, since he not only did not punish the murderers of Valentinian, but even received them into the circle of his friends, and moreover, forbidding the widowed empress to mourn the loss of her lord, within a very few days he constrained her to contract a marriage with himself.'

This scandal of his precipitate marriage with the widow of his predecessor, and the ruin which resulted from it for Rome, made evidently a deep impression on the minds of contemporary and succeeding annalists, especially in the Eastern Empire, and disposed them to put the harshest construction on all his previous actions. It is curious to note how the suspicion which is but faintly marked in the pages of Prosper, and is not even alluded to in those of Sidonius, deepens and hardens in the later historians.

The Spanish ecclesiastic, Idatius (*fl.* about 400–70), says that 'Maximus was racked by a disturbing fear of great commotions. Through desire of reigning he had contributed by his wicked advice to the deaths of the persons slain by Valentinian, and even to that of Valentinian himself.'

Marcellinus, a count of the Eastern Empire (whose chronicle ends at 558), says, 'Valentinian the prince, by the stratagem of Maximus the patrician, by whose deceit Aetius also perished, was mangled in the Campus Martius by Optila and Traustila.'

But the anti-Maximian prejudice reaches its height in Procopius (*fl.* about 500–60) who has unfortunately made the largest contribution to the history of this emperor with the smallest claim to be regarded as a trustworthy authority. In the long and disagreeable romance with which he favours us, Valentinian is represented as winning the ring of Maximus from him at play, entrapping his wife to the palace by means of this ring, and then seducing her. The dishonour of his wife fills the mind of Maximus with thoughts of vengeance, in order to accomplish which he first of all induces Valentinian to assassinate Aetius, and then, 'without any trouble, he killed the emperor and took the sovereignty'. He marries Eudoxia, and incautiously tells her one night that it was for love of her that he killed her late husband. As soon as day dawns she sends the fatal message to Gaiseric, knowing that she will receive no help from Byzantium.

It is not worthwhile to point out the internal improbabilities of this story, the jumble of different motives which it ascribes to the chief actors, the disparity of years between Valentinian the seducer and his victim (who was mother of a grownup son and wife to the elderly Maximus), and other points which might be remarked upon. The history into which it is inserted is thoroughly inaccurate in a chronological point of view (for instance, it represents the fall of Aquileia as succeeding the death of Aetius), and Procopius, even in reference to the events of his own time, is notoriously apt to let his history degenerate into a mere *chronique scandaleuse*, inserting apparently many an unauthentic piece of gossip, simply because it is unsavoury. Gibbon truly remarks that 'Procopius is a fabulous writer for the events which precede his own memory'. Whatever judgement we may be disposed to pass on the alleged share of Maximus in the murder of his predecessor – and I am disposed to ask for a verdict of 'not proven' – at least let the fables of Procopius no longer pass current as history.

V Chronology of the Vandal Kings

There are some difficulties besetting the subject of the chronology of the Vandal dominion in Africa, and though no question of importance turns upon them, and I have no reason to dissent (except in one particular) from the ordinary chronology as given in Gibbon's *Decline and Fall*, it may be worthwhile to point out what these difficulties are, and on what foundation the received chronology rests.

The first point, the only one that can now be considered a matter of controversy, is the date of the passage of the Vandals into Africa. As to this it may be well to quote the entry of Prosper in full:

Hierio et Ardabure coss. Bonifacio, cujus potentia gloriaque in Africa augebatur, bellum ad arbitrium Felicis, quia ad Italiam venire abnuerat, publico nomine illatum est, ducibus Mavortio et Galbione et Sinoce, cujus proditione Mavortius et Galbio, cum Bonifacium obsiderent interempti sunt: moxque ipse a Bonifacio dolo detectus occisus est.

Exinde gentibus, quae uti navibus nesciebant, dum a concertantibus in auxilium vocantur, mare pervium factum est, bellique contra Bonifacium coepti in Sigisvultum Comitem cura translata est. Gens Vandalorum ab Hispaniis ad Africam transiit.

*Felice et Tauro Coss.**

Then follow the events of this year which do not relate to Africa.

The author of the *Chronicon Imperiale*, or the so-called 'Tiro', says: *VIII Theodosii II post mortem Honorii. Wandali in Africam transfretantes, ingentem, lacerata omni provincia, Romanis cladem dedere.*† (This is evidently wrong, as Augustine's death during the siege of Hippo by the Vandals is quite clearly fixed to 430.)

Idatius writes: *V Theodosii II post mortem Honorii Gaisericus rex de Baeticae provinciae litore cum Wandalis omnibus eorumque familiis mense Majo ad Mauretaniam et Africam relictis transit Hispaniis.*‡

According to Idatius' chronology, the fifth year of Theodosius II after the death of Honorius would be 429, since he gives Honorius' reign a year more than its due, and thus puts his death in 424 instead of 423.

Still, as a matter of fact, the fifth year of Theodosius II after his uncle's death would be not 429 but 428; and it is clear that some of Idatius' dates require correction. Take, for instance, the papal accessions. Celestine I's accession is four years too late, 426 instead of 422; that of Sixtus III two years, 434 instead of 432; that of Leo I one year, 441 instead of 440. Evidently there is a tendency at this part of Idatius' *Chronicon* to bring down

---

* Hierius and Ardaburius, consuls. At the bidding of Felix, war in the name of the state was declared on Bonifacius (whose influence and glory in Africa were increasing) because he had refused to come to Italy. The leaders of the expedition were Mavortius, Galbio, and Sinox. By the treachery of Sinox, Mavortius and Galbio were slain while they were besieging Bonifacius, and presently he himself, being detected by Bonifacius in deceitful practices, was put to death. Thereafter the sea was made a thoroughfare to the [barbarous] nations which were ignorant of the management of their ships, their aid being invoked by the combatants: and the care of the war which had been begun against Bonifacius was transferred to Count Sigisvult. The nation of the Vandals crossed over from Spain to Africa.

Felix and Taurus, consuls.

† Eighth year of Theodosius II after the death of Honorius. The Vandals, crossing over the straits to Africa, caused great slaughter among the Romans, harrying the whole province.

‡ [Fifth year of Theodosius II after the death of Honorius. In May King Gaiseric crossed from the shores of the province of Baetica to Mauretania and Africa with all the Vandals and their households, and so left Spain.]

his dates too low, and this may be in part owing to his having made the reign of Honorius too long by one year.

Cassiodorus here, as elsewhere, for the most part, does little more than transcribe Prosper.

Marcellinus has no entry on the subject.

Victor Tunnunensis does not begin till 444.

Isidore, in his *Historia Wandalorum*, has under *Era quadringentesima sexagesima septima* (the 467th year of the Spanish era corresponding with AD 429): *Gesericus frater Gunderico succedit in regno annis quadraginta. Qui ex Catholico effectus apostata in Arianam primus fertur transisse perfidiam. Hic de Baeticae provinciae litore cum Vandalis omnibus eorumque familiis ad Mauritaniam et Africam relictis transit Hispaniis.**

Isidore appears here to be transcribing Idatius, and therefore adopts his chronology. Isidore's own Vandal chronology, as we shall see further on, is an inconceivable muddle of errors.

The *Chronicon Paschale* [or Alexandrian Chronicle] has the entry 'Eleventh year of the twentieth indiction [428] consulship of Felix and Taurus. Under these consuls the Vandals entered Africa.'

This date, 428, I believe to be the true date of the Vandal invasion of Africa. Herein, I differ from Gibbon, who puts it in 429.

My reasons for this view are—

(1) The *Paschal Chronicle*, which seems to be accurate in its dates at this point, is the only one, except Prosper, which mentions the names of the consuls under whom the event occurred. Anyone who studies the principle on which these lists are composed, will see how extremely easy it is for an event to be dated a year too high or too low, when only the number of the regnal year is given. Much less is the chance of error when the date is linked with the names of the consuls.

(2) It is generally admitted that Prosper's apparent date (427) is too early, since the war waged by the court of Ravenna against Bonifacius, which was the cause of the invitation, only began in that year, and there is some reason to respect the statement of Idatius that the Vandals crossed in May.

I am not sure, however, that Prosper is really an adverse authority to the

* [Gaiseric succeeded his brother Guntheric and reigned forty years. Formerly a Catholic, he apostatised to the Arian heresy. He crossed from the shores of the province of Baetica to Mauretania and Africa with all the Vandals and their households, and so left Spain.]

date 428. It will be seen that he describes under 427 at some length the war against Bonifacius, and then at the end of this entry, and immediately before *Felice et Tauro coss*, says *Gens Vandalorum ab Hispaniis ad Africam transiit.* He perhaps, therefore, means to describe under 427 rather the events which led up to the crossing of the Mediterranean than the crossing itself.

The over-running of at least four African provinces, and the capture of all their cities but three, are events quite sufficient to fill up the two years between 428 and the siege of Hippo.

The next event of importance in Vandal chronology is the taking of Carthage. This is fixed by the consenting voice of Prosper, Idatius, Cassiodorus (who must be looked upon as only an echo of Prosper), Marcellinus, and the *Paschal Chronicle* to the year 439 (consulship of Theodosius and Festus). 'Tiro', who assigns it to 444, may be safely pronounced inaccurate. Idatius and Marcellinus agree that the capture was in the month of October, Idatius placing it on the 19th and Marcellinus on the 23rd of that month. The *Paschal Chronicle* also places it μηνὶ Ὑπερβερεταίῳ, which corresponds with October.

Prosper says that Carthage was taken by the Vandals *anno postquam Romana esse coeperat* DLXXXV (alias DLXXXIII).* The Vatican MS of Prosper says *Cartago capitur a Vandalis anno postquam Romana esse coeperat quingentesimo octogesimo quarto.*† As the year of the Roman capture of Carthage was 146 BC, these dates correspond to 439, 437, and 438 respectively.

Still, as before said, there can be no doubt that the true date is near the end of October, 439.

The death of Gaiseric took place on or about the 25th January, 477. We get this date from Victor Vitensis (i.17), who says (reckoning from the capture of Carthage), *Duravit in regno annis triginta septem mensibus tribus:*‡ and who is confirmed by the appendix to Prosper (Augustan MS): *Post consulatu Theodosii xvii et Festi, Geisericus Wandalorum rex Carthaginem ingressus est die xiv Kalendarum Novembrium. Qui regnavit eandem Africam civitatem annis xxxvii, mensibus iii, diebus vi.*§

---

* [In the year 585 after she became Roman (otherwise 583).]

† [Carthage was taken by the Vandals in the year 584 after she became Roman.]

‡ [He reigned for thirty-seven years and three months.]

§ [After the consulship of Theodosius (his seventeenth) and Festus, Gaiseric, king of the Vandals, entered Carthage on the 19th October (439; the date given by Idatius). He ruled his African state for thirty-seven years, three months, and six days.]

Gaiseric therefore died the 25th January, 477.

Reigns of Gaiseric's successors. From the same appendix to Prosper we get our most accurate chronology of these reigns.

Post hunc regnavit Hunerix, filius ejus annis vii, mensibus x, diebus xviii [After him his son Huneric reigned for seven years, ten months, eighteen days]:

Accession of Huneric	25th January, 477
Death of "	13th December, 484

Post eum regnavit Guntamundus Gentunis ejusdem Hunerici regis fratrius filius annos xi, menses ix, dies xi [After him Gunthamund, son of Gentunis the brother of King Huneric, reigned for eleven years, nine months, eleven days]:

Accession of Gunthamund	13th December, 484
Death of "	24th September, 496

Post quem regnavit Trasamundis Gentunis filius annos xxvi, menses viii, dies iv [After whom Thrasamund, son of Gentunis, reigned for twenty-six years, eight months, four days]:

Accession of Thrasamund	24th September, 496
Death of "	28th May, 523

Post quem regnavit Hildrix filius Hunerici annos viii, dies viii [After whom Hilderic, son of Huneric, reigned for eight years, eight days]:

Accession of Hilderic	28th May, 523
Dethronement of "	5th June, 531

Quo regnante assumpta tyrannide Geilamer regnum ejus invadit in quo sedit annos iii, menses iii [During his reign Gelimer assumed the kingship and invaded his kingdom, where he sat (on the throne) for three years, three months]:

Accession of Gelimer	5th June, 531
End of reign of "	5th September, 534

But this brings down the dethronement of Gelimer a year too low, as we know that the expedition of Belisarius against Carthage sailed in June, 533, and had accomplished all its work, including the captivity of Gelimer himself, by March, 534. We find also that we have one year too many, from the summation made by Prosper's continuer himself. *Fiunt ergo ab exordio regis Geiserici usque ad exitum Wandalorum anni xciii, menses x, dies xi.**

But the numbers above given add up to ninety-four years, ten months, and sixteen days. We therefore reduce the reign of Gelimer to two years and three months (agreeing herein with the tenor of the narrative of Procopius), and thus the end of the reign of Gelimer is brought to the 5th September, 533: almost the exact date of Belisarius' landing in Africa. According to the view of an Imperialist chronicler the Vandal domination in Africa would end *de jure* as soon as Justinian's army entered the province.

Upon the whole it must be admitted that this chronology has been preserved with great accuracy, and it accords with the general course of the history.

Very different is the judgement which must be passed upon the only system of Vandal chronology which has any pretension to compete with that of Prosper and his continuer,† namely, that of Isidore of Seville. This Spanish bishop (who lived from about 560 to 636) in his *Historia Wandalorum*, which is compiled chiefly from Idatius and Victor Tunnunensis, gives us a series of dates, which is apparently very complete, but which must be the result of some bewildered back-reckoning of events, and is entirely and hopelessly inaccurate. His dates are given according to the Spanish era or era of Augustus, which corresponds with 38 BC; but translating them into dates of the Christian era they are as follows:

Irruption of the Vandals and allied nations into Gaul	AD 366‡	should be 406	
Their entry into Spain	408	"	409
Division of Spain between Vandals, Alans, and Suevi			411
Reign of Gunderic	18 years		

* [Thus ninety-three years, ten months, eleven days passed from the start of Gaiseric's reign to the destruction of the Vandals.]

† Not the author who is technically known as Continuator Prosperi in the Copenhagen MS.

‡ *Era quadringentesima quarta* [the 404th year of the era], but the omission of *quadragesima* [fortieth] is probably due to a transcriber's error.

Accession of Gaiseric			429
(who reigned forty years*)			
Accession of Huneric	463	should be	477
(who reigned seven years and five months)			
Accession of Gunthamund	476	"	484
(who reigned twelve years)			
Accession of Thrasamund	488	"	496
(who reigned twenty-seven years and four months)			
Accession of Hilderic	515	"	523
(who reigned seven years and three months)			
Accession of Gelimer	522	"	531
Fall of the Vandal monarchy	525	"	534

'Africa was recovered by Belisarius in the ninety-seventh year of the entry of the Vandals.' This agrees sufficiently well with Isidore's reckoning (525–429 = 96). 'The kingdom of the Vandals had lasted 113 years from King Gunderic to the death of Gelimer.' According to Isidore's reckoning this interval was 114 years (525–411 = 114), and moreover it was not terminated by the death of Gelimer, but by his defeat and captivity. It will be seen that the dates of Huneric's and Gunthamund's accessions do not correspond with the periods allotted for the reign of their predecessors. And the whole chronology is so hopelessly at variance with history that the expedition of Belisarius against Carthage is brought to the year 524–5, two years before the accession of Justinian to the Empire. It is clear that Isidore did not understand the rudiments of the subject about which he professed to inform his readers, and that his scheme of chronology is absolutely worthless.

Of the other chroniclers, Marcellinus Comes does not mention the accessions of the Vandal kings, but is of course acquainted with the true date of the completion of the conquest of Africa (534). He puts it, however, in the ninety-sixth year after the capture of Carthage by the Vandals. According to his own dates it should have been the ninety-fifth year.

Victor Tunnunensis is utterly wrong in his earlier Vandal chronology, but struggles into accuracy for the later period. He has evidently been the chief author of confusion to Isidore.

* The lengths of the Vandal reigns are those given by Isidore himself, though inconsistent with his chronology.

He puts the death of Gaiseric *anno regni xl** in the year 464 instead of 477.

This mistake, which vitiates all this part of his chronology, perhaps arises from a confusion between the accession of Gaiseric (which may have happened in 424) and the capture of Carthage in 439. But, even so, it is only in round numbers that Gaiseric can be said to have reigned at Carthage for forty years.

The reign of Huneric is said by Victor to have lasted seven years and five months (seven years, five months, and eighteen days, according to Prosper's continuer), but to have ended in 479, though his accession is placed in 464. By this arithmetical blunder eight years of the redundant thirteen, arising from the ante-dating of the death of Gaiseric, are silently cancelled and Huneric's death is made only five years too early.

Gunthamund comes to the throne in 479, reigns twelve years (instead of eleven years, nine months, and eleven days), and dies in 497. The whole of the redundant years are now cancelled, and Thrasamund actually comes to the throne a year too late (497 instead of 496).

Thrasamund reigns twenty-seven years and four months (instead of twenty-six years, eight months, and four days), and dies in 523, the correct year.

Hilderic comes to the throne in 523, and reigns seven years and three months (instead of eight years and eight days). This would probably bring his deposition to 530, but Victor agrees with Prosper's continuer in fixing it for 531. The fall of Gelimer is assigned to the year of Belisarius' landing in Africa, 533.

Probably these inaccuracies of the ecclesiastical chroniclers and their desperate attempts to remedy them by a suspension of the laws of arith-metic, are due to the fury of the Vandal persecution, which had caused the registers of the churches to fall into hopeless confusion.

VI Vandal Dominion over the Islands of the Mediterranean

It is clear that the Vandal domination (which, like that of the Athenians in the fifth century before Christ, was essentially a maritime domination) extended over several islands of the western Mediterranean, but it is not easy, from the scattered notices of the chroniclers, to draw up a precise account of the different stages of its growth.

* [In the fortieth year of his reign.]

Our chief information on this subject is derived from Victor Vitensis, who says that 'after the death of Valentinian III Genseric obtained the circuit of the whole of Africa, and moreover the largest islands – Sardinia, Sicily, Corsica, Ivica, Majorca, Minorca, and many others – and defended them with his wonted arrogance: one of which, that is Sicily, he afterwards granted to Odocacer, king of Italy, by tributary right, out of which Odoacer at certain times paid him tribute as to his lord, [Genseric] however reserving some part to himself'.*

It seems clear, however, that, at any rate as regards Sicily, there was no complete conquest of it by Gaiseric so early as 455 (the date of the death of Valentinian III). In 456, and again in 465, we find him ravaging Sicily, as if it were a hostile country.† At the time of the great combined expedition of 468 against Gaiseric, Sicily seems to have been made a base of operations by the Imperial flotilla: and it was in Sicily, after the failure of the expedition, that Marcellinus was murdered by one of his colleagues.‡ All these facts seem to show that at any rate the Vandal domination was not yet securely established over the whole of Sicily, though it is probable enough that Lilybaeum, and perhaps Palermo, may have been conquered and held firmly during these years of strife by Gaiseric.§ Apparently this is our last information as to Sicilian affairs until (as above stated) we find Gaiseric in 476 dealing with the whole island as his undoubted possession, and assigning it *tributario jure* [by tributary right] to Odovacar.

It is this fact which leads me to conjecture that in the treaty of 475 between Orestes and Gaiseric the island of Sicily may have been formally ceded to the Vandal king. The *aliqua pars* [some part], which Gaiseric reserved to himself at the time of his cession to Odovacar, was most probably the western corner of the island, including the fortress of Lilybaeum, though this does not seem to be anywhere distinctly stated.

Briefly to describe the later fortunes of Sicily, it evidently all formed part of the kingdom of Theodoric, till on the marriage of his sister Amalafrida with Thrasamund, king of the Vandals (*cir.* 500), Theodoric ceded Lilybaeum and the adjacent territory to Thrasamund as part of the marriage-

* Victor Vitensis, i.4.   † Priscus, excerpts 7 and 10.
‡ Cassiodorus and Marcellinus, for the year 468.
§ Baronius (*Annales Ecclesiastica*, for the year 454) infers the capture of Lilybaeum from the captivity of its bishop, Paschasinus, who wrote a plaintive letter as to his sufferings to Pope Leo. Idatius tells us that *Gaisericus Siciliam depraedatus Panormum diu obsedit* [Gaiseric plundered Sicily and long besieged Palermo] in 440, but we do not seem to be distinctly told of his capture of the city.

dowry.* To this period, doubtless, belongs the inscription recorded on a stone near Marsala, *Fines inter Vandalos et Gothos. Mil.* IIII.† On the fall of the Vandal kingdom Justinian claimed Lilybaeum (which had meanwhile been taken possession of by the Goths) as part of his prize of war, and the Goths' refusal to surrender it was one of the pretexts of the war, which for a time reunited not only Sicily but Italy also to the Empire.

As for the other islands mentioned by Victor – Sardinia, Corsica, and the Balearic isles – they appear to have been earlier and more firmly attached to the Vandal kingdom than Sicily. Sardinia was indeed recovered for the Empire by Marcellinus in 468,‡ but it probably fell back under Vandal dominion soon after the failure of the expedition of that year, since, at the conference between Catholics and Arians at Carthage in 484, the names of several bishops from Sardinia and the Balearic isles are mentioned, and these were undoubtedly subjects of the Vandal king. After that conference forty-six Catholic bishops were sent to Corsica to hew wood for the royal navy, a proof (if proof were needed) that this island also owned the sway of the son of Gaiseric.

All these islands were easily won back to their allegiance to the emperor after the fall of the Vandal monarchy in 533,§ though at a later period Sardinia and Corsica were for a few years subject to the Ostrogothic king Totila (*cir.* 545−52).

The foregoing faint outline of the history of the Mediterranean islands seems to be all that it is possible to extract from the secular historians. Probably a careful study of ecclesiastical documents would enable us to supply much that is here missing.

VII On the Alleged Immoralities of Avitus

The charges made by Gibbon (chap. xxxvi, n. 25), and repeated by his copyists, against the moral character of this emperor, rest on no solid basis of evidence.

(1) In the contemporary chroniclers there is no hint of anything of the kind.

(2) Victor Tunnunensis, who, though not a contemporary (he died

* See vol. iii, chap. ix.   † [Boundary between Goths and Vandals. Four miles.]
‡ Procopius, *De Bello Vandalico*, i.6.
§ Procopius, *De Bello Vandalico*, ii.5, and see vol. iii, chap. xv.

569), seems to have had access to full and trustworthy sources of information, calls Avitus 'a man of entire simplicity'. It is true that the MSS waver
here between Anitius and Avitus, but the latter is evidently intended.
Again, he says that Ricimer, 'sparing the inoffensiveness of Avitus',
allowed him to live after he had dethroned him. No doubt these expressions
are meant to be somewhat contemptuous of the intellect of Avitus, but they
would hardly be used of a man who was guilty of the wanton profligacy
which Gibbon ascribes to him.

(3) The very fact of his ordination as bishop, at that period of the
church, and under such a strict disciplinarian as Pope Leo I, is almost a
guarantee for the correctness of his private life.

What then are the opposing testimonies?

(4) Gregory of Tours (*Historia Francorum*, ii.11) says – 'Avitus, one of
the senators, and, as is very manifest, a citizen of Auvergne, when he had
schemed for the Imperial dignity of Rome, wishing to act luxuriously, was
cast forth by the senate, and ordained bishop at the city of Placentia. But
finding that the senate, still indignant, wished to deprive him of life he
sought the basilica of St Julian,' etc.

Gregory (who died about 595) is in no sense a contemporary, and is not
a first-rate authority for what happened in Italy at this period, Gaul, under
the Frankish kings in the sixth century, being the ground upon which he is
really strong. In this particular instance it is almost certain that he has overstated the share of the Roman senate and underestimated that of Ricimer
in the deposition of Avitus. It is true that Gregory, as being himself a native
of Auvergne, might have some special information as to the life of his
countryman. But let his authority be taken for what it is worth; it estab-
lishes, at the worst, a charge of 'luxury' against Avitus.*

(5) An anonymous epitomiser of Gregory, said by some to be Fredegar-
ius (who lived in the middle of the seventh century), but of whose name
and date we really know nothing, tells a disagreeable story about the capture of Trier by the Franks, which was occasioned by the dishonour
inflicted by the emperor Avitus on the lovely wife of the senator Lucius, a
crime about which the emperor was foolish enough to jest in the hearing of
the outraged husband, who, in revenge, delivered up the city to the Franks.

* It must be remembered however that *luxuria* has a distinctly worse connotation than
'luxury', and may well imply moral depravity: *luxuriae ac lasciviae perditae* [dissipation and
depraved wantonness] (Suetonius, *Life of Caligula*, 25). This of course does not affect the
vagueness of the charge.

But it is quite clear that this story, whatever its truth may be, relates to events which occurred more than forty years before Avitus' accession to the Empire, and that the insertion of his name is a mere slip on the part of the epitomiser. Paragraph 6 describes the usurpation of the Imperial title by Jovinus (about 411). Paragraph 7 contains the above-mentioned story about the cause of the fall of Trier, and that event, as we know from Gregory (*Historia Francorum*, ii.9), also occurred in or about the year 411. Paragraph 8 mentions a campaign of Castinus against the Franks (417). Paragraph 9 gives the accession of Chlodeo, assigned to 428, and the reign of his son Meroveus. Then at last in paragraph 10 we have a short notice (in the words of Gregory of Tours) of the real Avitus, his luxurious life, ordination as a bishop, and death.

It is plain therefore that paragraph 7 does not relate to Avitus the emperor, and that his name has been substituted for that of some other Roman emperor residing at Trier, probably Jovinus, by a clerical error of the epitomiser. Gibbon's attempt to transfer the story to Rome by the remark that 'it seems more applicable to Rome than to Trier' is quite inadmissible. The story is an account of the circumstances which led to the fall of Trier, or it is nothing.

Upon a review of the whole evidence it is contended that, except for a vague and feebly supported charge of 'luxury', the moral character of Avitus is without a stain.

SOURCES

I Early History of the Huns

This chapter is for the most part a mere compilation from a previous com‑
piler. Our chief guide is M. Deguignes, who published at Paris (1756–8)
a *Histoire Générale des Huns, des Turcs, des Mongols, et des autres Tartares Occi‑
dentaux, avant et depuis Jésus‑Christ jusqu'à présent* (4 vols, small 4to; the first
volume being divided into two parts). Only the second part of the first vol‑
ume (and not the whole of that) is occupied with the history of the Huns
properly so called. The fortunes of the different branches of the Turkish
and Mongol races fill up the remainder of the work, which might in fact be
called *The History of the Northern Turanians*, though that term was not
known to ethnology when Deguignes wrote.

During the period for which we follow his guidance he draws his mater‑
ials entirely from Chinese historians, whose names are scrupulously
quoted. The chief appear to be Kam‑mo, Lie‑tai‑ki‑sou, Han‑chou, and
Ssu‑ki. As he was one of the first Chinese scholars of his day, and as his
work has stood its ground for more than a century as an authority on the
history of central Asia, it is reasonable to presume that no gross inaccur‑
acies have been discovered in his manner of using his Chinese authorities.

It was stated in the first edition of this work that 'it would be prudent to
hold the theory as to the origin of the Huns as not much more than a possible
hypothesis'. Perhaps we ought now to go further than this and to discard that
theory altogether. Mr Howorth, than whom no English scholar, perhaps no
European scholar, is more qualified to express an opinion on points of
Turanian ethnology, pronounces decidedly against it in a paper contributed
to the *Journal of the Anthropological Institute* (iii.396–474). But upon the
whole, remembering the length of time during which it was accepted with
unquestioning faith, and considering that the Huns, who were undeniably
an Asiatic people, may probably enough have passed through some of the
experiences here recorded of the Hiong‑nu, even if they were not the people
bearing that name, I have thought it best to let this chapter stand nearly as it
was first written, referring the reader to [appendix i, pp. 365–6] for a brief

summary of Mr Howorth's arguments against the theory of Deguignes.

The article above referred to is incorporated with a translation of the Han annals by Mr A. Wylie. This, as far as Chinese history is concerned, goes over very much the same ground which has been already traversed by Deguignes.

II Attila and the Court of Constantinople

Priscus, born at Panium, a town of Thrace, probably about the beginning of the fifth century. He wrote (in Greek) a history in eight books, *Of Byzantium and the Occurrences connected with Attila*, which apparently narrated the events between 433 and 474. He is commonly spoken of as 'the rhetorician' or 'the sophist', and his pure, elegant, and lively style agrees with the supposition that he was by profession a man of letters. He was admitted to the intimate friendship of Maximin, one of the generals of Theodosius II, whom he accompanied on his celebrated embassy to Attila, and also on a visit to Syria. It is probable that both he and his friend Maximin were pagans. Only fragments of his work remain, but one of these, of considerable length, describing Attila and his court and the reception of the Roman ambassadors, is the most interesting piece of contemporary history which the fifth century has bequeathed to us.

III Attila in Gaul

At the outset we derive a little further information as to Attila's embassies from Priscus, but our chief source is again Jordanes. He gives, of course, always the Gothic version of the events which he describes; but the chapters relating to the invasion of Gaul and the battle of Châlons, rise to a far higher level of literary merit than the rest of the history, and seem to have something of the vividness and picturesqueness of contemporary narration.*

Apollinaris Sidonius, the Gaulish nobleman, wit and bishop, whose relation to the politics of the time will be portrayed [in chapter vii], writes about the events of this year in his usual declamatory style. He lived 430–88, and was therefore twenty-one years old at the time of Attila's invasion of Gaul.

* [For more information on Jordanes see vol. i, pp. 577–9, 581–2.]

Gregory of Tours, who wrote his *History of the Franks* [*Historia Franc-orum*] about 590, supplies some meagre details about Attila's invasion.

The Bollandist *Acta Sanctorum*, in the lives of St Geneviève, St Lupus, and St Anianus, give further details of a more or less legendary character. A student who should possess sufficient patience and discrimination to winnow the wheat from the chaff in the vast mass of ecclesiastical literature collected by the Bollandists, would bestow a great service on the history of the Middle Ages.

The *Panegyric of Aetius*, attributed to a Spanish poet named Mero-baudes, contains some interesting hints as to the life of Aetius previous to the year 446 (the date of the poem), but in its extremely fragmentary state it is difficult to extract much solid historical material from it. The imitation of Claudian's style is obvious.

IV Attila in Italy

A chapter in Jordanes and a paragraph in the *Historia Miscella*, with one curious anecdote from Suidas the well-known lexicographer (of uncertain date), are all the materials that we possess for the history of this immeasur-ably important campaign, except the brief memoranda of the annalists.*

V Extinction of the Hunnish Empire and the Theodosian Dynasty

For the disruption of the Hunnish empire, Jordanes. For the deaths of Aetius and Valentinian, Prosper, whose original chronicle ends with a long and eloquent paragraph at the year 455.

The continuer of Prosper (*Codex Havniensis*) is an important authority on the deaths of Aetius and Valentinian III.†

With the termination of Prosper's chronicle we are introduced to a new set of annalists.

Victor Tunnunensis flourished in the sixth century. He was bishop of a place in the province of Africa, the exact situation of which is not known. He wrote a chronicle continuing that of Prosper down to the first year of

* [For more information on the *Historia Miscella* see vol. i, pp. 612–13; for the annalists, vol. i, pp. 605–10.]

† [For more information on Prosper and his continuer see vol. i, pp. 605–9.]

Justin II (565). He can only be looked upon as a second-rate authority for fifth-century matters, but, writing from the neighbourhood of Carthage, he may have sometimes preserved the local traditions as to the acts of the Vandal conquerors.

Anonymus Cuspiniani is the uncouth designation of a mysterious MS which is our most valuable authority for the last quarter-century of the Western Empire. The MS of this chronicle is in the imperial library at Vienna. It was first published by a certain Joseph Cuspinianus, a scholar of the Renaissance (who died in 1529), and hence the name by which it is technically known. It begins with a mere list of names of consuls, very fragmentary, and of no great value. With the year 378, the point where St Jerome's chronicle ends, 'the Anonymous of Cuspinian' becomes more valuable. He begins to insert much fuller notices of passing events, and is exceedingly precise in mentioning the day of the month on which each event occurred. It would not probably be too much to assert that at least half of the dates recorded by historians who write of the accessions and depositions of the Roman emperors in the fifth century, are due to the Anonymus Cuspiniani. His information becomes perceptibly fuller and richer as the historical interest approaches Ravenna. From this and various other reasons it is conjectured that we have here an official record compiled at Ravenna, possibly by some minister of the Imperial court, or else part of the lost history of Bishop Maximian;* and some of the scholars of Germany have gone so far as to endeavour to reconstruct from it the original *Annals of Ravenna*. But putting aside all minute conjectures as to its origin and preservation, there can be no doubt that we have here an exceedingly valuable and nearly, or quite, contemporary record of the events between 455 and 493. There is an unfortunate chasm in the chronicle between 403 and 455.

Besides the above-mentioned sources we derive some details from Apollinaris Sidonius and Procopius, who will be described more fully [below].

VI The Vandals from Germany to Rome

For the events which happened during the Vandals' stay in Spain Idatius is our best authority.†

For the Vandal Conquest, Procopius. This historian, secretary, and commissariat officer to Belisarius is well known as the chief authority for

* See vol. i, p. 565.   † [For more information on Idatius see vol. i, pp. 609–10.]

the events of the reign of Justinian. He flourished from about 500 to 560, and wrote, besides other histories, two books, *De Bello Vandalico*. The Vandalic war, which it is his main object to describe, is of course that in which Belisarius overthrew the Vandal kingdom (533−4). But he devotes seven chapters of the first book to a description of the foundation of that kingdom by Gaiseric and the chief events of his life.

Although Procopius is an authority of the first class for the events of which he was himself an eye-witness, he is somewhat slipshod and inaccurate as to those events concerning which he had to gather his information from others. Hence his chronology is often erroneous: and when he is separated by a considerable distance of time from his subject, it seems clear that he cannot always have used the best material which contemporary historians might have afforded him. He has also an extreme love of historical gossip, and generally leans to the ill-natured view of a man's character. But the reader will see by the references how large a part of our knowledge of the Vandal settlement in Africa is derived from this source, only partially trustworthy as we must admit it to be.

Victor Vitensis, an African bishop, who was driven into banishment for the faith by Huneric, son of Gaiseric, wrote about 486 a *History of the Persecution of the African Province* in five books. He is therefore an all but contemporary authority even for the early part of the Vandal settlement.

He used to be cited as Victor Uticensis. It is now admitted that Vitensis is the correct form. Vita appears to have been a city in the Byzacene province, but its exact position is unknown.

The *Life of St Augustine* by Possidius, bishop of Calama, his disciple and friend, gives us some particulars as to the siege of Hippo and the death of the great African father.

VII The Letters and Poems of Apollinaris Sidonius

Apollinaris Sidonius: edited and translated by Grégoire and Collombet (3 vols, Lyons and Paris, 1836). The notes are full, but both in them and the translation the editors have a disagreeable habit of evading the real difficulties of their author.

VIII Avitus, the Client of the Visigoths

Our chief authority is of course Sidonius, the son-in-law and flatterer of the emperor.

The chroniclers Idatius, Victor Tunnunensis, and (especially) Anonymus Cuspiniani, notice this reign in their usual brief terms. Marcellinus is silent about it, reflecting probably the hostile feelings of the Eastern court towards the new emperor. A new chronicler, Marius, bishop of Aventicum (Avenches in Switzerland), takes up the work of Prosper and continues it down to the year 581. He appears to have been born about 530, and to have died after a twenty years' episcopate in 594. He is thus in no sense a contemporary, but he occasionally supplies some useful details, especially as to the movements of the Burgundians, who were masters of Switzerland at the period which we are now considering.

Joannes Antiochenus, an Eastern chronicler of the seventh century, throws some additional light on the fall of Avitus.

Gregory of Tours, born probably in 538, who began his *History of the Franks* about 576, and died about 595, adds some little information, of a questionable kind.

IX Supremacy of Ricimer. Majorian

It will be seen that our chief information as to this reign is again drawn from the poems and still more from the letters of Sidonius.

Of the annalists Idatius is perhaps the least meagre, and as the turning-point of Majorian's career was in Spain, this Spanish bishop may be quoted with some confidence for that event.

The Anonymus Cuspiniani, as usual, supplies us with dates and Procopius with romance.

X Supremacy of Ricimer (Continued). Severus II, the Lucanian, AD 461–5. Anthemius, the Client of Byzantium, AD 467–72

The *Panegyric* and *Epistles* of Sidonius, as quoted in the text.

The chroniclers as before, with the addition of Cassiodorus, minister of

Theodoric the Ostrogoth (480–575). Now that he no longer has Prosper to copy from, his chronicle becomes valuable as an independent authority.

We are also compelled here, in the great dearth of contemporary information, to rely occasionally on Theophanes, though a Byzantine historian of a poor type. Theophanes was born in 758 and died in 817. He was of noble birth, embraced the monastic life, and took part in the Iconoclastic controversy as a vehement upholder of the worship of images. His *Chronographia* extends from the accession of Diocletian to the second year of the emperor Michael I (284–813).

For the life of Marcellinus our chief authority is the *Lexicon* of Suidas (of uncertain date, possibly not later than Theophanes).

For the quarrel between Anthemius and Ricimer the main authority is Ennodius, *De Vita Epiphanii* [*Life of Epiphanius*], described in the text. Ennodius, bishop of Ticinum, lived from about 473 to 521.

For the close of the reign of Anthemius some valuable details are furnished by the recently discovered fragments of the history of Joannes Antiochenus. The author was an orator of Antioch, probably of the seventh century, who wrote the history of the Empire from the Creation to the great earthquake and fire at Antioch in 526.

Priscus of Panium (described [above, p. 388]) gives the diplomatic history of the times with some fullness. Unfortunately we have his work only in fragments, relating to the negotiations in which the Empire was engaged, but as far as his information goes we may trust him thoroughly, as a contemporary and a man of truthful character.

Paulus Diaconus (about 720 to 790) in his *Historia Romana*, a continuation of Eutropius, gives us some valuable fragments of information, but cannot be considered a first-rate authority for this period, though he will be invaluable for later centuries.*

XI Olybrius, the Client of the Vandal, AD 472. Glycerius, the Client of the Burgundian, AD 473–4. Julius Nepos, the Client of Byzantium, AD 474–5. Romulus Augustulus, Son of Orestes, AD 475–6

Cassiodorus, Theophanes, and Joannes Antiochenus have been described [above]. Marcellinus and the Anonymus Cuspiniani give the versions of the facts current at Constantinople and Ravenna respectively.

* [For more information on Paulus Diaconus see vol. i, p. 613.]

A new and most valuable source is opened out to us by the writer called
the Anonymus Valesii. The two fragments which pass under this name
were published by Henricus Valesius (Henri de Valois, 1603–76) in his
edition of Ammianus Marcellinus, and they have since been generally
appended to the history of that author, with which however they have no
natural connection. The first fragment deals with the history of Constantine the Great; the second and much longer fragment describes, in a very
peculiar style, the affairs of Italy from the accession of Nepos in 474 to the
death of Theodoric in 526. It is tolerably certain that the two fragments
which are thus classed together are by two different authors. With the question of the authorship of the first we need not here concern ourselves.
Waitz* has argued with much probability that we have in the second an
actual portion of the *Chronicles* of Maximian, bishop of Ravenna, from
546 to 556 (see vol. i, pp. 563–6). In favour of this conjecture is the
fact of the author's evident close connection with Ravenna and his knowledge of Eastern affairs, since we know from the story of his elevation that
he was for some time a resident at Constantinople. Holder-Egger (*Neues
Archiv*, i.324) argues, on the other hand, that the poor style and frequent
barbarisms of the Anonymus Valesii do not correspond with what Agnellus tells us† of the learning of Bishop Maximian, and his care to secure
accurate copies of the Scriptures and other ecclesiastical books. There is no
doubt some force in this argument, but on the whole Waitz's theory seems
to me a very probable guess: higher value than this we cannot assign
to it. One feature in the Anonymus Valesii, which it is not easy fully to
account for by any theory, is his strong bias in favour of the Eastern emperor Zeno.

XII Odovacar, the Soldier of Fortune

The two mysterious chroniclers, Anonymus Cuspiniani and Anonymus
Valesii, are our best authorities for this most meagrely furnished epoch.
Cuspinian's MS gives us all our dates, and that of Valois nearly all our
personal details as to the dethroner of the last Roman emperor.

It will be seen however that Ennodius' *Life of Epiphanius* is again a valuable source of information. So is the somewhat similar *Life of St Severinus*

* *Nachrichten von der k. Gesellschaft der Wissenschaften . . . zu Göttingen*, 1865, p. 112.
† *Liber Pontificalis*, 81.

by Eugippius.* Joannes Antiochenus and Jordanes also contribute some facts. The details as to revolutions and embassies at Constantinople rest chiefly on the authority of Malchus and Candidus, two Byzantine his- torians of the end of the fifth and beginning of the sixth century. They were read and abstracted by the all-devouring Photius.† Fragments of their works are published in the Bonn edition of the Byzantine historians.

* Head of the monastery of the Lucullanum (near Naples), who is said to have written this book about 510.
† [For more information on Photius see vol. i, pp. 611–12.]

TABLES

I The Chief Turanian Races

TURANIANS
Northern division[1]

TUNGUSIC FAMILY	MONGOLIC	TURKIC		FINNIC		
THE MANCHUS the last Tartar conquerors of China	(1) The great TARTAR conquerors of the Middles Ages GENGHIS KHAN AD 1225 and TIMUR BEG (Tamerlane) AD 1369 (2) THE MOGUL DYNASTY in India AD 1530–1857	HUNS in Europe AD 370–468		FINNS	BULGARIANS	MAGYARS or HUNGARIANS

SELJUKIAN TURKS
AD 985–1294

OTTOMAN TURKS
AD 1301–?

[1] The southern division, comprising races in Tibet and the two Indian peninsulas, we may omit as too distant kinsmen of the Huns, our present subject.

II Family of Avitus

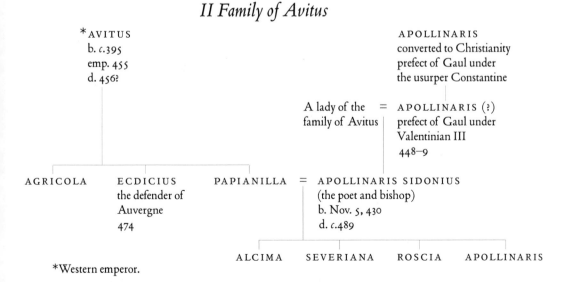

*AVITUS
b. c.395
emp. 455
d. 456?

APOLLINARIS
converted to Christianity
prefect of Gaul under
the usurper Constantine

A lady of the = APOLLINARIS (?)
family of Avitus   prefect of Gaul under
Valentinian III
448–9

| AGRICOLA | ECDICIUS the defender of Auvergne 474 | PAPIANILLA | = | APOLLINARIS SIDONIUS (the poet and bishop) b. Nov. 5, 430 d. c.489 |

ALCIMA   SEVERIANA   ROSCIA   APOLLINARIS

*Western emperor.

III Family Connections of Ricimer

WALIA
k. of the Visigoths
415–19

*ANTHEMIUS   A daughter = A Suevic chieftain

ALYPIA = RICIMER   A daughter = GUNDIOK
           b. probably   k. of the Burgundians
           between 410 and 420   437(?)–73
           d. 472

                                   GUNDOBAD
                                   k. of the Burgundians
                                   473–516

IV Family of Anthemius

PROCOPIUS
proclaimed emp. 365
killed 366

First wife = †MARCIAN = PULCHERIA   ANTHEMIUS
                                                     praetorian prefect
                                                     of the East under
                                                     Theodosius II

                              PROCOPIUS = A daughter

                 EUPHEMIA = *ANTHEMIUS
                            b. probably between
                            415 and 425
                            emp. 467
                            killed 472

RICIMER = ALYPIA   ANTHEMIUS[1]   MARCIAN[2]   ROMULUS   PROCOPIUS
the patrician   revolted against
                                    the emperor Zeno
                                    479

*Western emperor.   †Eastern emperor.

[1] Ariadne begged her husband the emperor Anastasius to bestow on this Anthemius the
office of praetorian prefect, but he refused, with some anger, saying that it ought to be held only
by men of letters (Joannes Lydus, *De Magistratibus* iii.50).

[2] Marcian married Leontia, daughter of the emperor Leo. He was therefore brother-in-law of
Ariadne, and through her, of the emperors Zeno and Anastasius (Evagrius, iii.26).

V *Genealogy of Olybrius*

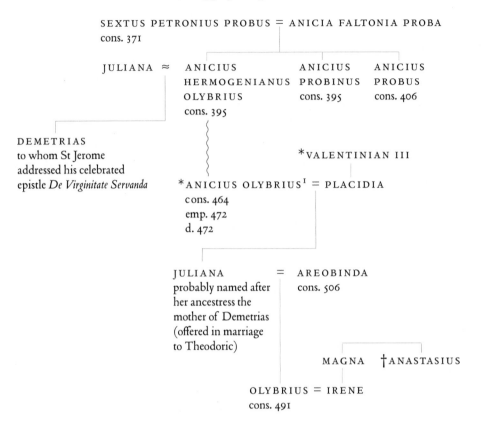

SEXTUS PETRONIUS PROBUS = ANICIA FALTONIA PROBA
cons. 371

JULIANA ≈ ANICIUS   ANICIUS   ANICIUS
       HERMOGENIANUS PROBINUS PROBUS
       OLYBRIUS   cons. 395   cons. 406
       cons. 395

DEMETRIAS
to whom St Jerome   *VALENTINIAN III
addressed his celebrated
epistle *De Virginitate Servanda* *ANICIUS OLYBRIUS[1] = PLACIDIA
                   cons. 464
                   emp. 472
                   d. 472

JULIANA   =   AREOBINDA
probably named after   cons. 506
her ancestress the
mother of Demetrias
(offered in marriage
to Theodoric)   MAGNA   †ANASTASIUS

OLYBRIUS = IRENE
cons. 491

*Western emperor. †Eastern emperor.
[1] [Anicius Hermogenianus] Olybrius was probably grandfather of Anicius Olybrius.

VI Genealogies of Eastern and Western Emperors, AD 474–5

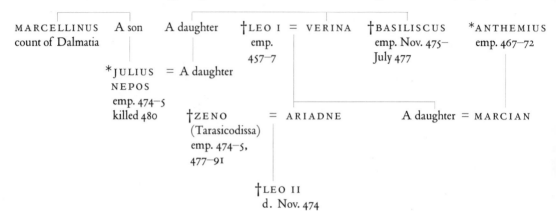

MARCELLINUS   A son   A daughter   †LEO I = VERINA   †BASILISCUS   *ANTHEMIUS
count of Dalmatia   emp.   emp. Nov. 475–   emp. 467–72
                                  457–7   July 477

*JULIUS = A daughter
NEPOS

emp. 474–5
killed 480   †ZENO   = ARIADNE   A daughter = MARCIAN
              (Tarasicodissa)

emp. 474–5,
477–91

†LEO II
d. Nov. 474

VII Genealogy of Augustulus[1]

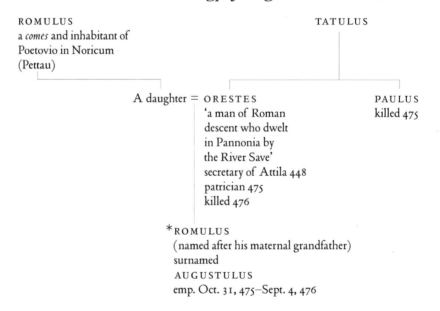

ROMULUS   TATULUS
a *comes* and inhabitant of
Poetovio in Noricum
(Pettau)

A daughter = ORESTES   PAULUS
                 'a man of Roman   killed 475
                 descent who dwelt
                 in Pannonia by
                 the River Save'
                 secretary of Attila 448
                 patrician 475
                 killed 476

*ROMULUS
(named after his maternal grandfather)
surnamed
AUGUSTULUS
emp. Oct. 31, 475–Sept. 4, 476

*Western emperor.   †Eastern emperor.
[1] Chiefly from Priscus.

INDEX

V Genealogy of Olybrius

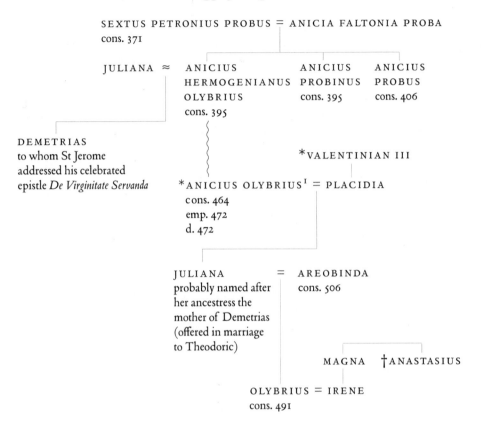

SEXTUS PETRONIUS PROBUS = ANICIA FALTONIA PROBA
cons. 371

JULIANA ≈   ANICIUS   ANICIUS   ANICIUS
            HERMOGENIANUS   PROBINUS   PROBUS
            OLYBRIUS   cons. 395   cons. 406
            cons. 395

DEMETRIAS
to whom St Jerome   *VALENTINIAN III
addressed his celebrated
epistle *De Virginitate Servanda*   *ANICIUS OLYBRIUS¹ = PLACIDIA
                                    cons. 464
                                    emp. 472
                                    d. 472

JULIANA   =   AREOBINDA
probably named after   cons. 506
her ancestress the
mother of Demetrias
(offered in marriage
to Theodoric)
                                    MAGNA   †ANASTASIUS

                       OLYBRIUS = IRENE
                       cons. 491

*Western emperor.   †Eastern emperor.
¹ [Anicius Hermogenianus] Olybrius was probably grandfather of Anicius Olybrius.

VI *Genealogies of Eastern and Western Emperors*, AD 474–5

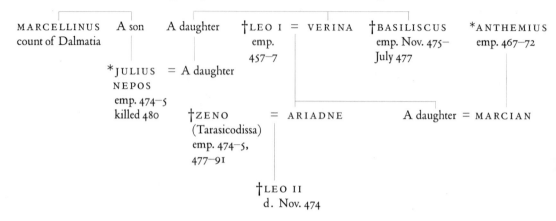

MARCELLINUS — A son — A daughter — †LEO I = VERINA — †BASILISCUS — *ANTHEMIUS
count of Dalmatia — — — emp. 457–7 — emp. Nov. 475– July 477 — emp. 467–72

*JULIUS NEPOS = A daughter
emp. 474–5
killed 480

†ZENO (Tarasicodissa) = ARIADNE — A daughter = MARCIAN
emp. 474–5, 477–91

†LEO II
d. Nov. 474

VII *Genealogy of Augustulus*[1]

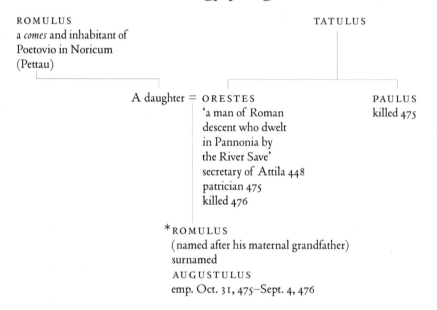

ROMULUS
a *comes* and inhabitant of
Poetovio in Noricum
(Pettau)

TATULUS

A daughter = ORESTES
'a man of Roman
descent who dwelt
in Pannonia by
the River Save'
secretary of Attila 448
patrician 475
killed 476

PAULUS
killed 475

*ROMULUS
(named after his maternal grandfather)
surnamed
AUGUSTULUS
emp. Oct. 31, 475–Sept. 4, 476

*Western emperor. †Eastern emperor.
[1] Chiefly from Priscus.

INDEX

Acatziri, 35n, 48, 49

Acincus (Buda), 237

Acta Sanctorum, 76n, 77, 389

Adige, river, 100–1

Aegean, piracy in, 149

Aegidius, 'Roman king of Soissons', 211n, 257–8, 259

Aetius, general: Aquileia siege, 92; Attila's invasion, 75–6, 79, 96; Attila's retreat, 99; battle of the Catalaunian plains, 80, 83, 84, 85–6, 259; campaigns, 223; compared to Attila, 111; death, 118–19, 235, 238, 316, 373; property, 256; relationship with Attila, 55, 57; relationship with Franks, 65; relationship with Huns, 25, 35, 85–6, 298; relationship with Marcellinus, 258; relationship with Valentinian III, 86, 117–19, 235; relationship with Visigoths, 69, 70, 75, 84, 85–6, 148; rivalry with Bonifacius, 147, 163; sources on, 389; title of patrician, 236

Africa: administration, 143–4; architecture, 142–3; astrologers from, 198; Belisarius' expedition, 391; culture, 141–2; diocese, 143; economy, 140–1; fall of Carthage, 148, 378; fortifications, 308; map at time of Vandal invasion, 137; provinces, 138–40, 143; religious controversies, 157–9; siege of Hippo, 145–7, 391; tribute, 335; Vandal dominion, 65, 155, 225, 305–6, 391; Vandal invasion, 133–4, 138, 144–5, 305–6, 375–8; Vandal settlement, 147–50, 391

Africa Proconsularis, *see* Zeugitana

Agintheus, general, 40

Agnellus, head of Lucullanum monastery, 394

Agricola, son of Avitus, 207, 224

Alamanni, 238

Alans (Alani): in Africa, 151–2; battle of Nedao, 116; conquest by Huns, 21; defeat at Bergamo, 259; in Gaul, 25, 70, 129; relationship with Vandals, 151–2; religion, 21, 53n; in Spain, 130, 131, 132; territory, 21, 104

Alaric, king of the Visigoths: army service, 298; burial, 88; capture of Rome, 175, 312, 330; compared with Attila, 26; compared with Gaiseric, 134; conflict with Stilicho, 33, 318; death, 96; escape from Stilicho, 85; invasion of Italy, 90, 220; leadership, 306; name, 235n; ransom from Rome, 45n

Alboin the Lombard, 220

Alexander the Great, 259

Alexandria, 319, 325, 328, 339, 359

Alexandrian Chronicle, see Chronicon Paschale

Alps, 24, 90, 241–2, 289, 301

Alypia, daughter of Anthemius, wife of Ricimer, 266, 269, 278

Amalafrida, sister of Theodoric, wife of Thrasamund, 383

Amals, 68, 80, 115, 117

Amantius, fortune-hunter, 195–7, 219

amber, 91

Ambri, leader of the Vandals, 127

Ambrose, saint, 92n, 275, 327

America: government, 364; slavery, 329–30, 331–4

Ammianus Marcellinus, historian: on Cilicia, 276n; edition of works, 394; on Huns, 21–3, 25, 271; religion, 327

Anatolius, ex-consul, 33, 34, 51, 60–1, 62n

Andages, Ostrogoth, 82

Andalusia, 131

RUGII

BRUCTERI

TORINGI

RIPUARIAN FRANKS

R. Rhine

SALIAN FRANKS

SAXONS

SAXONS (?)

ARMORICANS

R. Danube

R. Loire

VISIGOTHS
(SEPTIMANIA)

BURGUNDIANS
(SAPAUDIA)

Lyons

WESTERN

Milan

Aquileia
Venice

ALANS

Toulouse

Arles

Ravenna

Narbonne

Rome

SUEVI

Carthage

V A N D A L S

EUROPE IN THE YEAR 451

——— Approximate boundaries of the Eastern/Western Roman Empires

– – – Approximate boundaries of lands occupied by barbarians

0   100   200   0   100   200   0   100   200

Imperial miles   Roman miles   Kilometres